THE
COMPLETE
BOOK
OF THE
STRIPED
BASS

THE
COMPLETE
BOOK
OF THE
STRIPED
BASS

NICHOLAS KARAS

STOEGER PUBLISHING COMPANY

Published by Stoeger Publishing Company
55 Ruta Court
South Hackensack, New Jersey 07606

First Stoeger paperback edition, December 1975

This Stoeger Sportsman's Library edition is published by
arrangement with Winchester Press.

Distributed to the book trade by Follett Publishing
Company and to the sporting goods trade by
Stoeger Industries. In Canada, distributed to the book
trade by Nelson, Foster & Scott, Ltd. and to the sporting
goods trade by Stoeger Trading Company.

Printed in the United States of America

ISBN: 0-88317-062-0

This book is dedicated to the memory of

DR. ERNEST RAPHAEL

a physician of unlimited patience

who first opened the door for me to the world

of the striped bass

Acknowledgments

The world of the striped bass cannot be singled out as the realm of any one individual. It belongs to all those people who have ever followed this fish, with rod and reel, with net and trap, or with tags and rulers. It belongs to all those researchers and biologists who have studied, examined, and dissected the bass. It belongs to all those fishermen who have chased it for sport, food, and livelihood. It too belongs to all those writers and reporters who have gone before me, extolling the virtues of bass fishing. And it belongs to all those who will seek the striper after you and I are gone.

Therefore, I would like to acknowledge and thank the men who have come to know the striped bass, who have written about its habits, its life cycle, and its needs. And I hope I haven't borrowed too heavily of their ideas. I wish to acknowledge those who have given me guidance, direction, and encouragement to gather as much knowledge, technique, and lore as exists about this fish and then write it down.

Specifically, I would like to thank Phil Briggs, a marine biologist with the State of New York who helped me over some of the scientific hurdles in this book; Frank Woolner, Editor of *Salt Water Sportsman* magazine, who made sure my lore of the striped bass wasn't tainted with fresh water; and finally, my wife, who laboriously typed and helped edit the manuscript, and kept my enthusiasm in bounds.

Then, there are the researchers with whom I talked bass, primarily Byron Young, a young Downeaster who is helping to unravel many of the mysteries of the striped bass in the Hudson River for the New York Department of Environmental Conservation. There are scores of researchers with whom I've met, talked, and corresponded. These include Richard Schaefer of the National Oceanic and Atmospheric Administration; Irwin Alperin, Director of the Atlantic States Marine Fisheries Commission; Bruce Freeman, Stuart Wilkie, and Dr. L. A. Walford of the Middle Atlantic Coastal Research Center, Sandy Hook, N.J.; W. B. Scott, Curator of the Royal Ontario Museum; Fernando Fortier, for her translations; Gerard Beaulieu, Quebec Department of Fisheries; J. W. Baker of St. John, New Brunswick; Arthur Smith, Fishery Biologist, Prince Edward Island; Barry Sabean, Fisheries Biologist, Nova Scotia; C. P. Ruggles, Environment Canada; Lewis N. Flagg, Marine Resources Scientist, Maine; Richard Seamans, Chief, Marine Fisheries, New Hampshire; Bruce Rogers, biologist, and Thomas Wright, Rhode Island Department of Natural Resources; William Clede, writer, and Cole Wilde, Connecticut Department of Environmental Protection; Paul Hammer, New Jersey Marine Research Center; Arthur Bradford, Chief Pennsylvania Fish Commission; William F. Moore, Fisheries Manager, Delaware; Dr. Ted S. Y. Koo, Chesapeake Biological Lab, Solomans, Maryland; William E. Neal, Fish Biologist, Virginia; Michael Street, Marine Biologist, Donald Baker, Chief of Inland Fisheries, and James Tyler, biologist, North Carolina; Dr. Jack D. Bayliss, Marine Resources, Moncks Corners, South Carolina; Carl S. Hall, Fisheries Supervisor, Georgia; James Barkuloo and F. G. Banks, Fisheries Division, Florida; W. F. Anderson, Marine Resources, Alabama; Harry Barkley and Larry C. Nicholson, Mississippi Fish Commission and the Gulf Coast Research Laboratory; Bennie J. Fontenot, Jr., Louisiana Fisheries Commission; Harold K. Chadwick, California Delta-Bay Fisheries Project; C. J. Campbell, Fishery Division, and Robert T. Gunsolus, Research Division, State of Oregon; Scott Henderson, Arkansas biologist; Gary Edwards, Fisheries Specialist, Arizona Game & Fish Department; Ron Jarman, Fish Division, Oklahoma Department of Wildlife Conservation; David Bishop, Fisheries Biologist, Tennessee Game and Fish Commission; David L. Pritchard, Texas Parks and Wildlife Department; Charles C. Bowers, Director, Fisheries Division, Kentucky Department of Fish and Wildlife; and Dr. S. I. Doroshev, All-Union Research Institute, USSR.

I would also like to acknowledge the great field of researchers whose works influenced, guided, and contributed to my knowledge as well as the world's on the life of the striped bass. They are: A. J. Calhoun, John R. Clark, Albert C. Jensen, D. P. deSylva, William W. Hassler, Edgar H. Hollis, Robert M. Lewis, George C. Maltezos, Romeo Mansueti, W. H. Massman, A. L. Pacheco, Daniel Merriman, Walter S. Murawski, William C. Nevile, Paul R. Nichols, John C. Pearson, Alfred Perlmutter, John C. Poole, Edward C. Raney, Warren F. Rathjen Robert E. Stevens, James E. Sykes, R. E. Tiller, Wallace L. Trent, Vadim Vladykov, David H. Wallace and James R. Westman.

Contents

Foreword   xiii

Introduction   3

PART ONE   THE FISH

1   What Is a Striped Bass?   11
2   Distribution and Migrations of Striped Bass   24
3   Reproduction in Striped Bass   46
4   Growth and Feeding in Striped Bass   57
5   The Pacific Striped Bass   66
6   The Striped Bass in Fresh Water   73
7   The Future of the Striped Bass   85

PART TWO   FISHING TECHNIQUES

8   Early Striped Bass Fishing and Fishermen   113
9   From the Surf   128
10   From Bank, Pier, Jetty, and Bridge   144
11   From Boats   155
12   Fly-Rodding for Striped Bass   167
13   Chumming   180
14   Fishing at Night   191
15   Fishing the Striped Bass in Fresh Water   199

PART THREE   TACKLE FOR STRIPED BASS

16   Rods, Reels, Lines, and Hooks   209
17   Live and Natural Baits for Striped Bass   235
18   Artificial Lures for Striped Bass   276
19   Accessory Fishing Equipment   293
20   The Bass Boat   302
21   The Beach Vehicle   331
22   Striped Bass Cookery   346

Index   359

Foreword

In the introduction to this book, the reader is invited to view the world of the striped bass as the fish sees it. This technique of viewing the life of a fish through its own eyes and feeling its emotions is not wholly my invention. I first discovered the method in a wonderful book called *The Shining Tides*, written by Win Brooks. The book is described as a novel, but it is more a biography of a fish, and all the events occur in a very real way. Brooks was a newspaperman of the first order who wrote for the Boston *American*. Unfortunately, his premature death in 1963 robbed us of more works and this novel was his only book.

His technique so intrigued me that I felt compelled to borrow it. I believe that it is an ideal means of introducing readers to the watery world of the striper. It is a complicated world that often requires a grasp of scientific concepts and terminology to explain and understand. I have not been able totally to relieve the reader of this jargon, and he must bear with me in places where the going might get heavy. But in this new language lie the keys to unraveling the mysteries that surround this great fish, and I hope that the fish will be less of a mystery to the striped bass angler once he has completed this book.

The striped bass fisherman is unique among saltwater anglers. He is often endowed with a curiosity that reaches far beyond that of the average angler. The only counterpart he might have of which I know might be the salmon fisherman, found more often in fresh water. Both are interested in their fish and sport in a way that sets them apart from other anglers. To catch the fish is usually not enough: to know how and why it strikes is as compelling a force as the catching.

It is to satisfy this angler's curiosity that I have written this book. The initial intent is not so much to tell readers how or where to fish as it is to inform them about the fish itself, to enlighten them about their adversary. It is my maturing belief that you can tell other anglers very little about how to catch fish. But I believe that if a body of knowledge can be made available to a striped bass angler, he will ingest and assimilate it like a steak or loaf of bread, and it will become part of him.

There is a wealth of knowledge about the striped bass that is buried in the research reports of two dozen states and several provinces, and cloaked in a terminology that seems like another language to most readers. In effect, this information has been inaccessible to those who might use it best to practice their sport. This information, recast in readable language, constitutes Part One of this book.

How this knowledge can then be applied in practice is the subject of Part Two. The techniques for taking striped bass vary as greatly as the environments in which this great fish is found. They differ from harbor to harbor, beach to bay, as well as between states, provinces, and coast to coast.

The angler who has learned what he is after, and how it can be obtained, can then employ Part Three of this work, a description of the tackle and the mechanical aspects of bringing the fish from the water into the frying pan. This three-part approach to the world of the striped bass — and the striped bass angler — will, I hope, increase both the reader's understanding of the fish and the pleasure the fish can give him.

Nicholas Karas
Saint James, Long Island, N.Y.
April 1974

THE
COMPLETE
BOOK
OF THE
STRIPED
BASS

Introduction

Saxatilis edged closer to the massive granite boulder until its shadow completely hid her body. Along her side, she could feel the barnacles as she settled closer to the rock. Slowly, she let her massive belly touch the rounded pebbles on the bottom. The blackfish she had just swallowed had cost her more effort than she had expected. Now, it felt good just to rest, to let the rhythmic motion of the water lull her.

She realized that for the past few years she had grown tired more easily when her school of fish chased food. That was why she now preferred to feed alone. There weren't many fish left who had shared her young years in Chesapeake Bay, or had made the first trek into the clear waters of the Atlantic that spring when they were all three years old. Now she liked the solitude of hunting, feeding, and swimming alone. Only when the waters took on a chill did she feel a longing to be with other striped bass. They all schooled for protection. But she was large now, larger than most other fish she saw. There was very little she feared.

Old Silas had always been a good place to rest and feed. Saxatilis could always expect a blackfish or bergall to come around the corner of the large rock, picking at mussels or barnacles encrusted on the huge glacial boulder. It had always been a favorite hunting spot for her when she was younger, and now it was a good place to rest. The summer she found Old Silas was now a long time ago. Fifteen years had passed since she left Chesapeake Bay, and only occasionally did she go back. It had been more than two years since she had spawned and she could feel the urge in her to climb again the river where she was spawned. But that was still months away; it was now autumn in New York.

Saxatilis rested under the shadow of the rock until the waters began to darken. By then the blackfish was well digested in her stomach and she again felt the urge to feed. With the pectoral fins on her side, she lifted herself off the rocky bottom. The building tide carried her from under Old Silas and through the giant fronds of kelp that beat with the pulsating rhythm of the water. The tide was flooding into Long Island Sound and for a while she let it carry her sideways. Suddenly, Saxatilis resented the tide and with a flick of her giant tail took her own course.

She wasn't really hungry, but she realized that she needed great quantities of food to support her 50-pound bulk. As she worked her way downtide, the current suddenly reversed itself. She was now on the eastern end of Plum Island, and here the waters separated. Swimming along the north side of the island and against the current, Saxatilis had to use more of her energy, but she was powerful. More powerful than almost all the other fish of her kind that darted out of her way.

She sensed a taste or smell in the water coming toward her. The tide was swiftly carrying it to her nostrils. She couldn't see what it was but turned into the water that carried the flavor and followed it. In the kelp ahead there was a dark fleeting movement. It was Anguilla. The eel was intent on making headway against the rising force of the tide as it swept around Plum Island and through The Gut and didn't notice the striped bass approach.

Like a flash of light, Saxatilis overtook Anguilla. Before the eel could respond, she had grabbed it in her mouth and gulped it headfirst. Saxatilis liked eels; they had a flavor that was incomparable to her. The only food she liked better was Homarus, but lobsters had abandoned most of the coastal waters this summer because they had been too warm. Homarus and her kind were in deeper water, too far away from Saxatilis' natural haunts, so she gave up lobster for the summer.

After taking Anguilla, Saxatilis wanted to rest. She found the lee of a large boulder and tried to stem the current. But even here the tide moved too fast. To her, it seemed that all the ocean was trying to squeeze itself into The Gut, a watery gap that separates Plum Island from Orient Point on eastern Long Island. As she approached the fast water, the bottom gave way and fell to depths beyond her sight. In the distance, she saw a school of squid swim in with the tide, but they were too far away. She would have to leave the back eddy to catch them. There will be more food coming along, she said to herself, all she need do was wait and watch the tide.

Unexpectedly, Saxatilis felt a strange vibration. Almost simultaneously she heard the whine of two high-pitched propellers coming through the water. As she looked up, Saxatilis saw the darkening aspect of the sky broken by a momentary glow that swept from one side to the other. The beacon on Plum Island had been turned on early. The black silhouette of the boat's hull came close to her as the vibrations and noise increased in intensity. She knew she was in no danger and didn't move. There was more than 25 feet of water between herself and the surface.

As she had seen many times before after a boat passed, she saw two silvery lines slicing the water behind the craft. She was always concerned with them because she didn't fully understand how they moved through the water. Then she saw what looked like a squid, pulsating behind the boat. It moved with irregular, jerking movements and she thought it looked good to eat.

Slowly, Saxatilis changed her position as the white, pulsating squid came closer. She felt the force of the tide as she moved beyond the protection of the boulder, and it discouraged her. The squid was moving too fast and was too far away. Besides, she still had Anguilla to finish off. Saxatilis was lazy and returned to her lie behind the boulder as darkness flooded The Gut.

The night held no fear for her. Rather, she preferred this time. The bothersome bluefish would not beat her to any food she wanted. She needed no light to find the squid that were so bountiful in The Gut. All she required was her sharp nose.

Near midnight her satiation wore off as the tide began to loose its direction. In a fit of hunger, Saxatilis moved out from her rock and drifted with the tide into the Sound and into deeper and deeper water. Without warning, she suddenly drifted into a school of squid. She could feel the entire school moving in unison through the lateral lines on her sides. Saxatilis gorged herself until she could eat no more. In a burst of energy, she returned to the rocks under the lighthouse. The tide on the shore had already shifted direction and she took a new lie on the opposite side of the boulder and let it ebb as she digested the squid.

The weather above Plum Gut had turned colder during the night, colder than any night so far. Even a dozen feet below the surface Saxatilis was sensitive enough to feel the difference. And the sun rose in a slightly different spot that morning. The urge in her to move south became uncontrollable. During the following week, the large striped bass passed Gardiners Island and south to Montauk Point. There, she felt the bitter sting of sharp hooks in her mouth as she took a plug in the surf at Turtle Cove. But the plug had been too small for her and the line too light. She broke it without much effort.

The hook still dangled from the side of her mouth as she swam past Shinnecock Inlet. She tasted the water from the bay and felt it sweep over her skin. It was colder than the water that surrounded her. That changed her mind about entering it to feed. The hook had irritated her because she didn't understand it. Why had the fish she thought she had taken suddenly become a part of her jaw? She pouted and refused to eat even though it wasn't in the way. She was losing weight. A striped bass as large as Saxatilis must eat often and in large quantities when she is so active.

Off Moriches Inlet, as she headed farther west along the south shore of Long Island, the hook in her jaw fell victim to the acids in her mouth and stomach. It quickly rusted and fell free. When it happened, it was as if someone had signaled her to eat. She had been tagging behind a school of younger striped bass, fish 20 and 30 pounds in size. They had been feeding on a school of Brevoortia and she could taste the oily flavor of the menhaden for miles behind the school. Now it was her turn. The school of bass had forced the bunker into a deep pocket between the beach and an outer bar. Saxatilis wanted her food. She charged over the bar as a wave broke. Her belly scraped on the sand and she felt the momentary coldness of the air. The feeding striped bass parted to let her in and she slashed at the first Brevoortia that appeared. One, two, and then three fish later, she had enough. They were large bunker, 2 to 3 pounds. The big ones were reserved for her and her voracious appetite.

She didn't rest after feeding as she had done before. The chill experience of the cold air she felt while crossing the sand bar was a vivid reminder of how cold this part of the Atlantic could become. She must head south.

During all of December, Saxatilis swam. She cut south short of Sandy Hook and took a deepwater course because she no longer feared sharks. She could outswim them in a burst of speed. Off Cape May she was bothered by a school of porpoise, but they let her alone when they spotted the mackerel. By New Year's Day, Saxatilis was off the mouth of Chesapeake Bay. She could taste the water in which she had spent two years of her life before she left for the coast.

For a moment she wanted to turn west, slide past Fisherman's Island, and swim in the bay's turbid waters, but she hesitated. She had felt the swelling slowly enlarge in her abdomen as the millions of eggs she carried grew and grew. But the maternal feeling was still premature; it would be several months more before she would spawn. The coolness of the water from Chesapeake reminded her that winter was still locked on her home and that she could find the warmth she needed only in deep water, farther south.

In just a few days, she had passed the numerous piers jutting from the beaches in Virginia and North Carolina and spent a frenzied afternoon feeding on a school of small Brevoortia. Saxatilis had arrived at the turbid waters off Cape Hatteras. The waters here were cool, but warmer than those off Chesapeake Bay. Another current from the south mixes here with the cooler currents from the north and helps temper their sting. Still, the waters continued to cool, and she spent the next week feeding whenever she could. Gradually, the chill was slowing her life. She needed less and less food.

Eventually, Saxatilis drifted a few miles off the beach and joined other large bass. There she met a few with whom she had shared her home river. There were fish from the Roanoke as well. She had seen very few North Carolina fish go with the migrations north. Saxatilis spent February, March, and part of April in the semi-dormant state with thousands of other striped bass. In April she sensed the water beginning to warm and the bulging in her abdomen had grown much larger. It had filled most of the area her empty stomach had lost.

As the water approached 45 degrees, Saxatilis and the other large fish began to move from their winter grounds. It was a short swim into Chesapeake Bay and she felt good. She was eager to spawn and hadn't taken part in the ritual for three years. When she was younger, she had been more active. Now she did things more slowly. The bay waters were murky from spring siltation, but she could separate the smells of all the rivers that fill the bay and mix with salt water. She knew the odor of her river, and at Smith Point turned west and entered the Potomac.

She saw schools upon schools of younger bass, fish no larger than 5 or 6 pounds, all males, passing her, racing for the spawning grounds. There were other large females with her, but only one that was larger. There were very few small females. They waited their turn and would come to the river after the larger fish had spawned. Once past the big bridge near Morgantown, Saxatilis could sense a current in the river that had been too weak before to feel. Slowly, the taste of salt had left the water and she could now savor all kinds of exotic sensations. They all reminded her of her youth.

As she continued upstream she could feel the current mount, and strange feelings begin to stir within her. The water was still too cool as she passed the narrows at Quantico, but here is where she would drop her eggs. Thousands of small male bass milled around and came close to her. They never would have dared do that in the open ocean. For six days she stemmed the current of the Potomac off Quantico as the water temperatures slowly rose. Then one night it rained heavily near Hagerstown and the river was swollen with warm rainwater. It took two days for it to reach Saxatilis, but when it did she responded.

The young male bass became brazen and began bumping and pushing her as she tried to maintain her position in the current. Some would leap to the top of the water and splash about until the water was foaming. Even Saxatilis experienced a schoolgirl's delight and began racing about with the males. She turned on her side and slapped her massive tail on the surface and sent a geyser into the air. Males were everywhere about her, pressing on both sides and smothering Saxatilis. Together, they sank to the bottom and she relaxed as millions of tiny eggs flowed into the Potomac. The males about her exuded milt and together they churned the eggs and sperm until they were well fertilized.

Slowly, the eggs swelled in the water and a preordained phenomenon began to unfold within their clear, green envelopes. They drifted slowly with the current, on their way to where Saxatilis too had started her life. The cycle of life had come a full turn.

PART ONE

THE FISH

1

What Is a Striped Bass?

There is a saying that if you can get to know an opponent, he is yours. This holds true for the striped bass. If you can get to know the striped bass—its anatomy, its life cycle, the numerous forces that motivate it, the environment that surrounds it, and its responses to food, heat, cold, shelter, fear, and love—it is yours.

If you know the anatomy of a striped bass, you already have some idea of where it swims, how it swims, how it can feed, and why it inhabits the waters it does. If you know its range and distribution, you know where to intercept it and when to be there. If you know where and how it reproduces, you will understand why it is on the Roanoke River in April, why it is in the Cape Cod Canal in June, and why it is resting off Hatteras in January. If you know the foods it prefers, you will know what baits to feed it, what lures to select, and what levels in the ocean at which to present them. If you know what factors control the population of the striper, you can estimate its abundance and your own fishing productivity.

In my Introduction I attempted to communicate something of the nature of the fish by following a single sea-wise female through the months leading up to her spring spawning. But for a true understanding of the striped bass, a more conventional and ordered discussion is necessary, and in this chapter I will begin with the basic attributes of the fish—its classification among the fishes and its physical characteristics.

CLASSIFICATION

The striped bass, *Morone saxatilis,* is a typical saltwater fish possessing all those features it needs to compete successfully in an ocean of other fishes. Until just recently, the striped bass was grouped with the family of sea basses. These fish, of which the grouper is a good example, are warm- or tropic-water fish, and the striped bass was thought to be a northern contingent. But its preference for cool or even cold water puzzled the taxonomists and eventually they decided that it wasn't a sea bass. Today, the striped bass is considered one of a group of temperate-water basses that inhabit the ocean, and it is itself the best example of its group.

Striped bass have been tagged by a number of names ever since the first colonists discovered them swimming alongside Plymouth Rock. They were quick to call it a bass, because the fish closely resembled the sea bass or common bass (saltwater type) found swimming among the British Isles. The most common name now used is "striped bass," describing the striped appearance of the fish. An offshoot of this same line of thinking is the name "linesider." Bass have also been called "greenheads" and, because of their penchant for squid, "squid hounds." The second most common name in use today is "rock" or "rockfish," used more in Atlantic waters south of New Jersey. Farther south, in South Carolina and Georgia and along the Gulf Coast, it is known equally as well as the striped bass and as the rockfish. On the Pacific Coast, it is usually called the striped bass.

The name "rockfish" describes more the fish's feeding habits than its outward appearance or fleshy texture. This name evolved because striped bass feed commonly on food that dwells around rocks and other obstacles in the water.

The Indians of New England had their own name for the striped bass, "missuckeke," according to a book by Roger Williams, *A Key into the Language of America; or, a Help to the Language of the Natives in that part of America called New England.*

Scientifically, the striped bass has had three names over the past few hundred years. The earliest description of the bass labeled it as *Roccus lineatus* (Bloch). Bloch was thought to be the first man in scientific journals to describe the fish. *Roccus* is New Latin and refers to rock, the environment around which the fish was found. *Lineatus,* also Latin, refers to the stripes or lines on the side of the fish.

But *Roccus lineatus* wasn't a very appropriate name because it also applied to a Mediterranean cousin. Sometime around 1880, it was changed to *Roccus saxatilis* (Walbaum). This was accepted by most scientists until 1966 when the name was again changed. *Roccus saxatilis* is a bit redundant because it literally means rock that lives or grows around rock, or saxatiles. Saxatile derives from the Latin word *saxum,* meaning rock.

Somewhere in the literature, taxonomists discovered that another man—we don't know his name—had classified the fish before Bloch.

The convention is always to accept the older name. The genus is *Morone*. No one knows the exact meaning of the name. It could have been the classifier's own name, which was a common practice first used by researchers, discoverers, and taxonomists. The closest we can come to finding a derivation for *Morone* is the Greek word *moros*, which has two meanings, "death" and "stupid." The latter meaning may have been intended because in colonial times striped bass were so plentiful that they were extremely easy to catch, and if a fish is easy to catch it might be thought of as an unwise or stupid fish. Take your pick. In any case, since 1966 when the renaming took place, *Morone saxatilis* or "stupid rockfish" is what we must content ourselves with.

In relation to other fishes, the striped bass is a bony fish (some fish are made of cartilage rather than bone) and belongs to order Perciformes and family Percichthyidae. At one time the striped bass was included in the sea bass family, Serranidae, but because of the sea basses' like for warm water and the striper's preference for cold, and a few other physical differences, the striped bass has been reclassified. More recent classification has broken the Percichthyidae family into two groups, separating the warm-water sea bass of the south from those preferring slightly cooler water like the striped bass and its near cousins the white bass and white perch. This new family reflects the change of striped bass's generic name from *Roccus* to *Morone*.

Morone labrax, *the European version of our striped bass. It is the closest cousin of* Morone saxatilis. *Reproduced from* British Anglers' Natural History *by E. G. Boulenger.*

The only fish which is really more than just a cousin to the striped bass is *Morone labrax,* a fish that looks almost identical to our striper and to a British relation. The back of *Morone labrax* has a slight arch to it, and it does not have lateral lines. Its appearance is more of a silver or silver-blue; in color the fish looks a lot like the Atlantic salmon. It too is a marine species and frequently inhabits the estuaries and even fresh water, much like our striped bass.

This fish is found around most of the British Isles during the summer months but disappears south during the colder times of the year. In summer distribution, it is found in southern Norway and Sweden and from Denmark along the coast of France and Spain. Irish biologists have confirmed that it spawns in fresh water during May in the northern part of its ranges. Its way of life is almost identical to that of our striped bass.

In addition to *saxatilis,* the genus *Morone* includes five other species of closely related fish: *chrysops,* white bass; *interruptus,* yellow bass; *americanus,* white perch; *labrax,* European striped bass; and *punctatus,* from the Mediterranean.

ANATOMY

A striped bass is a fusiform fish. That is, its body is shaped much like a torpedo. Some fish are laterally compressed, from side to side, and most fish like this are extremely maneuverable—the permit is an example. Others are dorsally-ventrally compressed, like the flounder. This shape is best for fish which lie on the bottom much of the time, or fish which float through the water hunting, like skates and rays. Neither extreme is very swift. Fish almost round in cross-section are the fastest, but they lack real maneuverability. Good examples are the tuna and bonito of salt water and the trout and salmon of fresh water.

The striped bass falls between the extremes and is a somewhat average, unspecialized fish in shape. This lack of specialization, however, means that while it may not be at its best in certain unusual situations, it copes very well with the average conditions it faces in its daily life.

In all, the striped bass has a generalized fish body, the trunk of which is $3\frac{1}{2}$ to 4 times as thick as the body is long, from snout to its caudal peduncle (base of tail). The back is only slightly arched, while the bottom of the body has a heavy sway to it, especially in older examples and in striped bass from freshwater environments. The caudal peduncle is rather stout and gives rise to a large but only slightly forked tail. This large rudder gives the fish the maneuverability it requires for life in rivers, the surf, and estuaries.

The striped bass has a large, long head, almost as long as the body is deep. The moderately pointed snout isn't long enough to cover a slightly projecting lower jaw. The mouth is set on an oblique angle, making surface feeding a bit easier, and extends back under the eye. Two spines on the posterior margin of each gill cover are located on a level even with the eye and seem to make the head extend even farther back. Large eyes are set high on the head, again making surface feeding or feeding from below easier.

External anatomy of the striped bass.

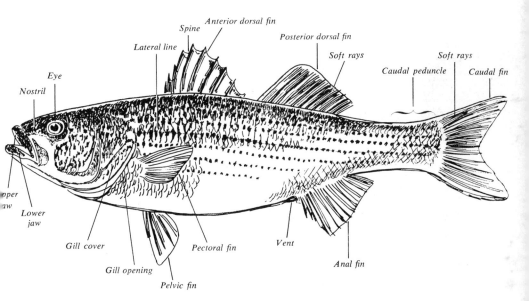

Fins

Two dorsal fins on the back are of equal length and just separated from each other. The anterior or forward dorsal fin is triangular in shape, much like a sail. It is supported by nine or ten stiff spines. The posterior dorsal fin is supported by twelve to fourteen softer pieces of cartilage called rays. They look as if they had been clipped by scissors because of their even edge. They grow smaller in size from front to back.

The anal fin on the underside of the striped bass just behind the anal pore looks a lot like the reverse of the soft dorsal ray. It has three short spines at its head and the remainder is supported by eleven cartilaginous rays.

During the course of the evolutionary development of the striped bass and other temperate basses, the paired pelvic fins migrated forward on the underside of the body to a point just behind the pectoral fins. They are of moderate size, similar to the pectorals. The paired pectoral fins are just behind the gill covers, on a line even with the mouth.

Internal anatomy of the striped bass.

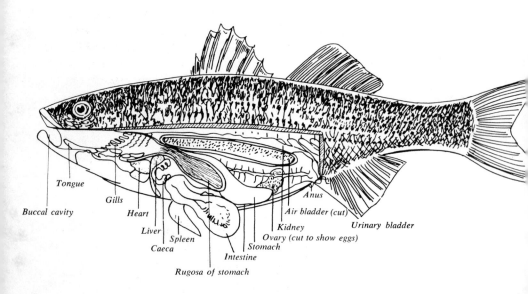

Tongue
Gills
Buccal cavity
Heart
Liver
Spleen
Caeca
Anus
Air bladder (cut)
Kidney   Urinary bladder
Ovary (cut to show eggs)
Stomach
Intestine
Rugosa of stomach

Scales and stripes

Scales on a striped bass are rather large compared to those of most other fish. Along the lateral line they number anywhere from fifty-seven to sixty-seven depending upon where the fish originate. They are ctenoid (toothed) in type and grow rings each season—helpful in determining a bass's age.

In the larval stage, striped bass are equipped with huge teeth to catch fish. But as they develop, the teeth regress. Adult striped bass do have teeth. They are small, and positioned at the base of the tongue in two parallel rows or patches.

In general coloration, a striped bass is white on the bottom with a gradual darkening up the sides toward the back. The darkening occurs because the seven or eight narrow dark stripes come closer together as they approach the back. The color on the back ranges from a dark olive green to a pale blue in some fish, black in others, while the stripes or lines on the sides are more of a black. Three of the stripes are below the lateral line on the fish, beginning behind the gill cover and the pectoral fin, tapering but not reaching the caudal peduncle. The longest stripe is that on the lateral line and extends to the very beginning of the tail fin. Three or four stripes above the lateral line extend rearward, merging as the body narrows.

The stripes under the scales are rather uniformly lined with only an occasional interruption. These stripes, as well as the scales on the back, will often take on a brassy, reflective sheen, especially in live fish. The fins and tail are somewhat dusky. Striped bass in a strictly marine environment are often lighter in color. Those that have been in an estuary for a while, especially an estuary with a dark bottom, tend to deepen in color, and so do striped bass living entirely in fresh water.

Skull of the striped bass. Reproduced from Fishes of the Vicinity of New York City *by John Treadwell Nichols.*

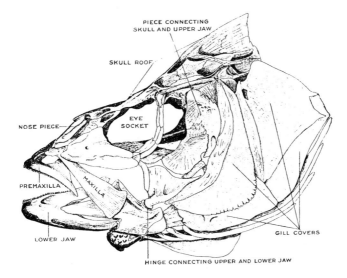

Drawing by F. A. Lucas

Locomotion

The striped bass is an excellent swimmer because of its generalized body shape. A fish swims by undulating its muscles and making its body move in waves. A wave starts at the head and moves toward the tail. Often another wave is started before the second wave is completed. The real power, however, for sudden bursts in speed and for maneuverability lies in the tail. The tail is supported by a series of bony rays founded on a broad peduncle. When snapped, it pushes the striper ahead.

Striped bass have been known to migrate as much as 12 miles per day, but can move faster with sudden bursts of speed. They can reach 14 miles per hour. A few fish, seen chasing fleeing menhaden, have been clocked at 20 miles per hour.

SENSES

Sight

The striped bass feeds by sight. It may use its hearing and sense of smell to find food, but the final approach or attack is made by sight. The eyes of a striper are a lot like human eyes. They can readily adjust to different intensities of light by controlling the size of the iris. Fortunately for the striped bass, its eyes are constructed with two types of light-sensitive cells in the retina, the area at the back of the eye. These cells, called rods and cones from the general character of their shape, are used for seeing under differing intensities of light in much the same manner as the rods and cones in the human eye.

Most fish have cone cells that are sensitive to color and are used primarily during the day. Those fish with only cone cells become inactive at night. However, the striped bass is an extremely active fish that feeds throughout the night. This is made possible with the rod-shaped cells. The rod-shaped cells are buried behind the cone cells during the day because they are extremely sensitive to light. But as night approaches they rise to the surface and replace the cone cells as the prime light and sensation gatherers.

The striped bass's nighttime vision is basically black and white. But with little light available to illuminate any colored objects, color vision at night would not give the striped bass any great advantage over other fish.

Unlike the lens in our eyes, the lens in the eyes of a striped bass are round instead of flattened. The effect of such a lens is to make the striped bass nearsighted. Without muscles to control the shape of the lens, as in our eyes, the fish cannot adjust its eyes and focus on far objects. This is one reason why lures and baits presented to the striper must be at close range. Striped bass get along rather well with myopic vision because most of the waters in which they swim have poor visibility; even the clearest salt water is filled with suspended particles. To find its prey, striped bass rely on the other senses and eyes become important only when they move in for the kill.

Striped bass lack complete binocular vision because their eyes are placed on the sides of their head rather than in front. The field of each eye can gather about 180 degrees of scope because the round lens projects slightly beyond the wall of the head. In many fish, there is often a void directly in front of the head because they do not truly gather 180 degrees of vision. It is interrupted by bony structures used to protect the eye. But in striped bass, the eyes are placed slightly forward and above on the head, and so it can watch the action on the surface without undue difficulty. This even gives the eye a bit of overlap, and a small degree of binocular ability and depth perception. It also explains why striped bass are so fond of surface lures and spend more time looking up than down.

Smell

Like a dog on land, a striped bass in the water really lives in a world of smells. This is probably the most highly developed of a striper's senses, followed closely by hearing. One could almost guess that a striped bass can smell better than see just from considering the environments it inhabits. In the large bays and rivers, the waters are turbid. Once in the open a bass doesn't go far from the beach, and in the wash the sand is always in suspension. Therefore, a striped bass is more likely to smell a lure or food before it ever sees it. If it's artificial, it had better smell good.

Reasoning in the other direction, we can tell a lot about how a fish feeds from the type of nostrils it has developed. We know from the construction of a striped bass's eyes that it has the ability to feed well after dusk. But to go along with this feeding on the dark side of the earth a striped bass needs a good sense of smell. The striped bass has evolved one of the best systems.

Instead of the one pair of nostrils on its head such as many fish possess, the striped bass has a double pair of nostrils, two on each side. The sensation of smell is carried in the water and picked up by olfactory cells in the lining of the nostril. These cells number a half-million to the square inch. The water that enters the nostril of the striped bass doesn't go out the same entrance through which it arrived, and it does not run into the throat as it would in a human nostril. Each nostril has an exit port. This means that the fish is always smelling a fresh supply of water passing over the olfactory cells. This is extremely important to fish that feed by smell or feed a lot at night, when the sense of smell is more important than the other senses.

The striped bass's ability to smell in the water is hundreds of times better than our ability to smell odors in the air. From miles away it can smell things that we would just be able to perceive from a dozen feet away in the air. Few experiments have been conducted to check the olfactory ability of striped bass, but it is very good — perhaps nearly as good as that of the champion Durante of the fishes, the American eel, which has responded to an alcohol of which one-billionth of a drop was diluted in a large swimming pool. This accounts for the ability of these eels to smell the Hudson River from as far away as the Sargasso Sea off Bermuda.

A striped bass can find its way back to a parent stream to spawn much the same way a salmon heads home. The homing instinct may be no more than a highly developed sense of smell that can identify the chemistry of a river immediately at the place where the fish was spawned.

Hearing

A striped bass needs a sensory system that will work in the black of night and in waters so polluted that the sense of smell is disrupted to the point where it is nonfunctional. Thus a sense of hearing is important too. The striper's auditory system is acute, and it can hear sounds well below our own range. One reason is that sound travels more than five times faster in the water than it does in air. The auditory range of a striped bass is also extremely broad, from as low as 15 cycles per second to as high as 10,000 cycles per second. Some fish can hear far above that. Our range in the air is between 20 and 20,000 cycles.

Sounds in the world of a striped bass are of two types: those that attract and those that make it run in fear. One means food and the other means a predator.

Fish have ears, but they don't protrude. Their ears are buried in their skulls, slightly behind and below their eyes. There are no external openings through the skin, but sound is transmitted to the inner ear through the flesh and bone on the skull. In addition to their ears, fish have another organ that functions in pretty much the same manner. After all, sound does nothing for the ear but set up sympathetic vibrations. These are then carried by an electric signal to the brain and recreate sensations of food, danger, or the like. So any organ sensitive to vibrations can function pretty much as another ear. In the striped bass and in most other fishes this organ is a series of sensitive canals along the lateral line. The sensors in the canals respond to low-frequency vibrations. The lateral line is used by striped bass to pinpoint the source of a sound, acting like a directional finder.

Taste

The sensation of taste is closely related to that of smell in both man and fish. Like man, a striped bass can differentiate between sweet, sour, salty, and bitter tastes. The two senses differ in range. The sensation of smell can be called the long-distance receptor and taste the short-distance receptor.

The sensation of taste isn't too important if you are fishing with plugs or artificial lures. But if you use live bait, the way it tastes to the fish is important, because striped bass will discriminate. If the bait is alive, then the taste sensations will take care of themselves and the lure won't be alarming to a striped bass. But if you use dead, frozen, or cut bait, its condition is important. The striper will reject foods that it finds displeasing in taste. There is an order of preference in baits: live bait first, followed by freshly dead bait, then frozen freshly dead bait, frozen old bait, and lastly just plain old bait that has been in the sun without ice. Some fish, like sharks and bottom scavengers, don't mind the state of a bait. But game fish like striped bass prefer live bait to all others.

I enjoy fishing for striped bass with live menhaden or bunker as bait. Bass will greedily and readily take this bait. But fishing a bunker in a heavily running tide while stemming the flow quickly wears out even the lightest-hooked bunker. They develop "lockjaw" and drown. Striped bass immediately shun the dead bunker and will pick only those lines with a live fish. The smell and taste of death is carried in the water.

Fish taste flavors in much the same manner we do, but their taste buds are not restricted to the tongue alone. A striped bass has taste buds on its tongue, in the throat, and around the roof of the mouth. But they don't stop there. They also have a battery of external taste buds on the end of the snout and lips. A bass can taste its food before it opens its mouth, and that may explain why it may seem to be "mouthing" but not taking a bait. It may only be nosing it to see how fresh it is before it strikes.

Sensitivity to temperature

Fish are coldblooded animals and have no heat-regulating mechanisms within their body. The temperature of a fish's body is the same as that of the water that surrounds it. When a fish undergoes strenuous exercise, the body temperature may rise a few degrees, but for the most part the fish has no real control over it. This life in equilibrium with the environment may be one reason fish are so sensitive to temperature and temperature changes. Research has shown that fish are sensitive to as small a change in their environment as 1/50th of a degree. This doesn't mean that they will respond to the change, just that they are aware of it and can use this sensitivity when selecting optimum water areas for feeding or resting. A fish feels the temperature through minute cells with nerve endings in the skin. These cells then transmit the temperature to the brain.

The outside temperature and thus the inside temperature of a fish affect the body's metabolism, or the vital functions of breaking down food, transporting oxygen, removing excrement, and the like. The higher the temperature, to a point, the more active is our striped bass. As the temperature falls, the body activities slow down. As these activities slow down, so does the demand for food to fuel them.

The active temperature range for striped bass is quite wide when compared to other fish. Striped bass wintering in the St. Lawrence River and in New England have been observed in water close to the freezing point—that is, the saltwater freezing point, which is a few

Striped bass grow large. Here the author holds a 51-pounder that fell for a white-bucktail/yellow-porkrind combination.

degrees cooler than for fresh water. In one Connecticut river, while the temperature of the water was at 35 degrees, a striped bass did take an artificial lure presented to it. However, striped bass go into a somewhat dormant state once the temperature of the water drops below 39 or 40 degrees.

On the high range of the temperature scale, striped bass have been known to tolerate water as high as 80 to 83 degrees, but they become extremely sluggish. The optimal ranges for striped bass are from 55 to 68 or 70 degrees. Their preferred spawning temperature is near the middle, at 64.5 degrees, and this may well be the optimal feeding temperature when they are not preoccupied with spawning.

One researcher found an interesting temperature effect on fish while working with tuna. In a struggle to rid itself of a hook, a tuna's temperature might rise 10 to 15 degrees. The total mass of the fish's body is so great that it cannot cool itself quickly, and it fatigues rapidly. Fish can take changes in temperature, but the adjustment is slow. If the change is too quick, fish will go into shock. Fish with large heads and small bodies can dissipate heat readily, but fish with large body areas, like the striped bass, cannot rid themselves of the heat quickly enough, and they succumb rapidly. And thus a striped bass taken while the waters are still cool (not cold) puts up a good fight because the water helps absorb and dissipate the heat. A fish taken in warm water, during August and early September, is less likely to put up a good fight.

SIZES OF STRIPED BASS

Striped bass can grow to great sizes. In past years, there have been numerous records of striped bass which weighed over 100 pounds being taken by commercial fishermen. There is a well-substantiated record of the largest striped bass ever hauled ashore from the waters of the Roanoke River. In April 1891, not one but several striped bass weighing 125 pounds were taken at Edenton, North Carolina. Another record comes from Orleans, Massachusetts, of a striper weighing 112 pounds, and in 1887 a 100½-pound striper was taken and recorded in Casco Bay, Maine.

The rod-and-reel record fish was taken in August 1913, a 73-pounder caught by C. B. Church at Vineyard Sound on the backside of Cuttyhunk Island in Massachusetts. There is also a well-substantiated but unofficial record of an 85-pounder taken in 1887 by Col. Francis W. Miner. Today, few fish above the rod-and-reel record have been taken commercially. Plenty of large striped bass, in the 50- and 60-pound class, are still caught each year, but the majority of the catches by sportfishermen range from 6 to 10 pounds.

2

Distribution and Migrations
of Striped Bass

It is rather well established that all fishes first evolved in fresh water, and then, through eons of time, some fishes gradually expanded their living space to take in the oceans. They adapted to the demands of living in salt water, and once this adaptation took place, most fish were unable to return to fresh water.

Several families of fishes, however, never lost the ability to change environments and are still able to return at will. For some, the adaptation to one environment after living in the other takes a good deal of time. For others, like our striped bass, the change can be accomplished quickly. This group includes, along with the striped bass, fish like sturgeon, shad, herring, smelt, white perch, salmon, trout, and eels. These fish are classed as anadromous species. An anadromous fish is one that lives most of its life in salt water and then returns to freshwater rivers to spawn.

There are some classes of fish that spend most of their lives in fresh water, but when they are in the proximity of the oceans, they may migrate to the estuaries for the summer to feed. A good example of this type of fish is our Eastern brook trout. It is typical of other chars living farther to the north. These fish make a regular habit of migrating to salt water to feed. Such fish are called catadromous. The Atlantic salmon is both anadromous and catadromous, depending upon which time in its life cycle you are watching it.

Over most of their northern range, striped bass are primarily anadromous fish; the great part of their lives is spent in salt water. When they do head for fresh water, it is to spawn. Striped bass quickly return to salt water after spawning. Even their eggs and young develop within a matter of a few weeks and are again in salt water because of the proximity of their spawning sites to estuaries. There are, however, some striped bass populations which spend all their lives in fresh water even though they are not blocked from returning to the sea. This characteristic appears to be a relatively recent development in modern striped bass, somewhat of a reversal to its ancient habits.

Distribution of the striped bass in marine waters of the United States.

The ability to live in either freshwater or saltwater environments is a function of a specialized kidney. When a striped bass is bent on spawning and enters fresh water, its body is faced with the problem of a salt loss in its bloodstream. There is also a tendency to absorb too much water. In order to make the change, the osmotic pressure—a force created by dissolved salts and minerals in the bloodstream—must be adjustable. Anadromous fish possess glomerular kidneys, which have the ability to respond to differences in urine volume that result from different salinities. These fish also possess gills and membranes in the mouth cavity that can handle the uptake and secretion of ions in the blood and tissue and protect it against undue diffusion. The glomeruli— small masses of capillaries within the kidney—take urinary wastes out of the blood, maintain an isotonic balance, and thus allow the striped bass to change environments at will. In many anadromous fish, the change requires a conditioning time, but in striped bass, it seems to be very minimal.

Distribution of the striped bass in fresh water, by states.

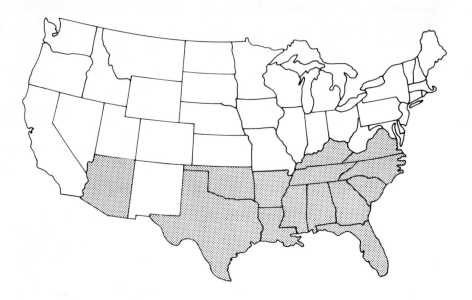

The striped bass is basically littoral in its range, though it is capable of swimming anywhere in salt water. Its life is closely associated with the shore, the estuaries, and rivers, and seldom does it stray far off-shore. In early evolutionary history, the fish was basically a river fish, one that eventually learned to go down to the sea and feed in estuaries. Today, the estuaries and large bays near rivers are still its prime living space.

During the earliest colonial times, striped bass were found in almost every stream that entered the ocean, from the St. Lawrence River south to Florida, and from western Florida to Louisiana. And almost every river had its own spawning population of bass that spent their summers at the mouth of the rivers, or in an area along the beach not too far from the ancestral stream. The one exception to this general picture today is a subpopulation of striped bass that originate in several rivers in middle Chesapeake Bay. We'll describe this phenomenon later on in this chapter.

After clearing the land and planting crops, the next order of business for our colonist forefathers was to develop a source of power to grind their grains into flour. As in England, they turned to the bountiful number of brooks and rivers, building dams and mills. As industrialization spread over New England during the middle of the nineteenth century, the demand for power to turn the wheels of progress became greater, and eventually the larger rivers of the Northeast were dammed. In effect, they had stopped all striped bass in this region from reaching the fresh water necessary for them to spawn. Very quickly, the fish was eliminated from this part of its range.

Rivers south of the Hudson still drained a land that was used primarily for agriculture. Industrialization is a recent event. For the most part, these rivers also lacked the landfall necessary to create mills, except in their upper reaches. Fortunately, these areas were far from salt water or where striped bass spawned. It is today these rivers of our Atlantic Coast which provide the major spawning and nursery grounds for striped bass.

DISTRIBUTION

Today, striped bass are still found over much of their original range, though in greatly reduced numbers. While they inhabit it, they no longer spawn where they once did. There are token spawnings in the St. Lawrence River, Quebec, that are independent of the rest of the system. There is spawning in a few streams in New Brunswick and Nova Scotia, and even occasionally in Maine. But for the most part, spawning is restricted to the Hudson River, a weak effort in Delaware Bay, and a great concentration in Chesapeake Bay. In North Carolina, spawning bass are restricted to streams that flow into Albermarle and Pamlico sounds. These include the Roanoke, Neuse, and Tar rivers. From South Carolina to the St. Johns River in Florida on the Atlantic and from streams in western Florida to Louisiana, striped bass are truly endemic fish, living most of the time in the rivers and only occasionally visiting the sea. The farther south one goes the more true this becomes.

Striped bass live and travel great distances up freshwater rivers in the United States and Canada. The most distant inland freshwater range on the Atlantic Coast for the striped bass has been recorded in Quebec's St. Lawrence River at Lake St. Pierre, approximately 400 miles inland. Other inland limits on the Atlantic include the Hudson River to Albany, though a few bass have even been recorded on the Mohawk River; the Delaware River, at one time as far as Port Jervis; the Susquehanna in past years to the New York state line; the Potomac at Great Falls; the Roanoke River to Roanoke Rapids; and the Alabama River to Montgomery and above. On the West Coast, bass have been recorded 250 miles up the Sacramento River in California.

Genio C. Scott, a fairly accurate recorder of fishing during the 1840s and 1850s in America, noted that he frequently fished for striped bass in the "upper portion of Lake Ontario." This was long before the first stocking attempt by New York State, so the fish must have been natural migrants.

Canada

The St. Lawrence River has always held an endemic population of striped bass whose cyclic abundance or scarcity does not seem to be affected by what happens along the remainder of the Atlantic Coast. Head of tidewater on the St. Lawrence is a widening of the river midway between Quebec City and Montreal, called Lake St. Pierre. Bass spawn at the rapids at the head of the lake in late June and July, then summer in the tidal river below Quebec City. In the fall, there is a migration out of this estuary and back up the river to the lake. At one time, bass were netted through the ice on Lake St. Pierre. Striped bass have occurred regularly up the river as far as Montreal. In 1865, a striped bass was even taken from Lake Ontario at the head of the St. Lawrence River by a Robert A. Roosevelt.

The striped bass is not found north of the Gulf of St. Lawrence, above the Laurentian channel separating Labrador from Newfoundland. In the Gulf of St. Lawrence it is found downriver along many of the streams that flow into the bay. In New Brunswick it has been found on the Miramichi River system and estuary, and at Tignisk; on Prince Edward Island in Malpeque Bay and Cheticamp, Nova Scotia. It also occurs in the estuary of the River Philip, N.S.; Summerside, P.E.I.; and the Richibucto River, N.B.

On the outer coast of Nova Scotia it is found on the Canso and in Mira Bay, Chedabucto Bay, and Mahone Bay. In the Bay of Fundy it is found in the Minas Basin area, and along the shores of St. John and Yarmouth counties, as well as in the St. Croix, Digdeguash, St. John, Kennebecasis, Shubenacadie, and Annapolis rivers. Some are even caught in Shubenacadie Lake.

On the St. John River in New Brunswick, striped bass at one time made an extensive upriver running spawn to the village of Mactaquac, just above Fredericton. A few years ago, the huge Mactaquac Dam was built astride the river, exactly where the bass spawned. The effects have been devastating.

From Maine south to the St. Johns River in Florida, striped bass are either seasonal or residential fish at one time or another throughout the year. The greatest concentration of fish appears between Cape Hatteras, N.C., and Cape Ann, Mass. During the summer months, from June to October, this concentration centers in the north half, between Long Island, New York, and Cape Cod. Before the opening of the Cape Cod canal, Buzzards Bay and Vineyard Sound were about the northern limit of the migration. During the colder months of the year, striped bass are concentrated just off North Carolina and in Chesapeake Bay. There is some holdover of fish in many of the large estuaries that contain a sufficient water depth, in the states of New Hampshire, Massachusetts, Connecticut, Rhode Island, and New Jersey. At one time, there was even an extensive winter fishery in several bays on southern Long Island, from Gravesend Bay East to Great South Bay.

Maine

Nowadays, striped bass in Maine are virtually seasonal migrants with only some slight winter holdover. At one time, there were records of striped bass spawning on the Saco, Kennebec, Androscoggin, Sheepscot, Penobscot, and St. Croix. Barrier dams at the head of the tide eliminated these historic spawning sites.

The concentration of striped bass in Maine waters varies from season to season, dependent upon the water temperature and the appearance of baitfish which striped bass feed on and follow. Consistently, when the fish do appear, the Saco is one of the best. Generally the fish appear from Kittery to Calais.

New Hampshire

In New England, the striped bass nowadays is a seasonal migrant except for the occasional holdover fish that becomes somewhat dormant and contributes only slightly to the fishery. In New Hampshire, the distribution of the fish is limited in the bays along this state's short coast. At one time, there was quite a fishery on portions of the Merrimac River in New Hampshire, but this has disappeared.

Massachusetts

The waters of Massachusetts become the northern limit for the summer migratory stock during most years for striped bass. They are distributed at the estuary formed by the Merrimac River and from Plum Island south to the waters surrounding Cape Ann and Gloucester. The greatest concentration, however, appears in the waters off Cape Cod, on the north side of Cape Cod and in all the bays, inlets, and estuaries along the seaward and southern sides of the hook. During the summer, striped bass are well dispersed about Nantucket, Martha's Vineyard, the Elizabeth Islands, and the numerous bays of Buzzards Bay, as well as in the Cape Cod Canal.

Rhode Island

Rhode Island has a good distribution in the waters of Narragansett Bay as well as on the outside, along the beaches from Sakonnet Point to Watch Hill. The western edge of Rhode Island, near Watch Hill, appears also to be the western limit of the summering populations of striped bass.

Connecticut

Connecticut receives striped bass from the Atlantic coastal migratory stock in its eastern waters in Long Island Sound. Along the western coast of the state, the fish are summering stock from the Hudson River fishery. From Bridgeport to Old Lyme, there is an overlap in the composition of fish from both the Hudson and Chesapeake Bay. Striped bass fishing activities are concentrated at the mouths of the Connecticut and Thames rivers, at Bartletts and Hatchett reefs, among the offshore islands in western Long Island Sound, and at the mouth of the Housatonic River.

New York

New York's striped bass fishery is composed of two differing stocks of fish and hence its distribution varies. The location of striped bass also varies with the season. Striped bass composed of the Atlantic migratory stock appear on the south shore of Long Island from April to November and even as late as December. These fish are on the move, though portions of the school do stay the summer in the eastern bays from Great South Bay to Montauk and in Gardiner's Bay and the Peconics, as well as in Long Island Sound from Wading River east. Part of this migratory stock becomes residential in the waters around Plum Island, in the Race between Fishers Island and the Gulls, and along the coast of Rhode Island during the summer.

The largest resident stock of striped bass in New York waters are produced in the Hudson River and influence distribution on western Long Island Sound. Until recently, the Hudson was thought to be only a minor nursery, but several studies have revealed that it is far larger than once believed. Striped bass inhabit the Hudson as far north as Poughkeepsie, with some fish present in the river as far as Albany during the summer. Nursery stock, for the first two years of life, remains in the area around Stony Point before taking part in a local migration.

Striped bass in the Hudson are migratory, but only in a local sense with regard to their immediate environment. About mid-April, adult bass and those that have spawned begin a southward migration in the Hudson. They eventually establish a summer population with its greatest concentration in New York's Upper Bay and Lower Bay and in the bays and estuaries of northern New Jersey, with a few fish moving as far south as Barnegat Inlet. Those fish that do enter the Atlantic move east along the south shore of Long Island and summer in Jamaica Bay. Some fish also enter the western part of Great South Bay.

Another portion of this fishery migrates out of the Hudson through the East River and into the western part of Long Island Sound. It disperses itself across the coast of Westchester County and as far east along Connecticut as Bridgeport. The fish are spread along the north shore of Long Island as far as Port Jefferson. The bass remain here throughout most of the summer and return to the Hudson as winter approaches. Some fish winter over in deeper rivers and bays of northern New Jersey and western Long Island Sound.

New Jersey

Unlike New York's, New Jersey's distribution is composed almost totally of a migratory stock except for a limited amount of juvenile fish that are spawned and reared along the southern part of Delaware Bay. The bulk of New Jersey's fishery is composed of the migrant Chesapeake Bay stock. This is distributed along the beaches from Cape May to Sandy Hook in the spring as they head northward and again in this same area in the fall as they return south.

A second contribution of migratory stock does come from the Hudson River. These fish are spread in New Jersey in waters from Barnegat Bay north to Newark Bay. They are summer residents here, in Raritan Bay and Navesink and Shrewsbury rivers. During their northward migration, some Chesapeake Bay fish will spread in the large bays of New Jersey and concentrate there for a while. To some degree, they will leave pods of summer residential stock. During the fall migration southward, many large bass do not elect to return to more southerly waters, and wintering populations have been observed at Great Egg Harbor and the Mullica River on Great Bay.

Delaware

Most of Delaware's fish are concentrated on Delaware Bay, and striped bass are distributed at times up the Delaware River to Wilmington, along the New Jersey portion of the bay, and about the estuaries near Wood-land Beach. The Chesapeake and Delaware Canal near the head of the bay has become a major migratory shortcut for the itinerant striped bass of Chesapeake Bay, and the fish are abundant at times in the canal. This waterway also contains a spawning population in the spring.

Chesapeake Bay

This vast body of water, shared by Maryland and Virginia, is the major nursery for striped bass on the Atlantic. Striped bass are spread through-out the numerous bays and rivers of this area at various times of the year. The coastal portions of Maryland and Virginia receive fish only during the migrations, and there is very little fishing for striped bass except after the migrations are under way.

Chesapeake Bay must be considered as an entity when dealing with the striped bass in this area. Most of the bay is essentially fresh water because of the great number of large rivers that empty into it. However, the effect of tides is felt to the very head of the bay on the Susquehanna River.

Striped bass in Chesapeake Bay populations can be divided into three groups, roughly based on their origin at spawning. There is an upper group of striped bass that are spawned in the Susquehanna River, the upper bay itself, the Chesapeake and Delaware Canal, and the Northeast, Elk, Bohemia, Sassafras, and Chester rivers. The second group of fish is produced in the Choptank, Naticoke, Wicomico, Manokin, and Pocomoke rivers.

The largest production of striped bass on Chesapeake Bay comes from the Potomac River. Also included with this population as a group are fish from the Rappahannock and York rivers of Virginia. The lowest river in the bay is the James River; its fish are the least migratory of the bass produced in Chesapeake Bay. They more closely resemble the striped bass of Albemarle Sound in migration characteristics as well as racial features.

During the summer, the waters of the bay hold large numbers of striped bass. However, the majority of these are small fish, one to two years old, and many of only zero-year stock. Large fish are present only during spawning.

North Carolina

The distribution of fish in North Carolina varies with the season. During the winter months, there is a large concentration of striped bass located offshore in the Atlantic that does, from time to time, approach the beaches from Cape Fear to Virginia Beach. The greatest catches are in the Cape Hatteras area. Inside the barrier beaches, in Pamlico and Albemarle sounds, the bays hold a large wintering population of smaller fish, similar to those age classes in Chesapeake Bay. During early spring, striped bass from outside in the Atlantic as well as those wintering in the bays make a spawning migration up the Roanoke, Neuse, and Tar rivers and several smaller tidal streams.

From Cape Fear south to Florida and along the Gulf of Mexico, striped bass are more or less confined to river systems during most of the year. Only occasionally are they found at the estuaries. The farther south one travels the more this characteristic obtains. In some systems, they are found 150 to 200 miles from salt water.

South Carolina

Estuarine environments conducive to holding striped bass are quite plentiful in South Carolina. However, the fish spend more time in freshwater rivers than in estuaries. Each river system has developed a self-sustaining population. From north to south, striped bass are distributed in the Waccamaw and Pee Dee rivers, which share a common estuary, and the Santee, Cooper, Wando, Ashley, Edisto, Ashepoo, and Combahee rivers. South Carolina shares with Georgia the Savannah River, a system which supports a fairly consistent striped bass fishery.

Georgia

At one time, Georgia's waters supported an active and extensive fishery for striped bass. Over the years, however, the rivers have been polluted by pulp operations, and construction on spawning sites has reduced natural production to extreme lows. A striped bass hatchery has been established at Richmond Hill, near Savannah, and efforts are being made to re-establish striped bass in the rivers. Today, there is a fair fishery on the Savannah and Ogeechee rivers. Migration runs on the Savannah itself have taken fish more than 180 miles upriver. The majority of Georgia's striped bass fishing is done along the coastal streams; the best angling is in the lower estuaries during the cooler fall and winter months.

Florida

To the surprise of most northern anglers, Florida possesses a unique striped bass fishery. The distribution is in two separate populations. One is composed of the southern limit of the Atlantic Coast population. The second is a Gulf Coast population that has no communication with the Atlantic fish.

On the Atlantic Coast, the striped bass distribution is limited to three rivers that empty into the ocean in the northeast corner of the state. St. Marys River, shared with Georgia as a border river, contains some striped bass. Within the city limits of Jacksonville and just south of the St. Marys is Nassau River and in Jacksonville proper is the St. Johns River, both with bass populations. The St. Johns flows north from Washington Lake for about 200 miles before it reaches Jacksonville. At one time or another bass have been taken along its entire course. Occasionally, striped bass have been taken along the Atlantic beach as far south along the Florida coast as Ft. Pierce, but these have been stragglers or wandering fish.

On the west coast of Florida, striped bass appear in all the rivers from the Suwannee west to the Perdido. These include the Aucilla, St. Marks, Ochlockonee, Apalachicola, Chipola, Choctawhatchee, and Yellow rivers. The Apalachicola is the most productive by far, and 40-pound striped bass are not too rare.

Alabama

Two Alabama river watersheds provide one of the longest migration routes taken by striped bass today in the United States. Both the Tombigbee and the Alabama rivers flow into a common estuary in Mobile Bay. North of Montgomery, the Alabama divides into the Coosa and Tallassee. Alabama's record striper, a 55-pound fish, was taken on the Tallassee. Striped bass are distributed along the entire route of this watershed system. They are rare in the estuarine portion, though in past years they have been taken there by commercial fishermen.

Mississippi

Seven rivers in Mississippi have varying concentrations of striped bass in their waters. They are the Pascagoula, Tchouticabouffa, Biloxi, Wolf, and Jordan. Mississippi shares with Louisiana two rivers with striped bass, the Pearl and Tangipahoa. There is little or no marine fishing for bass, and even in the estuaries their appearance is only occasional.

Louisiana

Striped bass reach the limits of their western distribution in the Gulf of Mexico in Louisiana. The occurrence of fish here is sporadic. In past years, a substantial population was recorded in the streams along the

Mississippi River delta, but today striped bass are rare. When they do occur, they are found in the two streams shared with Mississippi—the Pearl and Tangipahoa—and in the Atchafalya, Tchefuncta, and Mississippi rivers as well as in Lake Borgne, Rigolets, and Bayou Penchant.

Pacific Coast

Striped bass did not occur naturally on the West Coast of the United States. Today, however, the fish is quite plentiful, the result of two stockings of young fish taken from the Navesink and Shrewsbury rivers in New Jersey and planted in San Francisco Bay in 1879 and 1881.

Striped bass have been taken as far south in California as San Diego. However, these fish exhibit the endemic characteristic of Hudson River stock. The greatest concentration has been in the San Francisco Bay area. Bass are distributed in various parts of the bays and rivers at differing times of the year. They inhabit the San Joaquin, Sacramento, Feather, and Middle river systems at one time of the year and Grizzly, Suisan, San Pablo, and San Francisco Bays at other times. They are found in the Gate and outside, along the beaches immediate to the Gate. Seldom is the outer Pacific surf as productive as Atlantic surf fishing.

In Oregon, they are concentrated in Coos Bay, with additional runs into the Coquille and Umpqua rivers. The Columbia River forms a natural border between Oregon and Washington and striped bass are distributed in this system as well, but without the concentration found in Coos or San Francisco bays. Stray striped bass have also been taken by commercial trawlers as far north as British Columbia, but these are rare fish and do not constitute a population.

MIGRATIONS OF STRIPED BASS

Migration of fish is a natural phenomenon. Fish move about from place to place for a score of reasons. The motivation can roughly be divided into three categories: seasonal, spawning, and coastal. By far the most spectacular are the spawning migrations, as exemplified by the Atlantic salmon or the American eel. Few fish spawn where they live and eat, even fish contained in rivers.

Spawning migrations

Some fish, like the Atlantic salmon, return to the exact site in which they were spawned. To do their own spawning, they will travel hundreds of miles up rivers to reach that location. Pelagic species of fish spawn in bays, estuaries, or the open ocean. Striped bass, however, are endowed with an instinct similar to salmon and return to spawn in their native freshwater rivers. While the specificity of the salmon is uncannily exact, the striped bass needs only to return to the general area where it was spawned to satisfy the same urge.

The actual spawning areas of striped bass are far more limited than those of the salmon. This may result in some way from their lesser degree of exactitude. Also, striped bass larvae and fry immediately move into a saline or brackish environment to grow, whereas salmon parr may spend several years in a small locale before they take to the ocean as smolt.

Season migrations are often the shortest. A portion of the bass population seems to prefer to winter in fresh or nearly fresh water, often not far from future spawning sites. Others winter in the open ocean and make a pre-spawning migration to the sites. After spawning, the fish will migrate downriver and spend most of the summer and fall in the marine estuaries or along the immediate beaches only to return again in late winter to await another cycle.

Spawning migrations usually are composed only of adult fish. A striped bass is considered adult when it is capable of spawning. In male striped bass, this generally occurs when the fish is two or three years old. In the female, spawning occurs at three years of age in precocious females, but in the majority, fish are four or five years old. By six years of age, all female bass are capable of spawning.

Spawning migrations, then, are of several varieties. Bass that live most of their lives in salt water or estuarine environments will move from salt to fresh or nearly fresh water when their time to spawn is near. In river systems that are totally freshwater, striped bass will move from wintering or lower sections to upper spawning areas. In some river systems the migration is over tremendous distances. Striped bass in the Sacramento River will spawn just above tidewater, while other bass in the same river may move as much as 250 miles upriver. One of the longest migrations in the eastern United States is performed by the striped bass of North Carolina. The wintering fish will move from the offshore waters on the Outer Banks, migrate inshore over Albemarle Sound and then up the Roanoke River to Roanoke Rapids, more than 180 miles upstream.

In Chesapeake Bay, a basically brackish body of water, most spawning fish will winter in the deeper parts of the bay, or with a large contingent of old fish mixed with other itinerant bass off Cape Hatteras. Those fish that do stay in the bay take part in a southern migration to lower and deeper parts of the bay as winter nears. As April and May approach, these bass will begin heading for various rivers in the upper bay to spawn. In past times, before the construction of dams, striped bass entered the Susquehanna River and traveled up as far as Berwick, Penn., to spawn. Some fish have even been identified as far up this river as Binghamton, N.Y., but it was not determined if they were spawning.

A similar long trek to spawn at one time occurred on the Delaware River, and fish have been recorded upstream as far as Port Jervis in New York. Today, because of dams and pollution, these journeys are impossible and only fish capable of spawning at the head of tidewater, where the salinity is zero or nearly so, are able to continue their strains.

Delaware Bay at one time housed a rather large spawning population of striped bass. But as the valley became industrialized, pollution eliminated the major spawning areas. Today, spawning is confined to the Chesapeake and Delaware Canal and a few coastal streams on the New Jersey side of Delaware Bay.

On the Hudson River in New York, spawning takes place not in side tributaries, but in the main river itself. The Hudson is essentially fresh water, or brackish, from the George Washington Bridge north. Spawning takes place from Bear Mountain north to Cruger Island. The most intensive spawning occurs near West Point in water with no saline content.

Striped bass in the Pacific undergo limited migrations within their river-bay-estuary systems. There is no recorded mass coastal migration similar to that on the Atlantic. In the San Francisco Bay area, bass that have spent part of the summer outside the bay re-enter and begin a fall migration toward the delta of the Sacramento and San Joaquin rivers. As they move toward the delta, they are joined by fish that have summered in San Pablo, Suisan, and Grizzly bays.

Water along the many channels of the delta and the two rivers proper is fresh, and here the fish feed and wait the winter until spawning. On the Sacramento River, striped bass spawn in the vicinity above Courtland and on the San Joaquin between the Antioch Bridge and the mouth of Middle River. A post-spawning migration occurs as the fish drop down to the lower delta, and by the end of spring they are concentrated again in the bays.

In Oregon, striped bass inhabit five rivers and spawn to some degree in all of them. Coos Bay probably has the greatest concentration of fish, though the Umpqua and Smith rivers also have substantial populations. The fish are concentrated in the bays and near the inlets in the Pacific during the summer and fall and probably winter in the same area because the estuaries are so limited. In the spring, they ascend the rivers for short distances and spawn only to quickly return to their feeding and summer locations.

Coastal migrations

The model or typical striped bass populations in most areas of the fish's range make only two types of migrations — spring spawning migrations and winter-summer migrations to feeding grounds in the estuaries or

Migration routes. Illustrated here are the spring or northward migration routes of the striped bass. In the fall, the reverse paths are followed along the Atlantic Coast.

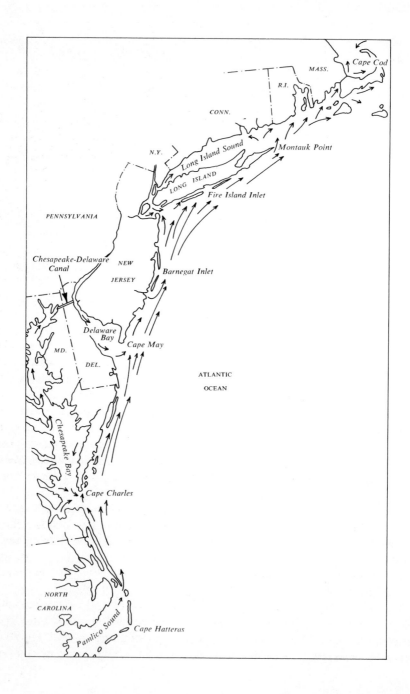

Fall migration in the San Francisco Bay area. Bass here abandon salt water to winter in fresh or brackish water in the delta formed by the Sacramento and San Joaquin rivers.

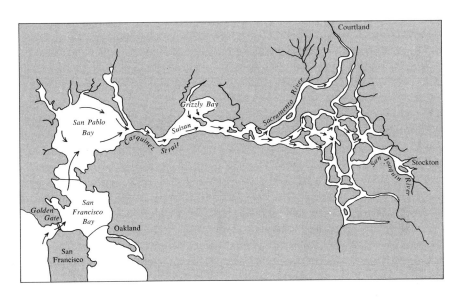

lower portions of their river system. Post-spawning migrations are usually to lower parts of the bays or to estuaries with the intent of feeding throughout the summer. Some of these are temperature-oriented movements so the fish can stay in water best suited to their metabolism.

However, there is one unique strain or race of striped bass on the Atlantic that is atypical of the striped bass model we are always trying to build. This group of fish undertakes one of the longest migrations possible for striped bass and is so spectacular in size that it often overshadows other bass populations and for a long time had confused the picture of cyclic migrations.

These fish stem from Chesapeake Bay. Actually, there are three, possibly four, definable populations of striped bass in Chesapeake Bay. There are those fish produced in the lower bay, on the James River; then another group on the York and Rappahannock that join with a major contribution from the Potomac River; and a third group from the rivers in the upper bays and eastern shore.

For some reason, striped bass spawned in the middle bay, principally the Potomac River, undertake a vast coastal migration. After these fish reach two years of age and begin their third year, primarily all females, there is a sudden urge to leave the bay. This is not a spawning run because all the females are sexually immature. Most now shortcut the exodus by using the Chesapeake and Delaware Canal and migrate up the Atlantic Coast. They are joined by much larger and much older bass in a post-spawning run, bass that have wintered offshore in North Carolina or have stayed in deeper bays and estuaries along the coast. The migration begins in April and May and the fish continue past New Jersey, eastward along the coast to Long Island and on to Cape Cod. During some years, they go as far north as the Gulf of Maine.

As this group passes north of Long Island it begins to fragment. Bass will drop off along the way and summer in the bays of eastern Long Island, Long Island Sound to Rhode Island, off the Elizabeth Islands, and on both the coastal and continental sides of Cape Cod. Some fish produced in North Carolina waters take part in the migration, but researchers have shown that this contribution is quite minimal. North Carolina fish, along with those of the James River in Chesapeake Bay, take up summer residence in Albemarle and Pamlico sounds or lower Chesapeake Bay.

Bass that are spawned in the Delaware estuaries and those that winter over in Delaware Bay and some of the rivers in New Jersey also take part in this grand trek. A few fish of Chesapeake stock may winter in upper and lower New York Bay, and they too contribute to this migration. All these wintering-over fish are believed, however, to be orginally composed of the same Chesapeake Bay population.

In the Hudson itself, fish produced in its waters make a relatively short southward migration, spending their summer in lower New York Bay, in several tidal rivers in adjacent New Jersey, and eastward along the Atlantic only as far as Jamaica Bay and western Great South Bay. In Long Island Sound, Hudson River stock summer on the western end, along the Connecticut shore as far as Bridgeport and on Long Island's north shore about as far east as Port Jefferson. Though this is a coastal migration of sorts, it is still considered a local move when compared to the great journey that is made by fish from Maryland and Virginia. In a real sense, all these waters are part of the estuarine system of the Hudson River.

Of the annual population of striped bass that are produced in the waters of Chesapeake Bay, only about 10 percent escape the heavy commercial and sport fishing pressure to take part in this coastal migration. Of the total of fish that do make the coastal migration, nearly 90 percent is believed to have originated in the Chesapeake Bay area. The remaining 10 percent is made up of North Carolina, Delaware, and Hudson River fish. The Hudson River contributes the least—not because it doesn't have the population, but because its fish are nonmigratory in relation to the coast.

Summer distribution of the Atlantic population of striped bass. The crosshatched area is the range of striped bass which originate in the waters of North Carolina, Chesapeake Bay and Delaware Bay. The diagonally shaded area represents striped bass from the Hudson River fishery. The ranges of the two races of striped bass overlap to some degree in Long Island Sound.

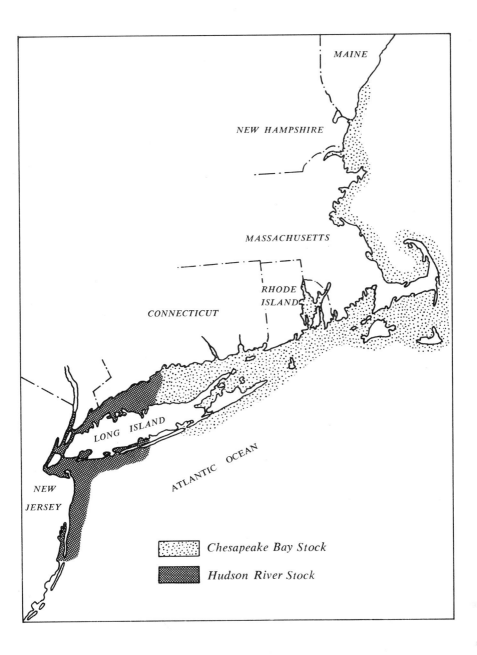

MAINE

NEW HAMPSHIRE

MASSACHUSETTS

RHODE ISLAND

CONNECTICUT

LONG ISLAND

ATLANTIC OCEAN

NEW JERSEY

Chesapeake Bay Stock

Hudson River Stock

Primary winter distribution of the striped bass along the Atlantic Coast. This does not include the Hudson fishery, which winters in the lower Hudson River, and the numerous holdover bass that find wintering spots along the Connecticut, New York, New Jersey, and Delaware coasts. Fish that winter in Chesapeake Bay and Albemarle and Pamlico sounds are mostly immature striped bass.

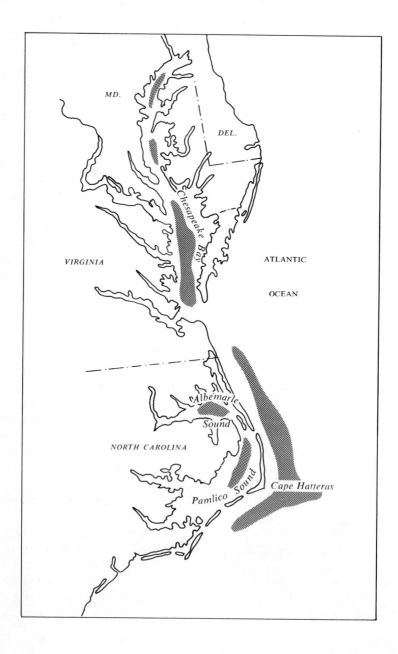

Seasonal migrations

In late September and October, this coastal stock of migratory fish begins a southward movement, spurred on by falling temperatures and shifting food-fish populations. The fish school and move southward along New England, west across Long Island, and south along the coast of New Jersey, Delaware, and Virginia. Many of the younger fish return to Chesapeake Bay to winter, but large numbers, composed of older bass, choose to winter in deeper coastal rivers and bays or in an area off North Carolina, between the mouth of Chesapeake Bay and Cape Hatteras. These large schools fall easy prey to high-speed offshore draggers because they concentrate in such dense schools.

As the water temperature falls below 40 degrees, bass in their various winter locations restrict their movement and enter a somewhat dormant stage. The exception to this are the smaller striped bass, one to three years old, in Chesapeake Bay. They have been shown to actively feed and move about the bay even under the ice. Their migrations are strictly of a feeding nature. During most of the months of December, January, and February, these fish will feed along the edge of deep water in the lower bay. When the temperatures rise during the day they will move into shallower water, only to return when it again falls.

The striped bass of North Carolina separate themselves somewhat like the large and small fish of Chesapeake Bay. However, here the separation is even greater geographically. The smaller striped bass will remain in Albemarle Sound during the winter, while larger fish move out the inlets to join wintering fish off the Outer Banks.

RACES OF STRIPED BASS

In order to manage a population of fish like striped bass, fisheries personnel must know where they originate, what is the parent stock, and if these various stocks can be differentiated and thus managed to the benefit of the entire fishery. Several years ago, studies were conducted along both coasts as well as the Gulf States to determine if striped bass produced in each area have physically different characteristics, features that were peculiar only to their fish. If they did, then the fish populations could be broken into what might loosely be called races.

Races are usually differentiated by their meristic features—that is, variations in the number or position of body parts. Groups of meristic features on striped bass were studied, and only counts of fin rays and counts of scales on the lateral line proved usable, the scale counts better than the fin-ray counts. After the studies were coordinated, it was established that striped bass had segregated themselves into races dependent

Migration routes during the spring in the Hudson River fishery.

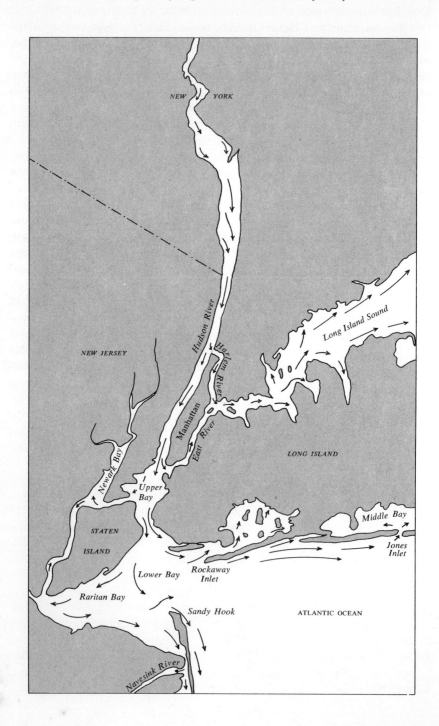

upon their brood stock or place of origin. It is only a weak guideline at best, but does serve to some degree as a fisheries management tool.

The number of scales on the lateral line differs on the average when compared between stocks from varying locales. Striped bass have been found to contain a scale range on the lateral line that varies from a low of 52 scales to a high of 67. Bass produced in the St. Lawrence River system contained an average of 61.3 scales on the lateral line. Hudson River stocks had 59.6 scales, Chesapeake Bay fish had 60.1, and North Carolina fish had 61.7. As one counts scales of local populations south of North Carolina they progressively diminish to a low number of 54.2 scales found on striped bass from the St. Johns River in Florida.

Another method in these meristic studies that attempted to separate breeding stocks was counting the number of soft rays in the anal fins of striped bass, but the differences were so slight as to make this a rather poor tool. The extremes ranged between 10.6 rays for Hudson River fish to 10.9 rays for Delaware and Chesapeake Bay bass. Most fish south of North Carolina, which had a 10.8 count, all possessed 11 rays except in western Florida and Mississippi, where they produced 9.8 rays.

Races were thus established for striped bass in the St. Lawrence River and the Gulf of St. Lawrence, for the Nova Scotia–New Brunswick area, and for the Hudson River. A weak separation exists between Delaware Bay and Chesapeake Bay stocks. Chesapeake Bay further complicated the picture by the discovery of at least three subraces and possibly a fourth that is closer related to the distinct race in Albemarle Sound than other Chesapeake Bay fishes. Separate stocks have also been identified for Santee-Cooper fish in South Carolina, and Florida has its own striped bass population. In the Pacific, the striped bass stock is the same as Hudson River fish because the few New Jersey transplants that started the Pacific on its way came from northern Jersey, of stock that had been spawned in the Hudson River.

3

Reproduction in Striped Bass

The evolutionary history of the striped bass as a freshwater fish is evident when the fish is ready to reproduce. Most marine fishes spawn in salt water and their conversion to this environment is complete. The striped bass, however, has never become an exclusively saltwater fish and still requires a return to ancestral spawning grounds in fresh water to reproduce its kind.

Where the seasons vary greatly during the year, the spawning will usually take place in the spring so that the eggs and growing fish have the advantage of the warmer months of the year to begin their lives. Striped bass throughout most of their range are influenced by seasonal fluctuations in temperature and thus are cyclic spawners, with marked activities all affecting when and where they will reproduce.

Spawning seasons

Striped bass spawn as early as February in the St. Johns River in Florida and as late as July in Lake St. Pierre on the St. Lawrence River, Quebec. These are the extremes. The bulk of striped bass populations spawn in April, May, and June. The time of spawning is more a function of the water temperature than of the time of year. During especially cold years, spawning can be retarded by as much as two or three weeks. The duration of spawning is also a factor of the water temperature, and as long as it remains in an optimal range bass will continue to spawn. Any change above or below this range will cause temporary or even permanent cessation.

Generally, striped bass in North Carolina and the Roanoke River spawn between the middle of April and the middle of May. At the head of Chesapeake Bay, bass have spawned from the middle of May to the middle of June at some years. However, during normal years, spawning beginning in April will last during most of the month of May. On the Hudson River, April and May are the preferred months. In California waters, the season can be considerably longer, beginning in April and lasting until mid-June.

Water temperatures

The temperature of the water is the single most critical factor in determining when bass will spawn. Bass will carry mature eggs about, but until the reproductive processes are stimulated by the correct temperature they will remain unshed.

Spawning will occur over a great range of temperatures, from about 57 or 58 degrees to 70 or 71 degrees. In an environment where the water temperature is rising rapidly, bass will spawn until it reaches 70 degrees and stop immediately, and they will not start spawning again if the temperature continues to rise. Fertilized eggs exposed to water 70 degrees or higher fail to hatch at this high temperature. Thus, water temperature can be a vital delimiting factor when searching for environments for self-supporting populations of striped bass.

Though the preferred spawning temperature does vary over a range of 10 to 12 degrees, optimal spawning temperature, no matter where the fish are located over their range, seems to be about 64.5 degrees. Rivers with slowly rising or steady temperatures at this range will find a complete spawning of fish in this environment. In the case of moving fish, as soon as they reach water of this temperature near the spawning ground they will begin to spawn. If the spawning population is a large one, as is often the case on the Roanoke River, spawning may last for three or four weeks, all with peak activity. In areas where the stock is small, spawning may be completed in two or three days, as is the case in the St. Lawrence in Quebec and the St. Johns River in Florida.

Spawning sites

Striped bass demand substantially fresh water in which to spawn. However, they will spawn in waters with chloride concentrations as high as 10–150/00 (parts per thousand). Today, it is difficult to generalize what the ideal striped bass spawning ground might be like, because so much of it has been altered or destroyed, or eliminated by dams and pollution barriers. Now striped bass spawn where they have been able to adapt to existing environmental conditions.

In a river situation, one with a large head of water and a long watershed, striped bass will still move 150 to 200 miles to spawn. Only the St. Lawrence River in Quebec and the Roanoke River in North Carolina,

100 miles above tidewater on the Atlantic, offer such long-run spawning sites. I'm sure that at one time, many of the rivers in Maine, the Connecticut River in New England, and the Delaware and Susquehanna rivers in New York, New Jersey, and Pennsylvania also offered such spawning sites.

More frequently nowadays, however, the major spawning rivers on the Atlantic are broad tidal streams with a large but slow flow of water. Striped bass will select sites just far enough above salt water with sufficient current that will allow the eggs to be buoyed off the bottom and hatch out before the current carries them into salt water.

The hatching time, another function of the water temperature, varies between 48 and 72 hours on the average. The higher the temperature, the shorter the development time. The eggs should not be carried to an all-saline environment by the current before hatching time. It is best if the environment is brackish, a mixture of fresh and salt water, for a substantial time. Because of such requirements, spawning on such rivers as the Hudson, Nanticoke, Potomac, Wicominco, York, James, and Rappahannock may take place in an area 10 to 40 miles above salt water. The actual distance is determined by the river current.

SPAWNING

Male striped bass usually appear on the spawning site days or weeks ahead of the females. Large females arrive before smaller females. The fish congregate in schools around rivers that have a gravel or sandy bottom and a substantial current. Some sites are even in the rapids. Pre-spawning rituals, often described as "rock fights," precede the actual spawning.

In the case of a large female, anywhere from ten to fifty younger males will act as suitors and surround her as she reaches the moment to spawn. The fish will thrash on the surface, often racing on their sides over the top, resembling wounded fish. The splashing may continue for hours until the appropriate time has come, usually in the late afternoon. Generally, most of the activity heightens as the day wears into night and spawning continues through the entire evening.

After the splashing and gamboling on the surface slows, the female sinks below the surface, and as many as five or six males may press alongside the larger fish, forcing her to exude her eggs. At the same time, milt from the males flows into the water, mixing with the eggs and fertilizing them. As the males become spent new fish take their place, and they continue to nose and bump the female until she has expelled all her eggs.

After spawning, the spent males and females begin dropping back from the spawning area and return to resting spots farther downriver.

During spawning and immediately thereafter, striped bass do not feed. But as soon as they are well off the spawning site they again begin to feed.

The fertilized eggs then drift downstream, with the current buoying them off the bottom. The eggs are protected from damage by the perivitelline space—the fluid-filled space between the outside membrane and ovum of a fertilized egg. As soon as the eggs are expelled they begin to absorb water through the outside membrane (vitelline membrane), and this fluid acts as a buffer to shock. The egg grows from an average size of 1.1-1.35mm to about 3.63mm. In about 6½ days the yolk sac is absorbed.

Fecundity of Spawners

As already stated, female striped bass are generally capable of spawning at four years of age, though the greater percentage of a year-class reach spawning maturity at age five. Males are more precocious; some records have revealed one-year-old males with mature milt, but the average age is three years.

Striped bass have the capability of annual spawning. In general, however, it is believed that they do not spawn annually. During the first five or six years of their adult lives, they may spawn annually, but as the females grow older they tend to become sporadic in their spawning habits. The number of males above fourteen years of age decreases rapidly in the population. There is evidence of dimorphism—sex change— in striped bass, and some researchers believe this might account for the change in population number. The possibility exists that they may alter their sex as they grow older and the population becomes female-oriented. Because no conclusive studies have been conducted this is little more than a hypothesis.

Hermaphroditism exists in about 4 percent of several Pacific Coast populations, and some researchers feel that this figure might go considerably higher if a more general study were made of sexual compositions. There are records of bisexual striped bass containing both ovaries and testes and both in perfect spawning condition.

Fecundity (the ability to produce eggs or sperm) in differing fishes varies with the amount of care the parents provide for their fertilized eggs and offspring. The more care the parent or both parents give the offspring, the fewer eggs are produced. Conversely, the less care the parents provide, the more eggs are produced to ensure the survival of that species of fish. It is nature's way of keeping everything within a reasonable balance.

There are three general though arbitrary categories of fecundity in fish. A minimal spawner produces less than, say, 50 eggs per individual.

A good example is the marine catfish. It produces eggs the size of marbles, and the male carries them around in his mouth until they hatch. The second or intermediate group of spawners produce up to about 1,000 eggs, and they provide a certain degree of post-spawning care. One example is the brook trout, a fish that prepares a gravel nest for the eggs, and after fertilization, the male continues for a while to guard the eggs.

The third category, the extreme cases of parental carelessness, includes fish like the mackerel, weakfish, and bluefish. Into this category also falls the striped bass. Spawners can broadcast as many as 50,000 eggs, and fertilization takes place almost haphazardly. The eggs are then left to fend for themselves. But such huge quantities are produced that survival is almost always guaranteed.

Duration of Spawning Ability

Fecundity of a female striped bass is in direct relationship to her weight. The larger the fish, the more eggs she is capable of producing. The average number of ova increases progressively from 426,000 in a 4-pound female to 4,200,000 in a 55-pound female. On the basis of this information, biologists believe that large striped bass do make substantial contributions in the spawning process. However, the large striped bass are so few compared to the astronomical numbers of 4-pound fish that the contribution of younger striped bass is much greater than that of the large fish.

Early regulations in Maryland (1929), followed by similar regulations in Virginia and Delaware, were aimed at protecting large female striped bass because of the great number of eggs they carried. The legislation prohibited the taking of striped bass over 15 pounds in Chesapeake Bay. With the rise in sportfishing the value of a trophy fish began to overshadow the legislation. Not only was the law difficult to enforce and unpopular, but the very concept was challenged by other biologists, who believed that the viability of eggs was reduced as a fish grew older. They felt that senility was in operation on these fish.

The 15-pound maximum affects males about nine years old and females about seven to eight years old, and Maryland's biologists reconsidered the restriction. They found no evidence of senility in the large female striped bass collected during the study, even four females that weighed over 50 pounds and were over fifteen years old. The eggs were artificially fertilized to see if they would develop and hatch. Fish were reared to the larval stage. Therefore, the evidence tends to support the concept that large striped bass are highly productive to the end and are valuable brood fish.

In 1962, the legislation was amended to allow fishermen to keep one large fish over 15 pounds each day, except during the spawning season, which is bracketed by closed dates beginning March 1 and ending June 15. The capture and sale is still prohibited to commercial fishermen. In reality, the change hasn't had too much of an effect on the brood stock or the striped bass fishery because large fish, 30 pounds or more, enter Chesapeake Bay only to spawn and immediately return to the Atlantic. They do this during the closed season. Outside the closed dates for the trophy fish, striped bass 30 pounds or larger are rather rare in the bay.

EGG MATURATION

Mature or ripe striped bass eggs are a transparent green, with a small amber-colored oil globule. In the ovary, they mature at different times, but as spawning approaches, all the eggs mature and are the same size. On the average, the large, mature ovum (egg) is about 1.35mm in diameter.

As soon as they are fertilized, the eggs take on a spherical shape and begin to swell and water-harden. They are nonadhesive and slightly heavier than water, and sink to the bottom unless agitated by a slight current. It takes but the slightest movement to keep them buoyed.

After fertilization and exposure to water, the eggs swell rapidly in size and in fifteen minutes attain an average size of 1.84mm. The sizes of the yolk sphere and oil globule or globules remain the same, and the chorionic membrane surrounding the egg remains transparent. It is, however, thin and fragile.

At twelve hours after fertilization, the egg shows a greater increase in diameter, reaching 3.2-3.8mm. Water absorption is just about complete. The blastoderm is in late cleavage and the periblast begins to turn a pale green.

All further expansion of the chorion ceases in the egg at twenty-four hours. By now the embryo has become differentiated and extends about halfway around the circumference of the yolk. Coloring now begins in the embryo, with small, black dots covering the dorsal or back of the embryo.

Thirty-six hours after fertilization, the embryo is about 1.6mm in length. The eyes have formed but are colorless, and the tail of the embryo is free from the yolk sac. If the temperature has been an even 64.2 degrees F., the egg is about to hatch. Increased embryonic temperatures will hasten the hatching, whereas cooler temperatures will prolong the development of the embryo.

Once the embryo is hatched it is referred to as a larva. At sixty hours after fertilization it is about 3.2mm in length, but the resemblance to a mature striped bass, or even a fish, is still rather distant. The globule of oil in the head of the yolk sac projects beyond the head of the larva. The fish still lacks mobility, despite a strong swimming action, and it settles

Striped bass eggs at fertilization and during embryonic development.

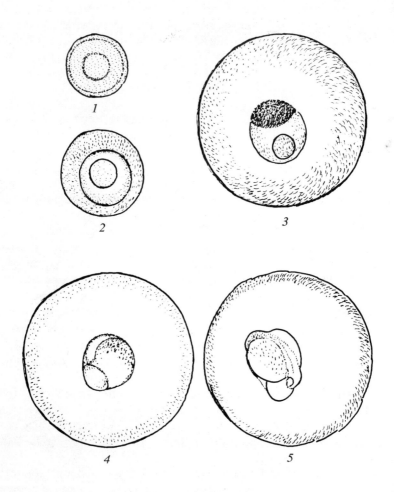

1. At fertilization, diameter 1.3 mm.
2. 15 minutes after fertilization, diameter 1.8 mm.
3. 12 hours after fertilization, diameter 3.7 mm.
4. 24 hours after fertilization.
5. 36 hours after fertilization.

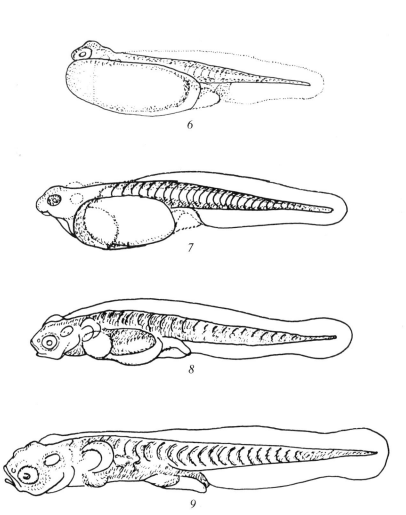

6. *60 hours after fertilization, length 3.2 mm.*
7. *84 hours after fertilization, length 4.4 mm.*
8. *144 hours after fertilization, length 5.8 mm.*
9. *288 hours after fertilization, length 6 mm; shows slight atrophy of organs because no food was available to fish.*

to the bottom of its environment unless a current is available to keep it suspended.

Eighty-four hours after fertilization the larval fish has attained a length of about 4.4mm. The head now extends beyond the oil globule, and a series of black dots begin to appear along the underside of the body behind the anal vent. The eyes still lack coloration.

Pigmentation finally develops in the larval fish at about 120 hours after fertilization. The larval striped bass now is about 5.2mm long, and the jaws begin to show development. Both the oil globule and yolk sac now show considerable reduction in size, and the beginnings of a digestive tract make their appearance. Pectoral fins now become recognizable.

Mouth parts and the digestive tract are much better developed in the larval fish at age 144 hours after fertilization. The larva is about 5.8mm long. At 192 hours the oil globule and yolk sac have almost disappeared, while length increase seems to slow down, 6mm, in deference to development of body structures. The coloration along the underside of the body is more strongly developed.

A ten-day-old postlarval fish begins strongly to resemble a mature striped bass. The head is still disproportionately large, and the caudal fin is still weak, with remnants extending on both the back and underside connecting it with other fins. The fish is approximately 9mm long. The second dorsal and anal fin rays become slightly differentiated, although the first dorsal and ventral fins are yet to begin development. The lateral line has become well defined and the musculature is evident through the thin skin. Mouth parts are well developed, and the pigmented eye seems especially large for the remainder of the fish.

By the eighteenth day after fertilization our postlarval striped bass is half an inch long and looks like a chubby bass. The two back (dorsal) fins are still connected and the spines are weakly developed in the anterior fin. All traces of the larval fin fold have disappeared.

At a length of about 36mm and an age of from three to four weeks, the young striped bass assumes the general fusiform shape of a mature fish. The most noticeable characteristic is the well-developed scales that now cover the body and fully developed fins and rays.

At ninety days old, our striped bass is a fingerling or fry and approximately 80mm in length. The characteristic lateral black stripes are almost complete, six to nine in number. Also, at this time there appear seven fainter vertical bars that extend from the base of the dorsal fins down the sides to the lateral line. After a short period, these lines disappear. Except for the eyes, which are large compared to the body size, the striped bass looks pretty much like an adult. All the development is complete, except the gonads, which will develop when the fish is three years old or older.

This fish developed at a temperature ranging between 60 and 68 degrees. From top to bottom: age 30 days, length 15.8mm; age 45 days, length 33mm; age 60 days, length 46mm; age 90 days, length 80mm. (Courtesy, Dr. S. I. Doroshve, VIRNO, USSR)

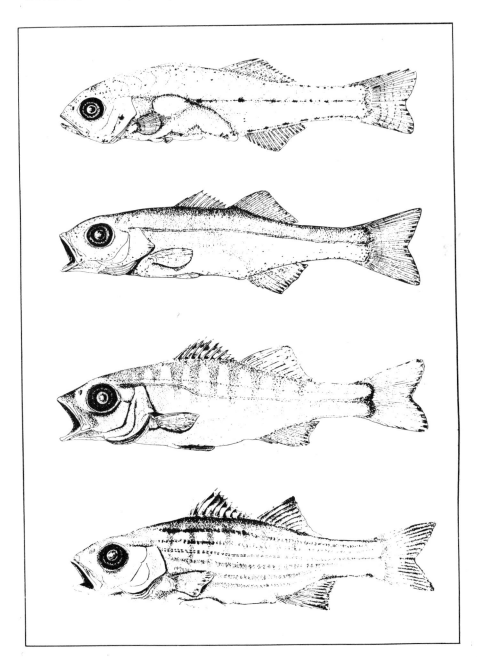

Ontogeny and Phylogeny

In the dogma of the biological sciences, especially the field of embryology, there is a saying that ontogeny recapitulates phylogeny. Ontogeny is the biological development of an individual, whereas phylogeny is the evolutionary development of a species. Many animals in their embryological development go through several body changes that reflect the different steps in the evolutionary development of the animal. These stages disappear before or shortly after birth. Of course, the final, adult forms mask all these levels and they are no longer evident.

In a very real way, the striped bass does this in several respects. Its embryological development gives us a clue to what the striped bass of old might have been like. It reveals a fish model with characteristics adapted to the ecological conditions of life on deltas in estuaries and reflects characteristics of both freshwater and marine fishes.

These characteristics include a high fecundity (females of 40–50 pounds are capable of shedding 3 million eggs), typical of pelagic marine species of fish. Add to this a short period of embryonic development (forty-eight to seventy-two hours) and a larval animal that is poorly developed, hatched before it is really capable of caring for itself. These are characteristics of a hurried development for life in an unprotected situation without much parental care or protection from predators. To compensate for these shortcomings we then have characteristics that produce sharp fluctuations in abundance under natural conditions, and adaptability to spawning in the lower reaches of rivers and to the variability of ecological conditions in estuarine environments.

The early development of a strong digestive system, the appearance of large teeth in the jaws, the excellently developed eyes, and the positive phototaxis (attraction toward light) all tell us that the striped bass is a flesh-eating fish from the very beginning, even before it has the mobility to chase its own food. At these stages it is still living off the yolk sac that was a part of the egg stage of the fish.

4

Growth and Feeding in Striped Bass

Striped bass, at every stage of growth and development, are voracious feeders. When compared to other species of fish, striped bass are rapid growers. However, after about ten years, the rate of growth tapers off rapidly, both in weight and length.

Within the sexes, there are also different growth rates. From the time of hatching in April or May to the end of the following winter is considered a single year in the life of a bass. During this first year, both sexes grow at the same approximate rate and attain a length of about 4½ to 5 inches. Thereafter, the males grow slightly faster than females until the fourth year. Female striped bass then put on a growing spurt, and by the end of their fifth year they have outgrown their male counterparts. Thereafter, throughout their lives, a female is larger than a male of the same age. The greatest growth spurt in both sexes of fish takes place during their second year after birth.

Male striped bass above the age of ten years are almost nonexistent in California waters and rather rare on the Atlantic. Records of old male fish come from the Elk River in Maryland with one twelve-year old male that weighed 24.5 pounds and was 37.2 inches in length. Thought to be the largest male striped bass recorded by 1952 was a fish that weighed 16.5 pounds and was 31.5 inches long.

From 1954 to 1963, Maryland conducted a series of studies of the sexual composition of striped bass 15 pounds and larger in Maryland waters. Over that period, forty-four male bass between 15 and 20 pounds were taken, eight males between 20 and 25 pounds, and six males between 25 and 30 pounds, and in 1954 one male striped bass that weighed 32 pounds and measured 40 inches fork length (from the tip of the head to the point of the tail notch).

The largest male striped bass eventually recorded was also the longest found during the study. It was a fish measuring 45½ inches fork length. The bass was tagged and released in the Nanticoke River (Chesapeake Bay) on April 19, 1958. Six weeks later it was captured off Barnegat Inlet, N.J. At the time the fish was tagged on the Nanticoke, its weight was estimated at 40 pounds and the fish was freely exuding milt.

The sex ratio during the Maryland study involved the capture of 672 striped bass that weighed 15 pounds or more; the largest was a 63.2-pound female. Females constituted 91.2 percent. Thus though male striped bass in the heavyweight class are rare, they do exist.

Once striped bass reach the age of nine and ten years it becomes progressively more difficult to tell how old they are. There are two methods used by researchers. The first is the length-frequency relationship of a population of bass. In a given haul or collection of striped bass on rearing grounds, the fish can be grouped rather nicely into specific length groups that contain only a few odd fish with measurements in between the averages. Most fish around 5 inches are part of the one-year group, those near 12 inches are two years old, those 14–15 inches are three years old, and those 17 to 18 inches are four years old.

After four years, the growth-rate spread between frequencies is less distinct and this method is less dependable. Another method that supports the diagnosis of age groups determined by the length-frequency method is counting the annuli on the scales, a growth mark that is similar to the rings on a tree. Each year, fish have a rapid-growth period during the summer and fall and then slow into winter. At the end of winter a ring or annulus is laid down that is darker than the rest of the scale. One annulus is laid down each year, and a fish's age can then be determined under a dissecting microscope by counting the dark rings on the scale. This works out well until about the tenth year, when the growth rate slows and the dark rings begin to pile one atop another, making accurate age determination impossible. From ten years on, the age-weight-length ratio is extrapolated to determine the ages of older striped bass.

Female striped bass weighing 25 to 50 pounds are believed to be between ten and fourteen years old. Some researchers feel that a 50-pound female striped bass is closer to eighteen years old. At these higher weights the length and weight closely approximate each other — that is, a 50-inch bass weighs about 50 pounds.

Recent research in growth studies with striped bass that have been spawned in fresh water and spend all their lives in fresh water has revealed that these fish grow at a rate approximately twice that of fish in a marine environment. However, there is a negative note: these fish have only half the life expectancy of saltwater striped bass and do not reach the same maximums in size.

Striped bass have grown to enormous sizes, though few fish over 100 pounds are known nowadays. In April 1891 several striped bass

This is a graphic summary of the relationship of a striped bass's weight to length and correlated with its age. The striped bass grows so uniformly in a marine environment that if you know a fish's length you can calculate rather closely its weight and age just by comparing it to the above chart. Female bass after age three are slightly larger than males, and hence in the graph males are shown dark and females light. Males over eleven to fourteen years of age are rather rare, but they do exist.

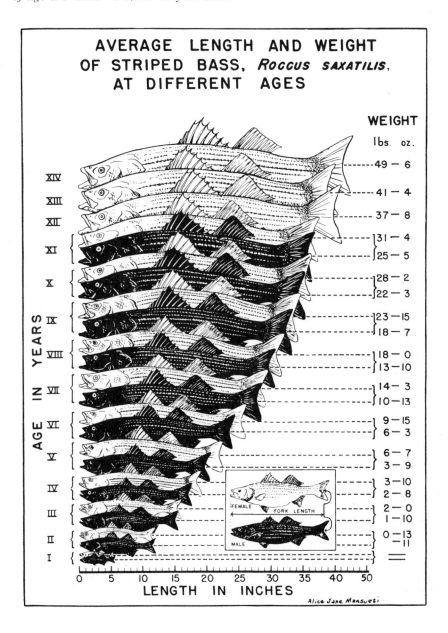

AVERAGE LENGTH AND WEIGHT
OF STRIPED BASS, *ROCCUS SAXATILIS*,
AT DIFFERENT AGES

WEIGHT

lbs. oz.

49 — 6
41 — 4
37 — 8
31 — 4
25 — 5
28 — 2
22 — 3
23 — 15
18 — 7
18 — 0
13 — 10
14 — 3
10 — 13
9 — 15
6 — 3
6 — 7
3 — 9
3 — 10
2 — 8
2 — 0
1 — 10
0 — 13
— 11

AGE IN YEARS

XIV
XIII
XII
XI
X
IX
VIII
VII
VI
V
IV
III
II
I

FEMALE   FORK LENGTH

MALE

0   5   10   15   20   25   30   35   40   50
LENGTH IN INCHES

Alice Jane Mansueti

were netted at Edenton, N.C., that each weighed 125 pounds. North Carolina seems to be the area for the larger striped bass, and this may be related to its longer feeding period because of a more southerly latitude. In a haul seine taken off the beach at Avoca, N.C., on May 6, 1876, 840 striped bass were netted that weighed just over 35,000 pounds. Of these 840 fish, 350 averaged 65 pounds each.

This is an enlargement of a plastic impression of a striped bass scale. The impression is easier to study than the actual scale. This fish was in its fourth year, weighed 5½ pounds, and was 60cm (24 inches) long. At the end of each winter of life a heavy annulus is laid down by the fish and marks one year of growth. Four distinct rings can be seen, similar to rings in a tree.

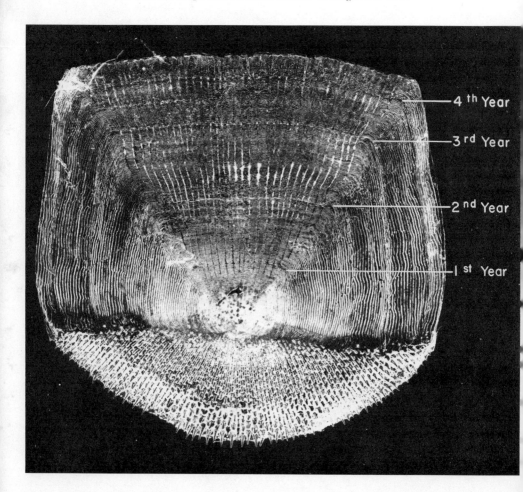

AGE AND LENGTH RELATIONSHIP (IN INCHES)

Age	Length, males	Length, females
1	5.3	4.92
2	11.7	11.5
3	15.0	15.3
4	17.0	18.4
5	19.7	21.9
6	23.4	25.4
7	27.7	28.5
8	29.7	30.0
9	32.7	33.7
10	34.5	35.4
11	35.7	36.8

The preceding figures are for fish taken in Chesapeake Bay. For California striped bass, the figures differ only slightly, with the males leading in length until the fourth year. In the Maryland stock, the males lead only to the second year.

Measurement of striped bass can be taken by three methods: the fork length (FL), already defined; the standard length (SL), from the snout to the base of the peduncle or tail; and the total length (TL), measured from the snout to the end of the tail fin. Most researchers use the fork length.

The following is the approximate growth rate for male and female striped bass produced in the San Francisco Bay area with averages for the first four years:

year 1	4 inches
year 2	9.8 inches
year 3	13.4 inches
year 4	18.5 inches

	Males	Females
year 5	20.4 inches	21.3 inches
year 6	22.0 inches	24.0 inches
year 7	24.0 inches	26.8 inches

FOOD AND FEEDING

If there is one thing that everyone will agree upon it is that the striped bass is a voracious, carnivorous, predacious, mainly piscivorous, and extremely active feeder. A striped bass will eat anything that swims, crawls, or floats in its environment, even its own kind. Cannibalism is not rare among these fish. About the only time striped bass stop feeding is when they begin spawning, and then it is just for a short period.

Foods of striped bass can be divided into three spans in the fish's life: the larval stages, as an active fry up to one year in age or 5 inches in length, and thereafter. The types of food can further be divided into crustaceans and other invertebrates, and vertebrate or fish foods.

For the larval striped bass the principal source of food is zooplankton, microscopic one-celled and multicellular organisms. Small fish, from the fry stage to about one year or 5 inches in length, begin aggressively hunting and feeding on marine worms and marine crustaceans. In some environments the freshwater shrimp, *Gammarus,* an invertebrate, composes almost 60 percent of a young bass's diet. The remainder is composed of annelids or sea worms. Even insects are part of the menu when they are available. In freshwater situations, insects form a large part of the diet in May and June. The average composition, however, is 50 percent marine worms, 48 percent crustaceans, and 2 percent small fishes.

The fish that juvenile striped bass eat are mostly herringlike fish, like menhaden, along with white perch, a close relative to the striped bass, and spottail shiners. The striped bass's eyes are often larger than its stomach, and a small bass often takes on food that is almost as large as itself. There have been reports of a 6½-inch striped bass trying to swallow a 3-inch white perch and a 7¼-inch bass having eaten a 4-inch minnow.

Large striped bass will eat almost everything in their environment. Favorite foods include such crustaceans as shrimp, crabs, and lobsters. They will eat all kinds of marine worms, sandworms or clamworms as well as bloodworms. Even shellfish aren't safe from bass; they will eat mussels, soft-shelled clams, and periwinkles. The range of finfish that bass find to their liking is unlimited. They prefer menhaden, silversides, and anchovies, and at certain times of the year they will feed on spot and croaker. On the West Coast, they have no qualms about feeding on trout and salmon, though these fish do not constitute a measurable part of their diet. Their favorite is the bullhead (sculpin).

Other preferred fish are killifish, shad, sculpins, sand lance, eels, squid, flounder, blackfish, tomcod, white perch, mullet, catfish, shinners, and blenny. Striped bass have even been recorded eating the Portuguese man-of-war, a poisonous jellyfish.

By weight, other fish constitute more than 95 percent of a striped bass's diet. So though a bass may occasionally dine on softshell crab, shrimp, or lobster, the real volume comes in the form of other fishes — most of them species of little or no economic value. This fish diet should be a hint to striped bass anglers who feed their potential fish a strict diet of sandworms. In a study of striped bass in the upper Chesapeake Bay area, around the Susquehanna River, fish as food varied between 46 and 100 percent of the total content in the stomach. Twenty-six different kinds of fish were reported in the study to be eaten by bass. Anchovy, menhaden, spot, and croaker were the most frequently ingested.

But in another study conducted off the south side of Long Island, where there were plenty of small fish in the surf and offshore, the bass had glutted themselves on sand fleas, mysids, copepods, and isopods while passing up huge schools of silversides (spearing) that existed at the same time.

If you know where and when a striped bass feeds, then your chances of meeting it at the dinner table can be increased. Our first place to look for a clue is within the fish itself, basically the mouth and the stomach. Striped bass have few real teeth—a double row in the back of the tongue and small rows along the maxillary bones or upper lip. Basically these are used for holding a fish or other food that has been grasped and to keep it from working its way out of the mouth. Therefore the food fish must be ingested whole, because the striped bass cannot bite off a piece—as can such fish as bluefish, which is well supplied with teeth and can feed on any part of a baitfish. Because ingestion in a striped bass must be in its entirety, the bait must also be taken head first into the mouth. Otherwise the spines and fins on a baitfish would open and the fish would become lodged in the mouth of the striped bass.

The next place to look is in the stomach. The wall is heavily lined with a greatly convoluted lining called the rugosa. It resembles a corrugated washboard. Using this type of lining increases the stomach's area of absorption of food without increasing its external size. This heavy rugose lining is a hint that digestion is rapid and the digested food large.

Such equipment makes the striped bass a sporadic feeder. That is, when it feeds, it fills itself and stops hunting for more food until everything in its stomach has been dissolved. Fish like the bluefish that can bite small pieces, and are hyperactive, must feed all the time and thus are continuous feeders. Studies of striped bass stomachs have supported the contention that striped bass feed in a rather short time and then go off somewhere to digest what they have eaten before they eat again. Nettings at various times of the day have revealed entire schools of bass with empty stomachs. Bass taken on rod and reel have been found with some contents in their stomachs or nothing at all. This indicates that a bass has just started to feed or hasn't completed feeding. Once it has fed, it is not likely to take your lure.

Striped bass are gregarious fish during their younger years; not until they become large "cows" or "bulls" do they become solitary in their feeding and schooling habits. Because striped bass feed most heavily on schooling fish such as menhaden, spearing, and anchovies, they then school together when they feed. As a result, a school that feeds together usually spends its digesting time together, and thus the feeding blitz will often stop all at once, over a rather large area of water. This is supported also by seining research. When a school or part of a school has been netted, the stomach condition of all the fish is about the same, either full, empty, or somewhere in between.

Another aspect of striped bass feeding habits is the great specificity for a certain type of food even though many choices are available at the same time. In other words, even though menhaden, anchovies, and spearing may all be at hand for the bass to feed upon, they may decide on menhaden and everyone in the school eats menhaden until the fad is over or the fish become too scarce to find without a great deal of swimming effort.

When do striped bass feed? During the year, the greatest feeding intensity takes place in the late spring and early summer for adult fish. There is again a flurry of feeding late in the fall. Fish do little feeding during the winter. When the water temperature drops below 39 or 40 degrees, the fish not only stop feeding but go into a somewhat dormant state, seeking out the deepest holes or warmest water in which to sulk. Juvenile fish seem to make their big meal in September and even October. One reason for this is that many of the forage fish that young bass may feed upon when they are one, two and three years old mature to the bite-size stage at this time of year. With a superabundance of food around, the young bass put on a feeding spree that lasts until the forage or baitfish have moved on and are no longer available to the young bass.

The time a striped bass feeds is also affected by other factors, including the temperature of the water, whether the fish are in a fresh-water or saltwater environment, the time of day, and the physiological condition of the striped bass, as well as its size. Just how much a striped bass will eat varies with the seasons as well as the time of day. From numerous collections of striped bass by biologists at all intervals during the day and studies of their stomach contents, striped bass appear to feed most avidly in the evening, just after dark, and they put on a second flurry just before sunrise.

Striped bass anglers have long known that fishing is far more productive after dark than during the day. This doesn't imply that striped bass don't feed during the day. It does mean that striped bass will feed better and more consistently after sunset and before sunrise. Schooling groups of smaller bass are more apt to feed during the night than the day, while large bass feed equally during the day and night.

While the striped bass's appetite is influenced by the water temperature, the feeding range is wide. The bottom of the range appears to be around the 40-degree mark. At this point, the body metabolisms slow down. Fish are coldblooded creatures and their life is one big chemical reaction that takes place at a rate directly proportional to the environmental temperature. This doesn't mean that you can't catch bass at the low range. Bass, large bass, can be taken on rod and reel, with live bait, and even with plugs. One angler on the Thames River in Connecticut successfully catches fish in January and February. He has taken fish 4 to 40 pounds from Norwich to the New London Bridge. His efforts have been most successful at night with underwater plugs, though he has taken bass during the day on live bait as well.

At the lower temperatures, those between 40 and 45 degrees, striped bass will feed, but less frequently. In the colder water digestion takes much longer. A 4-pound menhaden may take only a few hours for a large striped bass to digest when the water temperature is 70 degrees, but at 40 degrees it may take days. Thus, cold-water feeding is a much less frequent event.

The top of the feeding temperature range appears to be somewhere between 70 and 75 degrees. Fish will feed in warmer waters out of necessity. If they can't escape it they must still continue to feed. The effects of excessively high temperatures are rather similar to those of low temperatures on striped bass. They begin to move less and less and feed less and less. The best examples of this are the doldrums of August in waters along the New York Bight and eastern Long Island. The bass seem to be off their feed and will only strike irresistible baits; live baits and then eels seem the best lures.

The optimal feeding range of a striped bass is between 55 and 68 degrees. Fish then are most active. The cooler water temperatures are associated with post-spawning temperatures and migratory temperatures. At both these times in the life of a striped bass feeding is intense.

5

The Pacific Striped Bass

On the south shore of Carquinez Straits, in the city of Martinez, should stand a statue of two men holding a milk can. And at least once a year, preferably in July, all the fishermen in California, and some from Washington and Oregon as well, should walk by the monument and touch it with respect. And each should whisper a quiet thanks to the two men with the milk can.

At the base, the inscription should read: "Livingston Stone, Aquaculturist, U.S. Fish Commission." Under the other statue, "Stephen Rush Throckmorton, Chairman, California Fish Commission." Under the milk can: "132 Navesink Striped Bass." Lastly, the monument should be dated: "July 1879."

From these 132 striped bass, a part of the Hudson River stock in the Navesink estuary in New Jersey, and a later stocking of 300 bass three years later from the Shrewsbury River, the entire striped bass fishery on the Pacific coast had its origin. Most of the fish were small, between 1½ and 3 inches, but their potential was large. A recent estimate of the striped bass population in the San Francisco Bay complex placed the population at about 2 million fish 16 inches or longer.

The latter part of the nineteenth century was a great time for fish experimentation. Fisheries biologists were introducing new species to waters that had been voided of native stocks throughout the East because of industrialization and altered environments. It was about this time that the brown trout was brought over from Europe and introduced to American waters. Unfortunately, the European carp also came. It was a field day for the fish culturists with an adventurous spirit.

One such man was Livingston Stone, employed by the U.S. Fish Commission but on loan to California. Stone, long a devotee of the striped bass, believed that San Francisco Bay could support a population, and after netting a catch in the Navesink he nursed the fish on a long train

San Francisco Bay is the center of abundance for striped bass on the West Coast, similar in concentration of fish to Chesapeake Bay on the Atlantic Coast.

ride from New York to California. There he made the historic planting. Fortunately, it turned out to be one of the better moves made by fish culturists.

Today, the striped bass is plentiful in two areas along the Pacific Coast—the San Francisco Bay area and Coos Bay in Oregon. It is sporadic on the Columbia River system between Oregon and Washington. From time to time, striped bass have appeared in northern Mexico and southern California, but not with any degree of prediction or dependency.

In just ten years after their planting in San Francisco, the striped bass were so well established that further transplanting of these bass was attempted in other West Coast locations. Humboldt Bay had a stock planted in 1889, and in 1903 the Santa Ana River in Orange County (near San Diego) received striped bass. In 1916 and 1919, Morro Bay in San Luis Obispo County was given a collection of striped bass in hopes of establishing another population. The fish even spanned a big piece of the Pacific and in 1919 they were released near Honolulu, Hawaii. Unfortunately, all these stockings failed to take hold.

The striped bass were smarter than the fish culturists. In these areas conditions just did not exist that would support a striped bass population, especially one that would reproduce itself. The fast waters were there with plenty of spawning sites, but most lacked the large estuaries that bass like for summer feeding. These big run-outs before the open ocean often house the food supply and hold the bass in a place to grow and mature. Bass on the Pacific Coast had exhibited the typical local migration nature of most striped bass stocks on the Atlantic, and the somewhat indigenous attitude of Hudson River fish was carried over into the Pacific fish.

Instead of heading south, striped bass on their own headed north from San Francisco Bay. There is a natural biological dispersion of fish in any population on the search for more food and less competition from its own kind. This drift northward was not a migration similar to certain Chesapeake Bay fish but a natural tendency of a fish species to move into new areas, a phenomenon that is always in action.

On their own, the fish established themselves at Coos Bay, and it was to their liking. They thrived so well that by 1922 a commercial fishery was under way. Eventually, striped bass reached as far as the Columbia River, and here too they established themselves with a breeding population. There have been reports of striped bass being taken by commercial fishermen as far north as British Columbia and southern Alaska. But this has been rare.

CALIFORNIA

Today, striped bass constitute the major sport fishery in the San Francisco Bay area, supplanting native species of salmon and trout that had been reduced over the years because of changing environmental conditions in the bay and the surrounding watershed.

Success of the striped bass transplant is like a Horatio Alger fish story. Ten years after the initial planting, hundreds of striped bass were being taken in the area. By 1899 over 1,200,000 pounds of striped bass were landed commercially, and from 1916 to 1935, the annual catch of fish by commercial means averaged between 500,000 and 1,000,000 pounds. In 1935, all commercial fishing was stopped to protect the sport fishery.

Almost all of the striped bass taken in California waters comes from the San Francisco Bay area. California's 200,000 striped bass anglers catch about 750,000 fish annually. In order to make their fishing possible, these anglers each year spend $20,000,000 in pursuit of the striper.

Striped bass in California and other West Coast waters differ little in their characteristics and habits when compared to the same species of fish in the Atlantic. The only difference might be the food selection, and that is governed more by what is available than by their own choice.

Migrations

California biologists have intensively studied the striped bass and have established migratory patterns for fish in their area. The annual migrations are similar in pattern to fish in the Hudson. In the summer, the fish inhabit the lower bay and the beaches north and south of the Golden Gate. Their environment at this time is basically in salt water. In the fall, from September to November, they begin an upstream migration from San Francisco Bay through San Pablo Bay and the Carquinez Straits into Suisan and Grizzly bays. As winter approaches they are in the freshwater delta formed by the San Joaquin and Sacramento rivers. Here they over-winter and remain until spring. As spring approaches the fish scatter out over the delta, and some head up the Sacramento River to spawn. After spawning, they return to San Pablo Bay and adjacent waters to feed for the summer.

Just how many striped bass will trek back to the ocean after spawning varies from year to year. Smaller bass tend to stay within the confines of the bay, while some of the larger bass develop a bit of wanderlust and move outside the Golden Gate. These large fish have been taken with a fair degree of frequency as far south as Monterey and north along the coast as far as Tomales Bay.

Spawning

Two major spawning areas and a number of minor sites are used by California striped bass. The two principal areas are in the Sacramento River from Isleton to Butte City, and in the main branch of the San Joaquin River and adjacent sloughs from the community of Antioch upriver to Venice Island. The amount of water flowing in the rivers affects the location of spawning more than the bottom composition or other factors. Because spawning time is directly related to water temperature a great flow of water will cause fish to swim even farther upstream until the correct spawning temperature is reached. Because of these factors, during years of high spring water run-offs the fish will spawn farther upstream. During spring seasons of minimal flow they will spawn farther downstream.

The situation is somewhat different in the San Joaquin River system, which has more of a delta and thus greater diffusion of its water than the adjacent Sacramento. With less of a water flow, the location of spawning is determined principally by salinity, or lack of it, as in the Hudson River situation.

Striped bass demand extremely low salinity or virtually fresh water in which to spawn. In years when there is a high run-off on the San Joaquin, the saline block is pushed farther downstream and spawning occurs farther downstream. During years of lesser run-off the salt block occurs farther upriver and the spawning takes place ahead of it.

Spawning begins in these rivers when the water temperature passes 60 degrees and peaks out between 63 and 68 degrees, similar to spawning in the Atlantic. Thus, spawning in the Delta and San Joaquin usually precedes spawning in the Sacramento by about two weeks because of cooler water in the Sacramento. Approximate spawning times in the Delta have been from April 25 to May 25 and in the Sacramento River from May 10 to June 12.

As eggs are deposited they are fertilized by the male and begin drifting downstream with the current. They are just slightly heavier than fresh water; their specific gravity is 1.0005. Depending upon the water temperature, the eggs hatch between forty-eight to seventy-two hours. The young larvae obtain nourishment from the yolk sac still attached to their body, and though they attempt weak swimming movements it is the current that keeps them off the bottom. By the seventh or eighth day, their mobility increases and they begin active feeding on microscopic zooplankton. As they grow their food becomes larger.

From four to six weeks after spawning, the young fish are all found downriver in the Delta and Suisan Bay, where fresh and salt water mix. Through the remainder of their first year, opossum shrimp are the main food for the juvenile bass. As the winter months come on, the young bass begin feeding on smaller fish, which increasingly become the major part of their diet. The fish spend most of their juvenile lives in Suisan and San Pablo bays. As in the Atlantic, male bass mature sexually during their second and third years, while females mature during their fifth and sixth years. Once these fish are mature they take on the migratory habits of adult fish.

OREGON

Since 1879, striped bass have dispersed northward along the West Coast of the United States and established themselves in several locations. In Oregon, four centers have reproducing populations. The most extensive group exists on Coos Bay and two tributaries that flow into it; Winchester Bay where the Umpqua and Smith rivers meet; Siuslaw Bay and River; and Coquille Bay and South Fork Coquille River. Occasionally, striped bass are also taken from other small rivers along the Oregon Coast but without consistency, and there may be fish produced in one of the above four systems. It may have occurred much sooner, but the first striped bass recorded north of San Francisco took thirty-five years to travel there. In 1914, the first bass was taken in Coos Bay in a gill net.

Today, Coos Bay supports an extensive fishery for striped bass. The fishing area reaches from the Coos River Bar to the upper tidal reaches of the Coos and Millicoma River that enters Coos River from the north. At various times of the year, this area has four principal regions that produce striped bass for anglers. Fishing for bass takes place on Isthmus Slough; on Coos River–Millicoma River and Catching Slough; in Coos Bay at various tributary mouths and Haynes Inlet; and at the Inlet of Coos Bay to the Pacific as well as South Slough.

Spawning takes place from about the middle of May and lasts until the end of June. Spawning locations in this system are confined to an area where the South Fork Coos River meets Millicoma River and about a mile south of this junction on Coos River. As the eggs develop they drift downstream to an area near Enegrin Ferry. Hatching occurs in forty-eight to seventy-two hours and the young larvae remain in this part of the river for the next week to ten days. Young fry and juvenile bass feed in the bay and do not take part in migrations until they have sexually matured.

Migration studies of the Coos Bay area are still incomplete, but a few patterns have been established that are similar to other endemic populations on both Atlantic and Pacific coasts. There are two migrations of bass in Coos Bay, a spawning migration upstream in the spring and a second migration to the sloughs in the bay in the fall. Two to three weeks after spawning, the adult fish drop downriver into the bay and apparently leave the bay for the open ocean, because the bay is almost devoid of big fish until fall. The fall migration sees the bass return and winter in the sloughs. The large fish may spend the summer along the outside beaches and take short coastal migrations like the large bass in San Francisco Bay. They may even take extended runs, but it is unlikely, because commercial angling with otter trawls, long lines, shark nets, crab pots, and even salmon trolls have not yielded striped bass off the beach.

Oregon research on sexing striped bass taken from commercial catches (striped bass can be commercially fished in five Oregon rivers) reveals a considerable amount of hermaphroditism. Almost 3 percent of the bass samples were found to possess gonads for both sexes. Occasionally both the ovaries and testes were ripe. In all examples, the male organs or testes formed the anterior portion of the glands and the ovaries formed the posterior section. In both cases, the testes and ovaries were both ripe at spawning time.

WASHINGTON

Information on the striped bass in Washington is spotty. There is no defined fishery in the state. Occasionally, striped bass are taken near the mouth of the Columbia River or in Willapa Bay, and an occasional fish is caught in Holmes Harbor on Whidbey Island in Puget Sound. During recent years, a few juvenile fish have been seen on the Columbia, but little else has been noted and the fishery is virtually unexplored and unidentified.

6

The Striped Bass in Fresh Water

Even the early colonists knew from observations that striped bass spent a part of their lives in fresh water when they ascended the rivers to spawn. Throughout most of the Southeast and Gulf Coast states, biologists as well as anglers have always known that the striped bass here lived more of their lives in fresh water than in salt water. In many rivers in Alabama and Mississippi, the striped bass are hundreds of miles from salt water and never reach it.

However, everyone assumed that at least once a year, or maybe even only once in their lives, the striped bass descended from their freshwater environment for a rejuvenation of sorts in salt water. Then they returned to live upstream. Bass always had access to salt water and no one even considered the idea that these fish, out of their own volition, had decided to give up the saltwater phase of their lives and return to a more primordial routine. Or maybe these striped bass of our southern waters had never even gone to sea like their brethren along the northern part of the Atlantic range.

It was therefore quite startling when a collection of events began to unfold in a South Carolina reservoir. Quite by accident, a funny thing happened on the way to the ocean. In a vast program of rural electrification during the 1930s and 1940s, Southern and Central states began harnessing their rivers with hydroelectric dams. South Carolina's needs turned to two rivers not far from the coast, the Santee and Cooper, and here they created a double reservoir. On November 12, 1941, the gates of Pinopolis Dam were closed and the reservoirs, lakes Marion and Moultrie, connected by a 6-mile diversion canal, began to fill.

Lake Moultrie (the lower lake) had been cleared of trees, and Lake Marion could be cleared after the gates were closed because it would take more than a year to fill the reservoirs. But along came the war and the demand for electrical power intensified. The lake was filled as quickly as possible and the timber was left standing. Any fish in the streams became incidental to the urgency.

These two rivers had always produced good bass fishing, along with some steady panfishing. After the reservoirs formed the angling was phenomenal. Striped bass also inhabited the original rivers and had always traveled up their courses to spawn. The striped bass trapped behind the dam also grew large, like the largemouth bass. Though the striper, or rockfish, were few and far between during those first years, they were large fish.

Then, during 1948 and 1949, the striper fishing began to pick up in quantity. However, instead of the catch being composed of the behemoths of the past, a great variety of sizes began to show, even small striped bass.

These smaller fish meant that new fish were being produced. But everyone knew that striped bass were anadromous fish and that anadromous fish must spend a part of their life cycle in salt water. The single lock on the dam did open occasionally throughout the year for the few boats that traveled up and down the river. However, they weren't open for a duration that would support the large influx of striped bass that would be needed to come up from the ocean and perpetuate the population of the reservoir with young fish. Besides, the bass moved up from the sea for only two or three weeks in the spring, and the chances of the gates being open at the correct time were considered too small to be the explanation.

For all practical purposes, the striped bass had been cut off from the ocean. Those trapped behind the dam had to be the cause of all the puzzlement. South Carolina biologists began to study the phenomenon, beginning with a tagging program. Six hundred striped bass were caught below the dam, tagged, and released in its tailrace. Results showed that the Cooper River supported an endemic group of striped bass that made their home between Charleston Harbor and Pinopolis Dam.

The next study showed that young of the year—that is, striped bass produced in the spring—could be captured by nets along the shore of the lake above the dam throughout the summer and fall. From the vast numbers netted the population of the entire double reservoir could be estimated. Biologists determined that there was no way a sufficient number of bass could have come through the locks to spawn and produce this horde of young fish.

The final determination concluded that striped bass on the Santee-Cooper Reservoir had indeed become landlocked and were producing their own young without a need to return to salt water for a part of their life cycle. It did, however, pose another question that may never be answered. How did the landlocked strain of striped bass develop? Had it been the result of the dam, and had these fish spawned on what may have been primordial spawning grounds? Or had these striped bass already eliminated the trek to salt water, for all intents and purposes passing the complete cycle of their lives in an upriver environment? Had this new cycle started hundreds of years before the dam was built?

About 1950, a sudden increase began in the number of striped bass being caught in the reservoir. The increase turned into an explosion. The fishing was fantastic over the next several years. Anglers were taking striped bass at a rate of better than five fish per trip. It was too good to continue.

The cause of the population explosion was the availability of a great food supply for striped bass in the form of threadfin shad, gizzard shad, and herring. While the bass were repopulating themselves, these forage fish were not. The dam had effectively cut off their supply. Fishing began to fall, and finally the state's biologists put their fingers on the diminishing food supply as the cause. This was simply corrected by allowing shad and herring spawners to come through the locks during their annual migrations up the river from salt water. During March, the locks at Pinopolis Dam were opened twice a day. This let spawning-bent herring and shad into the lower lake to spawn and created more food for the bass, and in addition the adults themselves were trapped and contributed to the food supply. Since then, the population has risen and the annual locking-through of food has established a balance between predator bass and food fish.

At the same time Santee-Cooper Reservoir was established, other reservoirs were built throughout South Carolina. After they became stabilized their fish populations also increased, but the rough fish outshadowed the gamefish, glutting these impoundments. The solution was to add striped bass as a fish controller. Gizzard shad were the real culprits, and striped bass loved them.

Adult striped bass that came up the Santee River to spawn in the tailrace of the dam were netted and transplanted to other reservoirs. The bass went to work on the shad. However, self-sustaining populations could not be developed on these reservoir systems. Only Santee-Cooper had the precisely correct water environment to produce its own supply of new fish. What South Carolina now needed was a steady supply of fish for stocking; it needed a hatchery for striped bass.

North Carolina had established a successful striped bass hatchery on the Roanoke River before the turn of the century and has since continued to hatch bass taken from the Roanoke Rapids as they come upriver to spawn. South Carolina patterned its Moncks Corners Hatchery, next to the Pinopolis Dam tailrace, after the one at Roanoke Rapids. With a few improvements, it was ready to begin producing striped bass for all its reservoirs that couldn't create their own natural production.

Moncks Corners Hatchery, established on the Santee River just below Pinopolis Dam, which forms the Santee-Cooper Reservoir. Bass migrating up the river to spawn on these ancestral sites are shocked and netted, and then eggs and milt are taken and artificially fertilized. The eggs are hatched out in the jars shown inside the hatchery, and the young striped bass produced are used to establish a freshwater striper fishery in environments where natural reproduction cannot take place.

Still another problem crept up. South Carolina couldn't obtain many fish in a ripe condition to get the eggs and milt. North Carolina was lucky because it had such a vast supply of fish and anglers were paid to bring ripe fish immediately to the hatchery when they were caught.

How to get fish in a ripe state was a problem, but one researcher had heard of some work being done in Alabama with injected hormones that caused fish to produce ripe eggs. The technique was then refined at Moncks Corners with striped bass, and one of the most successful bass hatcheries in the nation was underway.

News of success on Santee-Cooper spread throughout the scientific journals, newspapers, and magazines. All states with big impoundments and rough-fish problems began looking to the striped bass as a solution. As a result, the striped bass, over the last ten to fifteen years, has been introduced in thirty-six impoundments from Georgia to California and from Tennessee to Louisiana and Texas.

Of the fifteen states working with striped bass in fresh water, only five have been successful in developing self-sustaining populations. Aside from South Carolina and Santee-Cooper, established fisheries are in Kerr Reservoir on the Roanoke River on the Virginia–North Carolina border; Keystone Reservoir in Oklahoma; the Colorado River in the Arizona-Nevada-California area; and most recently the Dardanelle Reservoir on the Arkansas River in Arkansas. Oklahoma has collected some evidence of spawning on the Texoma Reservoir, but firm establishment is yet to come.

States with freshwater striped bass populations are:

Arizona (California–Nevada)
Arkansas
Florida
Georgia
Kentucky
Louisiana
Maryland
Mississippi
Missouri
Nebraska
North Carolina
South Carolina
Tennessee
Texas
Virginia

Some of these states will be discussed separately below.

Arizona-California-Nevada

Between 1962 and 1969 both the Arizona and California game and fish departments combined their efforts in a program to establish a striped bass fishery on the Colorado River between Davis and Parker dams. Davis Dam is at the upstream section of this area and was completed in 1953. Parker Dam forms Lake Havasu, and the Colorado River flows 78 miles from Davis Dam to where it enters Havasu Lake.

Nine stockings of assorted sizes of striped bass fingerlings and yearlings were planted in the flowing part of the Colorado River below Davis Dam and Lake Havasu between August 1962 and August 1964. The stock for these fish came from California. In 1969, an additional planting of fish was received from Moncks Corners, S.C., and reared at a hatchery in Page Springs, Ariz.

Kentucky striped bass. The striped bass has been planted in several large reservoirs in Kentucky. Benny Polston of Jamestown holds a 34½-pound rockfish that existed for six years as the state record. In 1970 it was broken by a 44¼-pound striper taken on a cane pole and on a 1-pound freshwater drum used as bait by Ronald Warner. Note also the unique, deeper-bellied shape of a freshwater striped bass.

As early as 1964 the striped bass made a migration to the tailwaters of the Davis Dam to spawn. There was no evidence of a successful spawn until about 1969. In 1970, however, a strong year class was produced. The spawning took place from May to mid-June. An area about 10 miles below Davis Dam appears to be the primary spawning grounds for these Colorado River striped bass.

Catching a striped bass on the Colorado River was a rarity until 1966 when anglers finally found the bass and figured out how to catch them. In 1974, fishermen switched to whole and cut anchovies, and now most any angler can catch fish. The Bullhead City Striped Bass Derby has become an annual affair, and two other derbies in the area have been initiated.

Arkansas

Like many other states where the Corps of Engineers has been active, Arkansas is now endowed with a collection of large reservoirs where there once were river systems. And as in many reservoirs, threadfin and gizzard shad have multiplied beyond control. In 1956, Arkansas began its program to establish the striped bass in its waters. The first attempts involved trucking adult fish from South Carolina to Arkansas waters, but the mortality rate was so high that this method was abandoned.

In 1966, Arkansas biologists netted striped bass from Albemarle Sound in North Carolina, artificially stimulated ovulation with chorionic gonadotropin, and produced a batch of fry that were flown to a state fish hatchery in Lonoke, Ark.

The resulting fingerlings, in the fall of that year, were planted in the Dardanelle Reservoir on the Arkansas River. During subsequent years, Dardanelle, as well as other reservoirs throughout the state, has received additional stockings of striped bass. To date, seven reservoirs provide a striped bass fishery. In 1973, definite natural reproduction on one system, the Arkansas River, had taken place. The main impoundment in this fishery is Dardanelle Reservoir. Other reservoirs are supported by annual stockings of hatchery fish.

Florida

Florida's freshwater striped bass program began in the summer of 1968 when fish were established in six separate bodies of water. The source of the stock was South Carolina's Moncks Corners Hatchery. At first, striped bass from Florida's two freshwater river populations, the St. Johns and Apalachicola, were tried but proved unsuccessful.

During the first year, lakes Hollingsworth, Talquin, and Underhill received young fish. During 1969, lakes Hunter, Parker, and Bentley were stocked. Growth of the fish in these lakes was rapid and bass were around 11 inches long after the first year. The fish are maturing sexually, but natural reproduction is not expected in any of these environments, except possibly Lake Talquin. This lake has also been the best producer of striped bass compared to the other systems and in 1972 it yielded a fish weighing nearly 13 pounds.

Georgia

At one time, all of Georgia's coastal streams had substantial populations of striped bass. Because of industrialization, pollution, and dam construction, the fishery waned and was depleted in some streams. Today, the

Savannah and Ogeechee rivers still retain breeding populations. With the advent of reservoir building and the demand for a fish to reduce shad populations, biologists in Georgia also turned to the striped bass.

Georgia's initial attempts began in 1966 when some 250 large striped bass were stocked in Lake Blackshear, a reservoir on the Flint River that eventually flows into the Apalachicola in Florida. Some of the fish were 30 pounds in weight and the biologists hoped for a self-sustaining population. Next to be stocked was Lake Seminole, on the lower Flint, where it too flows into Florida. Lake Burton in northeast Georgia was stocked by accident.

The big boost in Georgia's freshwater striped bass program came in 1969 when, in cooperation with the U.S. Fish & Wildlife Service, 100,000 fingerlings were stocked in lakes Sinclair and Jackson. Since then, Georgia has constructed a new hatchery at Richmond Hill, on the Savannah River, close to where adult striped bass can be interrupted on their spawning runs. Here the fish are raised to fingerling size and used to stock the reservoirs. The aims of Georgia's striped bass program today are only to sustain nonreproducing populations on lakes Seminole, Jackson, Sinclair, and Blackshear. In addition, the state has begun a program of reestablished runs of striped bass on coastal rivers where the fish at one time were abundant.

Kentucky

Much of Kentucky's striped bass program has been carried out jointly with Tennessee. However, the program has not been as successful as in other states, with fishable populations just on the margin. This is not to say that "rockfish" are not caught in the half-dozen reservoirs and lakes in which it has been stocked, it's just that very few people go rockfishing to catch striped bass, and the catches are incidental to other fishing.

Kentucky's program began in 1957 when twelve adult striped bass were stocked in Cumberland Lake. Over the years, the program has expanded on Cumberland Lake and now includes Kentucky Lake, shared with Tennessee, and Herrington Lake. Natural production did not occur, though the fish grew, and one 34-pound trophy fish was caught. The latest addition to the system has been Barkley Lake in western Kentucky; the tailrace below the dam is one of the favorite angling spots. Fish up to 20 pounds have been taken from the discharge.

Hybridization is a chance occurrence that happens when striped bass and white bass populations inhabit the same environment. Natural hybridization, usually between a female striped bass and a male white bass, occurs in Kentucky Lake and some of Kentucky's efforts are now going into hatchery production of these hybrids, a fast-growing cross.

Kentucky's stocked waters include Cumberland Lake, Herrington Lake, Kentucky Lake, Barkley Lake, Gree River Reservoir, and Dewey Lake.

Tennessee

Tennessee was one of the earliest inland states to begin developing a striped bass fishery. Initial plantings of fish came from North Carolina and were stocked in Cherokee and Percy Priest lakes. None of these lakes has revealed any natural reproduction of striped bass, and the department has since resigned itself to put-and-take fishing.

Hybridization of female striped bass with male white bass at hatcheries in North Carolina and South Carolina produced a fast-growing fish. As a result, Tennessee began introducing hybrids to its lakes as well as Norris, Watts Bar, and Kentucky lakes. Striped bass fingerlings have also been regularly stocked in these lakes and reservoirs.

Tennessee now has created excellent fishing in two reservoirs, Cherokee and Percy Priest, good fishing in Norris, and limited fishing in the three remaining impoundments. Kentucky Lake, however, has the greatest potential for the self-sustaining population to develop because of the type of watershed feeding the reservoir and water quality. Efforts are likely to be made in the future to bolster stockings in this body of water in hopes of such a production.

The annual catch of striped bass in Tennessee waters now is close to 200,000 pounds. The largest bass caught so far was 20 pounds, and stripers on Cherokee Lake average about 10 pounds.

Oklahoma

A striped bass program was introduced to Oklahoma in 1965 with 125,000 small fish given by North Carolina. However, these fish were lost in the hatchery ponds. In 1966 both North and South Carolina again shipped fish west, at the rate of 4 million fry, and eventually 11,000 made it to the fingerling stage. These were stocked in Keystone Reservoir. In 1967, Virginia and South Carolina again supplied Oklahoma hatcheries with 5 million fry, and this time 190,000 were raised to fingerlings and stocked in the huge Keystone Reservoir.

Keystone wasn't the only favored body of fresh water for Oklahoma's striped bass program. In May 1967, 200,000 fry were planted in Lake Texoma, a reservoir that straddles the Red River between Texas and Oklahoma. Fishing was good in Keystone and even below the dam, on the Arkansas River. Stripers weighing 6 to 9 pounds have been taken and a 14-pounder came from the Grand River.

The big question, however, was that of natural production, something that at that time hadn't been achieved on any other water except Santee-Cooper and Kerr Lake. On June 18, 1970, haul seining along the shore on Keystone produced six fingerling striped bass and proved that fish had been successfully spawned in Keystone. Today, Oklahoma is able to replenish its own supply of striped bass with excellent production. Texoma has many of the characteristics of Keystone, and biologists in 1973 noted a few examples of natural production.

Texas

Texas became active in the propagation of striped bass in 1967 with the rearing of small fish obtained from sources in Virginia, Maryland, and North and South Carolina. The major emphasis on stocking has been in Navarro Mills and Bardwell reservoirs, with other stockings on lakes Spence, Granbury, and Bastrop. These stockings have supplied some fair catches of striped bass for Texas anglers. However, natural production has not occurred and the stock must be supported by hatchery production.

Current efforts are being directed to establishing a striped bass fishery in Lake Whitney, with additional efforts in Lake Granbury on the Brazos River system. This system has the potential for producing a self-sustaining population, which is more important to the hatchery programs than just the supplying of fish for these two reservoirs. If Texas can produce its own brook stock it can eliminate the costly practice of bringing in stocks from the East and increase its efficiency at the hatchery level.

Louisiana has stocked striped bass in the Toledo Bend Reservoir that is jointly shared by Louisiana and Texas. The largest striped bass so far in Texas has come from this reservoir, a 22¼-pound fish taken in 1973. Oklahoma also shares a fishery with Texas, on the Texoma Reservoir, where natural reproduction was recently identified. Texas intends to put more emphasis on the Brazos River system but has also recently stocked Pat Mayse Travis, Whitney, and Canyon reservoirs.

Virginia

The development of Virginia's freshwater striped bass fishery, or land-locked stripers as they are sometimes called, runs somewhat parallel to that of South Carolina. In 1952 the Kerr Reservoir on the Roanoke River was filled and created a vast inland lake over what had once been a rather productive striped bass river. Part of the river reservoir spills over into

North Carolina, and during the first two years after impoundment, the North Carolina Wildlife Commission stocked more than 3 million striped bass fry in the body of water. The establishment of a striped bass fishery occurred quickly, and biologists are not certain whether it was a result of the plantings or a natural population of striped bass that were trapped behind the dam once the gates were closed. Roanoke Rapids, a major Atlantic Coast spawning site, is not more than 30 miles downriver from the dam.

In 1957 and 1958, yearling striped bass were taken from the reservoir, confirming the belief that a self-sustaining population was in existence in the reservoir. Today, the total size of the striped bass population in Kerr Reservoir is probably second only to that in Santee-Cooper. In response to a need for more stock for other reservoirs in the state and other states, Virginia built a hatchery at Brookneal on the Roanoke River. Today, this hatchery is capable of an annual production of 35 million striped bass. It is now one of three major striped bass hatcheries in the world, but unique in that it is the only one using only landlocked brood stock for hatchery production. Other hatcheries, like that at Moncks Corners, S.C., obtain their brood stock from migrant fish that come to the base of the dam to spawn. These fish still have access to salt water.

Virginia has been active, because of the hatchery, in stocking almost every reservoir in the state with striped bass fry and sustains a good put-and-take fishery on most of them. Smith Mountain Lake, near Roanoke, is one of the better lakes maintained on this basis. Other reservoirs in Virginia include Clayton, Carvin's Cove, Prince, Meade, and Hardwood Mill.

HATCHERIES

The first attempts to hatch striped bass eggs occurred at the shad hatchery at Albemarle Sound in North Carolina in 1879. The young were sent to Druid-Hill Park in Baltimore, Md. Maryland eventually established its own shad hatchery at Havre de Grace near the head of Chesapeake Bay and the mouth of the Susquehanna River. In 1886, 20,000 striped bass were cultured at the hatchery and stocked in Lake Ontario, near the mouth of the Oswego River in New York State. Nothing was heard of these fish.

More recently, striped bass have crossed the Atlantic in hopes of planting them in Russian rivers flowing into the Black Sea. Shipments began in 1960. Since 1965, seven shipments of live striped bass were delivered to Russia. Four of the first batches were lost en route before techniques of transportation could be worked out.

The experimental rearing of striped bass larvae and young was carried out at the VIRNO aquarium at Moscow, on the Chernaya River

Trout Farm, and at a field point on the mouth of the Don River near where it flows into the Sea of Azov, an arm of the Black Sea. Russian biologists have done some fine original research concerning the development of striped bass eggs, larvae, and fry. However, there is little information now available on how successful the transplants were. In 1972, a two-year-old bass, weighing 1.5 pounds, was caught in the Black Sea. It was the first example of native production and indicates that natural spawning took place.

FRESHWATER VS. SALTWATER STRIPED BASS

For the most part, the striped bass in fresh water is the same fish as it is in salt water. Physically, the appearance of the fish might change only slightly. The adult freshwater fish does not attain the same length as in salt water. Freshwater striped bass also have a tendency to grow greater girth dimensions in comparison to length. This produces a fish with a somewhat heavier pouch, often not too unlike a largemouth bass in general body shape.

The only discernible difference between the fish in the two differing environments is the characteristic of growth. Striped bass in fresh water, as substantiated by growth records in Kerr Reservoir in Virginia–North Carolina, Keystone Lake in Oklahoma, and the Colorado River in Arizona-Nevada-California, grow at a much faster rate than the same fish in salt water.

The greatest year in growth for marine forms of the fish is the second year of their lives. In fresh water, it is the first year. Virginia research has established that striped bass in Kerr Reservoir grow twice as fast as the same fish in Chesapeake Bay. But there is a toll for this accelerated growth—the fish reach old age, seven to nine years, a lot sooner and begin to die off. Striped bass in salt water are not "old-age" fish until they get beyond fifteen years old. Saltwater fish grow more slowly, but live a lot longer.

The same rapid growth during the first year of life is also a phenomenon of Santee-Cooper fish. One of the reasons for this rapid growth might be the greater food supply in the impoundments. A second might be a warmer overall water temperature during the first year, allowing fry to feed for ten or eleven months instead of five to eight months, as may be the case in saltwater nurseries. To contradict this, however, the growth rate of fry planted in a reservoir was similar to the rate in a marine environment. Under the same growing conditions, as in Santee-Cooper, fry introduced showed a slower growth rate when compared immediately to fry naturally produced in the same environment. As a result, the causes of this faster growth rate are still obscure.

7

The Future of the Striped Bass

The abundance of striped bass has always been a topic of interest both to fishermen and to biologists. Striped bass were almost certainly more abundant in colonial times than they are today. In those days, numbers were determined only by biological and natural physical variables. Today, man has become a third element in the control of striped bass abundance along our coasts.

Striped bass played an important role in the earliest colonial times, and our first records of the availability of the fish come from Plymouth and Boston. In 1623, through misfortune, the Plymouth Colony had only one small boat. Yet with the aid of this boat and a net, the colonists were able to take enough striped bass to keep from starving.

Thomas Morton, writing in 1632, tells us:

The Basse is an excellent Fish, both fresh & salt, one hundred whereof, salted at market, have yielded 5 p. They are so large the head of one will give a good eater a dinner, and for daintiness of diet they excell the Marybones of beefe. There are such multitudes that I have seene stopped into the river close adjoining to my howse, with a sand at one tide, so many as will load a shipe of one hundred tonnes.

The famous Captain John Smith, who was governor of Virginia until that colony failed and then was Admiral of New England, wrote in a book published in London in 1631:

The seven and thirty passengers, miscarrying twice upon the coast of England, came so ill provided they only relyed upon the poore company they found, they had lived two years by their naked industry and what the country naturally afforded. It is true, there hath beene taken a thousand Bayses at a draught, and more than twelve hogsheads of Herring in one night.

The effects of civilization upon nature quickly began to take their toll, even of the seemingly inexhaustible supply of striped bass. Declines were first noticed in New England, where dams were built for power to run mills and where excessive netting of fish at times stopped the entire upriver migration.

Gradually, the decline spread throughout New England and then southward into New York, New Jersey, Delaware, and Pennsylvania. The decline was slow until after the end of the Civil War. Then the great American industrial revolution began and signaled the rapid decline of the striped bass. Catches along the coast of Maine, Rhode Island, and Massachusetts dwindled drastically. The fisheries in Maine collapsed, and striped bass clubs for wealthy anglers began to disband as the twentieth century approached.

Farther south, in Chesapeake Bay, long one of the oldest and richest fishing grounds along the Atlantic Coast, there was much less industrialization. Until the end of the Civil War, fishing there had been only to supply local markets. But the advent of the railroad and the dwindling fish-food supplies in the Northeast gave impetus to commercial fishing in Chesapeake Bay.

The original striped bass fishery along the New England and Middle Atlantic coasts was very likely totally self-supporting, receiving very little from the Chesapeake Bay fishery as it does today. The factors that encourage one race of Chesapeake striped bass to develop a great migration characteristic must not have been in operation at the time or they did not favor that particular strain of striped bass. If these fish had a migratory characteristic during the 1800s, they would have continued to populate the New England coast as they do today.

Very few records were kept before 1880, and during the years from about 1880 to 1930 only sporadic records of commercial landing were maintained by the federal government and many of the states along the coast. While the landings and populations of striped bass from Delaware north to Maine were steadily declining, those in Chesapeake Bay remained fairly stable, with local cyclic fluctuations but no steady decline. Landing figures from southern Atlantic Coast states, whose endemic populations do not contribute to the Atlantic migratory stock, also appeared to remain constant.

Since 1930 fairly accurate records of striped bass landings have been maintained by states on the Atlantic. Disregarding local highs and lows in the populations, there has been a steady increase in the catches of striped bass. In New England and the Middle Atlantic states, these landings surpassed those of the late 1800s. It is impossible to compare today's striped bass population to what it might have been in colonial times because of the greater fishing pressure nowadays and

Striped bass landings 1887–1929 (in thousands of pounds). Early records of striped-bass catches, or landings, are spotty and their accuracy is doubtful. However, they do give us a rough indication of the numbers of fish available and taken and their fluctuations. Since 1930, there has been a steady increase in the landings with rather accurate substantiation by the U.S. Bureau of Commercial Fisheries.

TABLE 1. Striped bass landings, earlier records (in thousands of pounds).

Year	New England Region						Middle Atlantic Region					Chesapeake Region			South Atlantic Region				Combined Total
	Maine	N. H.	Mass.	R. I.	Conn.	Total	N. Y.	N. J.	Penn.	Del.	Total	Md.	Va.	Total	N. C.	S. C.	Ga.	Total	
1887	—	—	20	11	46	77	115	615	15	116	861	1,140	505	1,645	500	182	11	693	3,276
1888	—	—	32	13	50	95	98	739	59	116	1,012	1,123	779	1,902	560	251	11	822	3,831
1889	—	—	25	80	39	144	212	306	24	110	652	—	—	—	526	11	13	550	—
1890	—	—	—	—	—	—	208	328	23	107	666	1,366	529	1,895	568	12	9	589	—
1891	—	—	—	—	—	—	205	298	25	95	625	1,265	483	1,748	—	—	—	—	—
1897	—	—	—	—	—	—	116	287	10	129	542	935	576	1,511	845	10	9	864	—
1898	25	1	13	102	14	155	82	274	—	—	—	824	528	1,352	—	—	—	—	—
1901	—	—	—	—	—	—	72	354	13	48	487	—	—	—	—	—	—	1,188	—
1902	16	2	28	50	40	136	53	66	6	40	165	721	451	1,172	1,175	10	3	—	—
1904	—	—	—	—	—	—	—	—	—	—	—	—	—	—	—	—	—	—	—
1905	4	—	21	32	19	76	—	—	—	—	—	640	504	1,144	—	—	—	—	—
1908	3	1	5	34	2	44	40	53	7	53	138	1,040	380	1,420	510	5	9	524	1,870
1920	—	—	—	—	—	—	95	70	—	5	170	—	—	—	—	—	—	—	—
1921	—	—	—	—	—	—	—	—	—	—	—	—	—	—	447	—	—	447	—
1923	—	—	—	—	—	—	—	—	—	—	—	1,414	821	2,235	—	—	—	—	—
1925	—	—	—	—	5	—	—	—	—	—	197	—	—	—	—	—	—	—	—
1926	—	—	—	—	5	—	87	64	—	46	—	—	—	—	—	—	—	—	—
1927	—	—	—	—	4	—	—	—	—	—	—	—	—	—	507	—	1	508	—
1928	—	—	8	44	4	56	—	—	—	—	—	—	—	—	—	—	—	—	—
1929	—	—	19	23	2	44	156	41	—	10	207	1,292	290	1,582	246	—	—	246	2,079

the lack of records for the first landings. Even the fish landings now from Chesapeake Bay area are four to five times greater than in the late 1800s. Considering that there was little fishing pressure prior to 1865 we could surmise that even Chesapeake Bay today has more fish than in the past. However, the fishery today is being utilized near its maximum point, and in 1865 it may have been strongly underfished. We can only speculate.

We can draw a general conclusion that the striped bass population over most of its range is in no danger of extinction. To the contrary, the striped bass fishery today is on a steady increase. Unfortunately, we do not know completely why. How long this trend will continue is anyone's guess. We can only predict its continuance over the short term. The striped bass population should continue its upward trend or maintain its present level if all factors, environmental as well as man-made, do not appreciably change.

POPULATION FACTORS

The current population has very little to do with the scope or magnitude of future generations of striped bass. This might seem a statement contrary to everything you've ever believed or learned about conservation. But the single most important factor that will determine the future populations of striped bass is its environment, especially the environment during the early life stages.

Striped bass are classed with the free-spawning fishes — that is, species which produce astronomical numbers of eggs, as explained in Chapter 3. If all the factors were favorable on spawning sites during hatching and rearing of striped bass from egg to larva to fingerling to adult, soon the oceans would be filled with nothing but striped bass.

But everything does not always go well with striped bass production, so we have what are called dominant year classes of fish. A year class is dominant when the fish produced during that one year are so numerous compared to production of other years that they seem to monopolize the striped bass population.

Because of the immense fecundity of even young striped bass, it doesn't take many mature fish to create a dominant year class. That's why future populations of striped bass are not so much dependent upon the number of adults that are around as they are on those conditions which make a successful spawning year. In fact, dominant year classes in the past have followed extremely low adult populations. The last decade or so hasn't totally held to this pattern; we have often had several dominant year classes in a row. That's why the overall populations of striped bass today on the Atlantic Coast are so high.

Striped bass landings 1930–1970.

Year	Mass.	R. I.	Conn.	N. Y.	N. J.	Del.	Md.	Va.	N. C.
1930	27	60	2	66	37	102	1,228	425	457
1931	48	39	4	64	18	52	635	481	327
1932	31	7	4	32	12	8	434	594	507
1933	20	39	2	19	9	12	314	519	—
1934	—	—	—	—	—	—	333	310	362
1935	5	16	+	37	8	17	928	375	—
1936	—	—	—	—	—	27	1,864	520	768
1937	121	317	13	132	241	32	2,011	1,005	713
1938	82	210	9	139	147	25	1,714	1,155	523
1939	63	213	9	184	243	20	1,729	964	339
1940	76	64	8	169	172	41	1,180	659	540
1941	—	—	—	—	—	—	1,223	865	—
1942	98	95	18	266	95	59	2,508	778	—
1943	100	73	25	317	160	37	—	—	—
1944	191	122	17	504	257	39	2,681	1,864	—
1945	186	95	27	301	418	63	1,545	2,119	609
1946	161	217	19	482	—	—	1,615	2,084	—
1947	55	52	11	244	60	109	2,338	1,725	—
1948	78	63	10	356	41	361	2,650	2,452	—
1949	72	81	9	626	21	255	2,629	1,913	—
1950	47	112	7	517	109	271	3,038	2,796	797
1951	132	112	22	626	140	215	2,336	1,804	702
1952	125	51	11	486	536	120	2,172	1,242	647
1953	105	82	6	482	435	106	2,303	803	757
1954	68	116	+	439	51	146	2,108	951	1,122
1955	72	34	+	506	35	88	2,572	894	736
1956	71	26	1	395	50	28	2,150	995	764
1957	56	23	1	553	132	16	1,859	929	597
1958	51	41	3	398	59	22	3,105	1,317	1,096
1959	81	31	8	538	196	12	4,349	2,097	872
1960	129	77	5	731	114	25	4,409	2,278	782
1961	210	167	20	910	276	66	5,408	1,854	550
1962	589	61	32	657	494	108	3,979	1,944	747
1963	480	71	30	673	753	48	3,749	2,747	736
1964	522	75	35	995	996	31	3,300	1,889	714
1965	463	60	—	740	761	32	2,949	2,803	484
1966	585	250	—	1,050	315	64	3,347	2,803	653
1967	662	132	—	1,630	327	66	4,150	1,677	1,817
1968	874	98	—	1,511	459	49	4,532	1,614	1,912
1969	1,038	132	—	1,535	311	42	5,088	2,671	1,568
1970	1,344	84	—	1,338	223	54	3,978	1,782	2,318

The best example of a small population of striped bass in the mature stage capable of producing a great year class or an entire population of striped bass occurred in 1881 and 1879, when 435 small striped bass from New Jersey were transported to the Pacific at San Francisco Bay. In 20 years, because of the immense fecundity of the fish and with the permission of the environment, a commercial catch of 1,234,000 pounds of striped bass was recorded.

Environmental limiting factors

Since it is the environment that controls the success of a year class, we should be able to isolate environmental factors and control them so that we can guarantee a striped bass future. That sounds ideal, but it doesn't work that way. Researchers believe that they know some of the factors that control spawning success, but they don't know all of them, nor how they interact with each other.

The most critical period in the life of a striped bass is the first week of its life, from fertilization to larval stages. The factors present at that time in the environment control the future of the fish. Factors that have been identified include water temperature, predation, current, drift, salinity, turbidity, and population equilibrium.

Water temperature at the time of spawning is the first hurdle. It affects the fishery in several ways. First, it controls the time of spawning. Striped bass in a ripe condition over their spawning grounds will release eggs and sperm when the water temperature reaches 58 or 59 degrees and will continue to spawn up to 71 or 72 degrees. These are the outside limits of spawning temperature. The preferred temperature, that at which the bulk of the eggs are deposited, ranges from 61 or 62 degrees to 68 degrees; the optimal temperature is about 64.5 degrees.

Water temperature also affects the duration of the spawning. If the temperature falls below the minimum required or rises above the maximum, striped bass will temporarily stop spawning until the temperature returns to the desired levels. If the temperature rises too far and does not return to the optimal range, the fish will not spawn and the eggs will be reabsorbed in the body.

The third effect of water temperature strongly influences the pattern of egg distribution. During a spawning season when the daily water temperatures rise gradually the number of eggs spawned steadily increases to a peak and then quickly drops off. This type of action is referred to as a "spawning bloom," and the duration of the bloom can vary from seven to ten days. During a season with vacillating daily temperatures during the spawning, bass will lay eggs in several peaks, each corresponding with the rise, fall, and then rise again of the optimum temperatures. Spawning periods under such conditions can be drawn out over six to eight weeks.

There is a correlation between the number of young produced during two such extreme examples and the temperature. During the gradual buildup of water temperature and a spawning bloom, the number of young striped bass produced is greater than during a season with changeable daily water temperatures. Whether the correlation is a direct result of this variability cannot be stated for sure except that the results are there and though the cause might be something else it does seem to mirror the temperature.

Water temperature also affects the larvae's chances of existence once the eggs hatch. During a three-year study period in Maryland's part of the Chesapeake Bay, researchers checked the viability of eggs spawned and fertilized. During the period studied, the viability of each year was approximately 30 percent. The differences were not large enough between years so that viability was a factor. However, during one of the years checked, the daily water temperature fluctuated greatly and during the other two it was steady. The year with a great fluctuation had the smallest production, and this led biologists to speculate that the mortality had to occur after the eggs hatched and were in the larval stage of the fish. Thus, water temperature is even more critical in the larval stage than in the egg stage. As an added footnote, striped bass eggs spawned when the water temperature rises above 70 degress have a reduced viability, almost nil.

Predation that might affect a year class of striped bass occurs during the egg, larval, and fingerling stages of the fish. To analyze predation during spawning, stomach samples were taken by a team of Maryland biologists of all species of fish found on the spawning areas. They included striped bass as well as competitive species. Twenty-seven species of fish were examined during one year at the head of Chesapeake Bay and almost all stomach analyses suggested that striped bass were not subject to measurable amounts of egg predation by other species of fish. The only exception was a few ingested by white catfish. Because of the deep-water egg dispersal characteristic of striped bass and the short incubation period, striped bass eggs are a minor food for other species of fish.

While the striped bass is in the larval stage it is still vulnerable to predation because of its limited locomotion. However, studies indicate that while bass are in this level of development, any other potential predators are also in immature stages or not present on the nursery grounds. Almost the same is true for the striped bass once it reaches the fingerling and juvenile stages. The fish is active and adroit enough in its swimming ability to avoid most of the would-be predators. The reverse is actually true: young striped bass become predators on other species.

There is some degree of cannibalism among striped bass—that is, larger or older-year-class fish feed on younger ones—but it has not been proved to be a major consequence. As a result, young striped bass are in a unique position during the early portions of their lives, with very few predators to affect their numbers. The number of fish and species that share spawning and nursery grounds with striped bass has been reduced over the years because of pollution and siltation, all this to the advantage of young striped bass. Striped bass have actually benefited by pollution. One well-known Maryland researcher, Romeo Mausueti, advances a rather sound hypothesis that civilization and striped bass populations are compatible in the Chesapeake Bay area because of increased enrichment and turbidity of the rivers. This is the only explanation offered so far for the increase in striped bass populations while almost every other species of fish along our coast has suffered a decline because of changing water qualities and physical alterations of their environment.

Current on the spawning grounds is also a factor that affects the development of a striped bass egg. The eggs have a specific gravity that is almost the same as fresh water. In a body of water with no current the eggs will gradually fall to the bottom. Siltation and a piling of other eggs will cause the eggs to suffocate and not hatch. It takes just the slightest degree of current to keep the eggs in motion, off the bottom and thus well oxygenated. Even in waters where siltation is quite high, striped bass eggs can survive because of their buoyancy. Eggs of other fish that have a greater specific gravity are likely to be buried by siltation in spring rivers.

Drift, or the distance eggs and larvae will be carried after spawning, becomes a crucial factor if the spawning sites are too close to salt water. With too great a drift in short rivers, the eggs will be carried into a saline environment too soon in their life and hatch can be adversely affected.

Salinity experiment studies have shown that striped bass eggs can develop in water with as high a concentration of salt as 20 o/oo. However, the larvae perish within twenty-four hours after hatching under these conditions. While striped bass eggs are perfectly capable of hatching in a purely freshwater environment, the normal mortality is between 10 and 20 percent. Ironically, the survival of larvae has proved highest in water with a salinity concentration of 2-3 o/oo in laboratory tests.

Typically, striped bass pick spawning sites that are often in totally fresh water but often still under the influence of tides. However, the nature of spawning sites can vary greatly, and fish have been known to travel as little as 20 miles and as much as 200 miles up a river to get away from salt water. Exceptions to the rule happen and fish do spawn in brackish water that can have a salinity range varying from 1.7 to 11 o/oo.

Turbidity — that is, murkiness caused by suspended solids in the water — is a characteristic of many alluvial streams where striped bass spawn. Given a choice, striped bass seem to prefer streams with some degree of turbidity over clearer streams. This is evidenced in North Carolina and in Maryland, where a diversity of watersheds is available. Perhaps turbidity reduces the activity of predators that require sight to feed on striped bass eggs.

One thing most researchers agree upon is that the dominant-year-class concept rather well explains the acyclic nature of striped bass fluctuations. As a multi-age species of fish, an unusually strong year class of striped bass dominates the population for two, three, or more years. Then, as the contribution of the dominant year class wanes, the population drops back to a low level and stays at the low level for two or three years until another dominant year class is born.

Numerous investigators have tried to explain the causes of dominant year classes. One found that dominant year classes were produced only in those years when the temperature was subnormal, but not all the years of low temperatures produced dominant year classes. The conclusion was that there must also be other factors with the subnormal temperature that bring about such production. Some have tried using another variable, like salinity, but couldn't develop a correlation. The only thing agreed upon is that there is no simple one-reason answer.

Population equilibrium is an interesting sidenote to be added to the dominant-year-class concept. Each year a dominant year class is produced, it is the result of a parent stock that is in numbers below the equilibrium size. Equilibrium in a population is attained when the recruitment or production is equal to the parent-stock loss; there is no gain or loss in the number of fish in a population. Also, as parent stock increases — that is, as existing fish grow older and larger — the annual recruitment, young fish added to the population, appears to decline slightly. One suggested answer to this is cannibalism by the adult bass. That is, when there are many large bass in a population they eat more of the eggs, larvae, and fry. But as the adult stock falls below the equilibrium level there are just so many young that the big fish cannot possibly eat them all, and thus we have a dominant year class. However, in food studies of striped bass there has been little evidence of cannibalism to support this conclusion. Also, the fact has been established that striped bass stop feeding for a period, maybe only a few days, while they are spawning, and this would certainly reduce the likelihood of spent bass eating their own eggs and larvae. At this point, the question has no answer.

Physical limiting factors

The physical limiting factors restricting the future of bass are the most apparent to even the untrained observer. Dams are the most obvious and were the first to affect the great abundance of the fish along the northern section of its range. In a few situations, fish ladders similar to those used for salmon were constructed, but their design was ineffective and striped bass couldn't or wouldn't climb them. The homing instinct, while a functional element in the striped bass, is nowhere as effective or precise as that of salmon. Thus, without a place to spawn and renew their kind, striped bass along the Northeast began to dwindle in numbers.

In some areas of the country, California as a specific example, the demand for irrigation water has lessened the flow over spawning grounds and proved a threat to the survival of the fish population. In other areas, water damned and used for hydroelectricity has reduced the flow on some streams and caused spawning sites to be changed, reduced or even abandoned. These factors then affect contribution of new fish to the overall abundancy of the population.

Pollution is a different kind of dam. Pollution blockages exist on other rivers of the Atlantic Coast: the Delaware River is one of the best examples. At times pollution by chemicals, including industrial and municipal wastes, is so great that it impedes the upriver migration of fishes. Shad and striped bass at one time spawned as far north on the Delaware River as Port Jervis in New York. The pollution block today has eliminated the vast shad runs, and the striped bass runs stopped so long ago that they are evident only in history. Spawning that does occur on the Delaware is in the Chesapeake and Delaware Canal and a few small streams that empty into the tidal section of Delaware Bay from New Jersey.

Here, the primary pollutants drastically reduce the oxygen content of the rivers and make passage upstream over a long length of river impossible. The situation is heightened during warm springs because of the lessened ability of warmer water to hold oxygen. The last blow comes to the young fish that are spawned and grow to fingerling size as they fail in their attempt to cross downstream through these pollution blocks and suffocate.

Pollutants also work against a striped bass population in another way, by affecting the biota upon which the striped bass depends in its food cycle. While a polluted river may not be directly harmful to the adult striped bass, it can disrupt the delicate food chain. Zooplankton form the bottom link in a long chain that eventually ends with striped bass and man at the other end. Striped-bass larvae, as well as young shrimp, upon which bass fry feed, depend upon such primary foods for their beginning. Sulfide pollutants are extremely detrimental to zooplankton and retard their multiplication. This is the chief pollutant in pulp processes and when dumped into rivers can ruin a striped bass nursery.

Atomic-energy plants are another threat. Power plants without internal cooling systems rely on marine or river waters to cool the great amount of heat generated in the atomic reactors. The use of immediate waters affects the fish in two ways. First, eggs, larvae, and often fry can be sucked into the water intakes and damaged or killed in the process, as happens in the Hudson River. The second threat is from the raised temperature of the discharge water. Water absorbs the heat in the reactor and comes out several degrees warmer than when it goes in. Discharge of water 5 to 10 degrees warmer might not seem great in a large marine body of water but it is more crucial than in fresh water. In freshwater environments, fish have learned to survive and adapt to rapidly changing water temperatures because of the relatively small water shield that surrounds them. The smaller water volume here is more readily affected by outside temperatures and responds to them. So do the fish. But fish in a marine environment are protected from rapid temperature change by a large volume of water. Thus, outside temperature changes take a long time to affect total temperature of the water. Saltwater fish have learned to adapt slowly to this gradual change. The effect of a 5- or 10-degree change in the water in a warm or cold environment can have immediate results when the plant is in the proximity of the spawning site of fish. This is even more pronounced in the egg, fry, and larval stages, when the temperature is such a critical factor. Eggs and larval striped bass have no locomotive ability and drift at the whims of tides and currents. They cannot avoid a hot-water discharge and can be killed if they drift into it.

Fishing pressures

Two other factors affect striped bass populations and their future: commercial and sport fishing. Until just a few years ago, the sports fishery had negligible effects on the fish population. However, it has grown so rapidly in recent years that it now rivals the commercial fishery in many areas of the fish's range. Chesapeake Bay is a typical example.

Haul-seining of striped bass has been a technique used by coastal fishermen since the first colonists landed in Massachusetts, and it is still in use in New York, Maryland, Virginia, and North Carolina.

There was very little sport fishing done during the early history of this nation, and what fishing did occur was to place fish on the table or to barter them for other items. The growth of our sport fishery parallels the availability of recreational time, which has increased enormously since the last world war.

The number of striped bass taken in the name of sport is quite large, though it it difficult to estimate accurately. In Chesapeake Bay and Albemarle Sound, the sport-fishing catch is reported to be just about equal to the commercial catch. Creel censuses for the average years at Santee-Cooper reveal that almost 500,000 pounds of bass are taken annually. On the Pacific Coast, the annual catch is estimated at about 3 million pounds, 2 million of which are taken from California waters where no commercial fishing exists. The annual take from the rest of the nation can only be guessed.

Commercial catching of fish is often described as "harvesting" fish, and I cannot always argue with this term. Whether a fish is being harvested or exploited depends when in the fish's life it is being taken. Almost all the biological evidence today suggests that the harvesting of mature striped bass does little to affect the future population.

During the colonial period, when commercial or economic netting of fish meant that one took all the fish possible with whatever means was available, the effect of this type of pressure was quickly felt. If you continually stretch a gill net across a stream at all times of the year for several years, quite soon you will effectively stop all the fish from reproducing or coming to that stream.

Numerous netting devices and rigs that would capture great numbers of fish indiscriminately have been outlawed or removed from the commercial fishery. Today, haul seines, gill nets (staked and floating), floating traps, and pound traps make up the bulk of the devices used to take striped bass. The control of mesh size in gill nets allows for smaller, immature fish to escape.

In Massachusetts the only way you can fish commercially for striped bass is with handline or rod and reel, while in Rhode Island floating traps take the major portion of bass. Haul seines and pond traps produce the most commercial fish in New York, otter trawls are used primarily in New Jersey, and fixed gill nets are the common device in Delaware. Fixed gill nets are also the most popular device in Maryland and North Carolina, although drift gill nets, pound nets, and haul seines contribute significantly to their commercial fishery. In Virginia, pound nets, haul seines, and fixed gill nets account for about 30 percent of the fish landed.

The commercial seasons vary from state to state. In Massachusetts the fishery is active primarily during the summer; in New York, from late September to late November; in New Jersey, winter; in Maryland and Virginia, March and April, just before the spawning season; in North Carolina, November to April. This pattern reflects the movement of large schools of striped bass from June until April, which dictates when bass can be taken commercially.

Commercial fishing, and sport fishing for that matter, only become a threat to a striped bass population when brood-stock numbers are so low in a given area that fishing can effectively remove all the stock or lower it to a level below the natural mortality. If enough fish aren't produced to maintain a minimal brooding stock, then the species in that locale is in danger of extinction. But because of the great fecundity of bass, modern commercial fishing and sport fishing have never become the real threat they have been accused of being.

Maryland and Virginia have similar laws governing the taking of striped bass from Chesapeake Bay. The minimum size limit is 12 inches. This means that the majority of fish harvested will be in their second or third year. If the size limit were raised to 16 inches, similar to the restriction in most of the other states, it would mean that Chesapeake Bay commercial fishermen would loose a lot of fish to the rest of the

Pound traps are fixed along the shore, and fish following the edge of land are guided into the trap and cannot find their way out. They are used on Long Island and in Maryland, Virginia, and North Carolina.

Atlantic states. Between the ages of three and four the fish go on a wandering binge. Most of the fish would leave the bay to take part in coastal migrations if they were not netted.

In effect, however, commercial fishermen and sport fishermen harvest almost 90 percent of a yearly production of fish. They do not harvest each year class during the first year because of the size limitation. However, when fish are between two years of age and as they approach three, just before they would migrate, they fall prey to the fishery. Thus two-year-old fish and some at the beginning of their third year, fish 12 to 14 inches long, make up the bulk of the Chesapeake Bay fishery. The 10 percent of those fish that do escape Chesapeake Bay then make up almost 90 percent of those fish taken along the coast during their migrations.

POPULATION FORECASTS

Biologists working in areas of the coast which produce striped bass and maintain a year-round nursery have developed techniques for predicting the future populations of striped bass in their waters. The forecasts, however, are short-ranged predictions that vary from as little as three years to a maximum of fifteen years. The shorter the forecast, the more accurate it is likely to be.

The technique involves sampling the fishery on the nursery grounds. In each haul with a net, the young fish are counted and their numbers compared against similar hauls in the same area during years past. The O-age group fish are compared with other year's production as well as with fish in the I and II year class to see how much of the current population they compose.

The relative abundance of young-of-the-year striped bass is sampled by extensive shore seining that begins during the summer and continues into early winter or before young fish leave the shallows and head for deeper, warmer waters. These are referred to as recruitment surveys and are based on a density index — that is, the number of fish taken in each haul with the net.

Catches by sportfishermen in many areas of the country, especially in New York and Maryland, equal or even exceed those taken by commercial fishermen. Here is a trophy catch of striped bass mixed with bluefish.

Dr. Edgar Hollis of Maryland's Department of Chesapeake Bay Affairs helped develop this technique. His experience with the striped bass recruitment survey indicates that seining is a very useful tool in determining rather quickly and inexpensively the relative success of spawning and annual production. The future availability of striped bass can be estimated from the relative abundance of young fish near shore in late summer and fall. This survey can be projected even further into the future because the abundance in one year of young striped bass is reflected three years later along the coast when these fish become migratory.

Population fluctuations

Striped bass catches have been fairly well recorded since 1930 and when graphed show a cyclic rise and fall, but with a general increase in the overall catches. The cycle repeats itself every six years. Beginning with 1930, a high year, catches were high again in 1936, 1942, 1948, 1954, 1960, 1966, and 1972. With the exception of 1954, the catches during all these years formed peaks on the graph.

These peaks in abundance are attributed to the dominant-year-class concept and reflect back to years of good production when spawning success was so great it overshadowed the previous year in the cycle. Therefore, a typical striped bass cycle represents three somewhat high years of catches and production with one a peak year and three relatively low catches and a low year. The spawning peak year predates the year of the big catch by three years in each cycle. The reason for this is that it takes the striped bass three years to mature and reach legal catchable sizes and take on migrations before they are fair game to the commercial and sport fishery.

Chesapeake Bay, because it contributes so heavily to the migratory stock along the northern half of the Atlantic range, has become a barometer for fish's abundance. The number of fish that will be available along Long Island's south shore can be predicted quite accurately, according to Richard Schaefer, fisheries biologist, from the size of each annual production in Chesapeake Bay. The only difference is a three-year lag.

Striped bass populations in Chesapeake Bay are checked each fall by extensive samplings. Maryland biologists then get their first look at how successful the spawning season had been that spring. These fish will stay in the bay until the beginning of their third year and then in the spring or early summer begin a migration northward along the Atlantic Coast. It is this population that Schaefer has been able to predict by working back to Maryland's analysis of annual recruitment of young striped bass.

STATE LEGISLATION AS A CONTROL TOOL

At the General Courte, holden in Boston, the 22nd of the 3rd M., Called May, 1639 — "And it is forbidden to all men, after the 20th of next month, to imploy any codd or basse fish for manuring the ground, upon paine that every pson, being a fisherman, that shall sell or imploy any such fish for that end, shall loose the said priviledge of exemption from public charges, & that both fisherman, or others who shall use any kind of said fish for that purpose, shall forfet for every hundred of such fish so employed for manuring ground twenty shillings & portionally for a less or greater number; pvided, that it shall be lawful to use the heads and offal of such fish for corne, this nothwithstanding."

The preceding act was passed by the Massachusetts Bay Colony in 1639, nineteen years after the initial settlement at Plymouth, so that striped bass could not be used for fertilizer. Thus it gives as a little insight into the condition of the striped bass population in just a short time after it was exposed to civilized man. The value and limited supply of the fish were immediately realized. Striped bass and codfish thus were one of the first natural resources in the New World to come under conservation measures. Even to this day, the striped bass and legislation to govern its taking are often topics of heated discussion.

New York was next to pass legislation protecting the striped bass, though more than 100 years later. A state law was passed prohibiting the sale of striped bass during the winter months because of "a great decrease of that kind of fish." In 1762 the people of Marshfield, Mass., also sought to control the striped bass fishery and preserve a bit of it for future use by passing favorably on a petition to the General Court to enact a bill for the preservation of the fish and to prevent its capture during the winter season.

Little legislation followed for many years as the population of striped bass slowly dwindled along the northern part of its range. Not until the 1930s, and then during the following thirty years, as the striped bass population showed steady growth, was there renewed interest in preserving the species. There was a rash of popular legislation, up and down the Atlantic Coast, as well as on the Pacific.

Today, regulations governing or restricting the taking of striped bass vary considerably. The expanded range of the striped bass into freshwater impoundments has generally seen the fish immediately placed in a game-fish category and protected by laws similar to those for largemouth or smallmouth bass.

Effects of legislation

The answer to how effective past and current legislation has been in preserving the species for the future is quite simple. The way to ensure a good future for striped bass is to maintain a healthy brood stock, all other conditions being favorable. And because the brood stock has never really been in danger, the legislation has never really had an opportunity to be effective.

Current legislation affects the population of striped bass by controlling the number of fish an angler might take, specifying either the maximum size by weight of fish that may be taken, or the minimal size that can be taken and the time of the year, or even the time of the day during which a striped bass may be caught. In general, most current legislation prevents the commercial fisherman in many states from competing with the sport fisherman. From a financial and sociological viewpoint, this is fine. However, it has no biological justification as a tool to guard striped bass from depletion.

Maryland has a 12-inch minimum limit on the size of striped bass that can be caught and sold. The reason for this limit is to discourage commercial anglers as well as sport fishermen from harvesting young-of-the-year fish, giving them an opportunity to grow and produce a heavier fishery. At one time the limit was 11 inches and a great number of young male striped bass were netted. It was feared that there wouldn't be enough left to migrate to the spawning grounds in their third year to perpetuate the species, so the limit was raised.

New York established a 16-inch limit, snout-to-fork measurement. The basis for this rule was not so much the biology of the fish but to keep 12-inch striped bass from the Maryland-Virginia fishery from the New York fish markets. This would lower the price of striped bass taken from New Jersey, New York, and New England. Maryland sells its fish before they reach the 16-inch limit (12 inches overall length), so there are few larger fish left to send to New York.

In some states, Massachusetts specifically, it is legal to fish commercially for striped bass only with a rod and reel. This effectively eliminates the large commercial operation and at the same time allows the sport fisherman to sell his catch without real competition from commercial anglers.

Dr. Daniel Merriman, a noted researcher and biologist who has concerned himself with the problems of the striped bass and occasionally with legislation concerning them, a few years ago summed up the feelings of other biologists in a speech to a New Jersey fishing club when he said: "It can perhaps be demonstrated that in certain areas it is *sociologically* and *economically* desirable to make the striped bass a game fish and hence to eliminate commercial fishing in those places. If that can be done in a democratic fashion, then let the legislation be debated on that basis. But don't let that legislation masquerade under the cloak of conservation."

An interesting note arises when one reviews the data on where the striped bass are caught and where they are not caught and the legislation in these areas. Those states that produce the fewest number of fish for the commercial market are the same states that are attempting to manage the resources by the most restrictive size limits and prohibitions. Ironically, none of these states is an important source of migratory stock. They only catch that small percent of striped bass which are able to escape the Chesapeake Bay fishery. Several biologists from Maryland made a statement that "Maryland anglers and netters would lose and fishermen in other Atlantic seaboard states would gain benefits if the minimum size in the bay were raised from 12 to 16 inches."

Among the mid-Atlantic and New England states, New York has the least restrictive regulations on the taking of striped bass, while contributing very little fish to the migratory stock in the Atlantic. But unlike other states in the group of noncontributors which have imposed numerous regulations, New York is harvesting the striped bass along its coast.

Most of New York's commercial fishery takes place between Jones Inlet and Montauk Point, with the greater concentration from Shinnecock Inlet eastward. It is basically a haul-seine fishery with a few pound traps in the bays and one along the shore which do not contribute significantly to the overall commercial catch. Other than the haul seine, the inshore otter-trawler methods contribute about 20 percent to the total catch. When all New York's landings are added together they only amount to between 8 and 9 percent of the total striped bass annually caught in the nation.

This figure needs a partial adjustment. New York's otter-trawler fleet contributes but 20 percent to the state's landing figures; however, the greater number of boats that trawl off Long Island's beaches are from New Jersey. New Jersey has banned all commercial fishing within its 3-mile jurisdiction, so its trawlers work beyond 3 miles and almost on the beach in New York waters. Their landings, however, are recorded as New Jersey landings even though the bulk of their catch has come from New York waters. New Jersey contributes about 1 to 1.5 percent to the overall commercial landings. However, with the development of high-speed trawlers needed to take striped bass, New Jersey's landings are increasing. During the 1973 season, a pair of Jersey trawlers working off southern New Jersey were reported to have run into schools of striped bass so large that they completely filled the trawls and stopped the boats in the water.

For the past fifteen or so years, sport fishermen in New York have tried to introduce legislation to restrict or prohibit commercial fishing for striped bass on Long Island. Their argument is that commercial fisheries there are landing large quantities of striped bass and that the sport-fishery landings are so low that if only they alone operated they would not affect or endanger the resource. However, in the light of continued increase of landings, and numerous dominant year classes that seem to excel previous years and thus contribute to an ever increasing supply of fish, this argument has little or no biological basis.

The striped bass area that New York can influence by management is the Hudson River, a fishery that is almost totally within the limits of the state and only shared in the summer months with a portion of northern New Jersey and western Connecticut. Ironically, the commercial landings for the Hudson fishery are nil. The fish have had a tainted flavor because of pollution and are not marketable locally. Thus a potentially large fishery is being underharvested.

SUMMARY OF REGULATIONS
BY STATE AND PROVINCE

Striped bass regulations vary greatly, and within each state or province they can be quite complicated. This listing is not intended to cover every area's regulations completely, but only to summarize the regulations. Before fishing, it is suggested that you obtain a complete syllabus of your state's or province's regulations.

Alabama — Legislation exists for the taking of striped bass in fresh water but not in salt water. Fish can be taken commercially in salt water and a license is required. They cannot be taken commercially in fresh water. Rod-and-reel bass can be sold commercially if a $1 hook-and-line license is purchased. There are no season dates in either fresh or salt water, but there is a freshwater creel limit of five per day with the same possession limit.

Arizona — The striped bass cannot be taken commercially, and a rod-and-reel license is required for sport fishing. There is a three-per-day limit and a 16-inch total-length minimum size. There are no season dates.

Arkansas — Striped bass cannot be taken commercially nor can they be sold. There are no season dates, nor minimum lengths or weights. The only restriction is a creel limit, three per day and six in possession.

California — Striped bass cannot be taken commercially from California waters, nor can they be sold when taken on rod and reel. There is a daily and possession limit of three fish with a 16-inch total-length minimum size. In five counties, however, there is no size limit. A saltwater fishing license is needed to take bass from marine waters.

Connecticut — Striped bass cannot be taken commercially nor sold when taken on rod and reel. There are no season dates nor creel limits on striped bass taken from Connecticut waters. However, there is a 16-inch fork-length minimum size.

Delaware — Striped bass can be commercially fished in marine waters and no license is required. Fish can be sold commercially. Netting bass is restricted to dates from November 2 to April 30. There is no sport-fishing season restriction. Minimum lengths are 12 inches measured overall, and maximum size limit is 20 pounds with no creel limits.

Florida — Striped bass cannot be taken commercially nor sold when taken on rod and reel. No license is needed in marine waters. There is a marine as well as freshwater creel and possession limit of six fish daily. The minimum size limit is 15 inches fork length.

Georgia — Striped bass cannot be taken commercially nor sold when taken on rod and reel. There is a five-per-day limit with no possession limit, and the minimum size is 15 inches total length. There are no season dates.

Kentucky — Striped bass cannot be taken commercially nor sold when taken on rod and reel. The minimum size is 15 inches total length, and the creel and possession limit is five per day. There are no season dates.

Louisiana — Striped bass cannot be taken commercially nor sold when taken on rod and reel. There are no minimum or maximum size restrictions or season dates. Anglers are restricted to two fish per day and four in possession.

Maine — Striped bass cannot be fished commercially in Maine waters, but fish taken on rod and reel can be sold. No license is needed to take bass from marine waters, nor is there a creel limit or minimum size.

Maryland — Striped bass can be taken commercially from marine waters, and no license is needed. There are no season dates or creel limits. However, fish must be a minimum of 12 inches in total length and not larger than 15 pounds. Maryland has trophy fish and season dates that allow freer taking of striped bass by sport anglers; regulations should be consulted for details.

Massachusetts — Striped bass can be taken commercially but only by rod and reel. Fish can be sold. No license is needed in marine waters. There are no season dates and no creel limits. However, the minimum size is 16 inches fork length.

Mississippi — Striped bass cannot be taken commercially from either fresh or marine waters. No saltwater license is required for sport fishing. The minimum size restriction is 15 inches total length, and there is a daily creel limit of three fish and possession limit of six fish. The marine limit is 50 fish daily and the possession limit is 100 fish.

New Hampshire — Striped bass cannot be taken commercially but can be sold when taken on rod and reel. No license is required. There are no other restrictions in New Hampshire except for a 16-inch fork-length limit.

New Jersey — Striped bass cannot be taken commercially, but bass taken by rod and reel can be sold and no license is required. The season

High-speed otter trawlers now are capable of catching large numbers of striped bass. Here a New Jersey trawler works almost in the wash of the surf along eastern Long Island. Commercial fishing in New Jersey waters is prohibited by that state.

extends from March 1 to December 31 and there is a 10-per-day possession limit. The fish must be 18 inches in total length and there is a maximum-size limit of 20 pounds for fish taken from Delaware Bay.

New York — Fish may be taken commercially and sold at any time from the waters of New York State. There are no season dates or possession restrictions. The only restriction is a size limit, 16 inches fork length. No license is needed in marine waters for either commercial or sport fishing.

North Carolina — Striped bass can be taken commercially and sold, and a license is required. The only restriction in marine waters is a minimum size of 12 inches total length. In fresh water, there is a daily creel limit of eight fish for inland waters and 25 fish for coastal waters.

Oklahoma — Only a freshwater fishery exists, and striped bass cannot be taken commercially or sold when taken on hook and line. There are no season or minimum-length restrictions. The creel limit is one per day and the possession limit two, except on the Arkansas River, where the creel limit is three and the possession limit six.

Oregon — Striped bass can be taken commercially and is limited to the estuarine waters of the Coos, Coquille, Umpqua, Smith, and Siuslaw rivers. There is no commercial fishing allowed above tidewater. A license is required to take striped bass both commercially and on rod and reel in marine waters as well as fresh waters. Striped bass taken on rod and reel cannot be sold commercially. Creel limit for striped bass is five daily. There is no possession limit. Bass must be a minimum of 16 inches fork length. There are no sportfishing season limits.

Pennsylvania — Striped bass cannot be fished commercially, nor can they be sold when taken on rod and reel. There is no creel limit for fish taken from marine waters. There is a minimum size of 12 inches total length. Season dates are from March 1 to December 31 with a daily limit of three fish and possession limit of six fish.

Rhode Island — Striped bass can be taken both commercially and by sport fishing and sold commercially. A license is needed to fish bass commercially. The only other restriction in Rhode Island waters is a minimum size of 16 inches fork length.

South Carolina — Striped bass cannot be fished commercially from either marine or fresh waters of South Carolina, nor sold regardless of the manner of taking. There are no season dates or size restrictions, but there is a creel limit of 10 fish per day.

Tennessee — Striped bass cannot be taken commercially nor sold in any manner. The season is open throughout the year. Minimum size is 15 inches total length, and anglers are limited to two per day and four in possession.

Texas — The striped bass fishery in Texas is restricted to fresh water. Striped bass taken on rod and reel can be sold and a license is required. There are no season dates or length restrictions but there is a limit of one per day and two in possession.

Virginia — A license is required to take striped bass with nets and to sell them commercially. No license is required to sell bass when taken by rod and reel. There is no creel limit except for trophy fish: two per day over 40 inches. The minimum size is 12 inches total length. The freshwater restrictions vary greatly with each body of water, and state regulations should be consulted before fishing.

New Brunswick — Very little legislation affects the taking of striped bass. A commercial license is required but no sport-fishing license is needed in marine waters. Fish taken by rod and reel without a commercial license cannot be sold. Taking of striped bass from non-marine waters is restricted to April 15 to September 15.

Nova Scotia — No license is required to take striped bass commercially, and striped bass can be sold regardless of the manner in which they are taken. There is a possession limit of 10 per day and the season extends from April 1 to September 30.

Prince Edward Island — There are no restrictions on the taking of striped bass.

Quebec — A license is required to take striped bass either commercially or by rod and reel. Fish taken by either method can be sold commercially. Season dates for marine fishing extend from June 1 to November 30. In non-marine waters, the date extends from June 15 to freeze-up. The minimum size is 16 inches total length. No other restrictions apply.

INTERSTATE STUDIES AND FEDERAL LEGISLATION

The role of the research biologist is to gather knowledge about the striped bass so that legislators can enact laws that will be effective in guaranteeing the future of striped bass populations. Legislative leaders should be able to rely on scientific facts about the environmental conditions striped bass require to survive, the changes allowable to the environment, and the effects of both commercial and sport fishing as well as industrial activities.

During the late 1940s and in the 1950s, as the abundance of striped bass increased, competition for the fish suddenly became keen. The growing number of sport fishermen now competed with the commercial anglers, and immediately a rivalry began. The contests were both immediate and political and made themselves felt in almost every state capital along the Atlantic as well as in Washington. Because of their growing numbers, sport fishermen were now an effective force, and they placed pressure on their legislators.

Because of the great lack of knowledge about the life history of the striped bass, legislators then demanded projects from their state conservation departments as well as the federal agencies. A rash of random studies was started by numerous states. Each state, however, concentrated on the fish as it appeared in its waters. Because of the migratory nature of the striped bass, a thorough study and any ensuing legislation would need a national scope.

In 1950, the Atlantic States Marine Fisheries Commission tried to coordinate the activities of each state by creating a striped bass study committee. It was strictly voluntary, but Massachusetts, Rhode Island, New York, New Jersey, Delaware, Maryland, Virginia, and North and South Carolina became active in it. But because of a lack of funding, shortages of trained personnel, and the lack of interest of some of the states, the main objectives were not achieved.

Georgia, Florida, and California had independent projects underway and contributed their results. California has been one of the leading states in striped bass research and produced several valuable studies on the fish and its life cycle. Reasons for California's success include the relatively endemic character of its striped bass, the occurrence of the fish in just one major watershed, and the state's willingness to support its projects financially.

The Atlantic Coast Marine Fisheries Commission then in 1957 established the Atlantic Coast Cooperative Striped Bass Program. The U.S. Fish & Wildlife Service acted as the coordinator of the various state projects. A large part of the funds were supplied to states through the Dingell-Johnson Program. The D-J Program was the result of an act passed by Congress in 1950 for the improvement of the nation's sport fishery and fishery-management programs. The amount of money given each state is based on the number of anglers in the state. The money comes from a 10 percent federal excise tax on fishing tackle. For each dollar of its money a state spends on the program, three dollars of federal funds are given.

The intent of the program was to encourage each state to concentrate on local problems and aspects of striped bass research while the U.S. Fish & Wildlife Service and its personnel investigated aspects that transcended state lines. Federal activities included racial studies of stock differentiation and tagging programs.

Anadromous Fish Conservation Act

In October 1965, Congress passed the Anadromous Fish Conservation Act. Its purpose was to increase the supply of anadromous fish in the United States by making $25 million available to the states on a matching basis for the next five years. In other words, the federal government would spend one dollar for every dollar that a state spent on studies to increase the number of anadromous fish running up our rivers. The Fish & Wildlife Service was given the chore of managing these monies and coordinating the programs of the states that responded. In 1970, the act was amended to extend it another five years.

Every state that had an anadromous fish, from migrating shad to the Atlantic salmon, took interest in the program. Striped bass projects were started up and down the coast. A majority of the research has centered around southern Atlantic coastal states and along the Gulf of Mexico. These states began to study the range and distribution of the striped bass in their waters, many in environments far from the sea. A lot of the monies were used by inland states to stock striped bass in reservoir waters and expand the range of this fish.

Migratory Fish Treaty

A striped bass on a migratory binge could cross twelve state lines and two provincial borders in one summer. In doing so it would be exposed to fourteen different sets of regulations that have its welfare in mind. This is not just conceivable, it actually does happen, every spring, summer, and fall, from the Outer Banks of North Carolina to the rocky shores of New Brunswick and Nova Scotia.

There is such great disparity in these regulations that their total effect on the striped bass population is more irksome than protective. Any rational program for the fish's management must be of national or international nature in its scope. So far we have had a regional approach to research and study, a regional approach to minimum-length regulations with little regard to the same problem just across the border, and a regional approach to seasons and limits. If the striped bass is to be well managed for its future, and is to receive the greatest benefit from our research, then we must consider the problems of the over-all population.

This same type of problem arose with the management of waterfowl. The management issues were much the same. These birds are migratory and seasonal, and each state had its own set of regulations, seasons, and limits to ensure the future of its waterfowl. But their numbers steadily declined. Finally, when some species were near extinction, the federal government stepped in and with agreements between Mexico and Canada, an international treaty was signed. It gave the three federal governments regulatory control over the entire population of waterfowl in North America.

The striped bass is not as international a traveler as our waterfowl, but the relationship is still the same between our states. Any new legislation that is proposed should be on the national level to monitor commercial and sport fishing and establish coast-wise regulations on seasons, length, creel numbers, and angling methods *when they are needed* as fishery management tools. Any proposal for research and study also should be on such a level, with each state contributing to the study what it can learn of the fish in its own waters. Even the study of endemic strains should be accomplished on a national level to avoid duplication of research and efforts.

The federal government should also enforce standards for water quality and usage to maintain the fishery on a national level. The control and regulation of the multiple use of waters for local energy sources should be based on the effects of such use on the entire fishery as a whole and not on just local populations.

PART TWO

FISHING TECHNIQUES

8

Early Striped Bass Fishing
and Fishermen

> The Basse is one of the best fishes in the
> country. . . . the way to catch them is with hooke
> and line: the Fishermen taking a great codline, to
> which he fasteneth a piece of Lobster, and throws
> it into the sea, the fish biting at it pulls her to him,
> and knocks her on the head with a stick. . . . the
> English at the top of an high water doe crosse
> the creeks with long seanes or Basse netts, which
> stop the fish; and the water ebbing from them
> are left on dry ground, sometimes two or three
> thousand at a set. . . .
>
> — William Wood, *New England's Prospects* (1635)

Our earliest striped bass fishermen weren't very sporting by today's
standards. They weren't fishing for sport, but for food that would see
them through the year in a land everyone thought hostile. Early settlers
along our New England coast created very efficient traps for taking
striped bass during the summer months as they stretched long seines
and weirs across the coastal streams at high tide.

As the water ebbed from the creeks the stranded fish were obtained
in far greater quantities than the fisherman could haul to land. The fish
were used either fresh, salted, pickled, or smoked. Pickled bass, along
with salted codfish, even became a medium for trade in the West Indies.
The earliest colonial record of the smoking of striped bass as a means
of preservation is by Wood:

They drie them to keepe for Winter, erecting scaffolds in the hot sunshine,
making fires likewise underneath them, by whose smoake the flies are expelled

till the substance remaine hard and drie. In this manner they drie Basse and other fishes without salt, cutting them very thin to dry suddenly, before the flies spoyle them, or the raine moist them having speciall care to hang them in their smoky houses, in the night or dankish weather.

Of course, Indians had been fishing for striped bass long before the colonists arrived, but the earliest accounts we have of their methods are relatively late and come from Canada. In the St. John River, New Brunswick, according to Adams (1873), the Indians captured striped bass at spawning time:

A few canoes would drop downriver, each with an Indian in the bow, spear in hand, and another in the stern gently paddling. A sudden splash closeby would indicate a spawning bass on the surface and like an arrow, the birchbark skiff shot toward the spot while the man in the front, resting on his knees, with much force and dexterity sent the three-pronged harpoon into the fish.

The art of fishing for striped bass as we know it today rested on the development of fishing equipment. Though rods and reels had been around since the fourteenth century, few if any found their way to salt water where striped bass could be caught. The rods and reels were designed more for light baits and flies with which to catch trout and salmon. They made their way toward salt waters as an alternate method only after the bait-casting reel was invented and perfected.

A good number of anglers, up until about 1825 or 1830, would take bass by handlines from boats and the surf. The accepted method had changed little since Wood's description. From the surf, a cotton or linen line was uncoiled in the sand and a large piece of bait—crab, shrimp, or cut fish—was secured on the hook. The fisherman swung the line around his head and then flung it into the surf. A fish was played on the hands or by running up the beach.

One of the most complete descriptions of this technique for fishing striped bass in the surf comes from a rather definitive work written in 1845 entitled *The American Angler's Guide; or, Complete Fisher's Manual, for the United States: Containing the Opinions and Practices of Experienced Anglers of Both Hemispheres.* Unfortunately, the author is not identified, but the book was copyrighted by John J. Brown, who may have been the author.

The title of the short chapter is *Basse Fishing on the Shores of Long Island:*

Off the south-east shore of Long Island, during the fall months, Basse are taken in considerable numbers. About the middle of August, fish from four to ten pounds begin to make along the coast from Montauk to Fire Island Inlet, and

Squidding. The original technique for fishing the surf was with a live squid as bait, tossed on a handline into the surf. The original sketch appeared in the 1899 Report of the Commissioners of Fisheries, Game and Forests of the State of New York. *The caption identifies the fish as a bluefish, but it is obviously a striped bass, and this is the technique used for bass.*

enter the Inlets, where they are generally taken upon the bar, or just beyond the surf, either by trolling, or by "heaving and hauling" from shore. The latter is a favorite mode of fishing, but laborious, requiring both physical strength and practiced skill. The squid for this purpose should be of block tin, full six ounces in weight, with large hook (no kirb), size Number 1 for Cod. This is attached to a *cotton* line, full twenty fathoms long, light and close twist, is made to gyrate around the head (the angler's) until it acquires sufficient velocity and momentum, when it is cast, with the full swing of the arm, into the breakers, carrying after it the line that is held loosely coiled in the left hand. The moment the squid strikes the water, it is hauled swiftly ashore that it may not sink, but play on the surf, and imitate the motion of a natural fish. At Montauk, they wind around a long squid-lead a strip of fresh skin from the belly of the basse, or draw and tie up over the lead the tail-skin of an eel. But hungry fish will snap at anything moving. I have seen taken a basse of twenty-five pounds that bit at a rag.

Even after the development of rods and simple reels that could throw a hooked bait into the waves, many anglers were still forced to use hand-lines because of the high cost of fishing equipment. A piece of squid on a cotton line (squid line) was the standard striped bass outfit for years even after tackle costs were reduced and within everyone's financial reach.

The squidding lines remained popular until monofilament came onto the market.

Striped bass fishing as a sport began to develop with the invention of the first bait-casting reel in the early 1800s. Between 1800 and 1810 — no one is sure of the exact date — George Snyder of Paris, Ky., developed a reel composed of a spool to spin and pay out line when cast and a handle to retrieve it. The lure had to be heavy to pull the line. Snyder had the background and inclination to develop such an idea. He was a watch-maker and a silversmith, as well as president of the Bourbon Angling Club. Others picked up the idea and by 1840 the reel was being mass-produced.

At first, most reels had a direct, 1:1 ratio. It was a simple trick next to add gears to the reel handle and spool. This created a multiplying reel, one with a ratio of 2:1 or more. Still, these reels had no drag or clutch — maybe a click, but nothing else to slow down the spool when cast or when a fish was running except one's thumb. Therefore, surf fishing was not as popular as it is today.

The nature of striped bass fishing and fishermen is rather difficult to determine for the early 1800s. We had to wait for the development of the American press as a keeper of records and teller of tales. From about 1850 on, the lights begin to go on.

One of the first writers of note was Frank Forrester, whose real name was Henry William Herbert. Herbert was a transplanted Englishman who condescended to make his living in America by telling us what was wrong with the way we practiced our sports. He assumed a rather snobbish posi-tion in much of his work but his descriptions of our early times and tech-niques are invaluable. His principal work was a pair of books on field sports and another volume on fishing. He wrote several other books that were more novels than factual description.

Herbert was a dedicated salmon and trout fisherman, but he also held the striped bass in great esteem. He likened it second only to the salmon as the most desirable fish along the coasts. His knowledge of the fish was less than he would have us believe, but still he tells us a lot about how the art of angling was practiced in the mid-1800s.

Herbert lived at "The Cedars" in New Jersey, and much of his striped bass knowledge is about the fish in the area of the New York bays. During his time, there was great striped bass fishing around Man-hattan, in the East and Harlem rivers, and in the meadows of New Jersey, as well as in the Hudson and around Staten Island. The New York *Sun* at one time used to run a daily account of the striped bass catches from the Battery bridge, on Manhattan's southern tip.

A far better account of the status of the striped bass in America during the 1800s is supplied by Genio C. Scott in his authoritative book

Fishing in American Waters. There is little doubt that during his forty years of fishing for the striped bass, Scott had become addicted to the fish. In an opening statement to his book of 1869 he apologized for putting a picture of the fish on the frontispiece and asked for "pardon in placing this beauty first on the list" of fishes he describes.

During Scott's day most of the striped bass angling for sport was either done from boats—trolling and some "still-bait" fishing—or was a weak form of casting off platforms above the surf and rock areas that striped bass had been known to frequent. At this time, the hot spots were on the western end of Long Island (though occasionally someone went to Montauk), among the Elizabeth Islands, from such renowned clubs as the Cuttyhunk Club, Pasque Island Club, the Squibnocket Club on Martha's Vineyard, the West Island Club off Sakonnet Point, and a few other choice spots off Point Judith, Newport, and Cohasset Narrows.

Scott even traveled north in New York State to Lake Ontario, and while fishing for salmon (landlocked) he also took caught striped bass "in the upper part of Lake Ontario" on several occasions.

In a brief summary of the methods of the day, Scott tells us:

The angler pursues many methods for capturing this beauty of the estuary, the chief of which is still-baiting from an anchored boat along the edge of the tide, trolling with live squid (small cuttle-fish), and casting with menhaden bait—but without sinker—into the surf off a rocky beach, along the shores and islands from New York to Martha's Vineyard.

It is also interesting to note the equipment of the day that Scott suggests. The illustrations are taken from his original book. The first rig is intended for the taking of small bass, fish probably no larger than 10 pounds that were fairly common in the lower Hudson during the season from June until October. The bait was often crab or shrimp. The rod was from 9 to 11 feet long, "bearing in mind that a short, stiff rod is best to cast with, but not so good to play a fish on light running tackle. The reel should be a multiplier type, without any stop, check or drag; it should be of brass, German silver, or bell-metal, run on steel or agate pivots, and with a balance crank."

Corks were of solid construction and tied to swivel sinkers. Rods in those days were of wood that would take a set or warp and therefore had guides back-to-back so that you could reverse your line every other time you went fishing and discourage warping. Hooks were of two styles, one with an O'Shaughnessy bend that better held shrimp while the other had an Aberdeen bend that was more suited to a shedder crab.

The second illustration is of a very elaborate set of gear for the day, more appropriate for fishing on the end of a bass stand, for larger fish in a

Genio C. Scott recommended this striped bass outfit for small fish in Fishing in American Waters *(1869).*

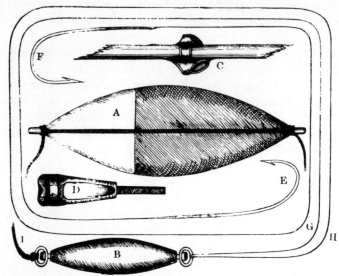

TACKLE FOR TAKING SMALL BASS.

A. Solid Cork-float. B. Swivel Sinker. C. Piece of the top of Rod, showing tne double guides ; on one side bell-metal, and the other agate. D. Agate or Carneli-an tip to screw into the top of the rod. E. Upper Hook, rigged a foot above the oth-er hook for shrimp. F. Lower Hook, for baiting with shedder crab. G, H. Single-gut Leader. I. Line ; of either linen twisted or silk braided ; very small, no larger than for trout, but from 300 to 400 feet in length.

boat, for angling from a bridge, or for venturing into big waters. Here, Scott recommends a rod 8 to 9 feet long, with butt and second sections of ash and the top section of lancewood. This would enable you to do battle with striped bass in Hell Gate, a part of the East River on the sunny side of Manhattan that was a favorite during Scott's time.

Probably no one could tell it better than Scott himself. I'd like to borrow a few pages from his book so that you can capture the flavor of saltwater angling as it was once practiced in New York more than a century ago.

When you decide to troll for a day over tumultuously-seething and hissing waters of Hell Gate, where an oarsman must know the tides and shoals to keep his boat right side up, you will require heavier tackle.

Those who employ a man to row and gaff the fish would do well to direct him to squid half a dozen hooks before starting, and lay them aside in the boat under some wet rock-weed before leaving shore. If you have ever been trolling—as I have—when large bass were biting generously, you will realize the force of this advice. It is unpleasant to be trolling in rough waters, and; when a bass strikes the back of your hook and takes your bait without fastening, to be obliged to stop and squid a hook before proceeding.

Now for the fray! Our boats are made by Hughes, fellow-apprentice of

Scott's recommendation for bigger striped bass and the surf.

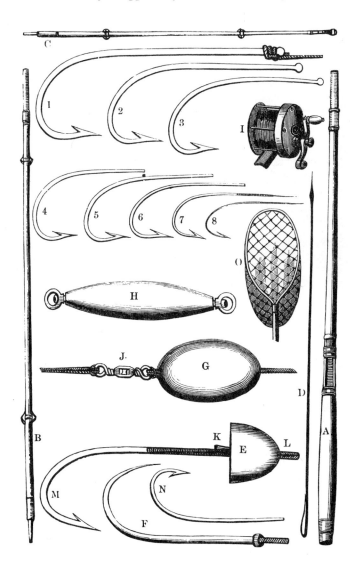

George Steers; and with Sile Wright and Sandy Gibson as guides and gaffers, we shall be sculled over all the favorite trolling grounds from the ferry below to the Drowned Marsh above Ward's Island. Our first move will be toward Tide Rock, swinging Big and Little Mill Rocks on the way; then we shall glide over the Hen and Chickens, swing* Holt's Rock on the Hog's Back, round Nigger Point,

*Swinging a rock is done by the oarsman holding the boat sixty feet from the rock and swinging it so that the troll will move about the rock on all sides and play as if alive. This art was possessed in great perfection by Hell Gate oarsmen.

Scott and friend fishing the waters of Hell Gate in New York's East River.

and, stopping at John Hilliker's to rest, enjoy a piece of incomparable apple-pie and a glass of milk served by two charming ladies. While indulging these ruminations one day, as my friend was swinging Holt's Rock, he hooked a large bass and played it all the way round the east end of Ward's Island to Chowder Eddy. Where, on landing, it weighed twenty pounds.

I was not so fortunate as my friend; for, as my squid was struck by a large bass, Sile said he heard the rod crack; but the fish made such a long, vigorous run, that I scarcely realized what he said, and, after turning the fish and reeling him in gradually, he broke water with a leap, clearing the surface, and revealing a forty-pounder. While turning and bringing him toward the boat for the third time, he darted down and snapped the middle joint of my rod in two, when I threw the broken rod down at my feet and took hold of the line; the fish made but feeble resistance, and I towed him alongside the boat and shouted to Sile for the gaff, but he had thoughtlessly placed it in the other boat. I then endeavored to put my hand in his mouth, and, while in the act, the fish turned over, breaking the hook and bleeding profusely as he settled off into the tide, leaving us astonished and almost desperate. On examination, I learned that a flaw in the hook had been the cause of our loss of the fish; but had we rowed ashore and towed the fish after the rod broke, we should probably have landed him.

Well, with broken rod and tangled line, I ordered Sile to row away from the scene of our misfortune. I found my friend at Hammock Rocks, his fish laid out in state on rock-grass, and he mutely bending over it with a face radiant with pleasurable satisfaction at his achievement. Trolling, to him, was a new-born pleasure, and his first capture a trophy of which a slayer of lions might be justly proud. It would be superfluous to add, we drank to the study for a Stearns or a Bracket as it lay shining on the pallet of sea-grass. Sandy commiserated Sile's misfortune at losing the large bass. In the centre of a radius containing the most picturesque landscape near the metropolis, we rested, wondered, and admired.

Having toasted the health and appetite of bass in that neighborhood in a glass of sherry, and replaced the broken joint of my rod with a sound one, we again seated ourselves in our boats, and commenced trolling the Little Gate, the Kills, and all about Randall's and Ward's Islands, and, after the usual alternatives of hopes, fears, and moments of ecstasy, we finished up a mess of seven bass between us, the largest nearly thirty, and the smallest four pounds in weight.

Well, having given you a taste of the sport on the waters bounding Manhattan Island on the north and east, let us anchor our boat near the lower hedges of New York Bay, and learn how different bottom fishing with a tracing sinker is from both trolling and angling with a float.

Just as a historical note, the George Steers whom Scott refers to is the same man instrumental in building the schooner *America* that went on to become famous, inaugurating the America's Cup Races.

The other accepted form of striped bass fishing of the day was casting, probably better described as heaving a bait into the water and waiting for something to happen. It was done mostly from rocks, and bass-casting platforms sprang up over almost every rocky promontory from Long Island to the Elizabeth Islands. There were platforms built at Montauk, along the Rhode Island and Connecticut coast, and on Block Island, Martha's Vineyard, and Nantucket. The more famous ones were on West Island off Sakonnet Point and on Cuttyhunk Island and Pasque Island in the Elizabeth Chain, paralleling Buzzards Bay.

Scott felt that casting menhaden bait for striped bass from the rocky shores of bays, estuaries, and islands along the Atlantic Coast constituted the highest branch of American angling. He says, "It is indeed questionable—when considering all the elements which contribute toward the sum total of sporting angling—whether this method of striped bass fishing is not superior to dry-fly fishing for salmon, and if so, it outranks any angling in the world. This style is eminently American."

Surfcasting is indeed a purely American invention, and Scott's statement might well serve as the credo for the modern surfcaster. However, the surf today is a little different from the surf of Scott's day or the surf at Cuttyhunk and West Island. The water was usually below the angler—the platforms saw to that—and only on a big comber did he become a part of it as is so frequent in modern surf fishing.

It was only natural that this type of surf fishing should encourage the development of clubs. Striped bass clubs in the past were considerably different from today's clubs. They were an extension of the polo fields, the race track, and the leisure life of the 1800s that only the

"A Fine Game — Sea Bass" is another reproduction from the 1899 New York State commissioners' report. This supposedly illustrates a bass stand somewhere in New York waters, but because of the rocky coastline, it cannot be Long Island and is more likely somewhere along the Rhode Island or Massachusetts coast.

Bass stands were extremely popular at Cuttyhunk during the latter part of the nineteenth century. Reproduced from Angling *by Leroy M. Yale et al.*

wealthy could afford. Maintaining a bass stand was costly and involved a good deal of work. And only if you were wealthy could you afford to play at fishing.

First, the boulders leading to the point were drilled and iron pipes placed in them to form the foundation of a catwalk. Then a wooden walk was built to the end. The end of the stand was often equipped with a chair in which the sport sat while a chummer employed by the club fed cut menhaden, crabs, clams, and even lobsters into the surf. If a fish was taken, the chummer did the gaffing. Even the best of fishing areas could provide spotty bass catches if the fish were not tolled to where a fisherman waited. Netting the fish for chum, digging the clams, and maintaining a clubhouse provided a lot of employment for the islanders and baymen, and the clubs were welcomed along the coast.

The oldest club was that on West Island, founded about 1862. The most famous was the Cuttyhunk Club on Cuttyhunk Island, the westernmost of the Elizabeth Islands. This club was formed on May 31, 1865, by a group of men at the St. James Hotel in New York City. It was composed of well-known businessmen, politicians, and industrialists from Philadelphia, New York, and Boston, who wanted a fishing retreat close to home and fitted out in the grand manner of their day.

This print from Alfred Mayer's Sport with Rod and Gun *(1883) depicts the clubhouse of the famous Cuttyhunk Striped Bass Club as it appeared in 1882.*

The same clubhouse, now in private hands.

Striped bass clubs existed as long as the striped bass were plentiful. However, during the latter half of the nineteenth century, the industrialization of northeastern America began to affect the striped bass population. The records kept diligently by many of these bass clubs are our only accurate sampling of the striped bass population for this era. The decline is evident in all their catches. The size of the bass seemed to be getting larger, but the number caught fell off. Eventually, the fishing became so poor that in 1907, the Cuttyhunk Club sold its holdings on the island and the organization was disbanded. Today, the clubhouse is a private residence. You can still walk the spacious lawn in front and look out over the rocks and beaches, all named and hallowed.

When a fish population is in danger, there are few or no young fish and large or extra-large fish begin showing up in catches. It would have seemed almost predictable that a large striped bass should be caught about the time the Cuttyhunk Club called it quits. In 1913, six years after the closing, the world's largest authenticated striped bass caught on rod and reel was taken almost within the shadow of the clubhouse.

During the bright of day, Captain Charles B. Church rowed through the Canapitsit Channel, which separates Cuttyhunk from nearby Nashawena Island, trailering a rigged eel behind his boat. He hooked and landed a 73-pound striper that today is still the world's record, though no longer official by IGFA standards. The fish measured 5 feet in length and 30½ inches in girth. The date was August 17.

Another of Mayer's illustrations. The club kept accurate records of all fish taken, and from 1876 to 1882 the largest annual bass weighed 51, 51½, 51, 49, 50¼, 44, and 64 pounds.

Large striped bass seemed to disappear from the fishing scene and almost from the Northeast coast, until the resurgence of the population in the 1930s and 1940s. Four large striped bass were taken between 1958 and 1967. After a fifty-four-year hiatus, the record set by Church was challenged by Charles Cinto of Mansfield, Mass. In 1967, while fishing with Captain Frank Sabatowski aboard the *June Bug*, Cinto caught the fish while trolling on the west end of Cuttyhunk. The fish exactly equaled the weight of Church's fish, though it was weighed several hours after being caught. Because the bass was hooked while trolling wire line with a plug having multiple treble hooks, it was not considered an official record by the International Game and Fish Association, the sanctioning body for such records.

Cinto's striped bass measured 56 inches in length and 35 inches in girth. It was gaffed after a twenty-minute battle at three a.m. in the morning while Sabatowski trolled over the Sow and Pigs Reef. Incidentally, Sabatowski was no stranger to big bass. In June 1963 he had boated a 67-pound 12-ounce fish in the same area.

Most recently, Church's record was challenged when Edward J. Kirker boated a 72-pound striped bass from almost the exact same spot Church had found his fish. Kirker, angling late in the afternoon on October 10, 1969, took the 72-pounder from Canapitsit Channel. He had been casting live eels in the channel when the big fish hit. It made five powerful runs before Kirker could get it to the scales at Cuttyhunk. The fish measured 51 inches in length and 31 inches in girth.

RECORDS OF THE LARGEST STRIPED BASS ON ROD AND REEL

Weight (lbs.)	Angler	Date	Place	Length (ins.)	Girth (ins.)
86.0	Francis W. Miner	7/?/1887*	Block Island, R.I.		
73.0	Charles B. Church	8/17/13	Cuttyhunk	60	30.5
73.0	Charles Cinto	6/16/67	Cuttyhunk	56	35
72.0	Edward J. Kirker	10/10/69	Cuttyhunk	51	31
68.8	Ralph Gray	10/1/58	North Truro, Mass.	50	34.0
68.8	John J. Solonis	9/5/67	North Truro, Mass.	54	32.5

The exact date on which this fish was caught has not been recorded, nor the length and girth measurements. The fish was photographed, weighed and documented. However, the documentation has not been found, and thus the fish's weight is not an official record.

During 1974, the International Game Fish Association reviewed its records. All those fish that had been taken on untested line were dropped from the official standings. Twenty-four records were affected, and Charles B. Church's was among those. The record that had stood for sixty years gave way to the 72-pound striped bass that Edward Kirker caught in October 1969.

The unofficial world's record striped bass, 73 pounds of fish caught by Charles Cinto on June 16, 1967, while fishing off the western end of Cuttyhunk Island. It just equaled Charles B. Church's record fish taken on the east side of Cuttyhunk Island in 1913. It too is now an unofficial record.

9

From the Surf

There's a certain mystique about fishing for striped bass in the surf. Surf fishing has a strong attraction for many thousands of fishermen. Ironically, it is also the least efficient and least productive of all the techniques available for taking striped bass. However, surfcasters are legion on the beaches, and perhaps it is not necessarily from the end that they derive such great satisfaction, but from the means by which they seek this end.

Certainly, it is one form of the sport in which the fisherman actually meets the fish on its own level, or in its environment. The surfcaster spends a great deal of time in the water, and maybe here, too, there is some explanation of the fascination. There is a ruggedness about surfcasting. Nothing delights a typical surfcaster more than to be immersed in cold water up to his chest, with a wind howling off his back and a comber threatening him from the front. With seeming impunity, he lashes back at the elements with a long rod that is often too heavy for comfort. Shivering in his insulated waders, a thermal hooded sweatshirt and a hooded rain coat tightly buckled around his waist by an outside belt, he will tell you that "this is great fun."

Quite often, I think surfcasting is more of a social exercise than a serious attempt at fishing. True, the cold water does steal away one's body heat, and true, the rods are usually long and heavy and the baits are even heavier, and therefore the surfcaster has good cause to take numerous breaks out of the suds. The upper beach will always see a score of anglers, butts in the sand and encircled, trying to determine why the fish aren't there, or when they will strike again. Truly, surfcasting has something in common with the coffee break as an American institution.

The striped bass is, however, a creature of the surf, and surfcasters do catch them. In their migrations north and south the fish are seldom more than a mile off the beach and more often are only a long cast away. Striped bass inhabit a more varied watery environment than any other fish. They can be taken in deep water, rivers, estuaries, and bays. They can be taken by casting, trolling, spinning, and even fly casting. Bass will hit almost every kind of lure imaginable. But of all these conditions and variables, the classic form of striped bass angling is still from the surf. It was probably the first technique, fishing with line and squid, that fathered everything else we today know as surf fishing.

Dr. Ernest Raphael, a devoted surfcaster, lifts a small bass from the waters of Moriches Inlet, L.I.

THE NATURE OF SURF

The surf is that region where water and land meet. An angler once described it as that place between a point on the beach where the highest tide reaches, out to where the farthest cast can be made. In a very real sense, he just about covered the entire realm of the surf and the surfcaster. Generally, the surf falls on two types of land, that made up of sand and graded and that composed of rocks and irregular. The greater majority of angling is done from sandy beaches, but along our Northeast, in Connecticut, Rhode Island, parts of Massachusetts, and Maine, there is a fair amount of rocky beach that has not yet been sanded.

A surf is created by moving water, and four phenomena can make the water move: wind, tide, ocean currents, and ground swells. At times, two or more of these phenomena work together and can create a huge surf. At other times, they may oppose each other and can cancel out some of their effects. And, at other times, they can work from different directions and the surf can be confused or mixed. When each phenomenon works independently, it can develop a surf with different characteristics. And each one can be counted upon to affect, either for the better or worse, the state of fishing at the time.

Most anglers approach the beach with little heed to the actual way the waves are formed. Not all waves are parallel to the beach and strike it at right angles, evenly at all points. Often a wave approaches the beach at an off angle. It can then be seen running along the beach as the leading edge touches and the remainder follows. At other times, the waves can be at direct right angles to the beach. This is best seen at a point of land. We even have situations where two sets of waves can be working onto the bars and beaches. One can be the result of ground swells far out at sea, created by large storms often hundreds of miles away. These waves may be approaching the beach in a parallel fashion, but the wind might be on a quarter off the swells and create a secondary pattern. We then have two sets of waves, together striking the beach.

Wave patterns. Three situations are shown. The first reveals the pattern of waves striking a beach on an angle and pushed only by the force of the wind. The middle pattern shows waves created by swells as they approach the beach parallel to its shape. The figure on the right depicts the combined effect of wind and swells that produces a mixed surf.

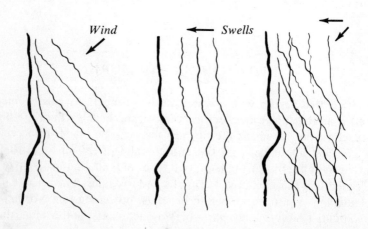

The result is a lot of white water, and white water means that striped bass are more than likely to be feeding. A confused sea has its effect on the baitfish, and the big fish are there to take advantage of such factors. If you watch your wind and weather, you too can figure where such a situation might occur. You should probably be there.

Slope

Not all sandy beaches are the same, nor are they a simple meeting place of water and land. If you have some knowledge of the factors at work in shaping a beach, then your chances of predicting where bass might be are substantially increased.

The steeper the slope of a sand beach, the greater will be the drop-off formed under the breaking water. Moving water approaching the beach is lifted over the outer bar and begins to break, loosing some of its force. Over the inner bar it again breaks, loosing more force, and then dissipates its energy as it rushes up the beach to the top of the tide line.

Scouring. The force of a wave rushing up the beach and then back to sea has a scouring or digging effect on the area immediately in the wash. How much of a hole it will dig depends upon the angle or slope of the beach and the depth of the water coming over the first and second bars.

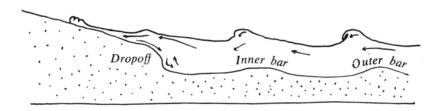

Dropoff   Inner bar   Outer bar

(Enlargement of above)

The spent water then returns to the surf. However, a second wave or force of water is immediately behind the first. As it approaches the beach, it overrides the returning water. The returning water is then forced to turn, circulate, and tumble against the force of the incoming water. This circulation has a digging or routing effect just under the surf. It creates the drop-off or trough.

This drop-off or trough area is an ideal location for finding small fish. They become confused by the stronger water currents. This concentration of baitfish forms a feeding area for striped bass. This bio-zone is also full of other food for striped bass. However, in this constantly changing and forceful environment, many life forms here have learned to survive by burrowing and boring into the sand. As the wave action disturbs the sand, sand fleas, crabs, sea worms, and clams are often disrupted.

On a gently sloping beach, it is far more difficult to locate where striped bass might be feeding without external signs. A gentle beach does not form such evident drop-offs or troughs and bars. There is a reduced wave action, and as a result, these are often the least likely spots along a coastline for finding bass. At low tide, the water may move far off the beach and many areas may not provide sufficient water for fish. Only at the higher tides is there a chance of catching fish on a slow or gentle slope.

Bars

Wave action on a sandy beach usually produces a series of ridges or bars along the bottom. More often than not, these bars are formed parallel to the contour of the beach. Their numbers vary anywhere from two or three to half a dozen, depending upon the depth of the water off the beach and the force of the wind, tides, and currents in the immediate area. Because of their distribution, a fisherman usually worries only about the first and second bar. That is about the limit of his casting range.

An average fisherman can expect to cast between 60 and 80 yards. If he can throw beyond 100 yards, he's in a select class. Bars can build as close as 3 yards from the beach or as far away as 65 yards.

Each bar is formed parallel to the others as well as the beach, making a corduroy pattern. It is the inner and outer bars that are frequently fished, because here is where the water most disturbs the sand and frees bait, and here is where bass are likely to come hunting.

The outer (or second) bar is usually the larger or higher and stops the initial force of an incoming wave. It can reduce it in size so that only a smaller wave or a flood of suds washes over the inner bar and the beach. Bars are not continuous along their entire length but are breached by channels and cuts of deep water. The force of the water returning from the beach gradually builds up, and the bars act as dams. This water is affected on top by the incoming waves and must eventually find its way back to more open water. It does so by cutting through a bar and developing channels.

These channels are hotspots for surfcasters. A pair of polaroid glasses is indispensable for looking into the water. Deep holes, pools, and cuts can often be spotted by a somewhat different color of water. Channels are throughways for fish and they enter the inner sloughs through such openings. Larger bass are more likely to stay in such channels while smaller bass come closer to the beach. Big bass are notoriously lazy and prefer to take a lie here, waiting for baitfish and loosened shore life to come streaming out to sea.

Winds

Winds have a direct effect on the size of the surf and can also contribute to keeping currents along the beach in motion. Onshore winds will increase the agitation and scouring effect of waves. Thus when a good wind is blowing onto the beach, the chances for catching fish are improved. Wind also has the effect of creating turbid water. In most cases, the turbidity is sand in suspension and unfortunately many anglers quit the beach, thinking that striped bass won't feed in such turmoil. I believe that a good, muddy surf is more productive than a clear surf. Striped bass depend upon their sense of smell for locating food and they can feed equally well in the riled water. Riled water means more loose food, so don't stop fishing or decrease your efforts because the water looks bad. It might look bad to you, but consider the picture from the view of a striped bass.

Wind is probably the single variable that has the greatest effect on the surf. On windless days, there is often very little action in the surf. Baitfish, and hence the striped bass, are farther offshore. An offshore wind has an even greater detrimental effect on the catch than days with no wind at all. It has a tendency to scatter fish farther off the beach. Baitfish seek protection in riled water, and if no riled water exists along the sand, there is no reason for the fish to come ashore. There is little confusion at work on a school of bait when there is no wind.

Swells

Ground swells can create a surf that is often as large as that produced by immediate winds. I have worked the surf on days when there was no wind at all but combers 4 and 5 feet high came rolling ashore. These waves are created by offshore storms, or by local storms that have passed and left the seas seething and falling. Their effect on the animal life is less than that of wind-formed waves, but still creates similar situations.

Currents

Local water currents can be created by wind, movement of the tide, and water flowing through inlets and rivers. The temperature of the water can also create currents. Water on the surface is stimulated to move by colder water rising and pushing to take its place. Effects along the beaches are minimal and are felt more by massive thermal currents spawned farther offshore.

Many parts of our coast have local currents generated by larger offshore currents. Along the Atlantic Coast the main current in the world of the striped bass is the Gulf Stream. This massive river within the sea originates in the Caribbean, moves northward along the coast from Florida, scrapes Cape Hatteras, and then follows the Continental Shelf past Long Island and off Cape Cod. Past Cape Hatteras, it creates a small back-eddy that comes down from the north, and with another coastal offshoot following it from the south, meets at the point and collides, forming a massive rip that extends more than 15 miles offshore. The fishing here is fantastic and attracts baitfish and game fish during all times of the year. It provides some excellent striped bass fishing during the winter months.

On the Pacific Coast, the currents head in a direction opposite to that on the Atlantic. Two streams, the Alaska Current and the Subarctic Current, flow east and strike the continent. They spawn a California Current that then sweeps down the coast from British Columbia, hugging the land until it touches Baja California. Here it abruptly turns west. While off Oregon and California, it brings the cold arctic water in touch with the coast and creates the fog that is so typical of northern California fishing. It may also be the reason that striped bass here prefer to winter in fresh water rather than in the cold Pacific.

Tides

Tides move only slightly from off the beach onto the beach, but work in a rather local way, moving in one direction up or along a beach and then reversing. Tides are independent from the action and direction of waves. However, tides and waves have a canceling or additive effect on each other, depending upon their direction.

Tidal flow then runs parallel to the bars, creating small rivers running up and down the beach. Striped bass will usually face uptide, the direction from which the tide is flowing, and this should be a clue as to the presentation of bait and lures. Also, lures work better against the force of the tide than when retrieved with it.

Tides also have a secondary effect on the beach and the water immediately adjacent to it: they vary its depth. The environment in the surf is constantly changing as the tide floods and ebbs. Parts of a beach at times may be devoid of feeding striped bass because of insufficient water. However, as the tide floods, bass will move in with it to search the newly covered sand and feed in the protection of the deeper water. The inner and outer bars also affect the possible location of striped bass. A bar with little or no water at low tide doesn't look inviting to a hungry striper. But two or three hours later, when there is more water over the bar, bass may feed upon it if it contains food.

The direction or state of a tide also affects where striped bass will feed on a bar. On a flooding tide, the fish are more likely to be on the inside of a bar, often between the inner and outer bar foraging for food. On a falling tide, they are more often located on the outside of the outer bar, and there is where you should concentrate your fishing efforts.

The state of the tide also affects the wave sizes and eroding action. A surf at low or mid tide can be monstrous and rolling up the beach with great crashing and force. But as the tide rises and more water appears over the bars and bottom, the waves diminish and lose some of their ferocity. High tide, with a reduced wave and scouring activity, can be a poor time to fish for striped bass.

Low tide along a beach is also a time to make notes, either mental or actual. It is a great time to study the shape of bars and sloughs, locating the cuts and channels and examining the bottom texture of the surf. Then you can return four or five hours later and cast where you think is best over a flat-surfaced ocean and have a fair idea of what lies beneath the waves.

Low tide is also a good time to study the composition of the bottom as a source of potential striped bass food. If the beach and bottom are finely textured sand, then you will have to depend a lot on migrating food and boring animals like marine worms, copepods, sand fleas, crabs, and clams. If the bottom has a muddy texture, sandworms will constitute a lot of the smells let loose in the water. If the beach is made of coarse sand and large pieces of stone, almost a shingle beach, then the food in the area is likely to be only passing fishes and drifting varieties of animal life.

Not far from Montauk Point on Long Island's south shore is one of the prettiest sections of beach one could imagine. However, it is constructed of glacial stones and boulders, millions of stones that were transported by the glacier and released from the sand and mud by the action of sea on the towering cliffs. The stones are all of a size between golf and tennis balls, and make walking impossible. With each wave, they shift into the sea and they come out with it. No matter how hard I have fished this section, or how inviting the environment looks, it has yielded few bass. There is nothing in this life zone that can take the pounding of the shifting gravel.

Also typical of this beach and the beaches east as far as Nantucket are large boulders deposited as the land wears away. At low tide many are exposed, and if you read them, plant them on your visual map, they can be productive sites when the tides return.

HOW TO FIND FISH

Now that you know what creates the surf, how do you find striped bass that might inhabit it? There are natural fishing locations along every beach, and these are where you begin. Fish will concentrate in an area if attracted to it for some reason. These attracting devices can be a collection of rocks on a normally barren beach, a bed of mussels, a point of land that juts into the ocean and will narrow the fish's passage to within casting distance. It might also be an inlet in the beach between the open ocean and back bays. Equally good are places where freshwater streams or rivers flow into salt water, either first as an estuary or directly into the briny. Piers and jetties are also places that will attract baitfish as well as weed and kelp beds. Baitfish have little protection from striped bass except to hide, and if any of these natural or man-made affairs can provide a sanctuary for them, then striped bass won't be too far away.

Rips—where two different tidal currents pass, where a river flows into the bay or ocean, or where back eddies are formed as the tide passes a point of land—are some of the best places to search for striped bass in the surf. Points of land, either off the main beach or on parts of islands, often have natural shoals extending from them. These natural shoals are more likely to be rocky and provide excellent small-fish habitat. The best example of such a natural shoal is Sow and Pigs Reef off the western end of Cuttyhunk Island. It has been a surfcaster's delight. Facing the opposite direction but quite similar in composition are the Long Island shoals off Montauk and Orient points.

Immediate signs

One of the most immediate signs revealing the location of striped bass is the activity of gulls and terns. Birds have been called the eyes and ears of the fisherman's fleet, and even beginning anglers quickly come to realize that a flock of screaming, reeling, diving birds are advertising the fact that they have found a school of feeding striped bass and are getting in on the leftover tidbits.

Gulls and terns have an ability to communicate with their kind that has baffled investigators. Through some unknown means, gulls and terns miles away know that their brethren have found food and come streaming to the spot. A surfcaster who keeps one eye on the skies watching the activity of birds can usually also cash in on the bonanza. If the birds around you suddenly get up and join other birds on the move, there is some reason for the action. And if you are not catching fish, there's no reason why you shouldn't join them.

There is a difference, however, between the credibility of terns and that of gulls. I have seen terns make a real ruckus over a single piece of small menhaden and have too often been left holding nothing when chasing terns. Years of birdwatching over the water has proved to me that gulls are better fishfinders for men than terns. However, don't totally discount the terns, because on some days they are all you have to watch or chase.

Bird life along the beach can be the fisherman's eyes and ears. They indicate baitfish and hence feeding striped bass, giving the alert angler a chance to get in on the action.

Hunting versus sedentary surf fishermen

What signs you look for will also be determined by which school of surf fishermen you belong to. One group firmly believes that it is best to stay put once you have located a natural area that should draw bass. If the fish aren't there when you arrive, then the chances are good that if you can wait long enough, the bass will eventually be there. There's nothing wrong with this. If you don't have a beach vehicle, then you may be forced to join this school of thought.

On the other hand, there is another group that is more active or aggressive in hunting feeding striped bass. This group seldom fishes unless they spot the genuine article or eminent action. They are usually quite mobile and in 4-wheel-drive vehicles will cruise miles of the beach looking for bird activity. In addition to the birds, they look for "oil slicks" on the water. When striped bass feed on schools of menhaden, spearing, or anchovies, something is released in the water that breaks its surface tension. It appears as a wind or oil slick on the surface. It doesn't really look oily, only that the wind-ripple is lessened or flat in the area.

Smaller hints, as you cruise the beach, are sudden swirls or boils in the water where a fish breaks near the surface as it chases bait. More evident are fish breaking water or a school of small baitfish suddenly leaping clear of the water. I have seen striped bass force schools of smaller fish into the wash and even out of the water. Striped bass, when in large schools, can be as vicious a feeder as bluefish, and everything runs in their way.

Two modern aids that are now aboard almost every beach vehicle that regularly hunts striped bass are a good pair of binoculars and a Citizen Band radio. Surfcasters who regularly fish together approach the problem of finding feeding fish with some forethought. They will set up watching stations at likely natural areas, combing the surf and offshore waters with their glasses. If the fish are spotted or actively feeding birds appear, the word goes out over their radios—in a code, of course. The other vehicles come running. If you can't figure out the code, just follow the crowd; a traffic jam is hard to hide.

WORKING THE SURF

This section might better be titled "Fishing Blind," because that is what the majority of your surfcasting techniques will involve. Even if you do find signs of fish you will still be fishing in the dark unless bass are actually breaking water. Your best weapon is a state of mind that will give you the determination to continue fishing when you don't see fish.

Every angler should fish a section of water just as if he were sure that fish lay beneath its hiding surface. It's surprising how often this approach does pay off. Some call this *concentration*, and in the long run it pays dividends. It keeps the above-average fisherman longer in the surf, it gets him there earlier in the day, and keeps him there into the night. It gets him out on rainy and cold days. Only by being in the water can you hope to catch fish.

Where to cast

I'm sure you've heard the statement that more fish are cast over than cast to by surf fishermen. However, I agree with it and it bears repeating once more. For some reason, beginning surfcasters, and numerous regulars who don't consistently take fish, feel that they have to cast as far as possible each time they decide it is time to throw bait or a lure.

There is a time for long casts, and if you are a long caster you will have a decided edge over the angler who has a case of the shorts. However, long casts pay off by increasing the territory you can reach. They also give you the edge when the ocean is flat and the fish are wandering off, with no natural reason to be at your feet or within your scope. But these days are rather rare in the surf—it is always seething or in motion. And it is that very motion that stirs the sand at your feet and tolls bass onto the beach.

I'm a firm believer of casting in a radius of 50 to 60 feet about the beach even before I wade into the suds. I don't want to stir or cast beyond any fish that might be in the immediate area. Gradually, I work my way away from the shore, but never more than 10 or 15 feet unless I want to reach the other side of the outer bar. It doesn't take much water to float even a 50-pound striper. If the water is up to my waist, the fish can be behind me.

Nor are all my casts always away from the beach. To cover the area adequately, you should sweep casts in every direction, up and down the beach, as well as over the bars. The cast downtide is my favorite because the lures always work better. Once I have covered a 50-foot radius, I extend my casts by 10 feet and again sweep the area. Then I extend my casts again, and keep doing so until I have cast all the water in my range.

Working downtide

Once you feel that you have exhausted an area, how and where do you move? The most productive direction is downtide. Cast on a quarter direction off the beach and let your lures sweep behind you. Then haul them directly back. Take a few steps and cast out again on a quartering angle shot. With this technique you eventually sweep the beach of all possible areas. If there is a bass in the water, your presentation will be natural.

Walking downtide also stirs the bottom. In a way, the drifting sand is a slight chum line. Fish face uptide in a running slough. In a fresh-water situation, the sudden appearance of muddy water might signal danger. But in the surf, riled water is a way of life and can only help you.

Retrieve

The speed of retrieves will depend on the equipment you use, the lure, and water movement. There is a certain minimal speed necessary to de-liver action to the lure. You can also override the action with too great a retrieval speed and have the same effect. However, no natural bait swims at a steady pace unless something is chasing it. You should vary the speed of your retrieve as you work an area.

Occasionally, really highballing a lure through the water does pay off, especially with bass. The action is unnatural but it is an attention-getter or an irritant, and many striped bass will fall for just such a trick. Floating surface lures have no minimal speed, and sometimes a plug left floating dead in the water has been hit by a striped bass that couldn't stand the tension. Popping plugs and surface lures develop their own characteristics, and a little experience with each type will tell you how best to work the lure.

When to fish

The best time to fish for striped bass is any time that you can get away to fish. As long as striped bass are around—that is, as long as you are fishing for them in season—then there are going to be some striped bass available at all times. There might be some times that are better than others, but somewhere there is always a bass that is hungry.

One group of anglers believes that the tide is more important than the time of day. Striped bass, like other game fish, use the current and movement of the water to help them feed. A moving tide carries more bait, and striped bass, being basically lazy fish, would rather wait and let the bait come to them than go actively after it unless they haven't eaten for a long time.

We know that striped bass are spotty or sporadic feeders and that they might all feed at one time. If the tide is the controlling factor, then it should be best when the tide is moving best—that is, an hour or so after it turns until an hour or so before it stops to reverse itself. This means that you have about four hours of prime fishing time on each tide and two hours of not-so-productive time. These not-so times are an hour on each side of flood and ebb tide. However, don't tell the striped bass that. I have had some great bass fishing when it was dead low and the fish didn't know it.

Another school of striped bass anglers believes that time of day is more important than the state of tide. The reasoning here—and there is some biological support—is that striped bass are more nocturnal than diurnal feeders. Best times, then, are from just after sunset for a few hours and then an hour or so just before sunrise. I know from experience that summer and early-fall fishing is best during the night. I have taken three or four fish at night for every one I caught during the day. I have fished throughout a night, taken fish regularly, and then felt the action slow down at daybreak and almost stop at sunrise. Raising a fish after that was all work, with strikes few and far between.

I think that the real answer is far more complex than what any one of these schools of thought offers. I believe that each factor, the tide and its speed, has an effect, as well as the time of day. Both have an interaction, and each affects the other in varying degrees at different times of the year.

Then, you must add such variables as the wind direction, water temperature, and fishing pressure in an area to develop a complete picture. Even more important is the availability of natural food in the spot where you might be fishing. All these factors must be considered, because they create so many possibilities that predicting the feeding habits of a striped bass becomes an art and not an exact science. Now maybe you won't think my first recommendation—that you should fish for bass whenever you have the time—is so flip or far-fetched.

Fishing from rocks

A "rock hound" in striped bass terminology is not a collector of stones, but an angler who fishes the surf from the tops of rocks located along the beach or some way out in the water. Very little rock fishing is available to anglers from North Carolina northward until they reach the eastern end of Long Island. Here, glacial boulders appear in the beaches, but they are transported rocks. The real stuff is just a bit farther north, along the coast of Connecticut, and then east and north past Rhode Island, parts of Massachusetts, and into Maine, as well as along most of the West Coast. Along their shores, the bedrock of the earth is exposed to the marine environment. Here is where the striped bass should be called a

rock or rockfish, because it is here that they truly inhabit the rocky
ledges, outcroppings, and boulders dropped along the shore.

Rocks are ideal areas in which to go bass hunting because kelp,
wrack, marine weeds, and other growth like to attach themselves to rocky
surfaces to perpetuate their kind. It is here that smaller baitfish will
come to hide from the marauding striped bass, and it is here too that the
striped bass fisherman will wade into the surf among the boulders.

*In the fishing sense, "rockhounds" are collectors of striped bass who use rocks
and boulders to get above the splash and force of the waves or to be able to
reach further into the surf. Here, Montauk Point bristles with rods during the
daylight hours of a fall migration of fish.*

Using the wave action in a rocky environment to help you determine
where the striped bass should be lying won't work. You need to read the
water at low tide and through polaroid glasses to get your first hints.
Real predictions can be made only based on fishing success in the past.
If you are near natural-attraction sites for bass you can cut down on some
of the odds.

SAFETY IN THE SURF

When a man walks into the surf wearing cumbersome waders that come
up under his arms and fights an undertow from each wave that tries to

Not all surf fishermen wait for the surf to lie down enough so that they can wade out to reach an outer bar. During recent years, a cadre has formed of dedicated surfcasters who don wet suits and walk into the surf to fish during any of the seasons the bass are there.

take him to the sea, there exists some degree of danger. Danger also creeps up when a surfcaster doesn't pay attention to a rising tide and walks out too far, climbs a rise, and forgets about the now deeper water behind.

The garb of a striped bass fisherman in the surf is primarily a high pair of chest waders and the top half of a rain suit. Outside the rain suit, a belt is worn so that if the fisherman is swamped by a large wave, the overlapping rain suit will not let the water fill his waders and carry him off. Even when a man falls in the surf, he can right himself quickly without taking on too much water if he has his belt snugly secured.

Not all the surf is on a sandy bottom. If rocks are around they are sure to carry moss, and that means poor foot traction. At one time, fishermen could buy chest waders with spikes in the soles of their shoes, like golf shoes. Today, about the only help you can get to keep from slipping off rocks are felt-soled shoes. They are good, but not as good as the spiked waders. Some diehards will use ice-creepers or glue on secondary soles that have had the spikes added. Some even place a pair of golfing spiked rubbers over their waders if they can get them large enough.

There is a new breed of surfcaster now on the scene that wears a scuba wet suit. These anglers walk into the surf, at all times of the year, well beyond the wading range of many men and even beyond the casting range. They take waves over their heads with little concern. If they get knocked down they just get up again. About the only safety device they need is an anchor, so that they won't get pulled out with the current, and an inflatable life jacket, in case they do.

10

From Bank, Pier, Jetty, and Bridge

To the landbound striped bass fisherman standing on the beach, fishing from a pier or jetty is almost comparable to wading to the outer bar for that first cast. These natural and man-made features—banks, piers and jetties, and bridges—all have the effect of bringing the fisherman closer to deep water and thus closer to the fish he seeks. While it offers the angler certain advantages over the man fishing from the beach it has a few inherent disadvantages.

When compared to a boat fisherman, these fishing situations restrict the angler's mobility. He can move only as far as the edge of the sod bank will allow him, or the limit of the jetty and groin, as it thrusts into the ocean. On the plus side, these situations provide a stable platform from which an angler can fish in almost any kind of weather. There are numerous occasions when the boat fisherman cannot get out of port or past the breakwalls. But it is seldom that the bass angler cannot walk along a sod bank, fish from a pounding jetty, cast off the end of a pier high above the waves, or troll back and forth along a bridge as he walks his lure.

BANK FISHING

Fishing from the bank in a marine environment is somewhat different from the picture you might conjure up of a bank-fishing situation in fresh water. Most marine banks are found in estuarine situations, in open bays and marshes where tidal rivers flow twice a day to flood the grasses and then drain back into the sea. Banks appear at the end of freshwater streams or rivers where they finally meet the sea. They also appear in large bays and along inlets, where the bottom might be too deep for sod formation, but where the shore is steep and chopped by constant wave and current action.

One of the more contemplative techniques of striped bass fishing is that used by bank fishermen.

Many fishermen naturally shy away from the sod bank found in a marine estuary, and with good reason. It is a part of the ever-changing scene of the tidal zone. The sod bank is in a constant state of flux. It is tricky going, and only those familiar with an area at low tide should begin walking the banks when they are covered with water, or when the tide is rising.

To those willing to spend the time to learn the intricacies of the channels and streams of a tidal marsh, walking and casting along the edge of the sod banks can be a highly productive and rewarding way to fish. Striped bass are especially fond of feeding along a sod bank, because it is an area rich in food. The bank with its covering of salt grasses provides a protective habitat for small baitfish, such as killifish and spearing, as well as a home for fiddler and green crabs. Barnacles and mussels line the bank from high to low tide marks, and numerous crustaceans swarm over the shell beds. It is a perfect banquet for the hungry striper.

Sod banks are usually in relatively shallow water and for the most part they attract school-sized striped bass, fish of from 2 to 3 pounds and up to 10 pounds. However, really large stripers occasionally enter an estuary to find food. The tendency for smaller fish to frequent such an environment means that the angler can use rather light tackle. Sod banks provide the perfect situation for light spinning gear with plugs, bucktail jigs, and spoons. It is also an ideal situation for the flyrodder.

Unlike freshwater bank fishing, marine bank fishing is not sedentary. The fisherman moves along the bankline, casting and searching the water as he walks. Most sod banks collect the sediment from the estuarine waters by stopping their current. As the holdings pile up the sod banks build. That is how the banks are formed. The banks are constantly building and shifting.

Their composition is not the best for easy walking. Mud is the basic element, held together by the root systems of the marine grasses that grow in it. They are rather solid but can give way without warning. The wise sod-hopper is always sure of his next step before he lifts his back foot.

A good bit of sod-bank fishing is done during the mid part of the tide. At high tide, the water depth may be too deep, even for waders. In a mid-tide situation, hip boots rather than waders are the preferred footwear. With hip boots you are not likely to be tempted into water deeper than you can handle. If you do find yourself on the edge of a collapsing bank, your maneuverability is better in hip boots than in waders. An inflatable life vest or flotation jacket is an even better bet when cruising sod banks.

The only time you may want to heave a lure or bait across the channel when fishing in bank situations is when you want to reach the water at the foot of the opposite bank. For the most part, you should be fishing the water adjacent to the bank you are on. The action of a current passing back and forth across and alongside a sod bank is to undermine the foot of the bank. As a result, most banks overhang slightly, and here is where you are more than likely to find striped bass foraging for food or resting in the current.

The most effective cast is one on a quartering angle downtide and then retrieved slowly as it swings under the bank. This means that you might need a 7-to-8-foot spinning rod to help you keep the lure away from the bank without walking too close to its edge. The line test might also be a bit on the heavy side — 10-pound, for most situations — because you cannot always follow your fish if it insists on going out with the tide. Too many sod banks are interrupted by side channels, some with deep water and others with mud bottoms too deep down for you to navigate.

The sod bank can also provide a good place from which to chum if you cannot cast to an area where striped bass naturally congregate. All the elements are there for successful chumming — a current, water not too deep, a stationary chumming location, and in all likelihood striped bass on the other end to be tolled to the bank.

PIER FISHING

At one time, the striped bass stands that dotted the rocky sections of our coast in striped bass country represented the height of pier development. They were individual piers placed where the chances of taking striped bass were at the maximum. Today, all these bass stands or piers are gone, an element of the past. The only comparable structures we have are the numerous large commercial fishing piers built along the East Coast, intended for any fish that pass.

Angling from bulkheads and fishing piers gets you farther into or over the water without getting wet, but it is far more communal than most other techniques. Usually, it's a family trip.

Some states have very active fishing-pier construction programs. But in the range of the striped bass, they are rather few. Fishing piers exist in North Carolina, Virginia, Maryland, Delaware, and New Jersey. From time to time, some good catches of striped bass are made, especially when the fish are migrating along the beaches in the spring and fall of the year.

The pier is the landbound angler's greatest extension into the ocean. It is a safe extension of the land onto the water and brings the caster closer to the fish. Some piers extend several hundred yards off the beach and give the fisherman a real cross-section of water in which to angle. A good many bass will be found between the end of the pier and the beach.

There are, however, several negative aspects of fishing for striped bass from a pier. The foremost is the height above the water level at which most piers are built. The caster will find that only the outer half or two-thirds of his cast is really fishable when using plugs or spoons. The elevation of his position begins to draw the lure higher in the water as it approaches the pier and angler.

Another drawback is the landing of a hooked fish. If the bass is large, the angler can be in a real bind. If the fish decides to head for the pilings instead of the open ocean, its chances of anchoring and breaking the line are good. If the bass is played to exhaustion, getting it into your hands can be another problem. If the fish cannot be lifted by the line and rod, it must be walked off the pier and onto the beach. However, most piers at their beginning have gates or fences extending out of their sides so that no one can fish the pier without passing through the tollgate. Getting around these devices with a fish on the line can be next to impossible. A few piers have ladders and catwalks on the lower level down to which you can climb or on which a gaffer can wait.

Another negative note is the great number of anglers who may be on the pier with you. At times, the pier may become so crowded that serious fishing is impossible. Not only is it impossible, it can also be dangerous when 6-ounce lead sinkers are being cast about. But if you don't like fishing alone and are willing to put up with a few inconveniences, then maybe angling for striped bass off a high pier is your cup of tea.

I know of one angler who loves to fish salt water but isn't much of a surfcaster. Nor can he stand the sea in boats, no matter how large or small—he always gets seasick. The pier is his answer and he has found a fishing home on them. In fact, he has specialized in pier fishing and gets as much kick out of it as the devoted surfcaster.

Areas around a pier are natural places for fish to congregate, and the pier itself does a lot to enhance the fishing on what might otherwise be a barren coastal beach. Pilings that support a pier quickly become encrusted with barnacles and marine plants, and these attract small fish. The small fish attract the larger bass, and the bass in turn pull the fishermen. The collection of pilings in the path of wandering bass are natural attractors to migrating fish. Striped bass on the move over a barren bottom are likely to spend a bit of time investigating the pilings after a long trek with no food.

Most pier fishermen work two rods at one time. Both rods are on the stiff side, and the line is usually 30- or 40-pound-test, capable of hoisting a fairly large fish out of the water. One rod is often finished off with a bottom rig, usually a 3-4-ounce sinker and a spreader with two or more baited hooks on it. The second rod can be equipped with a fish-finder or a float and a bait that doesn't rest on the bottom. Fishing off the downtide or downwind side, the pier fisherman can let the float drift as far as he wants and expand the range of his fishing from under the shadow of the pier. Bait is fished more from piers than plugs or spoons because of the height of the structure.

Pier fishing can be comfortable. Often, the pier operator runs a restaurant or concession on the pier, provides bait and tackle, and also has the latest fishing information. You can even fish in your own chair and set up a windbreaker on gusty days.

JETTY FISHING

Too often, novice anglers equate jetty fishing with a modified form of surfcasting. I must admit, it does look like a similar situation, but jockeying around on a slippery jetty in a storm is a far cry from fishing the surf with your feet in the sand. The entire approach is considerably different, from fishing lore down to the tackle you use.

Jetties and groins are rather new concepts on the marine scene and until the last few decades were rare along the Atlantic beaches. Jetties and groins are constructed to control the flow and erosion of sand. Most jetties are built on long, sweeping sand beaches, and their purpose is to interrupt the flow of current along the beaches, slowing it down and forcing it to deposit its sand load. They also are intended to keep the water from sweeping down the beach fast enough so that the sand is picked up and transported elsewhere.

Beach jetties were built to protect beaches and the houses built on them during the last forty or fifty years. Before such house-building began, the beaches were left to shift and move on their own. Other jetties were built to protect inlets to bays and harbors and keep the sand from silting in or filling up the passageway. Jetties paralleling an inlet or harbor are there strictly as aids to navigation.

Jetties can be extremely productive. A jetty that protects a river channel or harbor with moving currents is an ideal location for striped bass fishing.

In a sense, jetties are low-level piers, but they do not have the disadvantage of being too high, and as a result they appeal to the plug caster as well as to the bait fisherman. Construction of jetties and groins varies greatly, and so does their attraction to fish. The best fishing jetties are those constructed of large boulders or riprap. Huge boulders are placed in position with a crane, leaving innumerable pockets and spaces in between that eventually become havens for small fish and crustaceans that inhabit a shore. These are quickly covered with barnacles and marine plants and at their lower levels are extremely slippery for the fishermen.

Solid concrete jetties are nice to walk upon, but do little to attract or hold passing fish. They do get you out to deeper water, however. In many areas of the nation where rocks are not immediately available, jetties have been constructed of poured concrete blocks. These are piled together much like the natural boulders but leave plenty of space and openings in between which encourage fish to set up housekeeping among them.

The jetty jockey is a more stationary breed of fisherman than the surfcaster or pier fisherman. He picks out his rock and climbs onto it while other anglers take up other positions. A rock isn't the best surface from which to cast, and long rods and big reels for the surf are out of place in the jetty fisherman's precariously balanced world. Nor are long, reaching casts needed. As a result, the rods are somewhat shorter for this type of fishing, from 6 to 9 feet in length and usually with more build-up of the butt section so that the angler can persuade a large bass to stay on his side of the groin.

Pounding surf can make a rock jetty a rather hazardous place to fish if one comes ill-equipped. The most important item is on the jetty fisherman's feet. Steel or aluminum spikes in his shoes or waders are a must so that he can safely stand on the slippery rocks. Felt soles work, but the metal points work better. A few fishermen wear waders, but most wear knee-high boots because they don't intend to wade into the water. The angler is often swamped by a wave or spray, and a good rain suit with hood can protect him from that. Waders or even hip boots can be dangerous if the fisherman falls off the rock while hopping from one platform to the next.

The jetty fisherman is fishing on the edge of deep water, and his casts needn't be great. If he is fishing the rockpile by himself, his most productive casts are likely to be up and down the length of the jetty rather than away from it. Fishermen here read the water currents much the same as those on the beach. Water moves at right angles to the jetty, and a back eddy is formed on one side or the other of the construction, depending on the tidal direction. It is fished much like a natural rip off a point of land.

Most beach jetties and groins are built in New Jersey and Long Island in New York, where the beaches are being protected from erosion. Throughout most of the other sections of the striped bass's range, jetty fishermen must content themselves with rockpiles protecting the mouths of harbors and inlets. These are often more productive sections than beach jetties because they appear in natural areas where striped bass would normally be feeding or waiting to feed. When the weather is too rough on the outside to fish from a boat, jetties offer the striped bass angler still another area from which to practice his sport.

BRIDGE FISHING

Fishing for striped bass from and around bridges has become a way of life for some anglers. Bridges spanning saltwater streams and estuaries are favorite haunts for striped bass. They mean deeper holes for resting and natural collecting sites for food. Any obstruction in salt water means a place for smaller fish to hide, and if grass can grow there, so much the better. Bridges, with their pilings and stanchions, provide such areas.

There are two ways to fish a bridge, from the top or from the water in a boat. The latter gives the bass fisherman a bit more mobility but requires more gear.

Fishing around bridges is accomplished either out of a boat or from the bridge itself. Boat fishing near bridges is covered in Chapter 11. This section deals with those less-mobile fishermen who fish from bridges.

There are a few bridges in Pamlico and Albemarle sounds that are used for bass fishing, and the Chesapeake Bay Tunnel-Bridge is one of the largest in Virginia waters. But for the most part, bridges that really attract striped bass and bass fishermen are the causeway-and-bridge situations found crossing the many bays from the mainland to the outer barrier beaches. They number in the hundreds from Cape May in New Jersey north to the Atlantic Highlands, and along both shores of Long Island. From New Rochelle in New York, east along the north shore of Long Island sounds through Connecticut, Rhode Island, and Massachusetts, spanning the great number of streams and rivers flowing to the sea, we have another great addition to the world of bridges and striped bass. All along the Massachusetts coast and among several of the offshore islands there are more bridges. Each bridge, from Oregon Inlet to the Merrimack River, has its resident striped bass pro.

Before you try fishing from a bridge, however, you should know a little about bridge features and how they affect striped bass. There are two sides to a bridge, the front and the back. The front of a bridge is the side facing the current, and the back is on the lee side. In tidal situations, of course, front and back switch twice a day.

Most still-fishing with live bait is done off the back of a bridge. Casting can be done off the front or the back, with the front having somewhat of an edge. Bridge experts have found that striped bass will lie in two positions in relation to a bridge. Some of the fish take up a stand in front of the bridge, while others take one below the bridge. Few bass hold under a bridge; they move in only to feed or chase bait.

Water being forced between the abutments of a bridge will move faster because the pressures increase as the cross-section of the channel is reduced. This faster current under a bridge will dig out holes deeper than the bottom level surrounding the outer area of the structure. These deeper holes naturally attract bass and baitfish, especially during the day when there is no other protection except the depth of water in which to hide. Striped bass have come to associate bridges with food and will lie in wait near these holes because they are aware that all the food must pass through some sections of the bridge.

Tackle for bridge fishing can be either spinning or bait-casting with a level-wind reel. The latter is preferred for working bait because control over the line is so much better, and the line rides atop the rod, and there is less risk of its chaffing on the railing of the bridge. The spinning outfit is better suited for casting light lures and bait off the front of the bridge. The best retrieve is not one in line with the current, but on an angle, sweeping the lure in front of the pilings or abutments before it fouls.

Heavier lines are also in order because the abutments, pilings, and stanchions are often encrusted with barnacles and they are murder on a monofilament line. Then again, a bass may decide to head under another section of the bridge and you may have to let it run. Longer-than-normal rods also play an important role in bridge fishing. The longer tip helps the line clear any obstructions under the bridge while the fish is being played, and many of the casts will be lobs under the bridge or to one side, with little room for back-casting to avoid bridge traffic. The longer rod makes a snap-cast easier and puts more distance on it.

When trying to land a fish on a bridge, you are up against much the same situation as when fishing from a pier. Some bridges are not high off the water, and an extra long-handled gaff can work. On others, especially those connected to a long causeway, there is no place to beach a fish. I once watched one angler who solved the problem with a large treble hook, the size you might use for grappling or shark fishing. Around the shank of the hook he had poured about 10 ounces of lead, and he had attached the hook to a stout line. He simply lowered this rig under the hooked fish and used it as a sort of flying gaff. It worked, and he hauled his large fish over the railing with no trouble.

If you believe that bridge fishing during the day is good, then you should try it at night. The fish are spread out over a larger area around the bridge and they are more cooperative when it comes to striking. On a lighted bridge, the fish take up positions just inside the shadow cast by the bridge and here is where you must concentrate your casting efforts.

Trolling from a bridge is not as far-fetched as it might sound. The best action on a plug or spoon is when it is retrieved across the direction of the tidal flow, not with or against it. I have seen anglers walk their plugs back and forth across a long bridge and score well. This technique is fine as long as there aren't other anglers on the bridge. And like trolling from a boat, it is a good way to sample where the fish might be holding and which span of the bridge has the greatest potential. Then you can concentrate your efforts in that section of the bridge.

Chumming is also very effective from a bridge. If the bridge isn't too high above the water, you can create a fine chum line, leading the fish right to your baited hook. I have watched a bridgeload of anglers trying for striped bass and only one older gentleman seemed to have all the luck. I concentrated on watching him, hoping to spot what he was doing correctly and I was doing wrong. About every half-hour, he would set the rod in a portable holder and walk back to his car. In a minute he was back again. It wasn't a chilly evening, but still he wore a jacket and kept one hand in his pocket. Then I spotted him as he took out several grass shrimp and slowly, one at a time, dropped them unobtrusively into the water. Bridge fishing can be a crafty sport.

11

From Boats

Boats did for beachbound and bankbound striped bass fishermen just about what Abraham Lincoln did for the slaves. Boats freed them from the land and gave them a mobility on the water to chase his prey wherever it went. No longer must a surfcaster or jetty jockey watch a school of feeding bass chase menhaden beyond the reach of his cast — he could follow. No longer must he sit bound to his beach vehicle watching birds dive and feed over a school of fish — he could go after them.

Not only did the boat free him from the land, it also opened up an entire new realm of fishing techniques that increased his prowess. He could now troll for the bass, or anchor and take them by presenting baits in areas he could never reach from the beach. He could chum for them and bring them right to the boat, or he could seek the bass out in rips, holes, and eddies far from the beach.

BOAT HANDLING IN SURF, RIPS, AND OPEN WATER

One of the most productive areas to fish when striped bass are migrating is the surf. Most surfcasters, bound to the beach, can reach only a small percentage of the fish because they may be just beyond the range of their casts. Striped bass make two migrations a year along the Atlantic beaches from Chesapeake Bay to Maine. On the northward migration, there is a tendency to range a bit farther off the beach, sometimes never showing unless the angler can move out in a boat. During the fall migration, bass habitually take a course closer to the beach and more often than not are actually in the surf.

Surf fishing or inshore fishing from a boat can be the most rewarding of all techniques for taking striped bass. However, it requires a fisherman and boat skipper with a good knowledge of boat handling and a certain cool when the combers suddenly break on his gunwale. It also takes a good boat and a dependable motor, or two motors. Lastly, because the bottom rises and falls so quickly under a boat in the surf, a fathometer is indispensable.

The surf is worked either by trolling or by using the boat as a casting platform. Either way, the fisherman must read the waters as if he were still linked to the beach so that he can take his lures in and out of the channels and over the bars into the deeper sloughs. Trolling is the easier of the two methods because the boat is always under power and always under control. If a wave suddenly makes up too close, the fisherman can quickly turn the bow into it and avoid being swamped.

If a fish is hooked, an experienced skipper usually turns out to sea and fights the fish in deep water, beyond the origin of the breakers. Needless to say, fishing in the surf is a lot easier with two anglers, but a lone boatman can do the job if he has his wits about him. The rewards are usually worth a bit of daring.

Fishing the surf by boat requires that the boatman develop a sense of timing for the waves and a knowledge where they will break. He should be familiar with how much his boat can take along the side and when he must turn into the waves to avoid shipping water. Most boatmen will work the surf up to the back of the big wave. A wave moving toward the beach will lift a boat and pass under, breaking on the beach side. Waves consistently break at just about the same point on the beach while you are fishing, and if you watch them for a few minutes before you move in you can readily define this point. You can fish just to the outside and not worry about capsizing.

The small boat has revolutionized surf fishing. It allows the angler to fish the same water as shorebound anglers but from the outside. He is better able to work the bars and then move with the fish when they decide to move. The boat also makes an ideal casting platform.

When the boat is used as a floating casting platform, the same ability to read the waves and note where they break is just as important, if not more so. Once the wave pattern is established, the angler can let the boat drift as close to the breakers as the pattern allows so that he can cast over holes and channels around the bars. The engine is put into neutral.

Fishing the surf in this manner requires a good sense of balance and a pair of swivel hips. The boat is in constant motion and the angler is always in danger of falling out. Two fishermen can nicely work such a situation, one casting from the bow and the other from the stern. Together, they can sweep a large section of the surf.

Rips and rivers develop where the tide flows strongly over a shallow bar, about a point of land, or around an island where the tide on one side has not yet completely turned. Thus a rip is two tide flows meeting and working their edges against each other. A rip can also develop on a tidal river, in the estuary where the tide is flooding out of a bay or some constriction and meets the relatively motionless water of the open ocean.

These are all good locations to fish from a boat, and several techniques can be used. The first is to troll. The lures are trolled uptide as well as down. The downtide troll may require greater speed to keep the lures in action and is the less productive of the two directions. Lures are also trolled crosstide, sweeping back and forth on angles to the moving water. This is probably the most effective way to troll a moving body of water.

There is a third trolling technique, called stemming the tide, that is also quite effective. The skipper slows the boat's forward motion to a point where it just equals the force of the tide. He is almost standing still relative to the bottom. He can then sweep the lure back and forth over the rip and rocks by slight turns of the wheel, giving it a precise presentation. He can push the engines ahead to move it slowly uptide, throttle back enough to hold him on a new position, and begin sweeping again over a new area.

Tides and rips are also fished with the boat at anchor. The hook is dropped well ahead of where you intend to fish, and enough line is laid out to provide a scope by which the anchor can make fast to the bottom. You can locate yourself exactly over the spot you want to fish by paying out enough line until you are there. Obviously, you must anchor the boat near where you intend to fish or you'll need a lot of anchor line.

This technique has advantages over trolling or stemming because you can shut down the engines, fish quietly, and save fuel. It also frees your hands to work the rods and chum pot if you are chumming; this is a good technique when you are fishing alone. However, there are also disadvantages. You have no mobility and can fish only the area the length of anchor line allows. It can also be hazardous if you try to anchor in a swift current. Caution and common sense are important when anchoring.

The next technique is similar to fishing the surf from a boat but involves a lot less chance of swamping the craft. The current in the area provides mobility. Here, the skipper may believe that the noise of the engines is alarming the striped bass. He runs to the head of the water he wants to fish, turns off the engine, and drifts with the tide. He can use the boat as a fishing platform and cast to each side as the boat moves over new water, or he can even use cut bait and sinkers and drift the bait over the bottom.

If the current is too strong, live-bait fishing will not be as effective because the bait is apt to ride too high. Casting lures will also be less productive because the retrieve will be affected by the force of the moving water. Some lures work so strongly or have so much action that an uptide retrieve can be impossible and only downtide directions will work. Your best bet in a situation like this is to cast across the direction of the tide and fish it on a quarter. However, if the tide is moving fast the distance you can cover is limited.

In open-ocean and bay situations, where there is little or no effect by tides and currents, most anglers will spend their time trolling potential areas and keeping an eye on the birds for a sign of action. Here is where the boat comes into its own. However, chasing birds can be frustrating. Too often, once you arrive the birds disappear. Also, the skipper horsing around a boat must be careful not to put down the bait and fish.

The best approach to a school of feeding fish is from an upwind or uptide direction, whichever might be the strongest. If you are casting, then skirt the birds and feeding fish and come in again ahead of them. Cut your engines and drift down onto the fish. This is the safest approach. You can cast ahead of the boat and get several tries at the fish before they go down or move away from your line of drift.

If you are trolling, a similar approach should be used. Do not set a course through the birds and school of fish. Rather, swing wide around the school and then come in after you have passed them. The lures will swing in closer than the boat traveled, and you will pick fish off the edge of the school and not put them down.

FISHING TECHNIQUES IN A BOAT

There are four basic fishing techniques possible while using a boat for striped bass fishing. The first is casting or spinning, using the boat primarily as a platform from which to cast. The second is trolling, the third is jigging, and the fourth is bottom or still-fishing. Each method will be discussed below.

Casting

Casting and trolling are both widely used, but casting from a boat is held in higher esteem by many anglers. It is much like surfcasting but with mobility, and the type of equipment the complete striped bass angler might need is different. Instead of the long and heavy rods of the surf, boat sticks are modified and vary in size from 6 to 8 or 9 feet. Spinning reels are by far the most popular reel; they allow the angler to throw lighter artificial lures than if he were beachbound. This also means that the lures can be more lifelike and respond better in the water, since weight and distance are not prime factors. Casting ability and distance are nowhere near as important in a boat as on the beach. The boat fisherman can move closer to where he wants to fish if distance is a problem. This general, all-around lightening of tackle gives the boat fisherman more sport than he could have if he had his feet stuck in the sand.

No matter how large your boat, there is basically only enough room for two casters. I have seen three and four working closely and effectively from a boat, but it cramped their style. The reason is obvious. One man can nicely fish, even when alone, about 180 degrees around his station. If he is on one side of the boat, then he is working an area from the bow to the stern. That leaves only enough room for one other man to fish the opposite side of the craft. If he is in the bow, his sweep is approximately the same. There is also a certain amount of room needed for the back cast and this becomes very evident when you get more than two men working from a boat. It is even more complicated when one is not especially skilled in spinning.

Trolling

The word "trolling" is derived from the French word *trôler*, which means to lead or drag something about, like a dog on a leash or a lure on a line. That is exactly what you are doing when trolling. After you pay out a lure into the water with your line, you lead or drag it about until something comes along that is interested in what you have to offer.

Trolling lures and bait is not an especially new technique and was employed by fishermen even before engines were installed on boats. In the early days of striped bass fishing, a favorite technique was to set a single line with sandworms as bait in the water and troll about a bay by rowing. It was a slow affair. However, unlike bluefish or tuna, which can be trolled successfully at high speeds, striped bass are caught more often on the slowest possible troll. Trolling as a technique for striped bass becomes important when you don't know where the fish are or when there is no bird activity or other signs to tell you where to fish.

One of the most effective uses of a boat is trolling. The anglers can cover a great deal of water in exploratory fishing and can present baits too large or heavy to be cast. Here three charter boats work the seething waters off Montauk.

Like the two positions on a boat used as a casting platform, there are really only two positions for trolling—at the edges of the transom or the corner of the boat. On a big-game craft with an especially wide transom, this is still true. Even though outriggers are used to add lateral lines when a third rod holder is installed in the center of the transom, it is the two sides of the boat that determine the actual number of efficiently played rods.

Trolling for striped bass is an important technique when you cannot see fish activity or when the fish are at depths that never bring them to the surface. The depth at which lures or bait travel is determined by the speed at which you move relative to the water, not the bottom. A slower trolling speed will drop the lures deeper, and vice-versa.

There is a maximum depth at which a lure pulled through the water will fall. To get it deeper, you must change its shape, add lead weights to the line, add diving planes, or fish with lead-core or wire lines. A second factor that controls the depth at which the lure rides is the amount of line you have in the water. The more line you pay out, the deeper the lure will travel, to a point. However, this does not work at a fixed ratio. Beyond 100 yards, additional line may only drop your lure by inches.

The reason is that the water resistance on the line as it is dragged through the water affects the depth. The more line you have astern, the more the resistance increases. Eventually, a point is reached where the deepening effect of letting more line out is cancelled by the line's resistance in the water and no additional depth is achieved. This point varies with the speed at which you are moving through the water, with the diameter of the line, and with the texture of the line's surface—that is, braided nylon, copper, lead core, and wire surfaces all have different resistances to the water.

Not all baits or lures can be trolled effectively. When it comes to striped bass fishing, they are limited almost to artificial lures and those natural baits that can be rigged so they meet the requirements of being dragged through the water. A good example of the latter is a rigged eel.

How deep you want to troll is then a function of the amount of line. Most trollers have their lines marked with different-colored tape or swivels every 100 feet. Then they coordinate their speed or RPMs with the amount of line in the water to achieve a certain depth. An accurate determination of your real fishing depth requires knowing the depth of water over a certain point. This is best achieved with the use of a fathometer. Pick a shoal that comes up, as an example, to 20 feet. Make several passes over the shoal with different amounts of line in the water but keeping the RPMs of the boat constant. When your lures begin bumping bottom, you will then be able to match up the depth, in feet, with the RPMs, say 700, and you can note that you have 200 feet of line astern with that particular lure.

At first, this might sound a bit complicated, but it isn't. After a while you will be able to judge quickly how much line you need to take a 3- or 4-ounce lure to 20 or 30 feet. Usually, your trolling RPMs are constant for striped bass, between 500 and 1000, depending upon the type of engine and size of your craft. The lures will vary somewhat, between 1 and 4 ounces, and this weight will affect the depth between 2 and 3 feet. The remaining variable is the length of line, your easiest controllable factor. Also, don't forget that if you troll uptide the resistance is greater on the lure and line and will lift it off the bottom. At the same

RPMs, when you are trolling downtide your lures will be hanging up. You must compensate for these differences.

Trolling's great advantage over other techniques for taking striped bass is your ability to cover large amounts of open water with your lures. Trolling is an exploratory process, but it isn't all blind. You can read the surface of the water in much the same way you read the water outside the surf. Rocks and dips on the bottom will cause a current moving over them to raise up and boil. From the change in color between shallow and deep water you can tell that the bottom gives way, and striped bass love to hang around such a drop-off. Rips manifest themselves easily on top and tell you what to expect.

Trolling can and should be a methodical method for working an area to determine if striped bass are there, then to catch them. Most successful skippers develop trolling patterns when covering a new or even familiar areas. They do not aimlessly wander back and forth. In effect, they take a piece of water and begin slicing it, almost as if they mentally placed a grid over it and were searching out each square. They slice it back and forth, each time moving slightly to a new area. Each run should be taken in two directions. If the area is exhausted it is then criss-crossed at right angles until the correct presentation to the striped bass is determined.

After a strike, the skipper knows that there might be more bass there because of the schooling nature of these fish. It's impossible to put a marker in the water if there are other boats also working the area, and a marker with its line and sinker is apt to foul a trolled lure. The next best thing is to take a range on where the fish was struck. Taking a range involves finding two points, one on the horizon directly on the bow of the boat and a second off the stern. That gives you only one line and you need a point on that line. You pick another line at right angles to place your position on the first line, and here maybe only one position on the horizon is needed. Most skippers take a set of range points each time they start a trolling course, maybe only a mental note, but they know roughly where they were headed when the strike occurred. After a strike happens there isn't much time to take a reading and fight a bass at the same time.

In water where there are natural rips and boils forming, ranges are not quite as important. But as the tide shifts, these rips and boils will make up differently, so a few ranges in the back of the mind are never wasted.

Jigging

The synonym for "jigging" is "jerking," a word that describes the swimming pattern of the squid, one of the striped bass's favorite foods. The action is an abrupt up-and-down jerking, and this pattern of movement has come to mean food to every striped bass that has ever seen a squid. To imitate this, bait fishermen have devised two jigging techniques, both involving a moving boat as a fishing platform.

Drift jigging is the older of the two and accounts for a lot of striped bass over the course of a season. The elements necessary here are a favorite stopping place for fish, like the edge of an island or a bend in a tidal river, and a body of water in motion. In some typical constricted areas, like Plum Gut between Orient Point, L.I., and Plum Island, or The Race, between Fishers Island and Great Gull Island, jigging is fairly popular because of the fast-flowing tide.

The lure for drift jigging is usually a tin squid or heavy metal spoon like a Hopkins lure. It is allowed to fall to the bottom and then jigged a few feet up and down as the boat moves over the shoals. At the end of the drift, the lure is retrieved and the fisherman runs uptide to begin anew.

Jigging while trolling is the classic approach to striped bass fishing in deep water and is probably one of the oldest effective techniques. It can be worked by either large or small boat and is the favorite method for producing striped bass on charter boats. The jigging rod is a bit more limber than the average trolling rod and gives the lure an additional jerking action. The preferred lure is a bucktailed jig, composed of a lead head poured onto a large hook. Behind the head, the hook is dressed with dyed deer or polar-bear hairs. The hairs pulsate as the lure is jigged or jerked through the water, opening and closing, closely resembling the movement of a squid as well as the jerked swimming style.

Some jigs are made with an additional band of bucktail or marabou feathers tied facing the eye of the hook. This enhances the pulsating swimming action. Bucktails are jigged at a steady pace as the boat is trolled rather slowly over a possible striped bass area. The rod is jigged by the arms or held steady by the arms and the entire body, from the waist up, is jerked sideways, back and forth, to relieve the strain on the arms. Jigging while trolling is a tiring activity but it is a good producer of fish. And, when all modern methods of drumming up bass fail, skippers will inevitably fall back on the jig. Jigging is still in wide use today, and at the eastern tip of Long Island it is called the Montauk Jig, a play on the dancing connotation of the word.

Bottom fishing

Striped bass do more of their feeding along the bottom than at any other level. It's only natural when you consider that the bottom houses so much food. The goal of many anglers who cast baits and lures, as well as troll lures, is to get the lure as close to the bottom as possible. However, none works as effectively as bottom fishing from a drifting or anchored boat.

In a sense, the anchored boat represents an extension of bank or pier fishing except that the fisherman has more mobility. Another term for "bottom fishing" is "still-fishing," because the boat is usually stationary and the bait is held in one place by a lead sinker.

There are many situations in which an anchored boat is the only way to fish for striped bass. One is where shallow water, a distance away from shore, suddenly gives way to a deep hole or trough in a tidal river or along a bar marking a connecting point with land. Striped bass naturally congregate along such drop-off areas, and a boat anchored in the shallows with lure or bait trailing off into a deep spot is a sure producer. The proper depth can be attained by changing the weights of lead used with the bait; the bait can even be kept directly on the bottom.

Still-fishing from an anchored boat requires patience and it is not the most aggressive form of striped bass fishing, but to many it is one of the most enjoyable. Some baits can be effectively fished only from an anchored or slowly drifting boat. The live eel is a good example. The stationary boat over a potential striped bass hole provides the best technique for chumming, one of the deadliest methods for taking striped bass. Chum can be accurately distributed from an anchored boat and the fish tolled to the baited hook. Chumming will be discussed in greater detail in Chapter 13.

BOATING A BASS

Boating a bass from a trolling boat is approached differently by different skippers. My boat has two engines, and when I fish alone, trolling two rods, and have a strike, I will slip one engine into neutral and drop the other to its lowest RPMs. This keeps a light tension on the line and fish. If I am trolling uptide or stemming the tide, I don't change direction until the fish is alongside and ready to be gaffed or if the fish is so large that the water resistance is a factor in getting the bass into the boat.

Most fish taken on a trolled lure will hook themselves—or rather, the boat moving through the water does the hooking. I usually set the drag lightly with the click on, to contribute some pressure and also to act as an alarm to tell me a fish is on. Immediately after picking up the rod, I disengage the click and only slightly adjust the drag, letting the fish run. A bass, even the largest bass, will not run more than 100 yards. If it does, you can always follow it with the boat if you are fearful of running out of line.

An experienced fisherman can land a bass with the engine in neutral, taking up a charge by the fish when it comes toward the boat or giving line when it is needed. If you are not familiar with the charge of a bass, let the engine remain in gear, turn the wheel, with rod in hand, and drift away from the current on a quarter course. This will slightly reduce the drag created by the current. If the fish is really large and might test my tackle, I make sure the engines are out of the water when the fight reaches the see-saw stage of the battle along the stern of the craft.

Getting a large striped bass into the boat can be a problem, but if it is boated along the after gunwale with a gaff of the proper size, there isn't much chance for a mishap.

Whether you took the bass casting or trolling, the place to gaff it and bring it aboard is along the rear quarter of the boat. The lower gunwale here makes the job a lot easier. You should also fight the fish from this same area and be ready to stick the rod in the water if the bass should suddenly decide to head for the other side of the boat. The tip under the boat will guide the lines past the engine skegs or any obstructions on the hull of your boat.

Gaffing a fish is best done by someone else in the boat with you. When the fish is ready to be gaffed, don't reel in all the line, down to the leader and snaps, but leave enough so that you can slowly work your way to the bow of the boat and bring the bass abreast the side where the gaffer can easily get to it. You must get away from the transom or you will hinder his ability to swing easily after the fish.

12

Fly-Rodding for Striped Bass

Fishing for striped bass with a fly rod is not the most efficient method available for taking large numbers of fish. However, it makes up in quality what it might not offer in the way of quantity. The thrill of even a small bass surging, leaping near the surface, or bulldogging along the bottom is difficult to duplicate on any other type of equipment.

Fishermen who seek striped bass with a fly rod are probably the elite among saltwater anglers. Many of them look down their noses at the surfcaster or plug-tosser. Whether or not this attitude is justified, it is certainly a bit snobbish. I like to fish all methods, and I derive pleasure from all. Arguing over which fishing method is best is much the same as arguing over what is a good woman. In reality, they are all good—it is just that some are better than others, and which is better is a matter of personal taste.

And fly-fishing is a relative sport. It is the most frustrating of all the techniques. But when you do take a striped bass on a fly rod, you know there are few other techniques with as much reward.

Fly-rodding for striped bass is something best practiced by the experienced saltwater angler. Not that a freshwater fisherman can't take his fly rod into the briny, but success is more certain if he has a store of salty lore to his credit.

To the angler who is already accomplished in catching striped bass under all conditions and uses the numerous other methods and techniques available, the fly rod offers still another challenging method. At times it will even work better than the others. Fly-rodding for striped bass should thus be one of the techniques of the complete striped bass fisherman.

There is, however, an inherent limitation built into fly-fishing: the maximum size of the fish you are apt to catch. Fly-fishing equipment is great for small and medium-sized fish—that is, schoolies from 2 to 9 or

10 pounds and lone striped bass from 10 to 30 pounds. But prospects of catching larger bass are slight.

The basic reason is that bigger fish demand bigger baits. Really large bass look for a mouthful of food, and though they may nibble on shrimp and sandfleas during part of their daily search for food, they'd rather expend just the energy needed to catch a few 3- or 4-pound bunker. We approach the limiting factor when we try to make a fly or bucktail large enough to entice a big striper. There is just so much hackle and marabou that you can effectively or efficiently wield on the end of a fly line with a 9½-foot fly rod. Beyond an 8-inch fly, it becomes nearly impossible. I don't mean to imply that a good caster can never take a 50- or 60-pound striped bass, it's just that the odds fall off so sharply as to make it a fluke. But there's nothing wrong with catching 20- or even 25-pound stripers with some degree of regularity.

FLY-RODDING WATERS

Of course, you can take a fly rod after striped bass anywhere the fish swim. But the fly rod is more effective under controlled fishing conditions, those which you are more likely to find in a salt creek, a tidal river, along the edges of a salt marsh in an estuary, along the borders of great stands of grasses, or under the heavy sod banks cut by river channels in a large shallow tidal bay. You can fly-cast to striped bass in the open bays or on the outside when they show on top, under the birds, or along the outer tips of groins and jetties. But for the most part, the ocean is a big piece of water and you are fishing totally blind. Your chances for success are much lessened by the breadth of waters.

In a tidal creek, however, when the water floods into the marsh grass, you can feel pretty certain that if any striped bass are around, they will be poking their snouts into the banks, looking for shedder and fiddler crabs, killifish that are seeking the protection of the grasses, and mussels beginning to feed as they are covered with water.

My favorite striped bass haunt for fly-rodding is in my back yard, on the Nissequogue River. The Nissequogue is a typical tidal stream beginning as a small, spring-fed creek and then entering salt water. The tide rushes in to fill a large estuary, and striped bass flood in with the rising water. As the tide spreads over the mud and sod banks, the fish follow it over acres of grass and salt hay. Then, as the tide falls, the bass work back into the main channels of the stream, taking positions in each set of rapids or eddy much like salmon.

On a falling tide, I like to don a pair of waders and work the edges of the river much like a freshwater stream. The river is always changing character, and as the water rushes back to the sound, the bass take up new positions. I prefer working down, with the tide, casting along the

A saltwater estuary, especially along its banks and channels, is a nursery area for many fish upon which striped bass feed, and the imitations thrown by saltwater fly-rodders duplicate many of these small food fish. The sport is as enjoyable and rewarding as freshwater fly-casting.

sod banks, searching the rapids formed below a sand bar and letting a streamer or bucktail sweep through the pool, fathoming its depths.

I believe that this type of striped bass fishing is even more challenging than salmon fishing because you must learn the river and its moods in four dimensions. Not only must you know its width, depth, and length, you must learn these through a span of time as the tide rises and falls, keeping the other three dimensions in a constant state of flux. Time and tide affect the river as well as the fish, and the successful angler must comprehend each in the numerous combinations created in a saltwater stream.

Fly-fishing for striped bass is not something new or recently discovered, though during the last decade advances in equipment and technique have been so great that you might imagine that it is a brand-new sport. Fly-casting for striped bass has been done for more than a hundred years. However, it was always performed with freshwater or salmon tackle. During the last decade, maybe a little longer, the refinements of the fly rod and matching equipment have put saltwater fly-fishing into a category all by itself. In addition, the sport has become organized, and there are now clubs and associations dedicated strictly to the taking

of striped bass by fly and an international organization established to
oversee records and set standards for tackle.

FLY-RODDING TECHNIQUES

All the techniques of handling a fly rod in fresh water can be useful in salt
water when after striped bass. One difficulty that a saltwater fly-rodder
does not have, which often plagues his freshwater counterpart, is limited
space for back-casting. The openness of the marine estuary gives the
caster great freedom. But at the same time, he must cover a greater area
of water than must the freshwater angler in relatively confined river or
stream situations.

Wind can become a constant problem to the saltwater fly-caster,
and there is very little lee found on an open marsh. Most casters can
work in a wind up to 10 knots, but above that only the better men are
afield, and they, too, are hard put to make a fly rod work. This might be
the time to lay aside the fly rod and pick up another type of equipment.
There are few days on the marine scene when wind is not a factor, and
therefore ultralight fly-casting equipment is seldom seen in salt water.

Unless you are fishing a moving body of water, a tidal creek, or the
edge of a rip, there is very little movement in salt water compared to that
found in freshwater situations. As a result, most of the action imparted
to the fly must come from the caster. Stripping line becomes the most
important technique for the saltwater fly-fisherman.

Stripping line is simply the pulling or retrieving of your line and fly
by one hand after the line and lure has been cast on the water. The line
is stripped by the left hand (if you are right-handed) while it is guided by
the first or second finger of the right hand near the rod. The length of
each strip varies. Some fishermen prefer to haul their lures through the
water at great speeds and feel this is essential to getting a striped bass
to strike. Others prefer to work it with short hauls, 6–12 inches at a time,
with a lull between each pull or strip. Whether you prefer the full length
of your arm, 18 inches or so, or the short strips will be determined by
the water, its depth, the lure on your line, and how the fish are responding. Don't make up your mind too hastily; variety is the spice of life in
fishing and the successful angler is always willing to accommodate to
changing demands and conditions.

FLY RODS AND OTHER TACKLE

The first rods used in salt water for striped bass were often the long
salmon sticks of the East Coast or the steelhead rods of the West Coast.

Some anglers simply took their longest freshwater rods and adjusted them to saltwater fishing. Bass-bugging rods and popper rods were also adaptable, and one of my favorites is still a 9-foot bugging rod that works beautifully on schoolie bass.

Today, basic innovations in saltwater rods make them a separate class of fly rods. They often possess more backbone or power in the lower or butt section than standard freshwater rods. This is needed to set the hook on hard-mouthed bass and to fight the larger fish. Also, guides are constructed of noncorrosive metals, which are a real must in salt water. Normally, freshwater guides have a ¼-inch diameter, but to handle the heavier lines and to make stripping an easier chore, guides on saltwater rods, especially the first few, have been opened to ½ and ¾ inch. This also reduces the amount of drag or friction and makes casts travel a bit farther. Metal ferrules gave the early salty fly-rodders a fit. Once the rod was put together, it was often left together for the life of the rod. The perfect rod has no ferrules, but this is impractical if you want to take your rod traveling. The next-best thing is the glass-to-glass ferrule, which has been perfected to the point where it has little negative effect on the action and curvature of the rod.

On the butt end, the reel seats now are almost all constructed of anodized aluminum, which is highly noncorrosive and is also a weight-saver. A butt extension, a 2-to-3-inch extension beyond the butt, helps to balance the rod and gives the angler added leverage when needed. It also extends the rod down to the angler's elbow and reduces fatigue when fighting a large fish for a long time.

The saltwater fly rod comes in a range of sizes. Most are on the long side, between 8½ and 9½ feet in length. The average is in the middle, about 9 feet, and can often be matched with a No. 9 or No. 10 fly line. The actual length of rod should be determined by your handling ability and personal casting idiosyncrasies.

Fly lines

Like their freshwater counterparts, saltwater lines come in two basic types: the floating and the sinking line. Each is used under special conditions and with particular types of lure. A third type of line, a combination floating-sinking line, is also available. Lines for salt water tend to be on the heavy side because larger flies, streamers, and poppers are used. They range from weight classifications of 7 and 8 to as high as 12. However, 9 and 10 are the suggested weights for a 9-foot rod.

AFTMA FLY-LINE STANDARDS

Line No.	Weight (grains)	Line No.	Weight (grains)
1	60	7	185
2	80	8	210
3	100	9	240
4	120	10	280
5	140	11	330
6	160	12	380

Both the sinking and floating lines are tapered lines rather than the level lines that can be used in fresh water. The realm a saltwater caster must cover is so much greater that every advantage he can squeeze into his outfit makes that much more water he can sweep. The weight-forward (WF) fly line gives him an added edge. The WF10F line is a weight-forward line, No. 10 in weight and a floater. Such a line is used when casting in shallow water, 3 to 5 feet in depth, with streamers and bucktails or when using poppers and bugs that are strictly surface lures.

In deeper water, where a fisherman wants to haul his bucktail or streamer through the depths, a WF10S line can be used. This is a weight-forward line, No. 10 in weight and of the sinking variety. In mid-depth situations, where the fisherman doesn't want a lot of line to pick out of the water, he might select a WF10SF. This is a weight-forward line, No. 10 in weight, but with a sinking head and floating body. The front half of the line sinks and can reach water depths deeper than a floating line could. Some floater-sinker lines are double-tapered — that is, reversible — so that you can switch them around.

To achieve even greater distances over salt water, some anglers have gone to specialized "shooting heads," to reach out for fantastic distances. A shooting head is no more than a short section of fly line spliced to a light running line made of Dacron or monofilament. The latter is used more often because it creates less resistance in the guides and thus travels somewhat farther. The fly, lure, or even bait is cast with the fly line still in the guides, and as it escapes the fly line shoots forward, carrying the running line out of the guides. On false-casting, the caster should never work on his running line; it adds little or no appreciable distance and dampens the action of the tip. The weight of the shooting section should be heavy enough to bring out the action of the rod and is the same weight line that would be used to match the rod, regardless of the weight of the running line.

Leaders

A good rule of thumb for leader length is that it should approximate the length of the rod. Tapered leaders are heavy at the butt section and taper down to the tip to meet the eye of the fly. Tapers can vary in test from 50 pounds at the butt to 10 at the tip, and many lesser combinations exist. Some tapered leaders are constructed with a double taper, a second short taper at the butt section where it meets the fly line. This is preferred when you use a metal eye in the fly line and need the smaller diameter at the butt to tie a knot. Casters who don't use metal eyes generally tie a nail knot when fixing the line to the leader.

I prefer the eye splice. This device is an eye the size of a fish hook or smaller with a shaft about 1/2 inch long. The shaft has barbs on it that keep it from pulling out of the line. The shaft is skewered into the usually hollow center of the fly line. I have used these for years and have never had one that pulled out if it was properly inserted. I first use a small needle to open the core of the fly line before forcing the barbed shaft into its center.

Most eyes come in both iron or stainless steel for saltwater use. But even the stainless-steel eyes rust after a while when exposed to salt water, and they should be replaced regularly, depending upon how much use they get.

Leader material is usually made of monofilament and should be stiff enough to turn over the fly at the end of the cast. This isn't quite as necessary when fishing with streamers and bucktails on a sinking line. In fact, I often shorten the leader to 3 or 4 feet so that the fly is closer to the bulk of the sinking line and thus gets deeper into the water. Under such conditions, a tapered leader doesn't offer any advantages and I often substitute a piece of level spinning monofilament.

Reels

The first reels used for striped bass fly-fishing were salmon reels. But salmon in river situations don't have the wide-water prospects that a striped bass has and the reel's capacity often limited the fighting abilities of the fisherman. A saltwater reel today should be about 4 inches in diameter and capable of holding 40 yards of 10-weight fly line and approximately 200 yards of 15-to-20-pound-test braided Dacron or nylon line as a backing.

The reel should be single action—that is, one turn of the reel handle equals one turn of the spool. The spool should be capable of being removed so that the insides can be rinsed of salt water.

Earlier reels were rather heavy, and when added to a large saltwater rod and a heavy line capable of carrying large flies, the overall weight was a mankiller. Today, aluminum and alloys have made reels a lot lighter and often saltwaterproof.

Adjustable drags are often a part of a striped bass fly reel, but these drags add only slight amounts of friction pressure to the spool. The real drag that must be added when fighting a fish comes from the pressure of

Saltwater fly-rodding gear is like freshwater gear, but heavier, and the reels should be corrosion-resistant. Note the butt extensions on two of these rods.

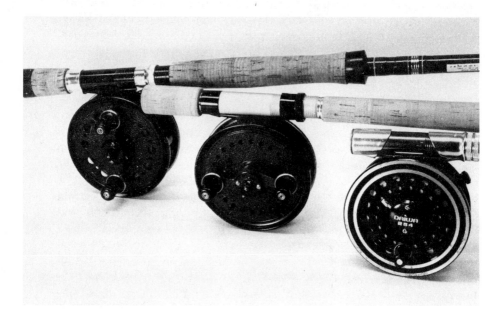

your fingers against the side of the spool. Thus fly reels with exposed spools on one side give the caster more control and are an advantage when fighting large striped bass.

In freshwater situations, most fish are played by stripping the line on the water or beach. But many fly-rodders after striped bass fish from boats, where all the line off the reel can cause immediate problems, and many anglers thus fight a fish from the reel. Small fish can be tackled by stripping, but the large bass that has practically cleaned your line is best handled by putting the line back onto the spool immediately.

FLIES FOR SALT WATER

Flies for striped bass originally were nothing more than large freshwater flies, bucktails, and streamers used for salmon or other freshwater species. However, saltwater fly-rodders quickly came to realize that color and pattern were not as important to striped bass as they are to salmon. Effective striped bass flies do not duplicate a striped bass's food so much as they act as attention-getters.

Colors are not as important as the shape and action of the fly. Colors were used to duplicate insects, and very few insects are part of the striped bass's world except in freshwater reservoirs. For the most part, saltwater flies duplicate small food fish—spearing, killies, herring, menhaden, and sand lances. Therefore, effective striped bass flies are built and shaped like these foods, or something with no comparison in real life except that it grabs the attention of the bass. The three basic patterns or styles of saltwater flies are popper or popping bugs, bucktails, and streamers.

Poppers

Popping bugs are surface lures made with either cork or balsa bodies and adorned with either feathers or bucktails on the backsides. The face of the popper can be cupped and angled, and performs as a true popping bug, making a thrashing noise as it is intermittently hauled over the top of the water. Other surface poppers have a flat but slanting face, one that lifts the popper onto the surface. This type really skitters or slides across the top of the water and doesn't set up quite the commotion a regular popper does. It is used when a fast retrieve is desirable. A third type of popper has a pointed or bullet head. This form is retrieved over the surface with a greater speed. It is the favorite of the fast fisherman with a full stripping arm. Each type can effectively take striped bass on the surface.

Poppers for saltwater fishing are generally larger than for fresh water and the hooks are made of nickel or steel. They can range greatly in size for presentations to either small or large bass.

There are a great variety of poppers constructed. One of the more famous poppers is the Kah-Boom-Boom, tied by Cap Colvin of Seaside Park, N.J. This is a slim, cup-faced edition, with a few bucktails, either red or white, on a red or white cork body and mounted on a 1/0 to 3/0 hook.

Bucktails

As the name implies, these lures are made of bucktail deer hairs. They are similar to freshwater bucktails except that they are tied on stainless-steel hooks. The lures are tied on long-shanked hooks, anywhere from 2/0 to 4/0 in size, though the majority of saltwater flies are tied on 1/0 hooks. Because striped bass take all their bait and food by the head, short-shanked hooks are equally in order and bass hit them as effectively as flies tied on the longer hooks. Longer hooks are used to increase the size of the fly and create a larger area for mounting the materials.

Bucktails are among the most effective flies used in salt water for striped bass because they can so effectively imitate a bass's natural food and a lure can be large enough to get the attention of a big striper. From left to right, these bucktails are: Mickey Fin, Loving Bass Yellow, Lyman's Terror, Brooks' Blonde, and Grizzly and Yellow.

Patterns or colors on bucktails are extremely simple. Most are two-color combinations with white predominating. Black and white, red and white, and even red and yellow, semblances of a Mickey Finn, are all effective. Since bucktails imitate small baitfish, the basic light-and-dark patterns require a lure with a light underside and a dark topside, like the shade patterns in live fish. Additional features are added to the sides of the flies to suggest stripes or bars.

A collection of the standard patterns would include a Palmer-Diller, (Harold) Gibbs Striper, (Frank) Gibbs Bucktail, Black Nosed Dace, and several of the Joe Brooks double-tied bucktails, including the Strawberry Blonde (red-orange), Platinum Blonde (white), Honey Blonde (yellow), and Black Blonde. These double-tied bucktails are constructed on a long-shanked hook. The first bucktail is tied just behind the eye as in a standard pattern and then a second tuft is tied on the shank just before the bend. In effect, it extends the bucktail, making it longer than possible with a single tuft. The double tie gives the fly more action and the forward tuft even imparts a breathing action. In addition, these flies are larger and will appeal to larger striped bass.

Streamers

Streamers are much like bucktails in construction, but made with feathers rather than hairs. However, this doesn't mean that hairs, tinsel, and artificial materials cannot be used in their construction.

Streamers are often of multiple-wing construction, either on long- or short-shanked hooks. They include four to six angled feathers that, when compressed by the action of water as they are drawn through the medium, bulk at the front to look like the shoulders or body of a baitfish. Most streamers, as well as bucktails and poppers, have large eyes painted on their heads, though some do not. These further simulate the small baitfish striped bass feed on.

Marabou feathers find their way into may streamers because of their pulsating effect when pulled through the water with an uneven haul. Newer concoctions are the series of shrimp flies that have blossomed during the past years. Because striped bass do a considerable amount of feeding on grass shrimp as well as larger shrimp, these flies have become especially popular and productive.

Fry flies are another group. They are composed of eyes, hackles about the hook, and long chenille or Mylar and Saran bodies to imitate long, slinky baitfish and small eels. Some have a tail tuft, and an example of this group has been tied by Fred Schrier of Toms River, N.J., long an advocate of fly-fishing for striped bass.

Streamers and look-alike lures can be in bizarre patterns that don't imitate anything living but they sure catch striped bass. Most of these concoctions came from Fred Schrier of Tom's River, N.J. From left to right they are: marabou streamer, marabou with peacock hackles, eelet with Mylar body, spearing with a good dose of Mylar, and a hackle streamer.

FLY-FISHING FROM BOATS

Not all the fly-fishing for striped bass is done from shore or in the water. A great amount is performed from small fishing boats, 12-to-14-foot car-toppers with flat-bottomed hulls that can drift with the wind across the tops of the grasses at high tide. The 12- and 16-foot Boston Whalers are ideal boats for fly-rodding. These boats are laterally so stable and the bow so clear of obstructions that they act as a perfect mobile casting platform

Water depth in a tidal estuary can vary greatly, and a wading fisherman's reach is limited by the tops of his waders. A small boat becomes invaluable in making the correct approach and presentation to feeding striped bass as well as increasing the area which the angler can cover. It also makes up for short casters. The 80-to-100-foot casters loose their advantage in a boat.

Most fly-casting from a boat is done drifting, either with the tide or current in a salt creek and marsh or with the current caused by a wind on the water. This movement is desired and constantly presents fresh or new water to the fly-caster. In one drift he can cover a surprising amount of water. In the case of a fast drift or too much wind, the boat can be slowed down by tying a bucket to a line and tossing it over the side, or by dragging a cinderblock or pair of sash weights that won't totally stop the drift.

In such shallow circumstances, it is best not to use an engine to put you onto the fish. Instead you pole to the spot or run upwind or uptide so that you can drift down onto the spot you'd like to fish.

You can also use a boat at anchor if you want to work a spot that is a consistent bass-producer. With a lot of anchor line, you can pay out a few feet after every cast and cover a lot of territory. In a similar situation, you can also use a boat to chum fish within casting range of your flies. I have chummed with grass shrimp at the edge of a tidal creek and tolled bass to my Mickey Finn. Shrimp patterns can be used in the chum line instead of bucktails or streamers.

13

Chumming

Chumming is an especially effective and highly efficient aid in taking both small and large striped bass. It is something of an art because of the great number of variables involved, and it takes certain skills. However, even the novice or beginning fisherman will have a better than average chance for putting striped bass into his cooler if he chums, and to become really expert at chumming requires only time and an alert mind.

Some anglers object to using chum. One objection is understandable: they object to the smell, the method of handling, and often the messy boat that results. But chumming does produce fish when other methods fail, and if you want to catch fish consistently then you may be forced to chum.

The second objection is that chumming isn't sporting. But certainly in saltwater fishing such a nice sense of what is sporting and what isn't is somewhat snobbish. Chumming doesn't make catching bass a sure thing. It certainly does help—a good chummer can fill his boat with bass when the fish won't strike on plugs or trolled lures. The complete bass angler, one who wants to catch fish, must add it to his bag of tricks.

Striped bass normally are very wary fish. In shallow water, their wariness seems to increase as the depth decreases. The chum line in effect helps subdue some of this wariness and enables you to bring bass closer to you and the boat. The prospects of a free meal are just too much for a striper to pass up, and when the fish are in schools they compete among themselves and become even more foolhardy.

Chumming is both old and new to the striped bass scene. A hundred years ago, it was the standard procedure when fishing for bass among the Elizabeth Islands and the bass stands along Buzzards Bay. The numerous striped bass clubs in Massachusetts and Rhode Island practiced fishing in a much different manner than we know it today. The wealthy sportsmen would sleep until the sun rose and then take their allotted place on the bass stands. However, hours before, their guides would have been on the stand and started a chum line going, doling out bushels of cut menhaden, eels, and lobster tails and parts. It seems inconceivable that someone would chum with lobster, but at $1.50 per hundred, lobster were chum.

By the time the sports were on the stands, the bass were well tolled and boiling in the surf waiting for tidbits. All the fisherman had to do was select a whole lobster tail, put his hook into it, and toss it into the melee. It may not always have been that simple but often it was.

During the same period, chumming striped bass with soft-shelled clams was practiced on Chesapeake Bay. Without lobsters, the Chesapeake Bay fishermen doled out what they had the most of, oysters and clams. This technique of clam chumming in Chesapeake Bay has never waned and for the past century has been among the standard techniques for taking rockfish. Today, most of the bay's 500,000 striped bass fishermen use the clam-chumming technique during at least some part of the year to take rock.

During the last forty or so years, the prevailing chumming technique along the coast from New Jersey to Long Island, Connecticut, and Massachusetts involved the use of grass shrimp. There are several varieties of grass shrimp along our coast and probably all are used at one time or another.

Grass shrimp were the preferred bait because striped bass like them and large quantities are readily come by. Grass shrimp are small crustaceans, about 1 to 1½ inches in length, and closely resemble the shrimp you pick out of a shrimp cocktail. They are easy to find and net in the grass along a tidal creek or marsh. But grass shrimp have been cyclic in abundance, their numbers seeming to parallel the availability of eelgrass along the estuaries. During the late 1940s and early 1950s a blight struck the eelgrass and the beds disappeared along the coast, along with the brant, weakfish, and grass shrimp. During the blight, chum was difficult to find. However, some enterprising Long Island bass chummers turned to the sea and found skimmer clams and clam bellies an equal if not superior substitute for grass shrimp. Eventually, grass shrimp returned when the eelgrass blight was over, but many chummers stayed with the clams.

Clam bellies are the waste product of skimmer clams. The offshore dragging industry on Long Island produces a great amount of clams that go into canned chowder or deep-fried clams. The waste is the softer parts and the lining of the clam, parts that cannot be used in the chowders. At one time it was thrown away or ground for bluefish chum. However, unground, the bellies provide a great striped bass enticer and now fishermen can buy a 3-gallon can of frozen bellies for about five dollars.

The purpose of chumming is to bring striped bass within the scope of your baited hooks. It is a tease or attraction that works something

Grass shrimp are kept in a bait car off the transom of the boat and doled out at a steady rate to chum bass to a baited hook.

like a smoke signal in the water. A chum line appeals to the striped bass's greatest sense, that of smell, and a chum line can extend a mile or so away from the place you are waiting, enticing any striped bass which enters the zone of smell and taste you are offering to come on up for more.

CURRENT AND CHUMMING

Aside from the availability of bass, there are several factors that will affect success while chumming. The most important is water current. This is more often a moving tide that will be used to carry your message to the fish, or it can be in an estuary where a river enters the briny. Whichever, you cannot chum effectively without it. Nor can you chum very well at the top of the tide or at dead low when the water flow has stopped. Too much current can also reduce your effectiveness. It can thin out the chum so much that fish will have a difficult time following it to its source or pinpointing the baited hook.

The amount of tide or current, then, is a factor you must consider above all others when selecting a site to chum. The current should be strong enough to carry your chum away from the boat so that you can fish a minimum of 50 feet downtide.

As the tide rises and falls, the degree of current will change. You must alter your chumming to meet these changes. In a faster current you may have to use more chum to keep the chum line connected. In a slow current, your chum should be reduced so that all the tidbits don't pile up and provide a mouthful for your bass. A good current is necessary to increase the length of your chum line. The longer the line, the more fish you are likely to attract. If you are fishing a defined area, like a deep hole in a shallow flat or the space under a bridge or along a sod bank, then you might not want an especially long chum line. In such cases, you have some idea where your bass might be. But in an open bay or along a beach, where you are chumming blind, the longer the chum line, the better your chances are for success.

WATER DEPTH

The next variable to consider is the water's depth. There is a minimum as well as maximum. I have effectively chummed striped bass while anchored in 3 feet of water. It was tricky and required real silence in the boat and a fair current so that I was taking fish 100 to 150 feet away. If I had to try to take them closer to the boat in a slower current at that depth, I'm afraid the boat would have spooked the fish.

It's difficult to say what might be the maximum depth. I don't like to chum in water more than 20 or 25 feet deep, but it can be done. The problem here is dispersal of chum. In deeper water, you will develop a broad spectrum of chum, in depth as well as width, and it places your baited hook in a larger area in which striped bass must hunt to find it. I believe the ideal chumming depth is somewhere between 10 and 15 feet of water, and the ideal current is one moving at 2 or 3 knots.

WHERE TO CHUM

Deciding where to chum can be a big problem if you are working a new body of water or at a stage of the tide during which you have not regularly fished. The best place to chum is where you know stripers can be found. Chum in natural areas that have something to attract bass. You can chum along a beach if the current is running parallel to it, you can chum off a point, off the end of a jetty or groin, along the edge of a sod bank where the water will eventually feed a hole, under bridges where striped bass come to feed on the life around the barnacles and grass, along the edges of a rip where bass wait for feed to come their way, or just about anywhere there is a current and a natural reason for striped bass to congregate.

Most chumming today is done from an anchored boat. However, in the past, most of the chumming was done from a point of land. Today, an angler can effectively chum from a bridge when he is landbound. Some of the best catches of striped bass along the south shore of Long Island are around the numerous bridges and causeways that criss-cross the several bays. In New Jersey, some of the better chumming sites are off the ends of the numerous jetties or groins — long, fingering piles of rock and riprap designed to keep the beaches from eroding.

The anchored boat, however, makes the presentation of the chum and bait far more easy. The angler can pick the place in the current where the chum line can flow most effectively to the striped bass.

HOW MUCH, HOW OFTEN, AND HOW LONG

The rate of chumming will be determined by the speed of the current and the depth of the water over which you are anchored. Chumming for bluefish is easily figured out. The chum line must be continuous, and you ladle the chum into the water at a regular rate. However, when it comes to striped bass, chumming is a miserly operation, and the danger here is to chum too freely. The object of chumming striped bass is to get them to your hook, teasing them with just enough tidbits to keep them moving up the chum line. If you feed them too much, then they'll lie back, waiting for the food to come, and never get to that morsel with the hook.

It is far better to underchum than to overchum. Chumming for stripers is an intermittent affair. You toss a few shrimp into the water, breaking the backs on some so that they will die and sink to the bottom. Others will swim slowly with the tide. I once fished with an angler who doled out one small shrimp every minute, and we did quite well. The rate is something that is determined by practice, and no one can tell you exactly how much to dole off the side of your boat.

How long to chum can vary greatly. Most chummers will give a spot they know, which has produced bass in the past, half an hour to an hour of time, if the current is moving well, before deciding that the fish just aren't in this hole. If the tide is slow at making up, they may stretch it to an hour and a half or two hours before finding another location. Once you have laid down a streak of prime bass food, giving it up too soon can be a waste of money as well as fishing effort. To move means that you must start all over again, and at best it will take half an hour if the bass are somewhere within the scope of your chum line before you can expect one to take a baited hook. The fish have, however, occasionally made a liar out of me and moved into a chum line less than ten minutes after anchoring the boat.

TYPES OF CHUM

Chum can be made up of anything on the menu of a striped bass, and that constitutes just about everything that lives in a marine environment, and some things that don't. The three most popular types of chum are grass shrimp, clam bellies, and clamworms. Grass shrimp are obtainable by netting along most creeks and tidal marshes, almost anywhere that a good stand of grass is available for protection.

At high tide, the shrimp are up into the grass and may be difficult to locate. At low tide, they may be out of the creeks and into deeper channels waiting for the water to return. Mid-tide will find them at a wadable depth, and two anglers stretching a small-gauge net across a creek and walking against the current should be able to fill their shrimp car in a few minutes.

Once the shrimp are caught, they are kept in a floating wooden box with screened sides to allow fresh water to flow through and a lid on top for retrieving shrimp when needed. The shrimp car is tethered off the stern of the boat. Shrimp held in a pail inside the boat need a lot of fresh seawater added to keep them alive. Two to three quarts of shrimp should be more than adequate to fish one tide. One tide involves about four hours of actual fishing time.

Shrimp are liable to swim away from your chum line if the current is not strong enough. In such cases, and even when there is plenty of current around, the shrimp should be fed slowly into the water and every second or third shrimp should be pinched to kill or wound it. If the current is swift, the shrimp should be tossed ahead of the boat so that they land on the bottom closer to the stern of your craft. In slower water, they can be broadcast off the back. Some anglers like to throw a handful of shrimp at a time and then not chum again for five or ten minutes. Others keep shrimp going over the side at a regular rate, with a few extra added every third or fourth time.

In many areas where sandworms or clamworms are plentiful, successful anglers chum with them. They are a natural bait, and striped bass are especially fond of worms during the spring and early-summer months. The technique is much the same as when chumming with shrimp. A sandworm is cut into six or eight pieces and then one or two pieces are dropped into the water every minute or so. One school of clamworm chummers prefers to cut up an entire sandworm and toss all the pieces in at once, then wait about five minutes before giving the water another dose of the same amount of worms.

Bloodworms or marine tapeworms work just as well as sandworms. However, with sandworms approaching two dollars a dozen today, this technique may become too expensive, much the same as has the chumming with lobster tails. However, if you are willing to dig your own worms and have a sand or mud flat at low tide nearby where you can do it, you can still chum with these baits.

Clam bellies as chum are increasing rapidly in popularity. One reason has been the increased cost in other baits and the ready availability of frozen clam bellies. Almost every coastal bait shop now has them available and the cost is about five dollars for a 3-gallon can. But this price is likely to increase, like everything. The frozen clams are just as good as those that have been thawed out the night before.

Mix the clam bellies with equal amounts of seawater to form a clam broth. This clam broth is just as valuable as the bellies, maybe even more so. And the broth gives clams an advantage over shrimp. It is so full of flavor, like a concentrated bouillon, that it is a great fish-attractor with very little food or calories in it. The technique for dispersing clam-belly chum is to scoop out a ladle of broth and bits and spread it over the water, then grab a belly or two in your hands and squeeze the juices out and into the water before letting the clam fall into the current. This is repeated about every five or ten minutes, depending upon how well the current is moving and how well the bass are responding.

To make the chum go even further, some anglers mix in a bit of sand. The sand takes on some of the chum flavor and in the water it drops first and paves a chum line on the bottom.

Soft clams can be used as well as clam bellies that come from sea or skimmer clams found farther offshore. Soft clams and bank mussels are pounded to a pulp with a potato masher or the end of a 2x4 to form a stew of meat and shells. This is ladled into the water every few minutes, and the shells do for these clams what the sand does for the clam bellies.

In the Chesapeake Bay area, where crabs are especially plentiful, a considerable amount of chumming is done with blue crabs, fiddlers, hermits, or any crab form available. Crabs are cut or chopped into small pieces and dispersed at intervals into the water. Large pieces are likely to fall too quickly and often pile just behind the boat. The smaller pieces are more likely to be carried farther astern and increase the length of your chum line.

Fish can also be used for chum and was the preferred material at the Elizabeth Island bass clubs. The oilier the better, and menhaden or mossbunker were the favorite. Mackerel also found their way into the chum slick, and these oily fish broadcast far and wide that there was a free meal to be had. These fish are cut into small pieces, some even ground, then mixed with seawater and doled off the boat or into the surf. The only drawback with this type of chum is that it also attracts bluefish and is best used early in the season and later, when the water is too cold for the blues.

Small baitfish are also used to chum bass. Spearing and small bunker are favorites. The small fish can be chopped up or just cut in two, with scatterings of whole fish mixed with the pieces. Securing this kind of chum can be a problem unless you have a fine meshed net with you or trap the young fish in a tidal creek when hunting for grass shrimp. Don't toss away any small fish; they can be used as bait if not chum.

FISHING TECHNIQUES WITH CHUM

The thoughtful chummer will quietly approach the place he intends to begin chumming, often drifting to the area after cutting his engine and then anchoring the boat. In a steady current with little or no wind, one anchor off the bow will be enough to keep the boat in place. But with a variable current and a wind on the surface, you can be swaying back and forth over 15 or 20 feet and produce a sloppy chum line, one difficult for the fish to follow toward your baited hook. In this situation, you will have to double-anchor your boat, straddling the current. The technique here is to drop one hook and see that it takes a bite, then motor back uptide, off the first anchor, and drop the second. By adjusting the length of the lines, the boat can be brought at a right angle to the current. This is an especially effective way to anchor when you have two or more anglers in the boat. They can all get an even chance at the chum slick. A word of caution here is in order: don't anchor cross-current if the tide moves with any great speed or you might capsize.

Another variation on anchoring with two anchors but still having the bow heading into the current is to drop your first hook and pay out enough line until you are well anchored and approximately where you want to chum. Then pay out an additional 30 feet and drop a navy-type anchor. Take up on the bow anchor line and when you are back to your original location you can then begin to snub up on the stern line. The navy anchor will hold more because of its bulk and weight, and while it won't keep you exactly in place you will not swing so wide of your chum as to lose its effectiveness.

Tackle in a chum slick can be either spinning gear or a conventional reel and rod. I prefer the latter because it is easier to handle the line, and line handling is an important part of the fishing technique in chumming. If you select a spinning outfit, it should consist of fairly stiff rod, one between 7 and 8 feet long, with an equally stiff tip so that you can set the hook firmly on large striped bass. You can chum up almost any size bass, from 1½-pound schoolies to behemoths of 50 and 60 pounds. However, if you are working a school of strictly small fish, you might better match the tackle to the size of the fish to keep some semblance of sport in the game.

If you are chumming near obstructions like docks, bridge pilings, and bulkheads, you will want a fairly strong line, and 20-pound-test monofilament should be your minimum. This should be piled onto a spinning reel capable of holding 200-300 yards and with a good drag in case you nail a large striped bass. With a spinning outfit, the line is payed into the current and chum slick with the bail open. After the current begins pulling it out, the bait is allowed to drift back at a pace just about that of the current. If it moves too fast, you can slow it down by forcing the line between your finger and the housing of the reel.

Retrieval is not with a steady, upstream pull. Instead it is jerked like a shrimp or squid swimming through the water. This gives any bass around the impression that the bait is swimming against the current. This action is more likely to catch the attention of a striped bass than a steady pull back to the boat. It can be imparted by reeling, but is better done with the tip of the rod.

I prefer to chum using a heavy freshwater bait-casting outfit or a medium saltwater outfit. I like a level-wind reel, equipped with a star drag and fished on a 6-to-7-foot rod. I have even chummed with a light trolling outfit when I knew that 40- and 50-pound striped bass were in the hole I was feeding, but even here, the action of the rod is rather light, a balanced 20- or 30-pound rod and line.

I think the trolling or level-wind reel is the better choice in a chumming situation because the fisherman can easily work his line on the downdrift of the bait. The reel can be put into free spool with a thumb on the spool in case of an unexpected strike and the line can be hand-pulled off the spool and fed into the current. I like to fish either 20- or 30-pound-test Dacron with a 10-foot monofilament leader of approximately the same test. The Dacron can easily be marked with a waterproof pen at 10-foot intervals. Knowing exactly how far your bait is astern the boat is invaluable after the first strike. With a marked line, you know just how far back the bass are lying and when you can anticipate a strike. Also, if you know that you are anchored 60 feet above a hole you can pay out the correct amount of line and be in the right place, rather than hoping you are there and maybe always too short or too long. Line measurements are just as valuable for the serious chummer as for the successful troller.

I don't like to fish more than 200 or 250 feet of line off the end of a boat in a chum slick. Beyond that distance, I feel out of touch. I let the current pull the line off the reel and occasionally slow it up to let the current lift it off the bottom. Otherwise, it is liable to lodge on something and nothing but a belly in the line will go out.

The baited hook should always drift just a slight bit slower than a free-floating or drifting piece of chum. This difference in drift rate within the chum line is likely to attract a striper that otherwise might be hesitant.

I will pay out the line until I have about 200 feet in the water and then begin the slow, sporadic, and jerking retrieve until the bait is again back to the boat. After a quick inspection, I let the current pull it out again after I have stripped off enough footage for the effect of the current to begin its task.

After three or four such retrievals, the bait is liable to become water-logged and loose most of its taste and smell. It should be changed frequently. Add the old bait to the chum slick and put on a new one; you can't afford to be frugal when it comes to the bait on your hook.

Hooking bass in a chum slick can be a ticklish problem. Live bait, or bait that once was alive, is approached differently by striped bass. They may taste it externally before ever mouthing it. Often, striped bass will swallow clam bellies before you have any idea that they have taken in the food. Other times, they may gently mouth the shrimp or cut bait and you can only tell they have it if you always have the line between your fingers.

When striking clam bellies or cut bait, bass may only take it into their mouths and swim off. It is important that there be little or no drag on the line. This can easily be accomplished with a conventional reel set on free spool but with the slight drag of a click left engaged. As soon as the bass stops or makes a telltale rush, the drag can be engaged and the fish hooked.

More often than not, striped bass feeding in a chum line will hook themselves if the hooks are sharp and of the proper shape. I use a variety of sizes, ranging from a 1/0 for grass shrimp to 4/0–5/0 on cut bait with clam bellies on a 3/0 hook. I also prefer the Eagle Claw shape and the bait-holding barbs on the shaft. These are also especially good when stringing on several sandworms or several clam bellies when they are used as the bait.

Which bait to use on your hook can be a matter of personal choice. The generally accepted rule is to bait up with a glob of the firmer parts of clam belly when chumming with clams, to use two or three shrimp on a hook when chumming with shrimp, or a couple sandworms, whole, when chumming with worms. The hooks and barbs are left exposed so that the fish can more readily hook itself.

However, there is no reason why you cannot chum with grass shrimp and bait your hook with worms, or mix any other combination. They have all worked at times. When I chum with clam bellies, I will also dig or buy a couple dozen skimmer clams, and use the muscles on the hooks and add the bellies to the rest of the chum. Clam bellies are nearly impossible to keep on the hook, and you are likely to find only small bits of muscle left over in the chum you buy. If you work the bait upcurrent properly, the bellies are likely to slip off.

When using crabs, half or even a quarter of a crab can be enough to bait a hook. The crab is hooked and then tied onto the shaft. Many anglers use a piece of Dacron line, but I carry a small spool of soft wire in my tackle box to save making knots with slippery fingers.

Most striped bass in a chum slick are likely to be found near the bottom at the end of your chum line, but they work progressively toward the surface as they approach the source. A good technique, especially when two or three anglers are fishing out of the same boat, is to fish a line on the bottom, one somewhere near the middle, and the third, a high line, often just under the surface. A line with just hook and bait is likely to float just under the top, buoyed up by the current. To get your line deeper won't normally require a lot of weight. I prefer split shot, 2 or 3 feet ahead of the hook.

In a really fast current, trying to keep the bait on the bottom while in close to the boat may require a 1- or 2-ounce bank sinker. But if you fish 100 or more feet behind your boat in 10 to 15 feet of water, all you will need is two or three large split shot.

Chumming can effectively take striped bass when all other methods fail. Striped bass must feed and if anything can get them to move for food it is a well-laid chum line. Chumming is also a contemplative method for taking striped bass and if anything ever impresses you on the first trip you take with an experienced chummer, it is the silence that is an integral part of his fishing method.

14

Fishing at Night

When the sun goes down and the stars come out, the view is just as different for the striped bass as it is for the striped bass fisherman. This nighttime world, however, is completely familiar to the fish. To most fishermen, it often seems a perpetual first-time experience, a kind of fishing to which he never really becomes adjusted. It is totally unlike striped bass fishing under the sun.

Night fishing can often be the most productive in terms of striped bass caught, for the angler willing to master an entirely different set of fishing techniques. The differences aren't caused simply by the lack of light. The entire approach and attitude of the angler must come about 180 degrees. Usually, those who are willing to make this adjustment and to put up with the various inconveniences of fishing in the dark are rewarded for their extra effort.

The most obvious reason for fishing at night is that the striped bass is a nocturnal as well as a diurnal fish, with perhaps more emphasis on the nocturnal aspects than most fishermen realize. The anatomical make-up of the striped bass — the rod development in the eyes for night vision, its great eye size, and its exceptionally well-developed olfactory system — all indicate a creature highly organized for living and feeding in the dark. Feeding studies conducted by biologists also point to this same conclusion: the most likely time striped bass will be on the move looking for food is from dusk to midnight and again before daybreak. If for no other reasons than these, you should fish striped bass at night.

There are other reasons. In some of the areas where striped bass are known to concentrate, the fishing pressures during the day can be so great that it is impossible to fish effectively for them. Sandy Hook, Montauk Point, Watch Hill, Sow and Pigs Reef, and many more such areas along our coast get such great fishing pressure both from private anglers and from charterboat skippers that effective and enjoyable fishing can be near to impossible. These conditions are compounded on warm, windless weekends during the summer months when the boating horde all but drives the fish off these natural feeding grounds.

But come sunset, the stream of boats heading back to port is like a traffic jam on the Long Island Expressway. The traffic in the other direction is almost nil, or so minimal that you occasionally like to see another red and green light bobbing next to yours just to assure you that you aren't on the River Styx.

Aside from the aesthetic disadvantages of crowded fishing, there are practical disadvantages. A lot of boat traffic, especially in shallow water, will alter the feeding habits of the striped bass. One of the best examples comes from my own back yard on Long Island Sound. A few miles west of where the Nissequogue River empties into Smithtown Bay is an area known locally as the Brickyards. Near the turn of the century a barge loaded with bricks was capsized in a midwinter storm and the bricks settled to the bottom in 10 to 15 feet of water, just 100 yards off the beach. A freshwater stream also seeps through a barrier beach in this area, and this combines with the brick-strewn bottom to produce some pretty good bass fishing during the summer months.

Striped bass are extremely active during the dark hours, and the nighttime angler is apt to get both more fish and bigger fish. Here the author battles a striper that fell to live eels.

When I first began fishing the Brickyards, it wasn't too difficult a chore to take the occasional bass from the area throughout the day. But as more and more people moved from the city to Long Island, bought boats, and began fishing, the daily pressure as well as the traffic increased greatly. The fish almost entirely abandoned the area during the daylight hours. During a typical August, I like to anchor my boat over the bricks and drift live eels off the transom. I will fish continuously, with steady success, until a powerboat approaches and whizzes over the area and the fish stop biting. An hour or so later, they begin again, if no more boats streak over the spot. During recent years, the traffic has been so steady that the fish refuse to come into the shallows, even with the best-looking eels from the pot. But as the day wanes and night approaches, the boat traffic all but dies, and the fish are less wary about approaching the shallows. They still feed there throughout the night.

Another reason to fish at night is a day-to-night migration that striped bass often make from deep to shallow water. Striped bass feel more at ease in the protection of deep water and as long as they are not feeding will more than likely stay put. But the protection of deep water becomes less of a factor as night approaches. Striped bass will abandon it to feed in water often so skimpy that their backs are in the air. At night, bass are more likely to haunt the beaches looking for food that normally wouldn't tempt them during the day, following bait into shallower water. Nighttime trolling in the shallows, or casting while your boat is drifting along the beach bumping into the bottom, will produce more bass than the same techniques during the day.

Even for the surf fisherman, nighttime is far more productive, and he needn't try to reach the outer comber or bar for bass. Often they will be swimming around his feet, and the best surf catches are consistently made at night. This might be one reason you see so many surfcasters who make a several-day jaunt of a fishing trip, and sleep in their campers during the day.

Another factor that can justify fishing at night is the routine of many striped bass foods. One of the favorite foods along the Long Island and New England coasts is the sandworm or clamworm. This salty annelid burrows into the sand during the day and leaves its hole only to feed and find other sandworms once the sun goes down. Striped bass are more active feeders at night just because the sandworms are then available, and the fish adjusts its feeding habits to that of its food. Likewise, the striped bass fisherman must adjust his fishing habits to the feeding habits of the bass.

Still another reason to fish during the night might be the occurrence of the right tide. Some bass anglers fish strictly by the tides, regardless of the time of day. A flooding or falling tide may be the only time that

striped bass will feed at a particular rip. And if that tide occurs during
the dark, then this is the time that you should be there.

Lastly, during especially hot summers, in late July and August, the
water in certain bays and estuaries can rise above 75 and 80 degrees and
put the fish off their feeding routine during the day. Until the hotspells
are over they will be active only at night. During the late night and just
before daybreak, the temperatures along the shallows and in the surf
can cool enough so that striped bass will come ashore to feed. Under
these conditions, this means that night fishing is the only approach to
success.

FISHING TECHNIQUES AT NIGHT

Of all the methods used to take striped bass during the day, only three
pay off in the dark: surfcasting, trolling, and still-fishing. It's difficult to
say which is the more popular or more effective, and after a while, it
becomes a matter of personal choice.

Surf fishing

Surf fishing is even more effective during the night than during the day,
as I have said. At night, striped bass abandon the deeper haunts and
chase fish into the surf and among the rocks and suds. The jetty jockeys
come into their own, and striped bass are taken where none could even
be chummed during the brighter hours of the day.

Needless to say, fishing the surf and jetties and among the boulders
at night can be hazardous if not approached with some degree of caution.
It is safest to fish in pairs and to keep a constant chatter flowing. Lights
are taboo except when gaffing a fish, so you can't keep shining a search-
light about to see where your buddy is or how he is doing.

Spinning rods and reels are less popular at night because of the
greater possibility of fouling. Level-wind bait-casting reels are better
suited to fishing in the dark, and even the larger closed-face spin-casting
reels are better because they are almost foulproof. But they aren't made
large enough for big surf fishing and not too many find their way onto
the marine scene.

At night, striped bass are apt to approach the top of the water as
well as come closer to the shore. Thus swimming surface plugs and
poppers may work well. On a quiet night, without wind and little wave
action, you can hear striped bass feeding and splashing about on the
surface as they chase baitfish. A popper plug is at its most effective

under such circumstances. But to cast at night requires some skill of the angler. It is difficult to cast into the dark, not knowing where or when your plug hits the water—or who it hits if you are a wild caster.

If you are fishing an established hotspot for stripers you'd better also come prepared with a large dose of patience, because everything that can go wrong usually does go wrong. And there are always other anglers in the surf who can help it come to such an end. A tangle of lines and lures, especially with a bass on the end that decides to run up and down the beach in the dark rather than out to sea, can put a score of surf fishermen out of action for hours. It requires the wisdom of Solomon to untangle such messed lines with everyone claiming the striper. It might be a good idea to scratch your name onto the plug before you go casting it into the dark.

Trolling

Some anglers consider trolling the most effective nighttime method, but it requires a good bit of boat-handling savvy. The first prerequisite is an intimate knowledge of the waters you plan to fish. You must know how to get out of the harbor, inlet, or port in the dark, and even more important, how to return in the dark. You must be familiar with the buoys and lighthouses as well as prominent land features. Street and shore lights will appear during the night that you never knew existed during the day. If you learn where they are, you can put them to valuable navigational use. Further, you need a lighted compass by which to travel and a fathometer that lights up brightly enough so that you can read its figures.

You should be able to handle your boat in pitch darkness. Be thankful for moonlit nights—they are added bonuses. Lights for night fishing are taboo, except those boat lights required for navigation by the Coast Guard. You can beat the problem of light shining on the water by mounting inside deck lights that shine down on the deck and not over the gunwale. Lights are required, but if yours are too bright, they will turn off the bass and even annoy other nearby anglers.

So much for navigation. Trolling at night should usually be done over areas with which you have become familiar during the day. You know, or should have developed, a set of ranges or trolling patterns over these home waters. The fathometer will help you keep these same patterns, and you can check them as well as against lighted landmarks on the beach. More than likely, you will be fishing closer to the beach at night than during the day, so you'd better be familiar with the bumps on the bottom and those that stick out of the water at all tides. The best way to learn them is to spend some time at low tide, during the daylight hours, mentally or actually plotting the locations of boulders, shallow bars, sunken obstructions, natural cuts in the bars, and kelp beds.

When trolling during the day, you can get some idea of the depth of your lure from the angle the line makes with the water. At night, this is difficult to do, so you must have measured and marked your line to let you know how much of it is in the water. A tachometer on the boat also comes into greater play. You judge your speed during the day by watching objects in the water pass the hull of your boat or landmarks slowly drift by. At night, you have only the tachometer as a friend.

Choice of bait and lures also changes somewhat at night. Eels are more active then and are thus preferred. The eels can be live, hooked through the lip, or rigged with lead heads for trolling. Eel skins and plugs with eel skins are also widely used. Sandworms and large spinner combinations trolled especially slow are also standard favorites in protected areas and places with little or no current. In areas where the water moves and rips, or where the tide piles over shoals, the white bucktail jig and white or yellow pork rind is an established winner. The jigging technique is the same as during the day.

"Fire in the water," or phosphorescence, can put the jinx on your nighttime trolling or casting. During the warmer months of the summer in northern seas, the waters are filled with uncountable billions of one-celled, microscopic plants and animals collectively called plankton. These drifting organisms provide the initial food for many crustaceans and fishes as the first link in a long food chain, often ending with man.

Fish, if they don't swim too fast, do not disturb the zooplankton enough to make it glow. But metallic lines, lures, boats, or almost anything else that moves at a rapid rate will cause the plankton to glow. The hull of a boat can set up such a glow that the rig looks like a meteor crashing through the water. The cause of all this firewater is a microscopic protozoan called *Noctiluca milaris*. Compared to other plankton forms, *Noctiluca* is rather large, with a swollen, bladdery appearance. It has one flagellum, and is colored a faint red under the microscope. It feeds only on living organisms. This protozoan is capable of an intense glow, but only when physically or chemically stimulated. It floats in our seas and is the chief cause of marine phosphorescence.

Striped bass naturally refuse such an apparition. On moonlit nights, the phosphorescence is greatly reduced or totally eliminated. But when the sun is on the other side of the moon, the minute animals glow with any disturbance of the water. There's nothing you can do about it. This usually occurs from July and August into September and even October in the more northern parts of the striped bass's range, from New Jersey north to the Gulf of St. Lawrence.

Trolling speeds at night should be conducted just as slowly as possible. The fish have lost most of their sense of sight, while smell and hearing take over except on brightly lit full-moon nights. Coupled with slow trolling is the use of small boats. It is far better to use a small boat — a car-topper, flat-bottomed skiff, or something like the 16-foot Boston Whaler — to duck in and out among the rocks than a large sportfisherman. Smaller boats also require less power and you can hang a smaller engine on the transom, one that will create less noise than the big mill used to push you about during the day. You are in no hurry while night fishing. If you do have a large, immovable unit on your transom, you can often augment it with a bracket and a smaller engine alongside for night trolling and getting you close to the beach.

Better yet, go with a really small boat and use your muscles for some row power. This is best conducted in a protected cove or bay, with a small engine for emergencies and getting to and from your fishing waters. With a pair of oars you can troll slow enough for the laziest of bass.

Still-fishing

Fishing at anchor or while drifting at night is a thoroughly enjoyable way to spend an evening. In addition, it can produce some large striped bass. If you aren't especially familiar with your waters at night, still-fishing is a gradual approach to learning what they are like. You can pretty well plot your way to a spot and get back, and rest without fear of running aground, while you are at anchor. You can learn the landmarks and coastal lights better from a sitting position and make them a part of your night-fishing lore.

Most still-fishing involves live bait, and again the eel is one of the preferred baits. It can be fished at anchor or while drifting. But you must know your bottom. Still-fishing with eel is best done around rocks or over a smooth bottom with some degree of running tide. The eel is left to swim and drift on its own. If there is a lot of kelp or grass in the area, the eel will bury itself in the safety of the grass and won't be working for you or any potential bass that might come your way. Chumming is also very effective at night and is easily practiced without boat traffic running across your chum line or someone else fishing the tail end of it for you.

Noise is kept at minimum while night fishing at anchor because the bass are relying more on their ears than their eyes as danger receptors. You can also anchor closer to the rocks and beach at night because the bass are more likely to approach your boat under night conditions.

The only time you are allowed to turn on the lights while still-fishing is when you are boating or gaffing a bass and sacrificing it for future fish. The only other exception is when you must flash your beacon onto another approaching boat. Usually your running lights are turned off while at anchor and the signal is needed to warn other boats of your presence and position.

In addition to live eels, live mackerel and bunker can be fished at night. The technique of drifting is as effective as working from an anchored craft. These baits are also fished by a boat underway, but while stemming a tide so that all effective forward motion is stopped. When a striped bass approaches live bait, like eels or bunker, the bait will become especially active. This is a warning that a strike might happen at any moment.

Fish taken on live bait usually hook themselves and you can let them run. In the case of eels or bunker, striped bass will take them by the head almost every time. As they do so, they turn with the baitfish in the water, swallow it head first, and hook themselves. The barb is usually exposed with such baits, making the self-hooking that much easier.

As a rule, heavier lines are used when fishing at night because of the obscurity of the waters. Hooked fish may head for deeper water or run along the shore, among the boulders and pilings, and the heavier line gives a slight safety margin from fraying. It is also a plus when you hook an unexpectedly large fish. Even the largest bass move in close to the beach to chase food, and you can never tell what has struck your bait until it heads the opposite way.

For an entire night's fishing, it might be a good idea to combine techniques. I like to troll for the first few hours after sunset. When it really gets dark, I head for a spot that has proved productive and anchor or drift live bait into the area. As daybreak approaches and I get itchy to move about again, I'll switch back to trolling if the action has been slow. However, if either method continues to pay off, there is little sense in switching. There's no need to.

15

Fishing the Striped Bass in Fresh Water

The freshwater environment is different from the saltwater environment, and the striped bass responds differently in it. A first experience chasing striped bass in fresh water is likely to be disappointing to the longtime saltwater angler if he does it strictly on his own. His cherished fish is a stranger to him and he must learn a whole new set of tactics.

But to the experienced freshwater fisherman, learning how to catch striped bass can often be little more than an extension of fishing lore that he already possesses. Nevertheless, even the knowledgeable freshwater angler, in a new environment and after a new species of fish, must do some homework before he can expect to take striped bass with any degree of regularity.

Many anglers in sweet water now find themselves in this position because of the great expansion of distribution the striped bass has had in just the last five years. Stripers are being planted in more and more impoundments as the techniques for transfer and hatchery reproduction are refined and enlarged. Impoundments that for years yielded bass, sauger, crappie, and several species of perch are suddenly producing cane-pole-busting fish, the striped bass.

There is no great mystery about how to catch the striped bass in fresh water if you can develop a bit of knowledge about the fish as well as the impoundments in which you are fishing.

The striped bass in freshwater environments acts neither like a saltwater striper nor like a freshwater largemouth or smallmouth bass. Instead it acts a lot more like the walleyed pike, sauger, or even the white bass, a close and kissin' cousin. The striper in fresh water is a schooling fish, and is not apt to spend a lot of time in shallow water except when its food is chased there. In fresh water, striped bass feed more often than in salt water, and they are where their food is swimming.

FRESHWATER SEASONS

There are seasons for catching striped bass in fresh water just as there are in salt water, but they are not as closely tied to migration as in the ocean. Striped bass can be caught in landlocked situations throughout the entire year, with the slowest period during the warmer days from mid-July to late September.

Much of our early freshwater striper lore was developed on Santee-Cooper, the fabulous impoundment in South Carolina which is responsible for most of the populations now stocked throughout the Southern states, from the Carolinas to California. But here the fishing season gets its annual rejuvenation or revival about the end of March, when the blueback herring migrate from the Atlantic and pass through the locks on the Pinopolis Dam. They are replenishing the herring populations in the lake.

Striped bass begin feeding on the bluebacks as they spawn and after they themselves take part in their own annual ritual. Striped bass spawn from late March through June in most of their range. After this act, they put on a feeding frenzy that is matched again only in the fall.

From about the first of March until near the end of April, striped bass are not as grouped or schooled as they are during the other times of the year. At this season, they also prefer, especially in Santee-Cooper, to feed near or on the bottom, and cut bait, especially herring, has proved to be the best striper producer. After spawning, however, they go for more wiggle in their food, and from the end of April to about the first of May, live herring, or gizzard and threadfin shad where herring are missing, are the preferred baits. This baitfishing falls off about the beginning of July because the bass have eaten most of the adults and those that are left are difficult to find, even for stripers.

July usually heralds a slowdown in striped bass activity. The fish have followed the bluebacks to deeper water and stay there throughout the summer. The best fishing technique to use until late September is trolling. And though it is difficult to troll in many impoundments, with their loads of stumps and brush piles, large plugs that swim and dive deeply are now the best producers of fish.

With the first hint of fall, the numerous herring and shad that were spawned in the spring are now bite-size baits for striped bass. The fish seem to come out of their doldrums as well as deep water and begin to feed ravenously on schools of these baitfish.

At these times of the year, gull-watching pays off. Gulls in fresh water are as helpful and useful to the striped bass angler as those found in salt water. Gulls spot schools of feeding stripers and follow them to take advantage of the bass's sloppy feeding habits and pick up anything that floats to the top.

Now is the time when a pair of binoculars and a fast boat pay off. Follow the birds and approach the feeding school slowly for the last 100 yards. If the fish are breaking on top, surface plugs will work nicely. If the birds are milling about and you can't see the bass, begin tossing bucktailed jigs and bouncing them along the bottom. The bass are down deep and the bucktail is the lure that will entice them.

Another technique that pays off at this time of year, from mid-fall and throughout the winter, is drift-fishing. If you run into a school of bass, you can stay with them until you limit out. In most parts of Santee-Cooper and Keystone Reservoir (Oklahoma), the anglers drift large live shiners. When they get a strike, the marker float is dropped over the side and the boat returned upwind for another drift. The advantage of drifting live bait over other techniques is that you can cover a lot of water and the opportunities of locating the bass are quite good.

Equally profitable for the bass fisherman during the fall months is vertical jigging. During the spring and summer, you should make note of all the brush piles on the bottom which you have snagged. Mark them on your topo map or use any other means, but be sure you can return to them in the fall. At this time, the numerous small baitfish are tightly schooled and they seek protection from the marauding striped bass in the cover that old brush piles or submerged brush rows along old creek beds afford. Stripers are likely to lie alongside such fish havens and wait for the smaller fish to come out. Brush piles are difficult to fish other than from a vertical position. The technique is to drop a metal spoon or jig into it and bounce it around. The lure most often used by Roland Martin, a striped bass guide for years on Santee-Cooper and now a resident of the Keystone Reservoir, is a Hopkins hammered spoon called the Shorty.

FRESHWATER TACKLE

Much of the tackle used for striped bass in salt water while fishing from boats, docks, or bridges can be used in fresh water. The conventional reel seems to be the preferred reel in most bait situations and is used almost exclusively except when casting with plugs on the surface. The reels are loaded with 10-15-pound-test monofilament or Dacron when fishing cut or live bait, or when drifting live shiners. When fishing over obstructions, the line test is increased to 25 or 30 pounds because any bass that are hooked must be hauled out before it retreats to the safety and tangles of the brush.

Live herring are fixed on a 6/0 to 8/0 O'Shaughnessy hook and fished either with a barrel sinker on the bottom or off a three-way swivel with a bank sinker on a 2-3-foot leader. The herring is hooked just ahead of its dorsal fin and passes only through the skin so that a minimal amount of injury to the fish occurs.

Rods for live or cut bait are about 7 feet long with a medium-action tip. The bait is fished in free spool with just the click on to keep it from unwinding. When drift-fishing with live shiners, the click is not enough to hold the spool and the drag is set very lightly to help hold it. When striking a bass, the thumb is momentarily used to keep the spool from rotating and after the strike, as the fish runs, the drag can be adjusted.

For vertical jigging, a somewhat stiffer and shorter rod is preferred. The stiffer tip is likely to give you a faster recovery when the lure is jigged. The technique is to drop the lure in free spool to the bottom, engage the reel, and retrieve 2 to 4 feet with the rod tip in a jerking manner. Then let the lure fall again to the bottom and jerk again a few feet from the bottom. Most bass will strike the lure on the free fall between jigs. You won't be aware that a fish is on unless you keep a slight degree of tension on it as the rod tip is lowered to let the Shorty fall. Too slow a dropping of the tip will ruin the fluttering action of the lure. Too fast, and you will lose touch with it until you retrieve it. The correct rate takes a little practice and know-how that comes only with experience.

FRESHWATER LOCATIONS

Finding striped bass in a large reservoir might at first seem like a difficult task. But if you know a bit about the fish—and we have already discussed the seasons—then you can begin eliminating a lot of the water by eliminating the other variables. Striped bass quickly fall into recognizable habits in a landlocked situation. They are schooling fish, even in fresh water, and they do like to move around a bit. However, there are certain environments which they prefer.

The drop-off is a typical bass cruising area. Here they can keep an eye on what is happening on the flats and watch out for any bait or larger fish that take off for the protection of deep water. Bass themselves feel skittish in shallow water and like to venture onto it only when they know that deep water is near at fin. The preferred depths seem to vary between 6 and 10 feet on a slope with water on the deeper side going down from 20 to 30 feet, or more. Follow such contours with a boat, mapping them on your chart or topo with the use of a fathometer. Drop a bucktail and bounce it along such slopes or troll a deep-running plug that can hug the bottom in 15 or more feet of water. As already stated, trolling a plug can be a problem in many reservoirs because of the submerged trees and brush, but there is no other way.

The other preferred bass residence is around old brush piles. From a topo that shows the bottom the way it was before the floods came,

The rapids on the Roanoke River near Weldon, N.C., have been a favorite river location for catching striped bass since the earliest colonial times. Striped bass migrate here from Pamlico Sound to spawn in the spring in the rapids just above Weldon.

you can almost pick good striped bass sites before you get there. Mark several on a map that look good, where old creek beds enter the main river, around old house and barn foundations, or along the edges of country roads that were lined with trees and shrubs. There are two simple methods for locating these spots you have marked on your chart and confirming that the brush is still there. The first is to have a sensitive fathometer on your boat that will record these, either on a paper graph or by flashing on a screen. The other is to make casts in the area with a heavy spoon or jig and sweep them until you snag or hang up. Ease your boat to the snag until you are directly over it and confirm it with your fathometer, then mark it on your map. Keep fishing the snag or brush pile while exploring and you are likely to get a striper.

During the colder times of the year, from December to the end of February, striped bass are likely to be off their feed and will not normally chase a lure far or run after a jig. For the most part, they have abandoned the shallows and are not around the brush piles. Instead, they have taken to deeper water where their body metabolism isn't affected quite as much as by the chilled upper waters. After 45 degrees, the world of a striped bass, even in fresh water, hasn't much activity.

Bass will feed, however, during these times of the year but on a modified dining plan and almost exclusively on bait. The best bait is cut herring or other baitfish that is fed slowly into the deeper spots of the reservoir. Search out the old riverbeds, and more often than not, the closer you are to the dam that impounds the reservoir, the better will be your chances.

Another idiosyncrasy of freshwater stripers is their preference for a certain depth in a particular reservoir when they are schooled and on the move. Of course, the depth that they choose will first be determined by what is available, but deeper reservoirs give them a wider range and more of a variable for you to solve. Roland Martin, who has fished both Santee-Cooper and Keystone reservoirs, has found that the bass will cruise between 15 and 25 feet searching for schools of baitfish. The prime zone appears to be between 20 and 25 feet but can vary, lower in deeper water and higher in shallower.

STRIPED BASS IN RIVERS

The striped bass throughout much of its distribution along Georgia, Florida, and the Gulf states often spends very little if any time in salt water. The fish has become landlocked of its own choice, though we'll never know if it ever really did go to sea in these sections of the nation. The striper here is a freshwater river fish and has been as long as Europeans have been in this land. And it reacts like most species, similar in habits and haunts to the white bass, white perch, and sauger.

There are two seasons for striper fishing, in the early spring, from February to April, and then again in the late fall, from November into December. The better of these is in the spring, soon after the bass have spawned. The location of the spawning sites is known and the angling concentrated on them or just downriver. In the rivers of Alabama, Mississippi, and Louisiana, striped bass are seldom fished for specifically but are taken incidentally while fishing for other species.

In several Georgia, South Carolina and North Carolina rivers, striped bass do constitute a major part of the spring fishery. Most of these fish, however, are not the purely fresh form. They have ready access to the sea and spend a part if not most of their lives in the estuary and along the shore. As one heads north from Georgia to South Carolina, this is even more true. The bass migrate up these streams when the time to spawn approaches. In South Carolina, these are basically estuary bass that migrate up the Santee and Cooper rivers, and a few lesser streams, to spawn at the sites of constrictive dams and return after their task is completed.

Another favorite freshwater river for striped bass is the Santee River. The Pinopolis Dam at Moncks Corners stops further upriver migration of bass. They spawn here in the spring and are taken by anglers fishing the discharges of the dam.

In North Carolina, this run is even more spectacular. The striped bass spend almost no time in the freshwater river except when they are about ready to spawn. Many spend summer, fall, and winter in the large bays as well as offshore. But as April approaches, the bass begin entering the rivers and will swim more than 100 miles to their primordial spawning sites. One of the best examples is the bass run on the Roanoke River near Roanoke Rapids. When the striper, or "rock," run is on, there is little parking room at the surrounding ramps and the many river channels are filled with boats and fishermen.

The best bait at this time is live minnows. The bass arrive often a few weeks prior to spawning, especially the younger males, and will feed up to the day they spawn. While they are spawning, they stop eating, but after a few days or even less, they resume their feeding. After the spawning takes place, the bass slowly drop downriver and by the middle of June they have abandoned the river to their fry.

PART THREE

TACKLE
FOR
STRIPED BASS

16

Rods, Reels, Lines, and Hooks

In 1869, Genio C. Scott's recommendation for a typical surfcasting outfit was a 9-to-9½-foot, rather stiff bamboo pole. And that is what was used on beaches until the late 1940s. I suspect, however, that anglers were always hoping better materials would come along, and when fiberglass appeared on the sporting scene, it revolutionized rod building and the thinking of a good many fishermen. At roughly the same time another important development took place: the introduction of spinning gear. This chapter will cover both traditional and modern bass-angling tackle.

RODS

Rods can be classified either according to type of fishing (surfcasting, boat fishing, etc.) or according to design (spinning, conventional, etc.). In the following discussion I will cover them from both points of view.

Surf rods

Today, surf rods have grown in length, some to as long as 15 feet, though most are a lot less. They can be divided into two general forms, depending upon the reels used: the spinning rod and the conventional surf rod. Spinning today has captured the imagination of almost every angler. Anyone beginning in the surf for the first time is more than likely to pick a spinning outfit, and most of the older beach regulars now tote one or more spinning rods along with their more conventional sticks.

Spincasting or spin-fishing or just plain spinning has grown rapidly because this system of reel, rod, and line is so easy to master. After just half an hour of instruction, a beginner can walk into the surf and seriously fish for striped bass — it is that easy. On the other hand, the conventional reel (also referred to as the free-spool reel, level-wind reel or bait-casting reel) takes weeks or months of practice before a fisherman can cast any great distance without fear of creating a bird's nest on the reel. Both types will be discussed separately below.

Surf rods, both spinning and conventional styles, can further be roughly divided into three classes — the lightweights, the medium rods, and the heavy stuff for big fish and big lures or baits. Light rods range from 7 to 8½ feet long, are easily worked with one or two hands, and are capable of tossing lures weighing 1½ to 2 ounces. They are equipped with lines ranging from 6 to 17 pounds in breaking strength.

Medium rods are a bit longer, between 9 and 9½ feet, with more power in the butt and with a somewhat stiffer tip so that the power imparted by the caster is not dissipated in the whip of the tip. Such rods easily handle lures between 2 and 3 ounces on line between 12 and 24 pounds in breaking strength.

Heavy rods are between 10 and 12 feet long. A few specialized rods are longer, but all in this class can be loaded with line up to 36 or 45 pounds in breaking strength. The lures they can toss range between 3 and 5 ounces. As you might imagine, some of these rods are real man-killers, used only under certain conditions, and by skilled fishermen.

Spinning and conventional rods differ in several ways. Most apparent is the size of the eyes or guides used for leading the line off the spools. On a spinning rod, the first eye is as large as the fixed spool on the reel. This is a standard construction principle. Then, there may be five to ten additional guides, diminishing in size as they approach the last or tiptop guide. In a spinning rod with a soft tip, more guides are needed so that the bent tip won't allow the line to slap. Slapping increases line friction and reduces the length of the cast. Too many guides, however, will ruin the action of the tip because of increased weight in that section of the rod.

On a conventional surf rod, the first eye or guide may have a diameter of ½ inch and the remaining three or four guides are all the same size but slightly less in diameter. More guides are not needed because of the somewhat stiffer nature of the conventional rod and the fact that the line comes off the reel in a relatively fixed position. As a result, a large first guide is not as important.

The butt section of either a spinning or conventional surf rod in the medium and heavier classifications is a two-handled affair. If the reel seat is fixed, the foregrip is then separated from the rear grip. In spinning rods, there is almost always a fixed reel seat, in the upper third of a 30-to-35-inch butt. On conventional butts, the reel seat may be no more than a pair of rings, or the reel is simply taped into the position that best fits the arm length of the fisherman.

Butt lengths average 31 to 32 inches. They must be fitted or picked for proper length when being selected, like the stock of a gun. A man with short arms will have difficulty casting a rod with a 34- or 35-inch butt. It is likely to stick him in the ribs with each cast. A good rule of thumb to remember when picking your rod is to match it to your sleeve size and you won't be too far off base.

Not only must a rod be matched to the bait or lures you are planning to cast, to the size line, and to the reel, but it must also be matched to your physical specifications and casting ability. A 5½-foot caster will have a tough time with a 12-foot rod, and a large man can overpower a 9-foot stick. Experience will be your best guide.

Almost all surf rods, either spinning or conventional, are constructed of tubular or hollow fiberglass. This material, given a minimum of protection and consideration, is almost indestructible. Butts are covered with specie cork or neoprene and come with chrome-plated brass or anodized aluminum reel seats. The first deterioration in a spinning rod is likely to be with the lines used to wrap the guides to the rod. If you coat them periodically with epoxy rod varnish, they will serve you a lot longer before the rod needs to be rewrapped.

The ideal surf rod is a one-piece stick. However, because long rods are difficult to travel with, or store at home, they are generally made in two-piece sections. The butt section runs entirely through the handle and is an integral part of the grip. In two-piece construction, the ferrule was formerly always constructed of chrome-plated materials, but more recently glass-to-glass connections have become popular. All-glass connections produce an almost perfect rod curvature; ferrule interference is so slight that it can be discounted.

Bank, pier, and jetty rods

The jetty rod can be either a spinning or a conventional rod, and it is nothing more than a shorter version of the type rods used in surfcasting. Adequate casting room is often a problem on jetties and shorter, snappier casts are called for, and thus the rod is shorter.

The jetty stick ranges between 6 and 7½ feet long for a conventional rod and between 6½ and 8 feet long for a spinning rod. Butt sections are shorter because of the tighter elbow room and range between 21 and 25 inches. The number of guides is likely to be reduced correspondingly, and the entire rod is somewhat stiffer, right to the tip, where the snap for such a cast receives most of its impetus after it leaves the wrists.

Most conventional rods for bank, pier, bridge, and dockside fishing are fairly stiff, short rods that are not called upon for great casting ability.

They are the typical bay or popping rods, 5 to 6 or even 7 feet long and equipped with a bait-casting or bay reel. They are used primarily for fishing live or cut bait and are as at home off the dock, pier, or bridge as over the gunwale of a boat.

Great action or response isn't a built-in characteristic of most popping rods, or rods designed for still-fishing from a boat. Sturdiness and an ability to handle a 4- or 5-ounce bank sinker and a big chunk of cut bait are the requirements. These rods are equipped with four or five guides with eyes made of chrome or stainless steel. The tiptop is made of tough tungsten carbide to withstand the cutting action of monofilament line. Most are designed for line classifications between 8 and 30 pounds.

The butt section is divided into grips, a smaller foregrip ahead of the fixed reel seat and a larger aftergrip. The butt is covered either with specie cork or neoprene. In less expensive models the butt is a hardwood, made of oak or hickory.

Boat rods

Rods for use in a boat vary greatly, from the spinning rods and conventional rods also found in the surf to the large trolling rods designed to handle large striped bass on 60-pound tackle. Between these extremes, we have specialized jigging rods and boat rods that are modified slightly from bank, pier, and bridge rods for use in a slightly more confined fishing area.

Spinning rods for boat fishing

The spinning rod reaches the height of its development when used for casting plugs and spoons from a boat because it is not required primarily to cast maximum distances. The typical spinning rod used in a boat is considerably shorter than the one used in the surf. Most noticeable is the reduced size of the butt—it may extend only 15 to 18 inches under the arm. Often it is also one-handed. Its overall length can vary between 7 and 9 feet but most are about 8½ feet long. The butt is equipped with a fixed reel seat and fore and aft butt grips of cork or rubber. In one-piece rods, the butt section is often removable, but a rod with the glass extending through and becoming a part of the handle has a better overall action.

A spinning rod used in a boat should be capable of throwing rather heavy striped bass plugs, lures weighing as much as 4 and 5 ounces. It is impossible to find one rod that can toss both small and large plugs equally well, so the properly equipped boat angler often will have two or three rods of different lengths and actions.

A boat spinning rod should have a fairly stout tip if it is used primarily for casting plugs. The added snap of the tip can put extra feet on every cast, whereas a willowy rod that is better suited for casting live bait will absorb some of the snap. Most spinning rods come with fixed reel seats of either anodized aluminum or chrome-plated steel or brass. The eyes are large wire or ring guides which match the spool of the reel being used.

Spinning rods for boats can be roughly divided into two classes according to length. The lighter group is composed of rods between 6 and 7½ feet long, and the heavier group of rods from 7½ to 8½ or even 9 feet long. Butt measurements vary from a minimum of 20 inches to a maximum of 25 inches. Smaller butts, even on longer rods, are somewhat preferred because of the limited space aboard a boat. Smaller spinning rods are often constructed with one grip section, with the after-butt construction typically that of a one-handed heavy freshwater rod.

Trolling rods

Trolling rods for striped bass generally fall into three classifications closely based on IGFA regulations for line-class distinctions. The lightest are 20-pound-class rods, and these, obviously, are equipped with reels loaded with 20-pound-test line. The midrange rods for striped bass fishing are 30-pound rods, and the heaviest are 50-pound rods. The last group is heavier than most sportfishing dictates. However, some charter-boat captains fish in crowded waters where tides run heavy and are forced into using heavy tackle to pull bass out of the rips and keep fighting time to a minimum. Rods in the 20- and 30-pound classes are nicely suited for trolling under most other conditions.

Most trolling rods are approximately 6¼ to 6½ feet long. A few may reach 7 feet. The butt section constitutes nearly 24 inches of the overall length and is built with a rather large foregrip, equal to or exceeding the after-grip section. The chrome-plated rod seats are fixed, and the butt is often detachable from the blade. The after section is exposed hardwood, and the foregrip is covered in specie cork or neoprene. The end of the butt is finished off with a cross-slotted gimbal nock.

The guide on a trolling rod closest to the reel (called the stripping guide) is usually equipped with double rollers through which the line is fed and controlled. Four hand-chromed stainless-steel ring guides run up the rod, and the tiptop guide is a roller guide to reduce wear on the line as it angles off the end of the rod.

Not all bass fishermen like to use such regulation rods. Some feel that the rollers occasionally jam the line at the most inappropriate times, though I have never had problems with them. Instead, they prefer rods with all eye guides, even on the tiptop.

The strain of heavier lures maintains a constant arch in trolling rods. The mate aboard Capt. Tom Wadsworth's sportfisherman Sunbeam *adjusts the third rod so that a full party can work the transom of his large boat.*

A variation of the regular trolling rod, one that handles either monofilament, Dacron, nylon, or lead-core lines, is the wire-line rod. This rod is used specifically for trolling with Monel, stainless-steel, or braided-wire lines. It is quite similar in construction to the standard trolling rod except that the roller guides are replaced with eye guides and all the guides are constructed of tungsten carbide, which is so tough that wire line cannot cut grooves into it.

A special kind of trolling rod has evolved for use with bucktailed jigs. This rod is worked with a jigging action from a moving boat. It has an extra resiliency that adds a bit of snap to the jigger's dance. Such a rod responds quickly to a pull and returns quickly to a straight position. It usually is equipped only with eye guides, though it may have a roller tiptop. Not many manufacturers carry or produce these rods, but nevertheless they bristle along the docks at Montauk. Most were made by a local maker, Johnny Kronuch, specifically for the charterboat skippers in the area.

There is another type of rod often used for vertical jigging in waters like Plum Gut and The Race, between Fishers Island and Gull Island. The rods are similar in construction to the trolled jigging rod but are often a bit shorter, 5 to 6½ feet long, and capable of working 30- or 40-pound-test lines.

REELS

Four types of reels are used in pursuit of the striped bass in addition to the fly-reel discussed previously in Chapter 12. By far the most popular seems to be the spinning reel, though actually trolling reels might run a close second if someone was capable of conducting an accurate survey. Reels for saltwater fishing differ from freshwater reels in but a few respects. Foremost among these is the materials used in their construction. A good saltwater reel must be resistant to the effects of salt. If it isn't, it is unlikely to last a season even with constant washing and care. Second, saltwater reels are generally larger than freshwater reels, both because the fish have more area in which to run when hooked and so require more line, and because saltwater fish are larger.

Spinning reels

The real value of a spinning reel lies in its ability to let a rod cast very light lures. On a conventional reel, the spool must revolve to let the line off and thus drag is increased on the line and the casting distance is reduced. On a spinning reel, the spool is fixed and the line spills off the end and out the guides, reducing friction considerably.

Spinning reels. Five size classes of spinning reels are available to striped bass anglers. From left to right: an ultralight reel, basically freshwater in design but corrosion-resistant and suitable for small or schoolie striped bass; a reel that is about the size of a standard freshwater reel and will work in many boat and bank situations; a special saltwater-size reel used for spinning from boats and light surfcasting; a standard surfcasting reel, for rods 8 to 10 feet long, and also found in use in many jetty situations; and finally a large reel used primarily with the longest saltwater rods and heavy lines and lures.

Since the spool on a spinning reel is fixed, another device must do the work of putting or laying line back onto the spool. This device is a bail, an arm that is flipped into place and guides the line onto the spool as it revolves about the outside of the spool.

Not only can lighter lures be used with spinning reels but lighter lines as well. And the lighter the line, the longer the cast. Another feature of the spinning reel is that there is no strain on the line once the forward pull of the lure has stopped. This means that the line will not continue to spill off, as it will with conventional reels. This has a secondary application. The beginning caster need not learn that fine point where he must apply pressure to stop the line and yet not cut short his cast, as he must with conventional equipment.

A drag mechanism holds the spool rigid and keeps it fixed. Though the spool is fixed when compared to the conventional reel, it can slip or give when intense pressure is applied to it — pressure that is greater than that exerted by the brake shoe or the spring-loaded mechanism that keeps it from revolving. These drags can be set extremely fine and they release in a very smooth operation, giving the spinning reel an exceptional drag for fighting fish on light tackle. This too has helped beginning anglers catch fish that they might have lost with other types of equipment.

The amount of drag is controlled by a knurled knob on the spool. This setting controls the drag tension only for that spool and is set at a slipping point under the breaking strength of the line. With pushbutton removable spools, the drag need not be reset each time; the setting stays intact with the transfer. In other spinning reels, the drag is set in the back of the reel and pressure is applied via a shoe to the gears or the shaft upon which the spool will be allowed to rotate. Both are effective.

The rate of retrieve — that is, how much line is added back onto the spool with one turn of the handle — is fixed in spinning reels and is determined by the ratio of the gears inside the reel. Larger reels usually have a smaller ratio because they deal in heavier strains. A 2.5:1 or a 2:1 ratio is rather standard. In medium and smaller spinning reels a faster retrieve is often desired because the spool diameter and the reel handle are smaller. In order to make lures work at normal speeds through the water, a higher gear ratio is often needed, anywhere from 3:1 to 5.5:1. But what you gain in speed, you lose in power, and so the higher ratios require more effort from the angler.

Spinning reels can be divided into five classifications based on overall size and the diameter of the spool. The smallest group is composed of the ultralight reels that match ultralight rods designed for freshwater fishing or school-sized striped bass under controlled conditions.

A slightly larger spool and reel characterizes the next class. This size is the standard found on most well-balanced freshwater spinning outfits. This size is readily adaptable to saltwater fishing. If the reel is made of corrosion-resistant materials it can be used in either environment. In salt water, this size reel is typically used in bank and pier situations when fishing with bait and light lures, especially small bucktails, and in boats on small striped bass.

The third class is the standard size found in most saltwater-spinning situations. It is often the same model as the freshwater reel we just described but slightly larger. The bigger reel is needed to provide the extra line required for saltwater species, as well as a large spool to match the larger eyes on a somewhat larger rod that is the typical plugging rod used on boats and in some bank and pier situations. This reel has a spool that will take 300 yards of 12-pound-test line. The spool is typically released by a pushbutton so that it can easily be replaced with a spool loaded with lighter or heavier line.

Almost all models and sizes of reels, except the large surfcasting varieties, come with both shallow and deep spools. The shallow spools are used with lighter-test line which would not fill a deep spool properly unless hundreds of unneeded yards of line were laid on. On reel models without shallow spools, a false arbor is often provided—one that slips over the axle of the spool and partially fills it. The line is then laid upon this filler device.

For the moment, let us skip the fourth class of spinning reels and go on to the largest class, the big spinning reels that are found in the surf. This class is almost exclusively for surfcasting because it matches the 10-to-12-foot rods, some even larger, that are used in a high surf to toss a large lure or chunk of bait to the outer bar. There is little place and little need for such a large reel on a boat. But in a big surf, when heavy lines are used, the reel must be large enough so that an adequate amount of line can be spooled. The reel is heavy, even when constructed of the lighter materials, and when it is coupled to a big rod, the total outfit can be a lot to maneuver.

The fourth class of reels are often the same model as the fifth class, the large surf reels, but are reduced in size and can be matched to intermediate surf rods. The largest stick is not always the most appropriate stick for the surf. In many plugcasting situations, you don't need to reach the outer bar, and a smaller rod and a smaller reel are called for. In addition, a smaller outfit is often better for shorter men. In a jetty situation, where the overall spinning outfit should be reduced, class-four reels and intermediate rods are perfect.

This class constitutes the largest number of reels found in the surf. Like most reels below it in size, it contains a pushbutton spool, while class-five reels often lack this device. This means that you must switch reels when you want to change to a different line test.

Conventional surf reels

The conventional reel for surf is a specialized form of the bait-casting reel, which has a revolving spool. It has been called the free-spool reel, the multiplying reel, and the level-wind reel, all descriptions of one of the reel's characteristics. The original surf reel was nothing more than a larger version of the freshwater bait-casting reel. It possessed no gears between the spool and the reel handle that would increase the retrieve ratio and had no drag but the thumb applied to the spool. The first innovation was to add gears so that for each turn of the reel handle, the spool might turn two or three times. Today, most conventional surf reels are built with a 4:1 or 3:1 ratio of retrieve.

On a cast, the engaged gears would slow down the revolution of the spool, and thus some device was needed to disengage the gears while casting. On most freshwater bait-casting reels the handle still spins while the gears are engaged. In the modern surf reel, the gears are disengaged by throwing the handle of a clutch and the reel is in free-spool. But a reel with no pressure on it can create a lot of backlashing, and the caster's thumb had to apply pressure at the correct time to stop the spool the instant the forward momentum of the lure and line fell to zero.

Built-in drags have been developed — counterbalances in some reels, magnetic devices in others, even air brakes in the form of fins on still others. For the most part, they are quite effective. Backlashes, however, still happen, and the reels must be finely adjusted at all times to make their anti-backlash mechanisms function properly.

The better-designed squidding reel, as a conventional reel is often called (a carry-over from the days when fishing in the surf began with squid and squid lines), is shallow and wide. This design allows line on the spool to spread and not pile or bury itself when a big fish runs. The line is laid back and forth with the thumb or by a level-wind device that moves back and forth across the spool, distributing line evenly as it moves.

Drag on these reels is controlled by a star-shaped lever on the side and a part of the reel handle. The drag works only when the clutch is engaged and when line is pulled out, not when it is reeled in. There can be an infinite number of settings with the star drag, and over the years it has proved to be an extremely hardy and functional drag in the surf.

A well-designed conventional reel should also have a quick and easy take-down so that it can be readily cleaned when out of the surf. One-screw designs are almost standard. The anti-reverse mechanism should be controllable by the caster so he can switch it on or off. Ball bearings have become standard and add smoothness to the spools. Spools can be constructed of either plastic or metal. Plastic spools work best with mono-filament lines, which when tightly wrapped on a reel can exert fantastic

A collection of conventional reels. The one on the right is for surfcasting and the other three for bay fishing. Bay-fishing reels are also called popping reels and used with popping rods for fishing from boats, bridges, piers, and banks where very little casting is needed. The conventional surfcasting reel has an adjustable antibacklash device, but an educated thumb is also required to get the maximum distance from every cast.

pressures on the spools. Metal spools under such strain can actually break or become warped. When using braided Dacron or nylon lines, metal spools are sufficient.

Bait-casting reels

The freshwater bait-casting reel has easy application in salt water if the reel is constructed of materials that can withstand the effects of salt on the metal. The simplest reels, used in boat- and bank-fishing situations, possess a simple star drag and a click that warns the fisherman that the line is going out when the reel is in free-spool. They are capable of holding from 100 to 200 yards of 15-pound-test line.

Most saltwater versions of the bait-casting reel do not have level-wind devices, and saltwater fishermen have come to thumb their line as a matter of course. Level-wind features add to the cost of the reel and increase the number of parts which could be affected by corrosion. Often called the bay reel, this simple version of the bigger trolling reels is fished off rather short rods, 5 to 6 or 6½ feet long. It is designed for boat or bank fishing from a somewhat sedentary stand. The line falls to the bottom with the reel in free spool, with the thumb on the spool to add pressure to stop it once the sinker reaches its destination. The clutch is then engaged and the drag set light enough so that a fleeing striped bass can strip out line until the angler is ready to pick up the rod.

Within the bait-casting or bay-reel group is another form designed almost entirely for use with monofilament lines. Monofilament is a little more difficult to spool evenly with a thumb on a small reel, so the need for a level-wind mechanism is greater. This reel contains all the features of the squidder, the bay, and even the larger trolling reels. It includes a gear ratio of 2.5:1 or 3:1, a clutch for engaging or disengaging the spool, a star drag for uniform resistance, and large handles for easy grasping and winding in wet situations. However, instead of a wide spool it has a narrow but deep spool. This allows the fisherman to add line quickly to the spool and build up a diameter at a fast pace. The increased diameter has the effect of changing the mechanical ratio and makes retrieving quicker.

Still another variation of this reel is the jigging reel. It has all the same characteristics as other saltwater conventional reels but has a narrow spool, an increased gear ratio of 4:1, and an increased handle length to increase the fisherman's mechanical advantage and compensate for the high gear ratio. Such a reel is matched to a special jigging rod.

This form of jigging does not involve the use of a bucktailed jig worked while the boat is being trolled. Instead a heavy diamond jig is fished off the bottom while the boat is drifting over deep water. The diamond jig is free-spooled to the bottom and then quickly retrieved for the first 15 or 20 feet. It is jigged a few times and then slipped into free-spool. The lure is again allowed to drop to the bottom, then again quickly retrieved when it hits. This constant up-and-down motion, at a fast retrieve, attracts striped bass. The larger gear ratio and the long handle on the reel makes this form of jigging easier.

Trolling reels

Reels used for trolling are modified versions of the simple conventional reel. Many features have been added but the basic design and principles are still almost the same as when the reels first appeared over a hundred years ago. The bigger trolling reels have been altered to handle larger fish, stronger lines, and heavier lures. There are more than a dozen different sizes of trolling reels, ranging from 1/0 to 16/0. For the most part they vary only in size and line capacity.

Not all of the numerous sizes of trolling reels are practical for striped bass fishing. The small reels, from 1/0 to 3/0, are extremely light, designed for small fish or for records, and probably only the 3/0 finds any use by striped bass fishermen. The 3/0 is capable of holding approximately 350 yards of 30-pound-test Dacron or 375 yards of 30-pound-test monofilament.

The 4/0 and 6/0 reels are better suited because of their larger size, drags that can withstand the powerful rush of a big bass in a roaring rip, and larger line capacity. Both 4/0 and 6/0 are considered light reels with respect to big-game fishing but they are the top of the line for the striped bass. A 4/0 will load approximately 450 yards of 30-pound-test Dacron, and 800 yards of 20-pound-test or 500 yards of 30-pound-test monofilament. The larger 6/0 reel is capable of holding 400 yards of 50-pound-test Dacron, and 1,050 yards of 20-pound-test, 650 yards of 30-pound-test, or 415 yards of 50-pound-test monofilament.

Seldom, however, is all this line used when trolling for striped bass. On a typical wire-line outfit, 100 or 200 yards of 30-, 40-, or 60-pound-test wire is spooled onto 200 or 300 yards of 30- or 50-pound-test Dacron as backing.

Trolling reels are essentially bait-casting reels modified for handling more line and heavier fish. For the striped bass, they vary in size from 3/0 to 6/0. Illustrated here from left to right: 4/0 Penn 209 with level-wind device and used primarily with monofilament, 4/0 Garcia Mitchell 624, and 6/0 Penn Senator. The preferred size for smaller bass boats is 4/0; the larger reels are for big game, heavy water, and heavy line.

On most trolling reels, the star drag or dragging device is still on the handle of the reel. In a few more costly trolling reels, the drag is a separate lever adjusted along the wall of the reel and calibrated with settings that don't always seem to hold true after being exposed to salt water for a while.

LINES

At one time, the saltwater fisherman was restricted to the use of cotton and linen lines as his only connection between hook and reel. The famous Cuttyhunk linen lines were standard for years. But linen lines had a tendency to rot when not properly dried, were inconsistent in strength, and changed in strength when wet or dry.

Not until the development of synthetic fibers, like nylon and Dacron, and eventually monofilament, was the fisherman freed from a woe of troubles. Heavy lines and undependable breaking points were all but eliminated. Nylon lines were the first on the scene. Braided nylon made a strong line with a fairly small diameter. It was quickly put to use by surfcasters using conventional reels. But nylon has a great amount of elasticity or stretch, and sometimes it was difficult to feel a fish or set the hook if you had a lot of line in the surf.

After nylon came Dacron, another synthetic fiber, and it was an improvement with even greater strength in relation to the diameter and less stretch than nylon. Dacron today is the preferred fiber for braided line. It is as popular as monofilament, a single strand of plastic line that has all but revolutionized casting and trolling. Today, both braided Dacron and monofilament are widely used. Though they have somewhat different characteristics, neither is truly superior to the other. It becomes a matter of personal choice and line application.

Monofilament lines

Monofilament lines are formed by drawing the fluid plastic material through a series of dies, each diminishing in diameter until the correct size and corresponding strength test is reached. The result is a fiber with a smooth surface, one that offers little resistance to guides and has an extremely small diameter but great strength. It therefore has become one of the chief lines used for spinning and spin-casting.

Monofilament lines also offer less resistance in the water than braided nylon or Dacron lines, and where a deeper-running line is desired it has a slight advantage over other lines. There is an inherent elasticity in monofilament lines, and when they were first produced, the stretch was so great that they were shunned by many trollers. But as the manufacturers brought stretch under reasonable control, the line was quickly adapted to casting and later even to trolling.

A certain amount of stretch is desirable, especially when a big fish strikes a lure going in the opposite direction. The stretch acts as a shock absorber and softens the force before the line approaches its breaking point. Too much stretch, however, will prevent the fisherman from feeling what the fish on the other end of the line is doing. It will make him strike a fish too late and in some cases make the setting of the hook difficult if not impossible.

Monofilament lines also have a "memory." If they are wound under pressure on a reel and allowed to stand, they uncoil with large loops that may foul if constant pressure is not always maintained. This memory also acts in a direction with the circumference of the line and will cause twisting if tension is not regularly relieved. Most anglers use high-quality swivels to allow the lure to swim or twist freely and not turn the line while doing so.

Monofilament lines are produced in the greatest variety of tests available, 13 classifications in all: line tests of 2, 4, 6, 8, 10, 12, 15, 20, 25, 30, 40, 50, and 60 pounds. Occasionally some odd strengths creep into the market, like 17- or 27-pound-test. These are usually lines that were designed for a higher or lower test but worn dies or other variable factors during production altered the specific diameter, and rather than destroy the lines, the manufacturer labels them correctly and places them on the market.

Dacron lines

While stretch can be controlled in monofilament lines, it is better controlled in braided-Dacron lines. Many dedicated trollers feel that a Dacron line is better suited to setting the hook and that the feel is maintained down to the mouth of the fish. On the other hand, because it is braided, Dacron will fray more easily than monofilament and thus will not last as long. Dacron line is also more expensive than monofilament. However, it is easier to work, and most big-game fishermen prefer it for tournament fishing.

Braided-Dacron lines usually correspond to the IGFA line groupings or classifications and come spooled in 50-to-1,200-yard quantities. There are eight classes of strength: 6, 12, 20, 30, 50, 80, 130, and 162 pounds.

Nylon lines

Nylon lines, still in production today, are often called squidding lines, replacing the cotton and linen first used in the surf. They are made of high-tenacity nylon that creates a smooth, flat, and supple line. The line's stretch can be controlled and then set with special heat devices during the winding. At the same time, special braided-in silicone lubricants are added to help eliminate internal friction in a line, and a special waterproofing reduces water absorption. Squidding lines come in numerous test strengths: 12, 18, 27, 36, 54, 63, 72, 90 and 110 pounds.

Lead-core lines

When you must go deeper than Dacron, nylon, or monofilament lines allow, and still don't want to adorn your terminal end with sinkers, you can switch to a lead-core line. The line is a hollow braided-nylon outer shell that surrounds a supple lead wire or strand in the center. It handles easily on trolling reels. Most lead-core lines are marked every 10 yards by changing the color of the nylon sheath. Lead-core lines are produced in coils of 100 or 200 yards and come in four strength classifications: 18, 25, 40, and 60 pounds.

Wire lines

Wire lines for trolling are used when the bass are deep and no other lines can get down without the addition of cumbersome lead weights. Wire has less stretch than any other type of line, and the feel you get is immediately transferred along the length of the line. The first wire lines were copper and were used for freshwater fishing, but because copper's tensile strength is low it had to be braided. Today, little copper wire is used in salt water, but a steel version of braided line is available. Braided steel line is especially strong for its small diameter size. However, the braiding increases resistance in the water, and the lines do not sink as deeply as single strands of stainless steel or Monel (an alloy).

Both stainless-steel and Monel wire are popular among striped bass fishermen, and it is difficult to state which might be the more favored. Stainless-steel wire is a bit more difficult to handle than Monel because it possesses a stronger "memory." Its tendency to coil is less pronounced in the lighter test wires and is used more often on these levels. Heavier tests are more apt to be Monel, a somewhat more supple wire.

Twist is not allowable with wire lines, and therefore they must be used with the best swivels or the line will fatigue and part unexpectedly. Wear spots in wire cannot be spotted as they can in monofilament or Dacron. If uncoiled improperly, wire will kink and the breaking strength of the line will be reduced by as much as 90 percent where these kinks occur. If a kink is unwound in the same direction it was created, it can be eliminated. This is easier to accomplish in Monel than in stainless steel.

A constant strain or pressure must be kept at all times on wire line when getting it into the water or when retrieving it to keep coils from forming. This is especially true of the more springy stainless-steel lines. Few reels are spooled entirely with wire; a heavier backing line, like 30- or 50-pound-test Dacron, is used to build up the diameter and then 100 or 200 yards of wire are added. I like to add small, high-quality swivels to my wire trolling lines. I place them at the 100-, 200-, and 250-foot marks and can tell how much wire is in the water simply by counting the swivels as they pass out. I have tried painting each swivel with red, white, and blue enamel paints but it seems to wear too quickly. At night, swivels make the task of marking the line much easier than colored tapes. The feel alone is often enough, and they can be heard as they rattle going through the guides.

In many instances, wire line is preferred when fishing for striped bass. The top illustrations show how to attach the line to the backing with a barrel swivel. The closeup shows a barrel swivel connecting two lengths of wire line. The proper "knot," the haywire twist, begins by evenly wrapping one line around the other. Swivels not only reduce kinking and eliminate twist, but also serve as permanent line length-markers to tell you how much line you are trolling. It's a good idea to mark the test strength of the line and its capacity on the side of the reel with plastic labels.

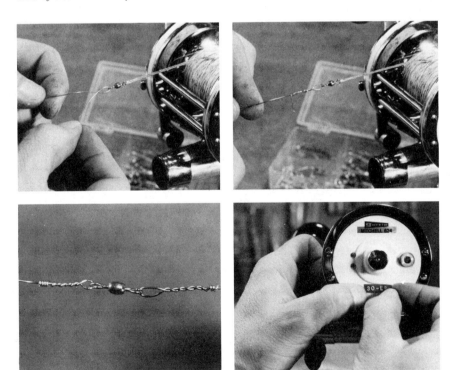

Many anglers use colored plastic tape to mark the differing lengths on their wire but I have had difficulty trying to keep them in position. With swivels in the line, you know your measurements haven't changed. There is also the added feature of the swivels eliminating any twist a bad lure or spinning fish might put in the line. Seldom does kinking or coiling become a problem when swivels are used in the line.

The International Game Fish Association will not recognize as records fish that are taken on wire lines. I fail to see the reasoning for this. A wire line is just as sporting as a Dacron or monofilament line. It works better to get lines down deep than the addition of drails or diving planes. A 40-pound-test wire line will break at 40 pounds of pressure just as a 40-pound-test nylon, Dacron, or monofilament line breaks.

In many crowded fishing situations, where you must troll close to the boat as well as deeply behind it, wire line is the only answer to catching fish. In areas where striped bass seldom come to the surface, few other lines can be used, and here again, wire line is the answer. In areas where rocks and barnacles make the ultimate landing of a hooked bass difficult, wire line again is the only answer. It's not unsporting, and it is far more sound in conservation terms than lines which would part with hooked fish.

Leaders

Leaders are terminal strands of line used between the main body of line and the snap, swivel, and hook on the very end. Leader material consists of either wire or monofilament, and it is used for one of two reasons. In the case of Dacron, nylon, and wire line, the terminal leader is usually a strand of clear monofilament. It is used where the sight of the main line might alarm fish or make them suspicious of the lure or bait. In this case, the leader is a level piece of monofilament, often considerably heavier in breaking strength than the main line so that it can resist abrasion or cutting by fish other than striped bass. When monofilament is used as the main line, the leader is simply another piece of much heavier monofilament.

In other situations, where bluefish and other fishes equipped with sharp teeth are apt to occur with the striped bass, and when fishing and trolling around rocky areas and those encrusted with barnacles, a 2-to-10-foot piece of stainless-steel wire is used as the terminal section of a line. It can be smaller in diameter than the main body of line and still be stronger than the rest of the rig. Wire resists abrasion better than much heavier monofilament, and where the presence of the wire will not alarm bass, it is the preferred leader material.

KNOTS

There are hundreds of knots that a fisherman can use at one time or another in maintaining his tackle. But for the most part, he can get by with six or seven. The form of knot to use is first determined by the line material. Knots in monofilament won't always hold in Dacron, and vice-versa. A knot is the weakest part in your line; if the line tests out at 20 pounds then you know that any knot tied in it will break at less than that. The fewer knots in your line the better. How and where you tie them can measurably affect the maximum size of the fish you can fight, so it pays to know the right knots and their best application.

The most efficient knot you can use in tying monofilament to hooks and swivels, and in some cases to other lines, is a jam-type knot called the clinch knot. There are a few variations, the improved and the double clinch knot, and all work well. This group of knots is one of the strongest you can tie and lessens the line's breaking strength by the least amount.

The blood knot is a variation of the clinch knot, a clinch tied on a clinch, and works well when tying two pieces of monofilament together or when tying one of slightly larger diameter to another. In tying two monofilament lines of greatly different diameter, the lighter line can be doubled for added strength and clinching ability. When their respective diameters are still too great, then you can switch to a surgeon's knot. This is the knot often used when tying lead-core line to a leader.

With Dacron or nylon lines, the last 15 feet are usually doubled for strength and wear resistance and the swivel is attached to the end by a simple Bimini hitch. In cases where wire and monofilament and Dacron must be joined, a swivel is a better bet than a knot. The backing is attached to one side of the swivel with the Bimini hitch and the wire to the other eye of the swivel with a hairwire twist. The hairwire twist must be evenly twisted by both strands of the wire and not simply one wire wrapped around the other. The end of the twist is finished off in a twist and then its free end is removed with a crank. The crank fatigues the wire immediately next to the twist and does not leave sharp edges on which to cut your fingers.

When finishing off monofilament knots, especially when using a clinch knot on heavy lines, the line should be cut fairly close to the knot to avoid "Irish pennants." The line might pull through if not jammed completely or cut this short. However, it can be secured by taking a match and melting the tip of the free line to form a small ball of monofilament. This will harden, increase the size of the line on the tip, and never pull through the jam. Caution should be used to keep the flame away from the rest of the knot or it will be weakened.

Useful knots for the striped bass fisherman.

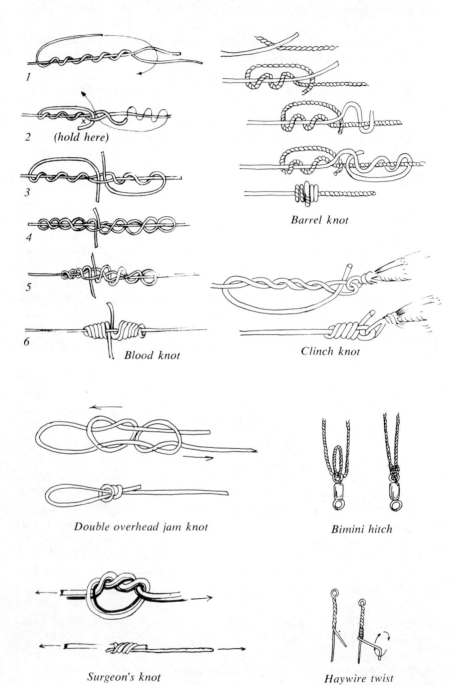

1

2   (hold here)

3

4

5

6

Blood knot

Barrel knot

Clinch knot

Double overhead jam knot

Bimini hitch

Surgeon's knot

Haywire twist

Some lures, especially plugs, will have their action hindered if the knot does not allow the eye to swing freely. In this case, a double overhand knot is jammed together to form a sliding loop. This knot is not as strong as the clinch knot, but if a clinch knot will affect the swimming action of a plug, it must be substituted for the double overhand loop knot.

SNAPS AND SWIVELS

Terminal tackle is often the weakest link in the line that fishermen throw into the water. Other than knots, it should receive the closest attention. The connection between line and lure or hook can be made directly. But in the case of some lures, they are likely to twist and thus weaken the line. In other cases, you may want to change lures quickly without a lot of knot-tying and the snap is your answer. Snaps and swivels come in combination or separately and in a great variety of shapes as well as sizes.

Snaps and swivels can influence the action of your lure if they are too large. Too often, I have seen snaps and swivels used for striped bass that would have held a giant tuna with ease. Don't use snaps or swivels any larger than the anticipated fish require. They should be kept small and unobtrusive for effectively enticing fish to bite. Even the smallest snaps and swivels test out at great strength, often far greater than the lines used.

For heavy trolling lures, the ordinary barrel swivel should not be used. Instead small swivels with minute ball bearings are available, and though they are somewhat on the expensive side, they will ensure that your lure swims properly and protect your line from excessive twisting. Other swivels are simply eyes with expanded ends encased inside a barrel housing. The two eyes are separate and revolve against the inside walls of the barrel. Snaps come in several shapes: lock snaps, safety snaps, Pompanette snaps, Coast lock, and McMahon snap. Each has its place and preference.

Swivels range in size — 12, 10, 7, 5, 3, 1, 2/0, 4/0 from smallest to largest — and vary in test from 20 to 350 pounds breaking strength. Thus, even the No. 10 swivel is large enough to handle the needs of most striped bass outfits. The size swivel should slightly exceed the strength test of the line you are using.

In cases where a lure and sinker must have separate leaders, then a three-way swivel is in order. These too vary greatly in size and strength and are available from No. 8, the smallest, through 6, 4, 2, 1/0, and 3/0, the largest. Even larger snaps and swivels are made for such specialized fishing as marlin, tuna, and swordfish and constitute still another class of swivels and sizes.

Snaps and swivels.

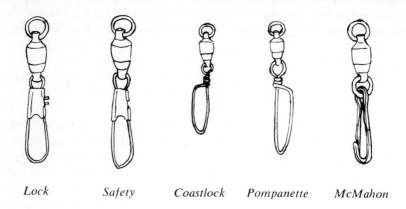

Lock   Safety   Coastlock   Pompanette   McMahon

SIZE AND TEST

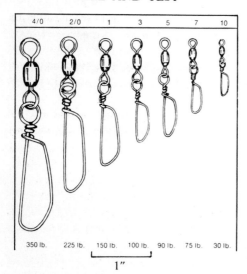

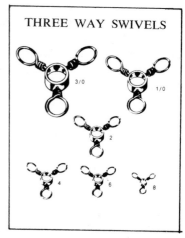

LEAD AND SINKERS

Even the most sophisticated striped bass fisherman must at one time
or another resort to fishing with lead if he wants to catch fish. If he is
dedicated to using nothing but a spinning rod and lures, he may never
reach this point, but then he may not be able to catch bass whenever he
wants to. To the versatile angler, there are times to fish on the bottom

and times to troll. To get you into these situations effectively, you may have to use lead, the universal weight. Our lead sinkers are seldom pure lead—rather a combination of lead and tin, with occasional other metals added that help it flow into molds and maintain its shape. Shapes are quite important.

The surfcaster appreciates the value of a lead sinker while fishing with bait in a running surf. Here a pyramid sinker is about the only way he can hold bottom and put his rod in a holder for a time to rest his arms. Pyramid sinkers come in 1-to-6-ounce weights. The line or snap is attached by a wire molded into the base. This means that any pull applied at right angles to the square base causes its edges to dig in and resist the pull. Pyramid sinkers are ideal when used with a fish-finder that allows the bait and line to run through an eye while the line is tethered and guided to the bottom until the strike occurs.

For anchoring by virtue of sheer weight, a bank or dipsy sinker is best. Because of their smooth shape and form, they are also good bets when trying to hold bottom among rocks and offer less opportunity for the lead to lodge in a crack or crevice. Ball or egg-shaped sinkers with holes through their centers can be used in the surf when it isn't moving quickly or in the bay and quiet areas where it won't be rolled about by a current. This type of sinker functions a lot like a pyramid sinker except that the line is allowed to pass freely through the sinker, and carried off by a fish. The weight of the sinker isn't noticed by the fish until the angler sets the hook.

Split shot or simple pieces of round lead partially sliced are the choice to add to your line when only small amounts of weight are needed.

Sinker styles, left to right: dipsy, bank, pyramid, barrel, and two trolling drails with beaded chain. One drail has a keel to discourage it from twisting while trolled.

They are directly attached to the line somewhere above the hook. Split shot shouldn't be clamped on too firmly or the pinching will weaken the strength of the line.

Drails are lead weights shaped in the form of a torpedo, mounted on beaded chains and used specifically when trolling. The beads allow the line or drail to rotate independently of each other and thus the line is not twisted. The front of the drail is usually equipped with an eye and the end with a snap. Some drails have slight keels on one side so that they will not twist when trolled. Other drails are even kidney-shaped to achieve this same no-spin feature. Drails come in weights from 1/2 ounce to 6 and 7 ounces, with intermediate weights in the 1/2-ounce increments.

HOOKS

The final link between fisherman and fish is the hook, and this little item deserves the utmost attention from the angler. There are scores of hooks

Hook sizes, shown life size. Hooks used should be appropriate for the size of the fish you are catching or intend to catch. For striped bass they range from

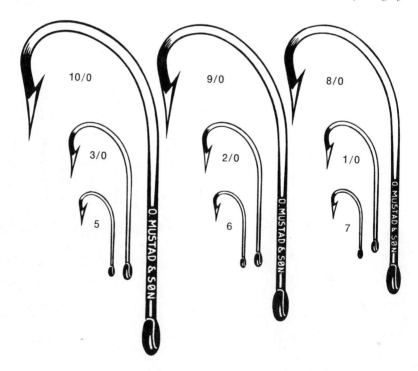

to choose from, each designed for a special task and each suited to the mouth of a particular species of fish or a type of bait. Not only is shape important, but the size is equally vital to a successful hookup.

There are 30 to 40 sizes in hooks, ranging from No. 22, the smallest, up to 16/0. If you want larger hooks, I'm sure that you can get them beyond the 16/0. Unfortunately, hook manufacturers don't all agree on the code number and hook sizes and so those used are often relative suggestions. A No. 3/0 by one manufacturer might be two or three sizes larger on the scale of another.

There are almost as many patterns for hook shapes as there are hook sizes, but here the striped bass angler is rather fortunate because only about three are ideally suited for striped bass fishing. These include the Siwash hook, best suited for trolling and hooking a following striped bass; O'Shaughnessy hook, well suited to a striped bass's underhung mouth and used on plugs and spoons; and the Eagle Claw or beak bend, used with bait, both live and cut. This latter is often equipped with barbs on the shaft to hold bait.

as small as No. 4 for schoolies to 10/0 for "cow" bass.

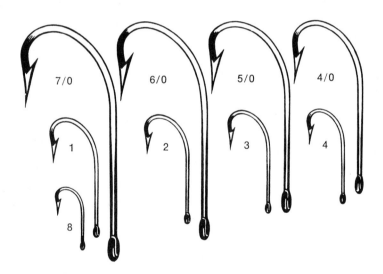

Bass hook sizes range from a small of 2/0 or 3/0, for school-sized stripers (fish up to 8 or 10 pounds), to the 10/0 and 12/0 hooks found on bunker spoons and large trolled lures. In a fair medium position are hooks in the 6/0 to 8/0 range. You can vary or adjust the hook size to the size of the fish you are taking. A complete bass angler is often equipped with a collection of hooks in sizes and shapes in his tackle box.

Treble hooks also find their way into the striped bass fisherman's box and are often the hooks adorning his plugs and spoons. Some live bait is better hooked on a treble than a single point, and every angler should be equipped with a variety of sizes. Hook shape is not quite as important in the treble as in the single hook, and the greater majority of plugs come equipped with Eagle Claw or Sprout treble hooks.

Treble hook eyes or rings come in three possible forms. The most common used on factory-made lures is the solid eye, with the shafts of the hooks brazed together. There is the open-ringed hook, where one of the shafts of a hook is not attached to the other two along their shafts and the snap on the line is run over the one free hook. Finally, there is the open-ringed hook, with an open eye that is closed with pliers after it is added to a ring.

Hooks come in bronze, stainless steel, and annealed iron, and plated with gold, nickel, cadmium, and tin. Cadmium plating is the best protection on large hooks. For saltwater use, insist that your hooks be stainless steel, nickel, or cadmium-plated. Otherwise, the lures won't be worth using more than once. Hooks that go into salt water, even if you wash them, quickly rust away unless they are made of the less corrosive materials.

Hook styles, left to right: Eagle Claw or beak-type with bait-holding barbs, same style but without bait barbs, Siwash, and O'Shaughnessy. At far right, fish-finder snap and swivel.

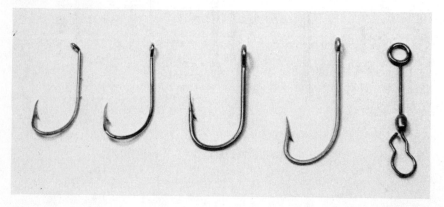

17
Live and Natural Baits
for Striped Bass

Natural marine baits account for a great number of stripers, from small, school-sized bass to those behemoths affectionately called bulls and cows by many anglers. Natural bait is an important part of fishing for striped bass and the angler who masters its use and presentation can take striped bass while purists whistle in the wind. Every well-rounded bass fisherman should be as familiar with the great variety of natural marine baits as he is with the great variety of artificial lures that will take bass.

There is a certain snobbishness about some anglers who swear by the plug and the rod and never seem to condescend to the use of live bait. I'm sure that part of this attitude is more the result of ignorance with natural baits and how to use them. Too often, live- or cut-bait fishermen are referred to as sinker bouncers. But presenting a live bunker or mackerel to a big bass waiting behind a boulder while stemming a 6-knot tide requires just as much skill as balancing on a boulder in the surf or fighting a headwind while on the proximal end of a fly rod.

The really serious striped bass fisherman who employs live bait when it is appropriate often knows as much about the bait he is using as the fish he is after. He should, because the lives of striped bass and the foods it eats are intimately entwined. To study one without any knowledge of the other is like wearing a set of blinders through life.

Thus fishing with live bait can be extremely challenging both physically and mentally, and often produces more striped bass than artificial lures. And if it is large striped bass you are after, just check the records. Almost all the big bass have been taken on natural marine baits, alive or rigged. There are certain times of the year when striped bass are vulnerable only to big baits, and many of the artificial lures just aren't large enough and do not swim well enough to entice a striped bass.

The striped bass is an omnivorous feeder. It will eat almost anything alive in the ocean. As a result, there is a horde of baits that can be threaded onto a hook or added to the water that will bring a striper to feed. These baits can roughly be divided into four biological divisions: the marine worms; mollusks, or clams, mussels, and squid; crustaceans, or shrimp, crabs, and lobsters; and the vertebrate fishes, including killifish, spearing, real eels, menhaden, sculpins (bullheads on the West Coast), and a list of game fish in small or large sizes that include mackerel, whiting, blackfish, bluefish, and weakfish.

Most of these baits can be found in our bays and estuaries, or in the inshore seas. They are found in the sand, over mud beaches, along the banks of tidal streams, and in the marine grasses from deep water to the intertidal zone. Some are in the swift water of the estuary outlet, while others are true pelagic fishes and you must seek them in deeper water beyond the barrier beaches and tidal rips. Most you can buy from a seafood store or a coastal bait shop. But for the most part, you can dig or net them yourself or set traps to collect them in large enough numbers to begin fishing.

WORMS

The three worms that interest the striped bass are strictly marine in their habitat and include the sandworm, bloodworm, and "tapeworm." The first two are annelids—members of a phylum of segmented animals generally called worms by most people and including the famous garden hackle, true tapeworms, and a host of marine worms. The "tapeworm" is really a ribbonworm and belongs to another phylum. Marine worms are more popular than any other bait and take a great percentage of striped bass. One reason is that they are so easy to dig or buy, are easy to fish with, and are extremely well-thought-of by striped bass.

Sandworms

The sandworm or clamworm is by far the most popular of the marine worms. *Nereis virens* is a polychaete annelid—that is, each segment contains several bristles. (The garden worm, a close relative, is an oligochaete, because it lacks the bristles.) In range, the common sandworm is distributed from Cape Hatteras north along all of the United States and into Canada. It is spread in the mud across the Arctic even to Europe and is found along the coast of Great Britain and Norway. Most North American specimens reach between 12 and 18 inches when fully grown,

The favorite three baits of saltwater fishermen are (left to right) the sandworm, bloodworm, and ribbonworm, all marine worms found naturally in the world of the striped bass.

but the European variety are considerably longer, up to 3 feet long and as much as 1¾ inches wide. Wouldn't that excite a bass in the Cape Canal?

The other common name, clamworm, gives us an indication of where the worm can often be found. Clam and mussel beds, especially if they are founded on a clay or mud base between the mid-tide and lower mark, are what sandworms call home. Their homes are often temporary, built between the ranges of tide, and are mucus-lined burrows which they inhabit during the day. During the night, sandworms take to wandering, swimming by undulations much like an eel or any other fish. That is why striped bass are such avid night feeders.

The sandworm is carnivorous, eating other worms and little fishes. Its pharynx can be thrown out of a mouth located at the very front end and armed with two black pincers that grasp food and help it down the gullet. Sandworms vary in color, and many anglers believe it is a characteristic associated with the surrounding mud or sand. This isn't true. Sandworms are sexually color-coded. Males range in dark colors from steel blue to green while females are olive-green with reddish or orange appendages that are used as side feet. When sandworms are in a healthy and fresh condition, their skin reflects with an iridescent sheen.

The best time to dig sandworms is on a falling tide on exposed mud flats. Usually below the half-tide mark, you can dig them out with a spade or fork. You must be fast, however, because they can disappear before your very eyes. Don't place them in a galvanized bucket or it will kill them. A wooden car or plastic bucket is your best bet. To keep them alive for any length of time, don't fill the bucket with water. Instead, drain the worms and add marine weeds like bladderwort or strands of kelp cut to form layers like a lasagne. Heat will quickly turn them into a stinking mess, so store them in a cool spot out of the sun. If you won't use them until the next day, better put them in a cooler or refrigerator, and don't get fresh water from ice on them.

Sandworms as striper bait can be used in several situations. One of the pleasantest ways to take stripers is by trolling for them in a small rowboat late in the day or early in the evening. The technique is carried out in shallow water, along the edges of bays and tidal estuaries, and in protected areas where the current isn't so great as to challenge your rowing ability.

The worms are fished on a spinning or popping rod, 100 or more feet astern of the boat, on 15- or 20-pound-test line. Small split shot can be used but aren't necessary in such shallow water. One or two large sandworms are placed on a 2/0 to 4/0 Eagle Claw or beak-type hook. The barb of the hood is pushed through the mouth of the sandworm and then immediately brought out the side. The worm is then slipped up the shaft and kept from returning by small barbs. The second worm is fastened in the same manner and left on the bend of the hook. Sandworms hooked only by their heads have the best natural appearance and look like they are swimming along when trolled slowly. Between the hook and the end of the leader, a small willow-leaf spinner can be added for extra attraction. The contemplative bass fisherman can usually handle two such rigs off the transom of his boat.

In areas where a fair current moves and an angler can get to its edge from a point of land, a jetty, or a pier, he can use sandworms effectively to take striped bass. The rig here differs slightly, with the use of a three-way swivel in the line and a dropper leader of less strength than that on the main line, tied to a 1-to-3-ounce bank or dipsy sinker. The rig is gently cast into the current and the slack in the line taken up until the fisherman can feel the sinker bouncing along the bottom.

To keep the sandworm from becoming hidden in the grass, a 1-to-2-foot leader is placed on the sinker and the festooned hook usually sails downstream on a 2-to-3-foot strand of monofilament. A few inches before the hook, many fishermen add a small cork or balsa float. It should just be large enough to cancel out some of the weight of the worm and hook but not lift it straight toward the surface of the water.

Often sandworms are used in conjunction with artificial lures. I couldn't believe it the first time I saw it, but one day at Cuttyhunk, on the famous striped bass ground, the Sow and Pigs Reef, I watched the regular charterboat skippers trolling with long surgical tubes. To the end of a tube between 2 and 3 feet long they would add a small piece of sandworm, maybe no more than 2 or 3 inches long. I laughed, but they caught fish and I didn't, because I didn't have sandworms for my surgical tubes. The sandworms must have provided that small bit of food odor that the lure needed to make the bass come up and strike.

Worms can be fished in a variety of ways. The top two illustrations are for terminal rigs with worms in the surf. A pyramid sinker anchors the rig and a fish-finder allows a bass to run with the bait. The second rig has a cork or balsa float added to it so that the worm is not directly on the sand, but on the bass's eye level. The third rig is a typical trolling rig, with a Cape Cod spinner added for attraction. The bottom illustration shows two worms attached to the same hook.

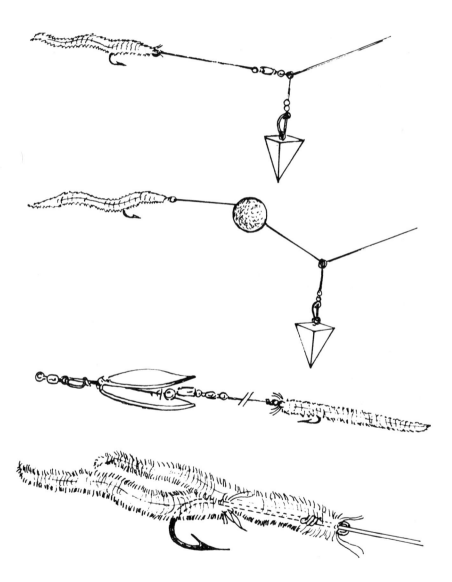

Sandworms are also effective baits in the surf for striped bass. They are used in conjunction with a fish-finder rig and a pyramid sinker. The size sinker, 1 to 6 ounces, will depend on the state of the surf and running tides. One or two sandworms are skewered onto a hook and gently heaved out to sea. The slack in the line is taken up with the rod in a surf spike (holder) and the drag adjusted just as lightly as possible to keep the surf from taking out the line or lure. The click is left on, and when a bass picks up the sandworms it can run, taking the monofilament or Dacron line through the large eye on the fish-finder without feeling the weight of the sinker. In many instances, a float is also used with the fish-finder rig to keep the sandworms just off the bottom of the surf and away from the sand sharks and sea robins.

Bloodworms

Bloodworms are used almost as much as sandworms for striped bass bait. *Glycera dibranchiata,* as it is known in scientific circles, has a somewhat less extensive range than its close cousin the sandworm. It is found along our Atlantic Coast from North Carolina to the Gulf of St. Lawrence and on the Pacific side from California to Mexico. It has been reduced in abundance and can be found in commercial numbers only in the land surrounding the Gulf of Maine, in Maine, New Brunswick, and Nova Scotia.

The bloodworm is somewhat smaller than the sandworm, about 12 to 15 inches in maximum length, and more closely resembles an earthworm than the flatter sandworm. It has a darker red color than the earthworm and a pointed head with a tail that diminishes rapidly in size. The bloodworm has no true system of blood vessels like other worms and the body fluids are filled with hemoglobin in corpuscles that slosh around its cavities and account for the purple-to-pinkish body color.

This open circulatory system also accounts for the profuse bleeding when a bloodworm is cut. Often after it stops and the blood is gone, there is little left in the area but the outside skin. It takes several bloodworms to adorn a hook the way one sandworm can.

Like the sandworm, bloodworms have a pharynx that can be flipped out, and they have a similar proboscis, but armed with four pincers or sharp jaws that can bite. The bite can be painful as well as slightly poisonous. Unlike the aggressive sandworm, the bloodworm is not a meat-eater but instead finds sustenance in organic debris in the soft, dark-colored mud it likes to call home. The strong jaws and the stinging bite are really defensive structures.

Unlike the wandering nocturnal sandworms, bloodworms are real homebodies and don't take to spending much time outside of their muck. Because of their softer body construction they can be found only around rather soft muds, away from well-packed sands, rocks, and gravel which are occasionally the home of sandworms. In some cases, both can be found together in a spadeful of mud.

Though the bloodworm is found almost the length of our Atlantic and Pacific coasts and most that are dug come from its northern range, it is used as a striped bass bait more commonly in the southern part of its range. Long Island seems to be an arbitrary dividing point, with anglers on the South Shore and from New Jersey to the Carolinas seeming to prefer the bloodworm to the sandworm. From the North Shore of Long Island to Maine and New Brunswick, the sandworm seems the first choice in baits.

Bloodworms can be fished in each of the situations described for the sandworms. They are just as readily taken by stripers as any other worm. But because of their smaller size, you may have to add more. Also, because of a weaker skin, they have a tendency to break apart, and smaller and thinner hooks make it easier to use them as bait. They are hooked like sandworms—that is, through the mouth and out the side. Often, however, because they stretch and break so easily, they must be hooked a second time near the tail. Because of this double hooking, they do not present as natural a picture when trolled as the sandworms. Given a choice, pick the sandworm for trolling situations and the bloodworm when you are fishing with lead, in the surf, or from a fixed position.

Bloodworms are more difficult to keep on the shank of a hook than sandworms. In addition to the hooks with barbs on their shafts as bait-holders, some companies manufacture a special sea-worm hook. This hook has a sharp wire point in the eye to which the first worm can be skewered if you are using more than one and if will hold its position.

Bloodworms drifted in a current with no weight attached to the line can prove a deadly combination on striped bass. The action of one or two head-hooked worms looks like the pair are wrestling with each other, and bass don't make good bystanders. Drifted off a low-lying bridge or pier, or off the end of a jetty or sod bank into a bass hole, bloodworms are one of the best baits available. If the current is too great for the worm to be live-lined, then one or two split shot, 2 or 3 feet away from the worms, will get them deeper and still not influence their swimming.

Ribbonworms

Commonly and erroneously called tapeworms, ribbonworms are the third group of marine worms used by fishermen to take striped bass. The ribbonworm is not an annelid because it lacks the body segmentation. Instead, it belongs to another phylum called the nemertean worms, a group that are not segmented and have a long, tubelike proboscis that is extremely muscular. Nor are the ribbonworms parasitic as are most tapeworms.

Ribbonworms, as their name implies, are extremely flat or dorsal-ventrally compressed, and closely resemble a ribbon. They are long worms, and seldom do you see both ends at one time. A 5-foot ribbon-worm can stretch itself to about 20 feet and maintain a width of about an inch.

There are several nemertean worms, but *Cerebratulus lacteus* is the one most often used by fishermen. It is widely distributed along the Atlantic, from Maine to Florida, but is concentrated from New Jersey to southern Maine and likes either sand or mud beaches as a place to burrow a home. It is an active burrower. It has a mucous covering over its body and is colored an ivory or creamy white with hints of pink. Ribbonworms are highly carnivorous and are active swimmers, leaving their burrows at night to hunt mainly other worms. They attack by rapidly everting the slender proboscis. The proboscis is not armed with teeth but simply wraps itself around the prey—a clamworm or blood-worm—and in effect squeezes it and works the food back into its mouth by retracting the organ.

Ribbonworms are difficult to buy because most fishermen are re-pulsed at the sight and only a small group are aware of what great striped bass baits they make. The common name, "tapeworm," also turns off a lot of fishermen. If you want your own, more than likely you will have to dig them, and it can often be a two- or three-man job. The worms are extremely fast burrowers, and once they have been discovered can rapidly move through the mud. To get one out intact requires fast work and often more than one shovel.

An entire ribbonworm would be too much to troll, even though striped bass are known to be head-hitters. Instead, the ribbonworm should be cut into 8- or 10-inch strips and hooked on the leading end several times to ensure it won't slip off. The other end is left trailing free. Small striped bass may often hit a long bait like the ribbonworm, or even long sandworms, on the tail or short side. This can be remedied by tying a second hook onto a piece of clear monofilament and then attaching it to the eye of the first hook. The length of mono leader should be a little shorter than the length of the worm. The second hook is just slightly passed through the trailering bait and should not appreciably affect its action. The leader material must be rather light and supple or it will override the undulations of the bait.

MOLLUSKS

Mollusks are soft-bodied animals that have developed external skeletons to protect them from the ravages of other animals and the elements. They include several classes, two of which are extremely important natural foods in the world of the striped bass. One class is composed of clams and mussels, and the second class is the Cephalopoda or squids, a closely related form.

Clams, mussels, and squid are high on the menu of stripers, and the linesider's penchant for squid has even earned it the name "squidhound" in some angling quarters. The striped bass is unable to do much damage to hard-shelled clams when they are in their element, but after a storm, when they have been smashed about by combers on the beach, bass readily take advantage of the situation and gorge themselves. Some soft-shelled clams and some mussels are another story; bass can break their shells with their strong jaws. In other situations, bass catch mussels and

Striped bass like clams as much as people do. Here is an assortment of the striper's favorites.

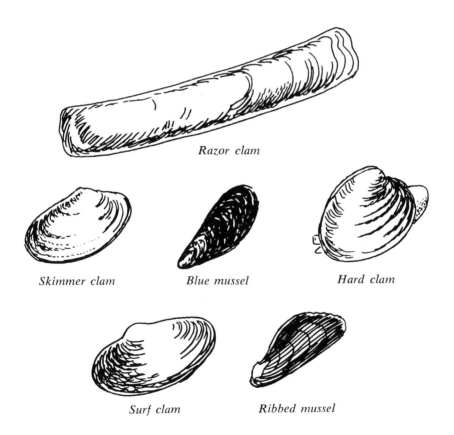

Razor clam

Skimmer clam   Blue mussel   Hard clam

Surf clam   Ribbed mussel

clams traveling—that is, with their best (and only) foot forward—and strike the mollusk before it can get its body back into the protection of the two valves.

Clams and mussels are used in two ways to catch bass: either impaled on a hook, or as chum to get them to a hook with more clams or other baits on it. The broadcasting ability of clam odor in the water is terrific, one reason clams are used so frequently in bass fishing. The squid are almost always used as the bait itself, either as an entire morsel or stripped and a part of artificial lures.

Skimmer clams

The skimmer clam, *Spisula solidissima,* is the most popular of all the clams and mussels used. It is locally known as a sea clam or surf clam and is often commercially sought for chowders and packaged seafoods. As a marine bait, the skimmer clam is unsurpassed. When shucked fresh from the shell, it has a large muscle that holds well on a hook, and the bait is full of juices that entice a striped bass to come looking.

A great abundance of skimmers also makes them the preferred bait over other clams, the smaller hard clams, soft clams, and razor clams. They can readily be purchased at seafood stores or bait shops along the coast, and at reasonable prices. They are easy to open, and if you walk the beach after a storm, they are more than likely to be in an open state. Pack a bagful away in your freezer while they are still fresh and you have the cheapest bait available.

Spisula solidissima is widely distributed along the North Atlantic coast, from Cape Hatteras to Labrador on the north side of the Gulf of St. Lawrence. Its greatest abundance occurs in the New York bight, between mid-New Jersey and as far east as Montauk on Long Island. Concentrations of skimmers are particularly large off the south shore of Long Island. This may explain the great popularity of chumming and fishing in this area with clams and clam bellies, the by-product of the clam-dragging industry.

Skimmers are our largest clams, measuring up to 4 or 5 inches across their widest part. They also produce large meats, and half a dozen big clams is usually enough for one man and an afternoon's fishing. They are great baits to use in the surf for bass because, if hooked properly, they will take a lot of heaving and casting and stay together in the pounding melee. The clam is strung onto the hook, preferably a long-shanked Eagle Claw or Siwash, between 3/0 and 5/0 in size. The soft parts are strung on first, if you can find them, and the muscle is then the last part over the hook and barb to keep the remainder of the clam from slipping off. If hooked in this manner, it is likely to stay on for a while. Such an affair is fished off the end of a fish-finder rig.

In other angling situations, clams are fished from a boat while chumming under a bridge, along a tidal creek, or in a river channel. The greater bulk of sea clams is ground or pulverized and fed methodically into the water. The bigger clam pieces or whole clams (without the shell, naturally) are hooked and drifted into the chum. A weight is seldom needed; the weight of the hook and mass of clams is enough to take it slowly to the bottom and keep it in the region of the chum. If the current is moving too fast, then a sinker is added in the line, 4 to 5 feet ahead of the bait. Clamp-on types with rubber cushions work well without pinching or weakening the line.

Most other baits for striped bass are fished with the hook and barb exposed. But because of the soft body of the clam, even its tougher muscle, the hook and barbs can be hidden whenever possible, and the bite of a bass will force the hook through the muscle. With the barb covered while fishing, the hook is less likely to collect drifting eelgrass or other debris.

Hard clams

There is only one hard clam, *Mercenaria mercenaria,* that is favored by bass and bass fishermen. It has three different names, and these are not colloquial handles, but instead refer to size. The hard clam was known to the coastal Indians of the Northeast as the quahog. Today, this clam in the larger sizes is used mainly for chowder and is often called the chowder clam as well as the quahog. Littleneck clams are the smallest hard clams, and cherrystone clams are the size between littlenecks and quahogs.

Hard clams are not frequently used for striped bass bait unless you have a surplus of quahogs, because they taste as good to the fisherman as to the fish.

They can be used in much the same manner as skimmer clams, but because of their smaller size, several might be needed in the place of one skimmer. Hard clams are dug or raked at the edge of low tide along the beaches or tonged up in shallow water in protected bays and estuaries. In many states where they occur, there are often seasons and regulations affecting their taking and use. You should be familiar with local regulations before you go clamming for bait.

Soft clams

The soft clam, *Mya arenaria,* is also locally known as the steamer clam. Steamers are as palatable to man as hard clams, but because they are far more numerous and easier to rake a bushel, they are more practical to use as a striped bass bait. Soft clams range from the warm, shallow protected bays of North Carolina to the frigid, ice-covered waters of the Arctic. They are most often found in soft, muddy bottoms between high and low tide, and more often nearer the bottom reaches of the tide.

Steamers group together more closely than hard clams, and when you discover a bed you can fill your bucket in a matter of minutes or a few shovelfuls of muck. They burrow just under the surface and their siphon holes can be seen pock-marking the beach. These clams are characterized by a long maneuverable siphon which can be extended beyond the shell to take in fresh seawater or hunt for food. Also, steamers have a softer, whitish shell that can easily be crushed between the fingers. The shell of a soft clam is more elongated in shape than the oval hard clam and has more pronounced ridges.

The meat of the soft-shelled clam is not as firm as that of the hard or skimmer clam, but the siphon, a tough, rubbery appendage, can be hooked on last, like the muscle of a skimmer clam, and will stay on for quite a degree of abuse. Soft-shelled clams are also used for chum. They are smashed or ground up, shells and all, and mixed with seawater to form a soup or broth. The substance is ladled into the water, and the hook is adorned with several soft steamers, minus their shells.

Razor clams

Like other species of clams, the razor clam, *Ensis directus,* can also be used as bait because it is everywhere found in the environment of the striped bass. The razor clam does a lot more wandering *on* the bottom, instead of *in* it like soft clams and quahogs, and thus is a more familiar bait to striped bass. However, their numbers are few compared to those of other clams and anglers are not as apt to use them.

Their long, curved shells, closely resembling the handle of a straight razor, can grow to 7 or 8 inches in length. And though narrow, they do provide a lot of meat for the hook. They are swift burrowers, and if you spot one in shallow water you might be hard-pressed to catch it. They are distributed from the southern tip of Florida to Labrador and are more fond of sand beaches than strictly mud environments.

Blue mussels

The blue mussel, or edible mussel, *Mytilus edulis,* is extremely plentiful along our coasts and is distributed on both sides of the Atlantic, from North Carolina to Spain. In Europe, it is a favorite seafood, but in

America it is seldom eaten by anyone except transplanted Europeans who aren't keen on spreading the word. Striped bass are also fond of blue mussels, but because their bodies are so soft, they are seldom used for bait. Instead, they are often pounded or ground into chum by bass fishermen and other baits are then used on the hook.

The elongated blue-colored shells are up to 2½ inches long. Blue mussels are extremely colonial, binding themselves into huge mussel beds by strong, yellow byssus threads that each mussel secretes. These beds are great hunting grounds for striped bass and clamworms alike and are good areas over which to fish and chum. The mussels do not burrow in the mud but live on its surface and pile colonies upon themselves. Their beds are located in the intertidal zone, in the lower portion, and clams shut their shells while the water is gone so that they do not dehydrate. Collecting a pailful is simply a matter of breaking them away from the mass. A fork works better than a spade.

Ribbed mussels

The ribbed or bank mussel, *Brachiodontes demissus,* is a close cousin to the blue mussel. It is quite similar in shape but is colored a soft brown to a yellow, or even an olive drab, instead of blue, and the shell is heavily fluted or ribbed along the longer axis. Bank mussels also prefer to live in vertical situations rather than build horizontally on the beach. Banks cut by tidal creeks and streams meandering through marshes are the fort of the bank mussel. Unlike the blue mussel, the bank mussel is not edible, and as a bait for striped bass it is difficult to place on a hook because of the extremely soft and fluid body. But as a chum ingredient, it is supreme for stripers, surpassed only by clam bellies, much the same product.

Nor are the bank mussels as colonial in their living habits as the blue mussels. You may have to hunt along the sides of a creek for a distance before you get enough to fill a bucket for chum. If you do insist on using them for bait, and they can fill this requirement, they will need a little help staying on the hook. The mass must be supported by twisting a soft wire around it or tying it on with a piece of thread.

Squid

It is difficult for anyone but a biologist to believe that a squid, that fast-swimming denizen of our inshore and offshore waters, is actually a mollusk. This extremely mobile creature has all but freed itself of its shell but still jets around like more sedentary clams. The squid is an aggressive carnivore, a highly organized animal that swims about in schools similar to real fishes.

The squid today is one of the most overlooked striped bass baits, though it was one of the first baits used by early sportfishers. Illustrated here are four possible squid rigs. The top rig is a whole squid with the tail cut square and then skewered onto a lead-headed hook. The tail is then sewn or threaded through holes in the lead head. The second rig is similar but the squid is tied to the head. The hook is attached inside to an eye and swings more freely with the body of the squid. The third rig is a series of hooks attached to each other and then imbedded into the squid. The bottom rig, the simplest, is primarily a surf rig, while the three others are used while trolling.

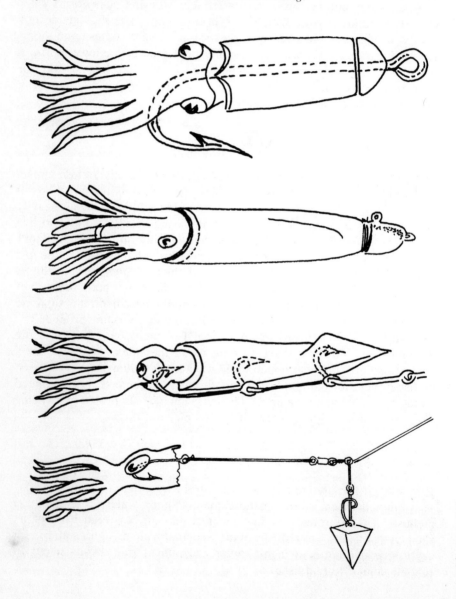

Because of its pelagic distribution, the squid has become a real favorite of striped bass and ranks high on its menu of preferred foods. Squid move about the waters by jet propulsion, squeezing water out of their bodies through a restrictive port that shoots them backward as they travel. The size of their schools can be extremely large and their only protection is sheer numbers so that some are always left to move on. Their prime source of food is small fishes, and a school of squid can decimate a school of sand eels or small menhaden with the rapidity of a ravenous bluefish.

The most common squid, *Loligo pealii,* can shade its appearance with tints of blue, purple, red, and yellow. It sports a spindle-shaped body, tapering in the back to an arrowhead point and trailering ten octopuslike tentacles from what is its front. To see where it is going, squid have taken the light-sensitive eye area of a clam and developed it into an organ comparable to eyes in vertebrates. The arrowhead back-side, which glides through the water first, has its edges modified into fins or diving planes similar to those of a submarine.

The range of this squid is from South Carolina northward to Cape Cod and occasionally into the Gulf of Maine. Its distribution covers both inshore and offshore waters. Most are caught by draggers traveling at high speeds or pound traps planted along the shore.

As bait for striped bass, squid can be fished on the bottom, rigged in a somewhat free-swimming form for the surf, or trolled. The last is the best technique and the one employed by the majority of anglers. The squid is used whole in most instances, though some anglers prefer to use only the head when casting or still-fishing. In this case, the head is pulled off the rest of the body and skewered onto a 3/0 claw-type hook, with barbs on the shank to keep the squid from slipping down. It can be cast into the surf, eased out of an anchored boat, or fished in shallow water with no weights. With a three-way swivel and snelled sinker it can be fished when the water is too deep or the current too strong to let the squid fall to where bass might be cruising.

The whole squid can also be rigged in several ways. One of the easiest is to hook three or four (depending upon the length of the squid) O'Shaughnessy hooks in tandem to each other—that is, through the eye of one and then the eye of the next to form sort of a chain. The last hook is passed beyond the barb, into the spaces between the eyes of the squid. The second goes into the bulk of the body and the third is planted not far from the pointed tail. If the squid is fresh and the meat firm, this may be enough to hold it on the hook, and it can be cast into the surf, fished off a three-way swivel in fast water, or trolled behind a boat. If the trolling is against a strong current, the squid can be further secured to the hooks by several pieces of light line or thread wound around the body of the squid and passed through the eyes of each hook.

Still another technique when trolling is to fix an 8/0 Siwash or O'Shaughnessy hook to a 12-inch length of wire leader. The tip of the leader can be cut at a sharp angle and the wire then passed up through the base of the tentacles and out the tip of the pointed posterior. If you want to troll the squid at deeper levels, then a small barrel sinker can be slipped onto the leader before the squid is pierced. The hook and sinker are drawn into the squid and covered by its tentacles and head. The wire is then fastened to the eye of a swivel and the free end cut loose. The softness of a squid's flesh is likely to give way at the point with excessive trolling and it is best kept in shape by sewing the tip to the eye of the swivel.

Still another effective technique, though not widely used because of a lack of materials, is the use of a lead head for squid. This is nothing more than a half-round ball of lead poured around the shank of a long-shafted 9/0 or 10/0 hook just below the eye. The pointed back end of the squid is cut off at a right angle and the squid worked on the hook through the center of the cut until the bend of the hook comes out near the mouth or eyes of the animal. To keep the squid from slipping down on the hook, a series of holes are drilled around the edge of the lead head and the squid sewn against its base.

This type of rigged squid can be trolled at good depths, or cast into the surf and slowly retrieved, or trolled with a jigging motion to simulate the manner in which a live squid swims. The jerky action also is a better attractor of striped bass than a steady, even pull.

Squid can also be cut into long strips for trolling, either by itself or at the end of a bucktail, spoon or other comparable lure. In this case, the head is cut off and the body sliced open. The outer covering is skinned off and the firm, white meat sliced into longitudinal strips that taper at their distal ends. The larger part of a strip of squid is always attached to the hook to give the tapered end a better swimming action. If you are drifting or still-fishing the squid strips, you can change their shape to add more meat to the morsel, with shorter but chunkier slices.

CRUSTACEANS

Lobsters, shrimp, and crabs are crustaceans familiar to all of us, but striped bass are on more intimate terms with these ten-legged creatures that swim and crawl in the marine world of the bass. They are favorite foods, and wherever they can easily be obtained, are good selections for bait. I doubt today that there is much fishing done with lobster tails as bait, as once was the accepted custom at Montauk and Cuttyhunk. But the lobster's close cousins are still in use, and even the famous blue crab that is equally satisfying to the striped bass and the striped bass fisherman is used in many areas of our country to subdue the striper.

Grass shrimp and sand shrimp

The grass shrimp, *Palaeomonetes vulgaris,* is the most popular of the shrimp used to catch striped bass. It can be used as the bait itself, with several strung on a hook, or as chum to entice striped bass to come to other baits. These small, 1-to-1½-inch crustaceans are liked by both large and small bass, though smaller stripers are more regularly taken with them as bait.

Shrimp can be used both as a bait and in a chum line. Both grass and sand shrimp are good chum material, while the common edible shrimp is more often used on the hook because of its larger size.

Edible shrimp (imported)

Grass shrimp

Sand shrimp

The grass shrimp has a translucent body, delicate and sharp-pointed, with a saw-edged spine that extends forward between the eyes to discourage diners. Grass shrimp are found readily in shallow bays, creeks, and marine estuaries where they are netted or out in deeper water, off the barrier beaches, and in deep sounds and bays. Given a choice, they prefer to live and feed over soft bottoms with good stands of eelgrass and other forms of marine vegetation.

The grass shrimp's distribution ranges from the lower Gulf of Maine south to Florida, and its abundance in many years has been regulated by the available amount of eelgrass or other protection offered by the marine environment. During years when eelgrass underwent a decline because of a coastwide blight, grass shrimp also declined and all but disappeared from their natural range.

The sand shrimp, *Crangon septemspinosa,* is more abundant than the grass shrimp but not quite as desirable. It can be distinguished from its close cousin by broad, fanlike expansions at the base of the antennae on the shrimp's head. The sand shrimp grows slightly larger, up to 2 inches, and is more abundant along sandy beaches and open environments than the grass shrimp.

Sand shrimp are distributed from the Carolinas north to Labrador, with the greatest concentrations located from Cape May, N.J., north to the southern Massachusetts coast. It is not quite as transparent as the grass shrimp but its pale-gray color and spotted mottling make it well camouflaged and nearly invisible to see until it moves.

Sand shrimp can easily be caught by sweeping the beach with a small-meshed haul seine, and a bucket can be filled in minutes. Grass shrimp are taken by seining the creeks and tidal bays at mid-tide by two men sweeping through with a roller-type net or moving downtide swiftly with the bend of the grasses. Both shrimp are stored best in a floating car attached to the transom of the boat and always exposed to a fresh supply of sea water.

Grass and sand shrimp, because of their small size, are often employed as chum for striped bass. When they are also used as bait, it takes several of them to fill a 2/0 beak-type hook to provide a mouthful for even a small striped bass. They can be frozen in plastic milk cartons, mixed with water so that all air is sealed from their surface. Freshly thawed, they are as effective as live shrimp except that swimming shrimp are not a part of such a chum line.

Edible shrimp

The shrimp you find swimming around in your shrimp cocktail belong to the genus *Penaeus,* and though they are generally native to the waters from Cape Hatteras south, they are found naturally from time to time as far north as Long Island. About the only way you can get them on your hook is by fishing around a seafood market, and if you are willing to use them without a sauce, the striped bass will feed on them. They are best used when chumming with grass or sand shrimp and the hook baited with *Panaeus*. But, like lobster, shrimp may be strictly a rich man's bait.

Blue crabs

The well-known blue crab, or blue claw, *Callinectus sapidus,* is common to the marine waters from southern Massachusetts to Cape Hatteras and is a denizen of the intertidal shore zone. When its summer migration brings it out of the deeper bays and estuaries, the crab is fair game in either its hard, soft, shedder, or paper stages. The greatest center of abundance for the blue crab is in Chesapeake Bay, in Maryland and Virginia waters. It isn't difficult to tell a blue crab from other crabs in marine waters because of its large size (up to 7 inches), sharply pointed, dark-green top shell (called a carapace), bright-blue trim, and dangling red-and-scarlet legs.

Like many clams and lobsters, blue crabs are protected by laws in several states, with seasons and size limitations on them. You might also be called upon to return female crabs, but they are easy to sex, with massive, bright-orange egg sacs attached to their undersides.

As bait, the crab is excellent and can be used in any of its stages, though soft crabs are preferred. Crabs, like other crustaceans, have an exoskeleton. Man has an endoskeleton. As we grow, the muscles are added to the outside of our skeleton, but crustaceans, crabs and lobsters, grow from the inside and soon fill their outer hard shell or skeleton. To grow larger, this skeleton from time to time is split and the crab emerges in a somewhat soft state and unable to swim. It is most vulnerable to striped bass at this time and it is several days before the new and larger exoskeleton is hard enough to protect it. Crabs may shed or molt several times during a summer season, depending upon how fast they grow.

One of the favorite methods for fishing a crab while seeking striped bass is to float it. The soft crab is somewhat buoyant, and when fixed to a 4/0 to 6/0 O'Shaughnessy hook will float long distances with the tide or current. The pull of the current against a fixed line helps buoy up the crab. It is almost impossible to hook a crab, nor should you while it is in the soft state. It can be fixed to the hook by two soft rubber bands, crossed over the back with the hook laid across the short axis of the crab, allowing its feet to be free and wiggle as an added attraction for bass.

Floating crabs is best done at night, from an anchored boat or off a point of land. At this time, bass will not hesitate to come near the surface

Crabs are one of the striped bass's favorite foods.

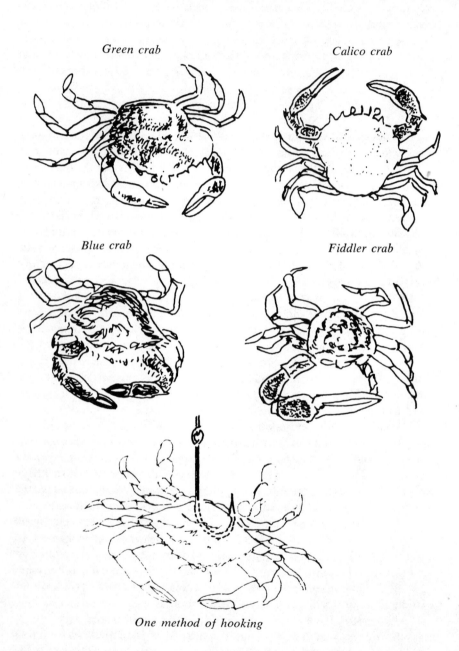

Green crab

Calico crab

Blue crab

Fiddler crab

One method of hooking

for a crab feast. The hook is best laid on the underside of the crab, and when the fish runs with the bait, some time must be allowed before setting the hook to ensure that the bass has taken the crab deeply enough for the hook to find a spot to lodge.

Hard crabs can be fished live or by passing the hook between both shells. They are better fished on the bottom with a three-way swivel with enough line on the sinker so that the crab is about 18 inches off the sand or mud. Nor need crabs be fished whole to be effective striped bass baits. A cut crab advertises its presence in the current of things in a striped bass's world by the odors and juices it exudes.

A crab can be cut in half or quartered and the pieces placed on a hook with the bend and barb hidden. If you have plenty of crabs, the legs and other materials can also be used to set up a small chum line. Don't waste anything that might entice a striped bass. Half and quarter pieces can be difficult to hold on a hook. They can be fastened with the help of a rubber band or light sewing thread. Crabs can be fished from an anchored boat, off a pier, dock or bridge, or fished while drifting.

When floated, the crab is allowed to be pulled away from the boat by the force of the current. The bail is open on a spinning reel or the reel left in free spool on a conventional type reel. The line is first pulled out by hand to get the crab into the current, and then its downtide drift is controlled by pressure on the spool from the thumb. When a bass strikes—usually a rather soft strike with crabs—it should be allowed to run until you think you dare not let out any more line. Then, the clutch is engaged on the reel and the hook firmly set.

Calico crabs

The common calico crab, *Ovalipes ocellatus,* is also known as the lady or sand crab. It is a brightly colored crab with a yellow to lavender back and purple spots. Calicos can be used when blue crabs are scarce or you'd rather cook them for yourself. The calico crab is fond of the outer beaches and sandy areas—more so than the blue crab—and is frequently found in the surf trying to race the water back into the ocean.

Its distribution is broader than that of the blue crab, from Cape Cod to the Gulf of Mexico. It is collected on the beaches by a rake equipped with a basket on its trailing edge. The calico will bury itself in the sand until only its eyes are exposed, but a rake drawn through the first inch or two of sand will easily pull it from its hiding spot.

Though smaller than the blue crab, the calico can be used in the exact same manner when trying for striped bass. Small ones can be doubled on the hook, and if you rake in a bushel the others can be cut into small pieces and used as a chum. Because it is more often found in the surf than the blue crab, the calico is preferred by some surfcasters who want to match the bait to the environment, and striped bass are less likely to be startled by an injured calico in the suds.

Green crabs and fiddler crabs

The green crab, *Carcinides maenas,* and the fiddler crab, three species within the genus *Uca,* often share the same environment. All can be used for striped bass baits. The green crab is a darker, mottled species of crab, medium in size, and is common from New Jersey to Maine. The bigger specimens, up to 3 inches, can be cut in two or used whole on a 2/0 hook.

Fiddler crabs are more gregarious than the green crabs and set up housekeeping in colonies along the banks of salt creeks and tidal marshes. As the tide floods in, striped bass are fond of searching all the fiddler holes to catch one too far out and make a meal of it. The pale-colored *Uca minax,* called "china back" by many anglers, is the species used most often for bait.

Hermit crabs

This rather specialized crustacean, *Pagurus pollicaris,* has given up its protective carapace or shell for a life of mobility but feels so insecure that it seldom wanders far from its makeshift home. Without a shell to call its own, the hermit crab, not really a true crab, will set up housekeeping in the abandoned shells of large moon snails or whelks. When the shells are crushed the soft, helpless hermit crab makes an ideal bait for striped bass. But because they are not often available in quantity, they are not too often used. If you are out of bait and spot a hermit slip into a whelk shell, don't pass it up—it may mean a bass for you.

Sand bugs

Not bugs in even the widest use of the word, this specialized crustacean burrows into the intertidal zone of a sandy beach and when knocked loose by pounding surf is eagerly sought by striped bass. At times, the sand bug, *Emertia talpoida,* is all that striped bass will seek out for food. During the striped bass's spring migrations along sandy beaches of the Atlantic, from Cape Hatteras to Maine, the sand bug is about the only bait, real or unreal, upon which they will strike.

I've never seen them for sale at a bait shop so the only way to get them is to catch them yourself. The bugs inhabit the tidal zone of sandy

Not really a crab, the hermit crab finds a home in the shells abandoned by mollusks while the sand bug or sand flea finds a home in the sand beneath the surf by burrowing.

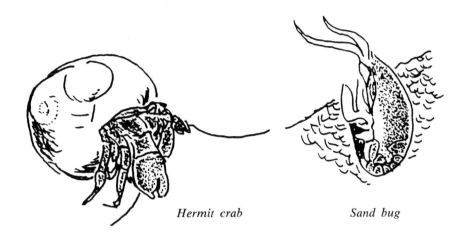

Hermit crab   Sand bug

beaches from Massachusetts to the Yucatan. They rush up the beach with the waves and then race it back into the wash. They are best taken with a wire scoop, because they move so quickly that the hands are neither large enough nor fast enough. They can burrow rapidly and disappear as you watch them if you don't react fast enough. Sand bugs are rather large as far as beach life goes—up to 2½ inches long, with a curved or arched back that is covered by a smooth, tough carapace colored tan or yellowish-white. It sports a pair of "feathered" antennae that are half as long as the bug's body.

Because of their small size, it takes more than one average bug to make a tempting meal for a bass in the surf. Fishermen prefer to string two on a hook and hide the barbs.

FISH

Striped bass are primarily piscivorous feeders—that is, the bulk of the food in their diet, by weight, is composed of other fishes. Though there is a great variety of foods that the fish will feed upon, once a striped bass reaches the fry or fingerling stage, it begins shifting from small crustaceans to small fish as its main food source.

There are two general groups of fishes that appear on the striper's menu. The first are primarily food and forage fishes, those that seldom grow large and are not sought after by fishermen as gamefish. With regard to the striped bass's likings, these include the killifish, spearing, sand eels, butterfish, and menhaden, the last being the largest of this group.

The second group of fishes that are food for stripers constitutes the young stage of many gamefish or even the adult form when these fish are not especially large. This group includes mackerel, whiting, blackfish, bluefish, weakfish, sculpins, and eels. Of all these species of fish, the American eel and menhaden or bunker are by far the most effective baits, and sophisticated and complicated angling techniques have evolved around them. Further, there appears to be a real correlation between the size of the bait and the size of the striped bass caught. Generally, the larger the bait, the larger the striper.

Killifish

The common killifish, or mummichog as it is called along the New England part of its distribution, is a plentiful forage fish and constitutes a fair share of the striped bass's diet when the fish are in estuarine and river environments. The killie, *Fundulus heteroclitus,* is a tough little fish, inhabiting some rather polluted waters along our coasts, in places other species have long abandoned. These fish prefer moving water. They are often swept in and out with the tide, flooding creeks and marshes, and often dallying too late and becoming stranded in potholes without water until the next tide. Remarkably, they survive.

The sand eel (top) and the killifish form a large part of the diet of a growing bass.

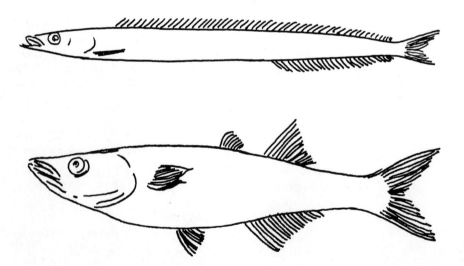

There are several related species and subspecies, and most of their range covers the coastal waters from the Gulf of St. Lawrence south to Texas. *F. heteroclitus* or the common killifish has a rather stout body, heavy caudal peduncle, and rounded caudal fin. Males are dark green with white and yellow spots and silver vertical bars and yellow bellies. The girls of the species are rather drab, uniformly a pale to medium olive.

Killies are extremely hardy and take a lot of punishment while being cast about. They survive being hooked for long periods. If they grew a bit longer, they would be the perfect striped bass bait. The maximum is up to 6 inches long but most are between 2 and 4 inches, and they appeal more to small bass and even then must be doubled on a hook.

They are almost always fished whole, hooked by No. 1 or No. 2 O'Shaughnessy hooks through the lower lip or just ahead of the dorsal fin. These fish must be fished—that is, hooked so that their action and swimming appears natural. When caught and frozen and then fished again, they can be used for chum either whole or cut and account for plenty of small bass.

Spearing

In the more open bays and larger estuaries, striped bass will herd and corral whole schools of spearing or silversides, *Menida menida,* and harass these little food fish to the point where they literally jump from the water by the hundreds. Unfortunately, spearing are rather fragile fish and won't take a lot of abuse or wear on a hook. They are a slender, translucent species, with a forked tail, pale green above a bright white or silver stripe that extends along the lateral line from the gills to the tail.

The fish is distributed from Maine to Chesapeake Bay and in lesser numbers farther south. During the summer months it concentrates in the numerous bays that surround Long Island, especially Long Island Sound. They have a habit of sweeping in and out of these bays with the tides and are almost as much at home in the *Spartina* grasses as in the deep bays and kelp beds.

Because of its fragile nature the spearing is seldom used as live bait. More often, it is caught and frozen in blocks and melted for use as chum, ground or cut into small pieces and fed into the slick of a boat. When baiting, several are fitted onto a hook at a time and allowed to drift in the chum line.

Sand eels

The sand eel or sand lance, *Ammodytes americanus,* is a more hardy food and forage fish and can take punishment almost as well as the killifish. It grows somewhat longer than the spearing or the killifish, up to 7 or 8 inches, and can play a more important role as a baitfish. However, it is thin, elongated for its length, and doesn't appreciably bulk on a hook. It has a pointed snout—hence the "lance"—and a long slender dorsal fin. The body gives off an iridescent luster that is a bluish-green sheen above the lateral line and silver and white on the underside and belly.

These fish move in dense schools both onshore and offshore and are distributed along the Atlantic from Cape Hatteras northward to Canada, across Greenland and Iceland to northern Europe. They can best be used for striped bass when hooked through both lips, with a light hook and behind a small willowleaf spinner and trolled from a rowed or slowly motored boat. In mass, they can be used as chum, ground or cut in pieces.

Menhaden

The menhaden, mossbunker, or bunker, *Brevoortia tyrannus,* has more than thirty common names. It might more appropriately be placed with the later group of fish used as a large bait for striped bass because of its size. But because it has no sporting value, or fish food value other than to be reduced to fish meal, it is associated with the smaller baitfish. Migration times and routes for striped bass are often heavily influenced by what the bunker decide to do. Within bounds, menhaden play a vital role in the life and times of the striped bass because the linesiders feed so heavily and consistently on these fish. From the time they are small fingerlings to the time they are 3- and 4-pound adults, striped bass chase and follow bunker. When the bunker head north in the spring along the coast of the Atlantic, the striped bass are usually immediately behind, following their dinner as it swims.

It is also a widely used fish by anglers because it is readily available from pound traps and caught easily by commercial draggers and purse seiners, who are after the rich oil it possesses. Bunker are members of the herring family, and like other herring are pelagic swimmers that work their way from Florida to Nova Scotia and back again during the course of a year.

Menhaden are deep-bodied fish, somewhat straight across their backs, with deeply forked tails, a rather thin caudal peduncle, and a large head that is almost a third the size of the body. The mouthparts are somewhat transparent and delicate, with an underhung jaw that extends well beyond the top lip. Coloration in a bunker is quite variable, but generally it has a blue back with an ivory or silvery cast and a strong, brassy luster along the sides. The sides are marked with various-sized spots that grow smaller as they pass caudally to form weak rows. One large dark spot is usually located just above the lateral line and behind the gill cover on each side.

One of the favorite foods of the bass, as well as baits for the fisherman, is the plentiful mossbunker, or bunker. The top figure illustrates one method of hooking dead bunker. Occasionally, the head alone is a good bait and the hook is passed through the back and down to come out near the bottom of the gills. Live or dead bunker can be fished from the surf by hooking the fish in the tough flesh just ahead of the pectoral fins.

Younger menhaden spend the greater part of their growing years in the numerous bays and estuaries of the Carolinas, Maryland, and Virginia, and migrate north during the spring to summer and grow in the bays of New Jersey and Long Island.

Bunker are almost the universal striped bass food and are used extensively ground up in chum, cut in halves and strips, and fished dead or alive. Because of their deep bodies they don't troll very well when dead but are excellent live baits when trolled at a snail's pace or stemmed against the tide.

As a cut bait, the bunker's best portion is the head, sliced just behind the gills, or long slabs cut out from each side. When used as head bait, a 5/0 to 10/0 Siwash or O'Shaughnessy is buried from the back and curved back through the bottom jaw, keeping the hook hidden at all times. As a bait strip, it is sliced into a wedge-shaped fillet and the hook pinned into the wider section. In these two hooking techniques, the bunker is best fished in the surf or off a boat or bridge with a three-way swivel or a fish-finder. This cut form can withstand a lot of casting if correctly hooked and can be tossed into the suds or fed off a bridge with a light

Live bunker or menhaden is a devastating striped bass bait. Illustrated here
is a treble hook in the nostrils, with a free hook and wire leader for short blue-
fish strikes, a flexible braided-wire leader leading to a trolling drail, and a
short wire leader just before the line.

sinker and bounced out with the tide and away from the fisherman.

Whole bunker are fished dead along many parts of northern New Jersey, from Barnegat Inlet to Sandy Hook and along western Long Island's South Shore, from Lower New York Bay east to Jones Inlet. Here, two variations of the technique are practiced. The big bunker, 1 to 2 pounds, are best when freshly dead or fresh-frozen. Old baits have their effectiveness diminish rapidly with age. The first method, basically that employed in New Jersey, is to drift the dead bunker. This requires a minimal amount of wind or a moving part of the tide. The bunker is hooked through the eyes on an 8/0 Siwash hook and lowered over the side. If there is a fair amount of current or wind, the bait is liable to rise to the top. It is kept down by adding a sinker in the line. This is often a 1-to-4-ounce drail, depending upon the speed of the drift, or a dipsy sinker on the end of a three-way swivel. The first is the preferred terminal rig because a bass can't use the dropper-sinker to help open the hook-hole and free itself in a fight.

On the drift, 100 to 200 feet of line is payed out in free spool and then the click put on. The line is kept from going out farther with thumb pressure. Once a bass picks up the dead bunker it will move off, and the click alone will not offer enough resistance to frighten a fish. Bass pick up live bunker by the head, but a dead bunker can be picked up in several ways so an unimpaired run is necessary before throwing the clutch and setting the hook. Needless to say, the drag should be set to the correct tension before the bait is ever lowered into the water.

Rigged eels are one of the most effective baits that can be trolled for striped bass. Here is all the equipment needed: a spool of waxed line, weighted head with hook, threading needle, second hook on a sash chain, and, of course, an eel.

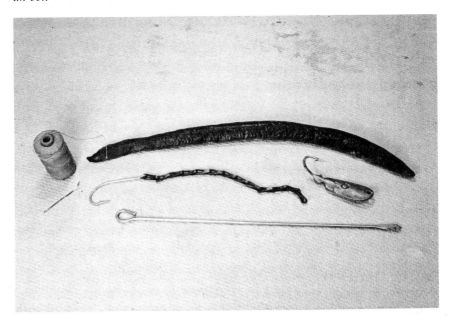

Off the beaches of western Long Island, the technique is somewhat different but still with enough similarities to be lumped together. Here, menhaden are hooked in the same manner and weighted similarly. But instead of fishing the dead bunker on a drift, the boat is slowly run almost onto the beach or alongside a groin. Then the bait is lowered over the transom. With the reel in free spool, the boat is slowly run away from the beach and the bunker stays approximately where it was dropped. When the skipper has run out as much line as he thinks possible, sometimes 200 or 300 yards, the boat is stopped and the fisherman slowly retrieves the bunker in a series of stops and starts.

Both techniques catch a lot of bass during the spring and again while the fall migrations are on. A few fishermen in these areas angle with live

The threading needle is passed through the eel's mouth and forced through its body out the vent.

At the vent, a length of waxed line is tied to the slot in the needle. Then it is pulled back out the mouth.

The line is attached to the sash chain after it has been measured to the eel and a hook is fastened to one end. Then the free end is drawn through the eel until the back hook just shows out the vent.

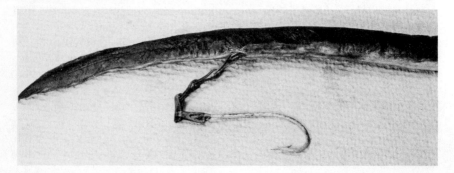

The front hook is threaded through a link on the chain.

The hook is pushed through the mouth of the eel until it comes out between the gills. The mouth of the eel is wrapped tightly shut around the lead head. A notch is cut into each side of the lead head to give the thread a gripping groove. The eel's mouth must be completely secured so that no water will flow into it and affect its swimming action.

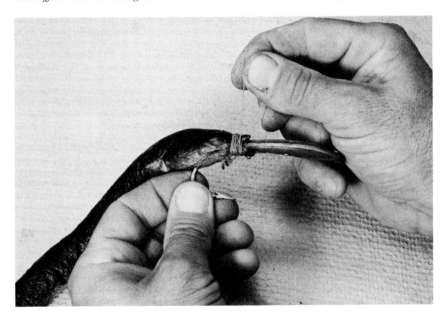

bunker, and they too are quite successful. In areas where striped bass won't hit dead bunker or where there is too much current, only live-lining pays off. Live-lining is far more effective, but requires more gear and sophistication on the part of the fisherman.

Before a fisherman ever thinks of fishing with live menhaden he must equip his boat with a live-bait tank. Bunker are extremely active swimming fish and must swim all the time to move sufficient water over their gills and obtain enough oxygen to stay alive. Therefore, a tank must be large enough to hold from one to two dozen bunker, 15 to 18 inches in length. This means that the tank should be 3–4 feet long, 18–24 inches wide, and about 18 inches deep. Water can be aerated in two ways. You can buy a large aquarium pump or build a two-pistoned affair that shoots a steady stream of air into your water. Or, you can modify a bilge pump or similar pump and pour fresh seawater into your tank. This latter is the better system and will maintain more fish for a longer period of time. It also demands that you have some hosework to take in the water and an overflow or stem in the tank to take off the excess water.

Bunker are peculiar fish and if you build your tank with corners in it, they will stick their snouts into them and suffocate without swimming. But if you have rounded sides, no corners, they will swim continually and stay alive. The direction they swim is almost always the same; they swim in a counterclockwise course. All pools, sinks, and toilets drain in a clockwise direction north of the equator and in a counterclockwise direction south of that line (the Coriolis force). Fish swim always against a current, and so should the fish in your man-made current. This is important and must be taken into consideration when you construct a tank and fix the direction of the inflow pipe. It should enter the fish box in such a manner that it sends the water circulating in a clockwise direction. If it does, you won't lose current or pressure trying to overcome the Coriolis force.

Such a live-bait system works equally well with other forms of large baitfish used for striped bass — mackerel, blackfish, whiting, weakfish, sculpins, or even the hyperactive bluefish. This form of the art is practiced to some extent by fishermen on western Long Island and northern New Jersey, but it is more highly developed by anglers on eastern Long Island, at Montauk Point, on Gardiners Island and Shelter Island, off Orient Point, and east along Great Island and Little Gull Island, across the Race in New York to Fishers Island, and up to Watch Hill, R.I.

Obtaining live bunker can be achieved by one of two ways: by snagging your own, or by making friends with a pound-net fisherman. Then be there every morning, often before daybreak, to get them from him when he lifts his nets. Live bunker must be gently handled to keep them alive. They bruise easily and develop red blood spots on their flesh if hurt in the transfer. They are best transferred with a long-handled net and kept in the water whenever possible. Fresh seawater should fill the tank before the bunker are added and it should be capped with a lid when not withdrawing fish. I have had bunker leap out of the tank when they panic and jump more than 15 feet into the water.

Many species of fish that are live-lined, like mackerel, herring and whiting, are hooked by a single large hook through the flesh just ahead of the dorsal fin. However, they cannot be trolled in this hooking position. Bunker, however, are best hooked through the nostrils with a treble hook no larger than 6/0 and can thus be trolled. The larger hooks open the nostrils too greatly and break the thin piece of cartilage that bridges the two openings. Once this wears through, the bunker is free. Hooking a bunker through the nostrils doesn't damage the fish. Nostrils on fish are used only for smelling or tasting water, not breathing. With both jaws able to function, the bunker can breathe and easily swim. From this anterior hook position on the fish's head, bunker can easily be trolled.

I have found that the treble hook is better than a single hook for live-lining striped bass. The single hook too often lies alongside the fish and if a bass strikes there are times when it misses the hook and does not hook itself. With live, moving bait, striped bass invariably hit it at the front, the head. A treble hook ensures that it stays hooked. Nor would I use smaller hooks, because I have had 40- and 50-pound stripers bend open very good hooks. I would prefer to use an 8/0 or 10/0 treble hook, and do when I get an exceptionally large bunker, but because of the nostrils, I don't regularly use the larger hooks.

Seldom do striped bass strike the rear of a bunker. But bluefish in the same waters are equally fond of bunker and when they strike there is no question about it. They leave a cleanly cut fish with no tail. To solve this problem, I attach a second treble hook, one about 4/0, to the eye of the first hook by a piece of wire leader. This second hook can swing freely in the current and will usually lie alongside the tail of the bunker. It is a nice surprise for the ravenous bluefish.

Bunker hooked in the nostrils can be trolled, but at very slow speeds. My favorite method is to find a point of land where large boulders are sunken off the shoal and where the tide passes over at a fair speed. This is a natural spot for big striped bass and such locations can be adequately fished at a snail's pace. I stem the tide in such situations, letting the bunker, or two if someone else is fishing with me in the boat, slip back and forth across the boulders. I can work ahead ever so slowly and present the bunker to new spots or drop back and sweep again over the area until the striped bass come to the top fighting for the bunker.

It is an awesome sight to watch three or four large striped bass, fish over 40 or 50 pounds, chase a live bunker to the surface and eventually strike it. This to me is one of the real highlights of striped bass fishing, to watch the actual strike. Live bait or not, it is a rewarding thrill.

In areas of running water the current's speed will change as the tide floods and ebbs. In water with some depth to it, the live bunker may have to be lowered. This is done with drails, and I continually change them as the current speeds up and then falls off, from as little as 1 ounce up to 6 ounces of lead.

The standard outfit for such fishing is usually a trolling rod and reel loaded with 20-pound-test Dacron line. In trickier situations, with a lot of boats around and the boulders closer to the top, I use a similar combination but switch to a 30-pound-test outfit. This strength line is all you need to handle a 50-pound bass with little or no worry about its breaking the rod or line.

The terminal end of the Dacron is finished off with 15 feet of 50- or 60-pound-test monofilament, and if bluefish are around, the last 5 feet is wire leader instead of monofilament. It is amazing how little line is fished in such stemming or trolling situations. The bunker may hold about 5 feet below the surface, but the striped bass will quickly rise to them if they are alive and swimming properly. Often I fish with as little as 40 feet of line astern of the boat and seldom more than 100 feet, and the bass show little or no fear of the boat or running engines. The water averages between 20 and 30 feet.

Bunker will last a long time swimming by themselves, and the only casualties come when the tide moves exceptionally fast. In this case, the fish develop what anglers normally call "lockjaw." The constant fight against the current weakens them and their lower jaw drops open. Eventually it cannot be retracted and the fish drown and die. Dead bunker never seem to catch fish in these situations and they are returned to a fish box alongside the live-bait tank.

Butterfish

The butterfish, *Poronotus triacantus,* is really more of a baitfish than a gamefish. It has a very small mouth and takes only the smallest of lures. It is a relatively small fish with a real value as cut bait for some species and whole bait for others. It is seldom fished alive but caught by commercial netters and frozen, only to be sold to tuna fishermen or chummers for striped bass who use the butterfish as the hook bait. Butterfish have a deep body with a small, sharply forked tail and reach a maximum length of 12 inches, though 6 or 7 inches is generally considered large. From time to time, butterfish move into the estuaries, bays, and rivers along our coasts, especially when small, but for the most part they frequent the near-offshore waters and find protection in its depths and expansiveness. They range from South Carolina to Newfoundland and Nova Scotia, prime tuna grounds in the summer.

American eel

I would be hard pressed to choose between the bunker and the eel as the best striped bass bait. Both produce a lot of big fish and both require a somewhat skilled and sophisticated angler to fish them properly. I think that more eels are used to fish striped bass than bunker, only because they are more easily obtained, are easier to maintain, and can be used in a greater number of ways.

The common or American eel, *Anguilla rostrata,* is spawned and born in the Sargasso Sea, in the middle of the Atlantic in an area north and east of Bermuda. While the eels are still in the juvenile stage, they begin swimming for North America, and it may take some of these little fish more than a year to make land. It takes several years more to grow to maturity and they do so along our coastal estuaries, bays, and tidal rivers. Not all are confined to the coasts, however; large numbers begin an upriver trek and will swim hundreds of miles upstream to spend one or more years in a strictly freshwater environment. When the urge to reproduce creeps into them, the males and females head back for the ocean, make that long crossing back to the Sargasso Sea. There they mate, and reproduce, and the mature fish die.

While along our coasts, eels have a special place in the diets of striped bass and fishermen. Striped bass are great feeders on eels and will readily strike at them. By the time the juveniles reach the continental shelf, many are 6 to 10 inches long. These "shoestring" eels are great baits for smaller bass. Adult eels grow as large as 3 or 4 feet but most range between 2½ and 3 feet. Bass feed on eels regardless of size.

Many fishermen prefer smaller eels for striped bass, thinking that the longer eels discourage smaller fish from striking. I don't believe this is so. I have fished with eels of every size that happen to swim into my pot and have taken small bass, fish 7 and 8 pounds, on eels that were twice as long as they were. Bass are gluttonous as well as omnivorous.

The American eel.

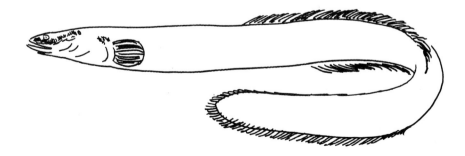

Eels spend a great deal of time in the mud and burrow there throughout the winter in a state of semi-hibernation. During the warmer days of the year, they spend their daylight hours in the mud and come out at night to feed. That is why striped bass are such avid night hunters, seeking eels on the move. Eels are basically scavenger fish and easily lured into an eel pot or trap by just about anything dead.

One of the most effective ways to fish an eel is while it is alive. Eels will take considerable punishment and handling. An eel hooked through the lower and upper jaws will last through hours of casting. The fish is best hooked with a 4/0 Eagle claw or beak-type hook, one with a substantial barb and curve to keep the eel from squirming off the hook. It can be fished from a drifting or anchored boat, under a bridge or from the edge of a jetty or dock. The bottom should be fairly free of cover so that the eel won't dig into it and hide, or swimming striped bass are likely to pass it by unnoticed. Eels can also be cast and then slowly retrieved or trolled while rowing or pushed by a small, quiet motor. In the latter case, a lot more line must be used to separate the noise from the food.

Eels designed to be trolled at higher speeds and fished with wire line are rigged on lead heads that provide weight. The shape of the lead also gives a dead eel realistic swimming action as it is pulled along by the boat. One technique for rigging an eel is illustrated here; there are several others. One that is popular among the islands of Massachusetts is the eel skin. The first step is to cut a ring around the head of the eel and pull off the skin. The skin is then added to the back of a large plug that has had its tail hook removed. The eel skin is secured to the plug (stapled, nailed, or sewn) and a few slits are cut in the skin near the head to let in water. While trolled, the plug and its diving plane give the eel skin an exceptionally lifelike action. Water fills the eel skin and it undulates almost as well as the real thing.

Other variations on rigging eels are similar to the leaded hook used for squid. An eel, minus its head, is impaled on the hook and the skin sewn to the holes on the lead head. Almost all forms of fishing with a dead eel require that a lead of some sort be added to the head to control the depth at which the eel settles and to give it a lifelike action when trolled.

Pieces of cut eel are also used for striped bass. The eel is sliced into 3- or 4-inch lengths and then halved. The half pieces are then hooked as you would any other piece of cut bait. Eels make especially good bait because of the great oiliness of their flesh which sends out odor messages as it lies on the bottom of the surf. They can be used with a fish-finder rig or a three-way swivel. But because the cut eel is such an attractor, it also calls other fish as well, and often the scavengers, sharks and sea robins, will get to your cut eel before a striped bass.

One of the most versatile lures for striped bass is the eel, either in parts, skinned, or whole. Illustrated here are several versions, and for each one here there is at least a dozen variations in use. 1. Typical Cuttyhunk eelskin. 2. Trolling rig for an eelskin. 3. Short eelskin attached to a swimming plug after the rear hooks have been removed. 4. Eelskin attached to a metal squid or tin spoon, a rig that swims well in the surf. 5. Whole eel attached to a sash chain. 6. Rigged eel attached to a chain and lead head designed to make the eel body swim when trolled. 7. Eel with head removed but replaced with a lead head to make the rig sink when trolled.

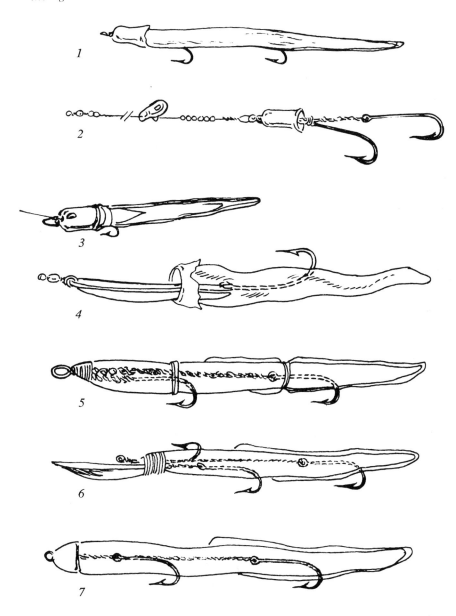

Atlantic mackerel

The common mackerel, *Scomber scombrus,* makes a great live bait as
well as cut bait for striped bass. Early migrations of mackerel up and
down our coast make them the harbingers of spring and winter. In most
parts of their range they are transients, but to anglers off Massachusetts
and in the Gulf of Maine, mackerel take up summer residence and can be
used through the fishing season as a bass bait.

Mackerel are not used as often when trolling for bass as is the live
bunker. Instead, mackerel are fished on a liveline, or free-swimming.
Though not totally free-swimming — it has a hook and line attached to
it — the mackerel is still able to swim about tethered on the line. This free-
swimming method is used in an area striped bass frequent and mackerel
usually avoid, and can cause pandemonium among a pod of bass.

Mackerel fishing is a lot simplier than angling with bunker. The
requirements for catching mackerel are simple. They are easily obtained
by attaching half a dozen small diamond jigs off dropper lines or directly
to a main line and finishing off with a large diamond jig or Hopkins lure
on the terminal end. Keeping them alive requires the same technique
as for bunker. Once you have solved these problems, fishing with this
bait is easy. Unlike bunker, mackerel are usually hooked just under the
skin and through only a small part of the flesh, just ahead of the dorsal
fin. Some anglers use single hooks, 4/0 O'Shaughnessy, while others
swear by treble hooks. I prefer the first for mackerel.

Large spinning outfits are used for mackerel, and with caution, they
can be cast away from the boat. The accepted technique, however, is to
use a fairly stiff spinning rod, one about 8 to 8½ feet long, a light surf
reel, and about 250 yards of 20–30-pound-test monofilament. The line
is attached directly to the hook without sinkers and the live fish is allowed
to swim away from the boat with the bail open on the reel. Once the fish
has taken 100 to 200 yards of line, the bail is closed and the drag set
especially light on the reel. After striking a fish, the drag is readjusted —
this takes a bit of skill so that you don't tighten it too greatly. Instead of
putting too much pressure on a drag, many anglers develop the habit of
fingering the spool, applying pressure to its edge with the index finger to
add more drag without adjusting the reel.

The technique of live-lining mackerel is done from an anchored boat,
a bridge, or a point of land. It is a lot easier, however, and somewhat
more effective while drifting. This slow movement keeps the fish off the
bottom and exposes your bait to new water and potentially more striped
bass.

Bullheads

There is another form of forage fish that often finds its way into the stomachs of the striped bass, but only rarely do anglers on the East Coast use them for bait. These are the sea robins or sculpin, belonging to the families Cottidae and Hemitripteridae. Their species are so numerous and varied that a listing would thrill only the taxonomist. The fisherman is interested in them only as bait, and they reach their highest perfection in the hands of West Coast striped bass anglers. In San Francisco Bay and the surrounding area, fishing with bullheads (sculpin) is a finely tuned art and is used most when the bass are off the estuaries and in the bays during the summer.

Bullhead are fished dead and backwards. The hook is forced into the fish behind the head and in a forward direction. It is brought outside through the gills and laid alongside the bait with the tip and barb exposed. The eye is tied against the body with a half-hitch and the thread passed back to the tail, where another half-hitch is wrapped, keeping the fishing line close to the body and tail of the fish and giving it a directional pull off the tail end. Otherwise, any pressure on the line would make the fish turn sideways and offer a lot of resistance.

The sculpin of the Pacific Ocean is a favorite striped bass bait. Here are two methods for rigging the spiny fish.

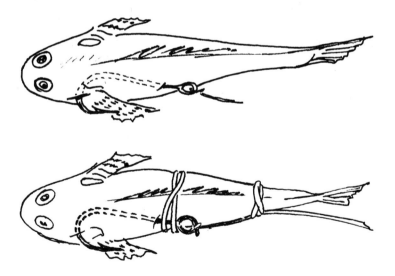

Hook sizes are 5/0 or 6/0, depending upon the size of the bullhead, and usually O'Shaughnessy or Siwash in style. The terminal end is finished off in a 5-to-10-foot heavy monofilament leader. A barrel sinker is used with such a rig so that any soft-mouthed bass won't flinch at the first resistance. The bait is taken head first and because of the exposed position and direction of the hook, there are very few missed fish.

Sardines

The California sardine, *Clupanodon caeruleus,* is a close relative of the common herring found on the East Coast. But California fishermen make better use of the bait and it is fished on the West Coast as much as the bunker is fished by Atlantic anglers. The sardine is seldom used in the live state; it is more often cut and filleted. The side of a sardine is sliced free of the bone and when the entire piece is used, it is skewered onto the hook in much the same manner as a worm. Really large pieces are pushed on the hook and up the leader. Smaller chunk baits are made by slicing the sardine fillet into pieces. The hook is run completely through the piece, out the other side and the point and barb are brought back into the meat to be hidden.

Three methods of rigging the sardine, another West Coast favorite.

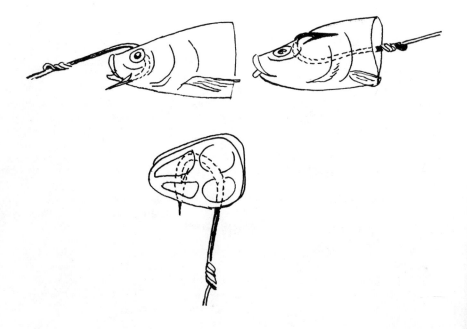

The sardine head is a valuable piece of bait and after the fillets are removed, the remainder is cut squarely, a little behind the gills. The head can be hooked through the eyes and out the side, or from the open cut into the head, and the hook then turned up to come out just behind the eye. Slabs or steak cuts are also popular and are cross-sections of the entire fish with the fillets intact. This is a valuable cut because the hook can be pushed in from one side, guided around the backbone, and brought to the surface on the next side, and most of the hook, except for the very tip, is well hidden in the flesh. Hooks for cut sardine range from 2/0 to 3/0 for small pieces to 8/0 for bigger slices. The Eagle Claw is an extremely popular pattern and the O'Shaughnessy a close second.

Other fishes

There are several other species of fish, often younger stages of game-fishes, that make excellent bait for striped bass. These include other herrings in addition to the menhaden, the occasional mullet that works its way north in the summer, blackfish (tautog), black sea bass, weakfish (squeteague), bluefish, and whiting. Most of these as baits are fished like mackerel when alive and like bunker when dead.

The typical hooking of a dead bait is through the eyes if it is not to be trolled. Dead baits, unless adorned with lead heads and special rigs, are poor choices for trolling. Fish like sea bass and the blackfish are especially hardy and will last a long time in the live condition. In this case, hooking just ahead of the dorsal fin or through the nostrils is the best method for keeping them alive and active.

18

Artificial Lures for Striped Bass

It's difficult to determine just when the first artificial lures were introduced to salt water. Though flies made of cloth and feathers had been used to lure salmon to the hook even before the Romans came to Britain, their application to salt water and other species of fish was extremely tardy. Saltwater fish were best fed real foods as bait, and the lowly squid was most often tossed into the surf with a hook in it to entice striped bass to feed.

Squidding, as the technique was called, was strictly a handline operation for generations. Even after rods and reels for saline fishermen became cheap and common, handlines were still favored by local beach bums and bayrats. The use of artificial lures for striped bass even predates the development of rod-and-reel fishing. Bass were taken from the surf by bones and feathers fastened to hooks, spun over the head, and then flung into the water.

The retrieve was determined by how fast an angler could pull in the line, hand over fist, or how quickly he could race up the beach to keep the lure moving. If a striped bass hit, it was a tug-of-war. If the hook held, the bass usually lost.

The first artificial lures to be cast in salt water were probably metal jigs or tins designed to imitate a squid. The tin squid, poured from tin mixed with lead and other metals, and often adorned with feathers or bucktails, was strictly a saltwater lure with no freshwater ancestry. The earliest plugs for saltwater fishing were adaptations of freshwater varieties, designed for black bass and northern pike. The development of the saltwater plug came only after the development and diversity of tin squids were almost complete.

The tin squid worked well for several reasons. The first was its weight. A wet linen or cotton line, after a few casts, created a lot of resistance in the guides and along the rod. A heavy tin squid could overcome this drag and still be sent a nautical mile to the beginning of the comber. Eventually, large saltwater plugs replaced the freshwater versions and with their added weight, they too could be tossed quite well with a conventional reel.

Even with these modifications in lures, and conventional reels with built-in anti-backlash devices, the artificial lure still lagged far behind live or cut bait in popularity when it came to saltwater fishing. What the sport needed was the development of new equipment. The spinning reel was the answer. It came to the United States shortly after World War II. In just a few years, it was introduced to salt water and the boom in artificial lures was underway.

Today, the saltwater angler has a great selection of artificial lures from which to choose. Their variety is even greater than the natural animals they intend to imitate. Each group of lures is also expanded by color variations, finish, and specific actions, so to the beginning saltwater bass fisherman, the world of artificial lures might seem a hodgepodge. But it can easily be put into order.

Lures are effective and work because they are based on several principles that make them inviting to fish. If they did not, fish wouldn't strike. Lures are most often designed to imitate smaller fish upon which larger fish feed, or to stimulate the fish's sense of smell, sound, and sight. Lures are colored either like the real bait or with vivid combinations that do more to attract a fish's attention. Color combinations and patterns need not necessarily resemble the real thing to make a fish bite. Some of the best plugs are colored red and white, and I haven't found a striped bass food that is colored red and white.

Other lures appeal to the receptors on a striped bass that respond to sound or vibration. This can mean food to the bass or just act as an irritant, making it angry or excited, or goading it into hitting the lure. Some lures have hollow bodies and contain weights that rattle, others make popping or gurgling noises that appeal to a bass's curiosity.

Another class of lures possess a smell or have an odor about them that can attract striped bass. The sense of smell is far more keenly developed in a striper than the ability to hear or see. This area has long been overlooked by lure manufacturers. Recently, the Woodstream Corporation produced lures coated with a Hydron spray, a highly concentrated bait scent that is supposed to attract fish. I have used it on freshwater fish and found that it outfished noncoated lures. I have yet to try it on striped bass but I expect it should work just as well.

Artificial lures for striped bass can be divided roughly into several categories—plugs, spoons, jigs, tubes, and copy-cat lures. Plugs for striped bass can be further divided into classifications determined by the zone in which they work. First, there are the surface lures, including poppers, chuggers, darters, and propeller lures whose basic function is one of noise and attraction. Then there are the medium-running lures. Some are subsurface lures that swim rapidly just under the top of the water. Others are floating-diving lures. These lures will float when at rest and the pressure of being pulled through the water forces them to dive.

The last category is the deep-running or diving lures. Many of these lures achieve their depth because they are heavy and sink in the water. Others have large diving planes in the front that when pulled through the water force the lure to head down. Others are combinations of sinking lures with diving lips and they search out the deepest waters when cast or trolled.

Spoons are not as numerous or as variable as plugs. They are small, solid, rather heavy spoons and chunks of metal or else larger spoons that are thinner in build and imitate large baitfish. Jigs are of two basic types, the all-metal or diamond jig, which is a hybrid between heavy spoon and jig, and the feathered or bucktailed jig, with a lead head that can be made in numerous shapes and sizes.

Tube lures are rather new, though earlier turkey- and chicken-bone lures are quite old. Today, the tube lures are designed to imitate everything from a school of baitfish to a long sandworm. The final classification of lures is the look-alikes or the copy-cats, and their development paralleled the development of soft, plastic materials that could be molded into bait shapes and adorned with action heads and hooks.

PLUGS

The plug came into its own with the development of efficient conventional reels and the spinning reel. A plug on either system provides the weight which takes out the line and makes a cast possible. Lures are measured in two manners. The first is by their weight, which can vary from fractions of an ounce up to 6 and 7 ounces. The other measurement is one of length, and plugs vary from 2 or 3 inches up to 8 and 9 inches. Some larger plugs can be cast, but most are designed to be trolled rather than heaved.

Top-water plugs

Quite naturally, these plugs are designed to float on the surface and are built of wood or hollow plastic, or molded condensed plastic materials that are lighter than water. The first requirement of a top-water plug is that it be able to attract fish by one of several methods. One is the creation of sound by popping or chugging. Many top-water plugs or poppers have faces cut on various angles to the water. If they are cupped, they

Top-water plugs. Top row, left to right: Gibbs Satellite Darter, Heddon Big Chugg, Raja Goo-Goo Eyes. Second row: Old Pal "817," Rebel Popper, Rebel Popper-Bucktail. Third row: Odap Bullet Popper, Old Pal Hydron Popper. Bottom: Arbogast Dasher.

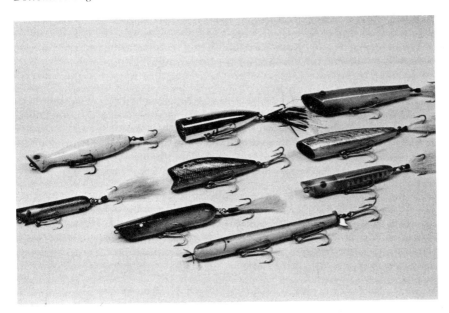

will make a popping plug, and this noisy nature is used in several situations. The most common is when a school of surface-feeding bass have been spotted. The commotion on top puts the popper right in the action and bass readily strike it. In shallow-water situations, along a beach or river bank, poppers will catch the immediate attention of nearby bass and usually bring on a strike. Poppers can also be used effectively when fishing blind, over deeper water. A popper working frantically over the surface can cause a deep-lying bass to rise and strike.

A second group of surface plugs are called darters or swimmers. These two styles are closely allied. Darters have a face or control plane on the head that causes the lure to dash off to one side or the other when pulled against the waters. This simulates the erratic swimming of an injured baitfish and is a real bass attractor. The swimming surface plug sets up a heavy vibration pattern that is transmitted through the depths and attracts interested bass. A modification of this is a swimmer with propellers on head and tail of the plug. These not only set up vibrations in the water when retrieved, but the metal rattles and has an added noise attraction. These plugs can be just as effective on striped bass as on fresh-water species of fish.

Medium-depth plugs

These plugs can also be classed as subsurface and float-diving plugs. Some are designed with shallow lips at the head so that they do not run very deeply into the water. This is a desired feature when fishing in water 2 to 4 feet deep and filled with weeds that do not quite reach the surface. A popper plug might cause too much noise or action, but a shallow-swimming plug nicely fills the bill for attracting any hiding striped bass.

Also part of this group are the floater-diver plugs. When at rest, these plugs float on the surface of the water, but because of a slight diving plane on the front, they will descend when pulled through the water. This type of plug has a special fishing action that, with several fast turns of the handle, will make the plug dive. Then the retrieve is stopped. In the stopped position, the plug rapidly floats to the surface. Then the retrieve is resumed. This dive and float, dive and float resembles an injured minnow and is a real bass seducer.

Still a third type of plug that works in this zone of the water is a slight variation on the floater-diver plug. It has a density just slightly less than that of the water and will float when first cast and allowed to rest. It is faster to dive, however, and does not recover as rapidly to float back to the surface. This is a true medium-running plug, a lure that is controlled more by the shape of the diving lip than the density of the plug.

Subsurface and medium-running minnows. Top row: Raja Goo-Goo Eyes "Big Daddy." Second row, left to right: Old Pal Raposa, Rebel Super Minnow. Third row: Cordell's Big Red Fin, Cordell's Red Fin, Rapala Salt Water Minnow. Last row: Rapala Magnum Minnow, Boone Bait Minnow.

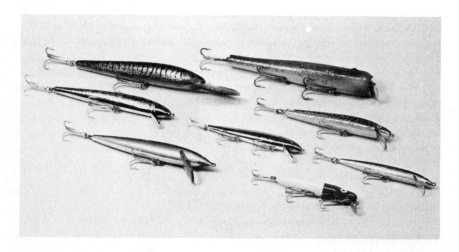

The lip on a diving plug provides all the swimming action, as well as the rate of dive. The angle the lip makes with the horizontal line of the body will determine how deeply it travels. The width of the lip determines how well and how often it undulates. A lip that is close to the angle of the horizontal will dive deepest. The lip that is steeply sloped spends more time wiggling than diving. The length of the lip also controls how fast it dives as well as its wiggle. A long, wide lip on a slight angle means that the lure dives deeply and shimmers wildly. Lip angles vary from lure manufacturer to manufacturer but fall into three general ranges: shallow, medium, and deep divers.

Deep-diving plugs

Deep-diving plugs achieve their goal by using one of two construction techniques. The diving plane is the first and we have discussed it rather thoroughly. The second technique is to weight the lure—that is, make it heavier than water so it will sink. Some lures are weighted and provided with a shallow lip. The weight takes the lure deep while the lip makes it swim. Medium-running lures equipped with big, slow-angled lips become deep-diving lures.

Deep-running plugs. Top row: Reb 2 Shorty. Second row, left to right: Rapala Blue Mullet, Rapala Magnum Minnow. Third row: Rebel Diving Minnow, Rebel Diving Minnow (medium). Bottom: Old Pal Flash Raposa Deep Troller.

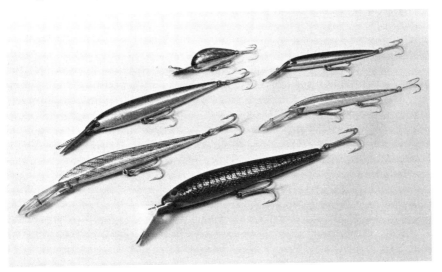

The ultimate in depth is the big-lipped lure with a sinking body. These are often large lures, too heavy for easy casting, and are designed primarily to be trolled. A large lip, one big enough to take a lure deeply into the water, can be cumbersome and collect weeds. That is why the sinking lure, with a modified lip, is used in combination to achieve almost the same effect. The eye or ring to which the line or snap is attached on some plugs can also affect whether it dives, runs on top, or is a deep-diver. The position of the eye has its effect on the direction of the pull and controls the angle the diving lip makes with the surface. Actual lure choice is determined by where the fish are feeding, with your sole objective to place the plug as close to these striped bass as possible.

SPOONS

The first spoon-type lure was just that—a spoon, cut off at the handle. A hole was drilled on one end for the ring or line and another drilled on the other end for a ring and hook. A school of baitfish swimming through the water, or even an individual fish, will flash or reflect sun regularly. This flashing gets the attention of gamefish.

The action of a spoon is produced by its wobbling effect. It sets up a flashing sequence which bass can follow. The wobbling technique imitates the side-to-side undulations of a swimming fish and is quite effective in its duplication.

Light spoons

Light spoons rely more on their shape to produce the desired action than on other factors. As a result, weight will kill the action in this type of spoon and for the most part they are thin and large. The reduced weight allows them to flutter better against the force of the water, and the large sides increase their surface area so that this action can be exaggerated.

Most spoons used for striped bass in saltwater situations are chrome-plated and metallic in appearance. Painted spoons can be effective, but the metal finish endures longer. Spoons of this nature are attention-getters in proportion to their light-flashing abilities. Some magnify their effectiveness with real swimming action. One of these is the large bunker spoon. It is designed to imitate one of the striped bass's favorite foods. Smaller spoons are often adorned on their hooks with feathers or bucktails to add a swimming action, while still others are finished with strips of pork rind that extend the length of the lure and create a tail for added interest.

Spoons, heavy and light. Top row, left to right: Hopkins Red and White 550, Hopkins Hammered Spoon 550, Hopkins Hammered Spoon 388, Hopkins Hammered Spoon 3½ No-EQL, Hopkins Hammered Spoon Shorty 150, Hopkins Hammered Spoon S-1. Bottom row: JAG Mooselock Wobbler (1¼-oz.), Spearing Spoon, Luhr Jensen Krocodile (5-oz.), Abu Toby (⅝-oz.), Abu Toby (½-oz.), Tony Acceta Pet 15, Tony Acceta Pet 13, Squid Spoon 2.

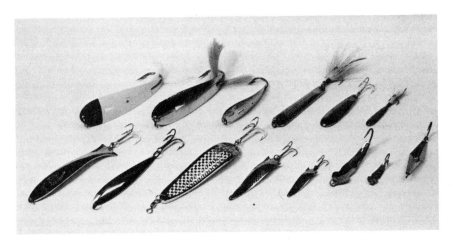

Heavy spoons

These striped bass lures might not be considered spoons by some, but for the want of a better classification or name, they are referred to as spoons. These include the famous tin squids, castings of lead that must be periodically brightened by polishing, and the famous Hopkins collection of pounded or hammered metal lures.

Both lures have some action in the water when retrieved or trolled at an even pace, but it is minimal when compared to the lighter, hydrodynamically responsive spoons. The reason is their weight versus exposed area. They are just too heavy to be retrieved smoothly. They were made heavy so that they could be small in size yet cast a long distance.

The secret to working these lures is to vary their retrieve, and the action is imparted more by the fisherman than the design of the lure. A jerking retrieve, one simulating the swimming pattern of a squid, is a surefire bass-producer. These are favored lures when fishing blind because you can cover great amounts of water and set up an enticing swimming pattern.

The tin (really lead) squid is seldom fished without a bucktail or set of feathers attached to the hook. This increases the illusion of a swimming fish. Hopkins lures can be fished without a tail dressing, but when the hook is covered in feathers or adorned with a pork rind, it stands a better chance of catching the eye of a striped bass.

In addition to being retrieved like other lures, the hammered metal spoon can also be fished as a jig, because of its weight. Striped bass in freshwater impoundments are regularly taken by vertical jigging of a small hammered spoon, and the action is carried on in a vertical rather than horizontal plane.

JIGS

Two widely used striped bass lures fall under the heading of jigs, not so much because of their construction or shape, but in accordance with the way they are fished.

Bucktailed jigs

The bucktailed jig is one of the oldest and probably still one of the most effective striped bass lures available to an angler. Its design is still rather basic, composed of a hook that is fished turned toward the surface, a lead head on the shank near the eye, and a dressing of bucktail deer hairs around the trailing edge of the lead head. There are some variations to the dressing. Recently, synthetic filaments have been used when bucktails are scarce. They can be made in any length whereas bucktails are rather fixed. Marabou feathers are also used and give the jig a pulsating effect similar to the squid they are trying to imitate. There is also a reverse bucktail that works quite effectively at times. Some anglers have just discovered it, but John Naimoli of Amityville, Long Island, has been tying and fishing the reverse bucktail since the early 1930s. This lure is dressed similarly to the standard bucktail jig but with somewhat fewer hairs. Then, a second mass of hairs or artificial fibers is tied in a forward direction, all but burying the eye. This also produces a pulsating effect similar to the marabou feathers.

Bucktails can be fished just as they are but they are far more effective when used in combination with a pork rind. The pork rind-bucktail combination is a standard lure in most Northeast bass waters and is fished best on wire while trolling and jigging. At one time, the bucktail was built with a swinging hook. The head was molded onto a shank with eyes on each end and the hook was attached to the trailing eye. When coupled with a 4- or 5-inch split pork rind, the action was so great that it could be fished without being jigged. For some reason, this type of jig is impossible to purchase nowadays.

Bucktailed jigs. Left to right: Beri-Jig, Reverse Bucktail by Sea King, No-Alibi Jig (4-oz.), Boone King Jig (3-oz.), Boone Bean Head (4-oz.), Nickelure (1-oz.).

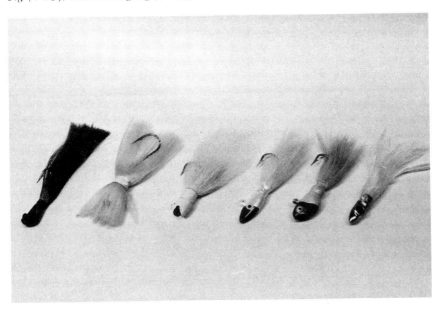

Jig heads come in a variety of patterns and shapes, from blunt-headed chunks of lead designed for bouncing along the bottom to bean- and bullet-shaped heads used in faster trolling situations. The weight of jigs also varies greatly according to the size of bass you are after and the depth and speed at which you are trolling. They range from ½ and 1 ounce to 4 and 5 ounces. Colors also are used, with white the favorite. Matching colored pork rinds are used or switched for red or yellow versions.

Diamond jigs

Diamond jigs are quite similar to tin squids and hammered spoons in their use, weight, and hydrodynamic reaction. Basically, the diamond jig is shaped like an elongated diamond, often ½ to ¾ inch at its widest and 5 to 7 inches at its longest. The jigs are made of cast metal and then chrome-plated so that they reflect light. They act like a baitfish and are jerked up and down off the bottom to look like a squid. The jig is finished with a treble hook on the business end and a fixed eye on the other end.

Diamond jigs can be fished alone, with pork rind or strips of cut squid. In some cases, the treble hook is replaced with a single O'Shaugh-

Diamond jigs. Left to right: Abu Egon (2⅛-oz.), Bridgeport Diamond Jig (10-oz.), Bridgeport Diamond Jig (2-oz.), Bridgeport Diamond Jig with imbedded hook (½-oz.).

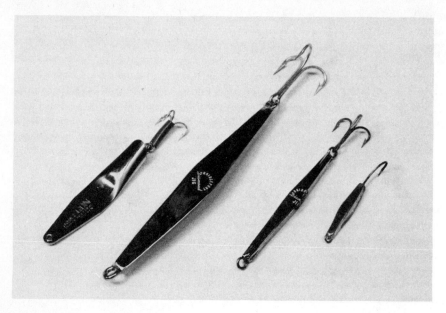

nessy or Siwash. Diamond jigs range greatly in size, from ½-ounce jigs for mackerel to 2-pound jigs for cod. Diamond jigs for striped bass range between 4 and 8 ounces. The speed of the water in which you are jigging and its depth will determine the weight of the jig you should use more than the size of the fish you hope to catch.

Most jigs are fished with their natural, chrome-metallic finish. However, one year in Plum Gut, off eastern Long Island, the fishing had come to a temporary standstill for everyone but one charterboat skipper. A close look through a pair of binoculars proved that he had painted his jigs a fluorescent red, and the bass liked it.

TUBE LURES

The striped bass fisherman is usually an innovative person and can readily adapt materials outside the world of the striped bass to the fishing scene. One of these innovations is the use of surgical tubing. This tubing, in its natural state, is a tan or translucent brown and doesn't look very appetizing, nor would one imagine that it could catch fish. But when cut into 1-foot lengths, with a lead head added, with or without eyes, and a pair of hooks, one on a wire leader inside the tube that comes near the head and a second hook a few inches from a split in the tail, you have what closely approximates the action of an eel or long sandworm moving through the water.

For added effect, some of the early forms that actually used surgical tubing were dyed red to simulate a healthy sandworm or black to imitate an eel. They all took plenty of bass. The surgical tube now ranks in number two spot, close behind bucktail–pork rind jigs as a bass-getter.

In early editions, the head was little more than a bullet-shaped piece of lead. Eyes were added for extra effect and the planing heads to make it swim in the water. Later, some of the long tail hooks with exceptionally long shanks were bent slightly and the action was further increased. Today, surgical-tube lures are a favorite with charterboat skippers who cannot get their fares to jig a bucktail.

Surgical-tube lures. Left to right: Trifin Eel (10-oz.), Tube Alou (3-oz.), simple surgical tube, Raja Tube (3-oz.), Trifin (2-oz.).

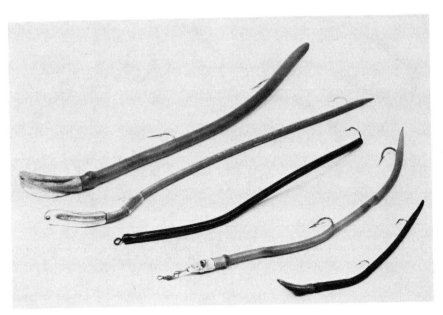

Umbrella lures

Large pieces of surgical tubing worked so well that some fishermen, mostly the charterboat captains, began using smaller-diameter tubes to imitate smaller baitfish. A single-plane spread was in use on striped bass as long ago as the 1930s. In this rig, two or more lures were strung together on a trolling plane and used to simulate several baitfish swimming together in a school. Usually they all had hooks and a striped bass could get caught on any lure. When the tubes became available about the middle 1960s, one Montauk charter skipper switched the plugs to tubes and strung them on what looked like a coathanger. It really caught striped bass and it was a well-guarded secret lure for months.

This is one example of an umbrella rig, the Whirling Dervish by Garcia. This umbrella is collapsible. The arms are opened and locked into place by a nut and bolt imbedded in a grooved lead head that also acts to weight the lure.

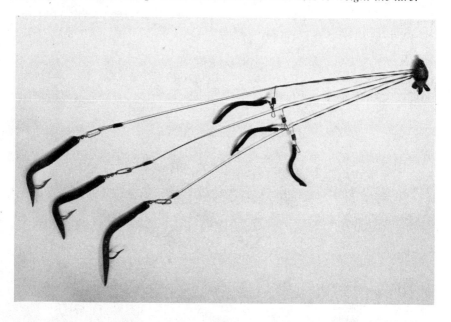

But the single plane of the lures gave him trouble. The lures and coat-hanger spun too much, twisting his line, overriding the swivels, and there weren't enough tubes. Also, the coathanger wire wasn't heavy enough and collapsed when trolled against the heavy rip off Montauk. If one plane is good, then two must be better, he reasoned to himself, and set two at right angles to each other. Thus, he had four spreader arms, each trailering a tube lure. Then he poured a lead head at the point where they came together and a swivel to which the line could be added. He further modified the lure by adding teasers halfway down the spreader rods. He also now used brass welding rod because it was tougher and springier, and fished four hooked lures on each rib. It began closely to resemble an umbrella's ribs and a school of small, whirling baitfish. Then he added a larger tube on a leader that emanated from the center. He made this the hooked tube and cut off all the hooks on the others. Now they wouldn't foul so easily and the larger lure almost always got the strike.

The umbrella rig now truly looked like a school of baitfish and the striped bass fell for it in such record numbers that there was a lot of talk about it being unsportsmanlike, or even illegal. But the rig got so expensive to produce that if you hung one on the bottom and couldn't break it loose, you could leave $10 to $15. The umbrella rig is still in use today, but is not the "hot" lure it was once supposed to be. It is still effective, but like many lures, if you don't use it, it won't catch fish. Often anglers seriously believe that a fish changes its preference for a lure. If the food upon which fish feed happens to change, then lures can change. But too often a lure loses popularity not because the fish have switched, but because fishermen have lost faith in their artificial bait.

Dave Spohn of Orient, N.Y., a master rigger of umbrella lures, sets the swimmers straight after unhooking a fish.

COPY-CAT LURES

These are lures made possible because of advances in our technology. Plastics that are lifelike in both texture and coloration have produced a host of lures good enough so that they regularly fool striped bass. They are modified with lead or metallic heads that enable them to be fished at various depths and give them the action to make the plastic look like the real thing.

Copycat or look-alike lures. These are only a few of the many that are today available to the bass fisherman. Top to bottom: Alou Bait-Tail, Alou Shoe-String (1½-oz.), Alou Eel, Sevenstrand Squid, Boone Shrimptail, Beri-Eel, Trifin Whip-Tail, Cordell Tattle-Tale, Garcia Eelet.

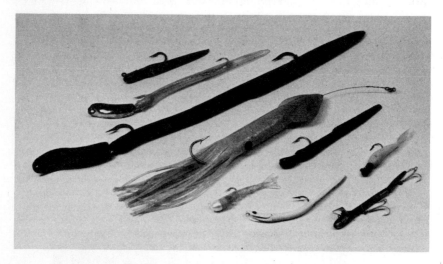

Foremost among these lures are imitations of eels. It is only natural that the eel be duplicated so often; it is a prime striped bass food. The Alou eel was one of the first, designed by Al Rinefelder and Lou Palma, and made in varying lengths to please both fisherman and fish. They swim effectively because the head for the plastic body has been well designed.

An offshoot by the same designers is the bait-tail, a cross between a jig and a plastic lure. The head is similar to that used on bucktailed jigs but modified in shape and weight so that it can be fitted with a plastic tail or body. It is fished similarly to the jig and probably should be classed with that type of lure.

Along lines similar to the bait-tail are the numerous shrimplike baits. These too have a jig-type head, a hook that is fished up, and soft, pliable tails that respond to the water's force. They are actually jigs with plastic bodies and were introduced to striped bass fishing after the great success plastic worms had in fresh water. Many imitate shrimp in size, shape, and coloration and are quite effective in taking striped bass.

The plastic squid was an engineering breakthrough. To duplicate the many curves and folds of a squid took an engineer with some degree of artistry. The look-alikes are quite effective when trolled and jigged. The problem is to weight them properly. Barrel sinkers inside seem to work, and the action comes not from the shape of the lure or the sinkers but the way the lure is worked by fisherman and rod tip.

There are a great variety of lures that seem to rise and fall in popularity with fishermen. Some are based on sound principles, others are bizarre in concept, are accepted for a while, and then fade away. One that seems to rise and fall is the Eelet, a small, thin lure made of hard plastic. It is probably better classified as a plug, if you can make a plug look like an eel. It is basically a freshwater lure, jointed in the center and with a small plane in the front designed to give it a swimming action rather than depth. The depth is controlled by the lure's weight, which is heavier than water, and it will sink rapidly unless pulled against the resistance of the water.

There are several other freshwater lures that make good plugs for striped bass. One is the large minnow made by Creek Chub for northern pike and muskellunge. Both solid and jointed minnows are good and work well either trolled or cast. The bigger lures are better trolled slowly. Some of these lures are modified by removing the tail treble hook and adding an eel skin. Most of these plugs are floaters and dive because of the shape of the forward lip. The lip can be easily adjusted to modify the degree of dive.

SELECTING YOUR LURES

Some lures are constructed so that you can get all the action you need simply by steadily retrieving them through the waters. They are hydrodynamically designed to react to the force of water flowing over their lips and heads, or against the sides of the body. These are good lures for beginning striped bass fishermen to choose. It takes the guesswork out of how to fish or retrieve them.

Other lures have no inherent action in them and are designed so that the fisherman can make them work in the exact manner he likes. These lures are almost always retrieved at variable speeds so that their depth can be controlled by the angler. Lures of this nature often require rods with educated tips to help the fisherman in the task and reels with higher retrieve ratios so that he can vary the speeds easily.

Whichever lures you choose, make sure you give them the care and maintenance necessary so they are always ready to work for you. Bent diving planes ruin the action of your plug. Weak rings, rusted or partially sprung, can give way when you are fighting a fish. Dulled hooks can make it impossible to set the hook on a tough-mouthed bass. Even the best quality saltwater hooks eventually fall victim to the effects of corrosion. You can retard this effect by rinsing the lure and hooks in warm fresh water before storing them after each trip and definitely after each season. Rusted, battered, and bent hooks should all be replaced.

19

Accessory Fishing Equipment

The serious bass angler cannot go fishing armed with rod and reel alone and hope for consistent success. He needs more gear—accessory equipment—to take striped bass under all the varied conditions he may encounter. Weather alone requires him to pay heed to his personal gear so that he can be out whenever the bass are running. Because of the great variety of fishing techniques by which stripers can be taken, the duffle of the bass angler must be more complete than that of other saltwater fishermen. Striped bass can be taken at night, from boats, from bridges, from jetties. They can be taken by casting, trolling, chumming, spinning, and drifting, and there is a great assortment of equipment that makes this task a bit easier for the fisherman.

Accessory equipment for the complete striped bass fisherman can roughly be divided into two groups, that designed to help you catch fish or get you into a position to catch fish, and that needed to make you safe, comfortable, and warm while you are doing the fishing. Of course, you can catch striped bass without any accessory gear, but it lets you concentrate longer on your fishing, allows you to be out when the weather is miserable, and makes those good times just so much more enjoyable.

CLOTHING AND PERSONAL GEAR

Clothing starts with insulated underwear. If you plan to fish the surf, even during early summer months the water can still be cold enough so that you get chilled after standing in it, in waders or hip boots, for even a short time. Insulated tops and bottoms are a must when it comes to night fishing on all but the warmest August evenings.

Closely associated with thermal underwear is the thermal or insulated sweatshirt. This heavy hooded shirt has almost become part of the standard uniform of the surfcaster, and with drawstrings around the hood it neatly fits under the hood of your rain jacket or foul-weather gear. CPO or chamois shirts are almost as popular as the hooded sweatshirt and are worn to keep the chill from getting you around the neck.

Foul-weather gear

Foul-weather gear is usually of the two-piece suit type. In the surf, if you have waders that come up to your chest, only the top half of the suit is worn. It is tied around the bottom and then further secured with a web or leather belt to keep out the surf if you happen to fall. If you ride a jetty or don't plan to get into the surf, the suit with top and pants is sufficient. This combination is also used by boat fishermen, even on dry days. Rain gear is good protection against wind too, and there are wet times in heavy seas when the boat sets up a spray as you run through it.

Some forms of foul-weather gear don't "breathe" and can get you as wet as no gear on a rainy day. Your body gives off a lot of moisture, even during the most routine activity. If there are no vents in your foul-weather suit, or if it is made of sealed nylon or plastic, then the suit will not let this moisture pass through. It condenses on the inside of the suit, and in an hour or so, you are just as wet and chilled as if you hadn't worn a suit.

Good rain suits are loose-fitting and allow moisture to escape through the sleeves, collar, and front. Trousers should be of the bib type with supporting straps over the shoulders. Rain pants with elastic in the waist hold well but they don't let the heat rise and moisture dissipate out the top. In a boat, if you wear knee-high boots and a finger-length top parka, you can get away without wearing rain trousers.

Waders

There are several brands and styles of waders on the market and none is very cheap, except the light plastic type that is good for a single day's fishing and is intended to save you on the day you forgot to bring your real waders. They are worn over the shoe, weigh almost nothing, and cost between $1 and $2.

Most surfcasters have two pairs of waders. Both have built-in boot-shoes. The first is a heavy-duty type with insulated feet. If you fish early in the season or very late, then this type of wader is a must. It is built of somewhat heavier-gauge material than lighter summer gear, and the foot, from about the knee down, is finished in double layers with a slight air space between that acts as insulation.

The well-dressed surf fisherman dons a pair of chest-high waders, then pulls over a hooded rain jacket, straps a web belt around his waist, and puts on felt-soled sandals. On his hip he sports a short hand-gaff and over his shoulder a lure bag. If he is lucky, he'll walk out of the surf with a 34-pound striped bass like this fisherman.

Surfcasting equipment. Shoulder-bag lure carrier and headlight with belt battery pack, web belt, sand spike, felt-soled sandals, Bimini belt, leather rod holder for belt, and ice creepers.

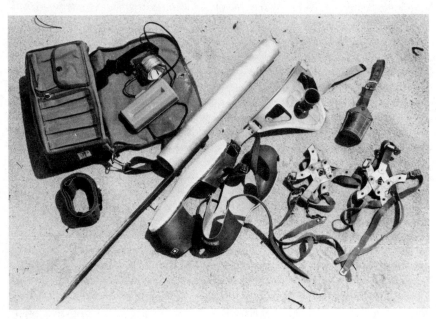

Waders should have a pocket on the inside to keep important items near and handy; a ring or grommet well attached to the outside in case you want to add a stringer of fish; and belt hoops to help you thread your belt around the waist. Wader fit can be a problem. During recent years, there has been a tendency on the part of many manufacturers to reduce the number of sizes they produce and this may make it difficult for you to find the perfect size. The wader is measured by the boot size, and it is usually about one size larger than your street shoe of the same size number. Very few manufacturers make half-sizes.

The other important measurement is the leg length. At one time you could order them almost as you do trousers, by length in inches. Today, you have only long, medium, and short from which to choose. Don't pick a wader if it fits you just right while you are standing up. It is too short. Bend the knees and sit down. If you are not pinched in the knees when you do this, then you have enough room and the waders fit. They may look a bit sloppy when you stand up, but you will be able to move around easily and sit down on the tailgate of your vehicle when you want to.

Hats

Hats have become another symbol of the surfcaster and boat fisherman. Typically long-visored, the hat plays an important role in a fisherman's ability to see what's happening on and in the water. Many of the long-visored hats have their sun shade composed of blue or green transparent plastic. This reduces the amount of light hitting the eyes but still gives the fisherman a chance to scan what's going on above without lifting his chin.

The boat fisherman has a somewhat modified surf hat, with a hard, plastic visor, usually not transparent, but proof against rain and spray. A good hat costs a little more but will often last a lot longer. Some of these hats, especially those with extra-long visors, occasionally come equipped with flipdown sunglasses attached to the underside of the visor. These are great, and when they have polaroid filters they are even greater. If you'd rather not have them attached, then polaroid sunglasses are your best bet. If you wear prescription glasses, then polaroid snap-ons can meet your needs, or you can have prescription polaroids made.

Polaroid lenses help you fish better in two ways. First, they filter out the stray rays of light and let you see deeper into the water. You can spot moving bass or read the bottom for signs or navigation. Second, they reduce the glare on the water during a warm, summer day, and this can make fishing much less fatiguing. Glare can have a negative effect on your fishing attitude if you can't escape it.

Shoes

The best shoes to wear in a boat have bottoms that grip wet or slippery surfaces, do not carry sand and dirt into the boat with each step, and do not mark fiberglass decks. Some boat shoes fill one or more parts of these requirements, but it doesn't take much more effort or money to find the proper boat shoe. Getting chewed out just once by a boat skipper or a fisherman who has invited you on board for the day is embarrassing enough to make you wish you'd given more thought to footgear.

Most boat shoes have canvas tops and can readily be washed when dirty and dry quickly if they become wet. But early in the season, wet canvas shoes never seem to dry, and they become especially cold after they are wet. You can get boat shoes with the same gripping soles found on canvas shoes but with leather uppers. I don't know how wet feet affect you, but as long as my feet feel dry and warm, the rest of my body can be wet and I won't mind it too much. If my feet are wet, I'm unhappy.

FISHING ACCESSORIES

There are numerous accessories for the fisherman both on the beach and on the boat. Some he can do without, others are more of a necessity than an accessory. I have listed just a few which I feel are important. Other skippers can always add their own personal necessities to the list to make it complete for them.

Bimini belt

Most spinning rods can be worked standing up and held in both hands. But a 20- or 30-pound-class trolling outfit, loaded with wire and worked from a moving boat, makes a portable gimbal or Bimini belt a real necessity. Reeling in often to check for weeds has a tendency to enlarge your belly button if you don't have a belt or rod pocket handy. When it comes to the actual fighting of a fish, you'll find it is much easier to handle a big bass on a belt. You can then use your legs and back to take some of the strain off the arms.

Gaffs

Freshwater anglers often seem shocked when they first see a gaff used on a fish. They prefer the idea of a net. But adequate nets are just too big to handle when it comes to boating a big fish. Lures or rigs with multiple hooks foul a net so badly that very soon even the most considerate angler switches to a gaff. A gaff is an efficient, effective device to get a fish quickly into the boat. Gaffs for boat use come in several lengths and sizes. I'm a firm believer that every boat should have two on board, one a large, double-handled affair for really large fish and a second somewhat smaller, but still with a handle at least 2 feet long, so that you don't have to double over on the gunwale to gaff a bass.

In the surf, long-handled gaffs are out of the question if you are doing your own gaffing. A short-handled gaff, often with just enough wood on it to hold the hook, is used. Many come with tip covers or holders that attach to the belt to hide the tip so that the surfcaster won't gaff himself. Some come with coiled line, much like a telephone cord, attached to the handle so that the gaff isn't left behind or dropped in the water.

One thing that should be common to all gaffs, regardless of their size or where they are used, is a sharp point. A dull gaff can help you loose a fish quicker than someone crossing your line with a boat. The point should be sharpened with a file and then finished off on a stone.

Sand spikes

Sand spikes come in assorted shapes, sizes, and constructions. Basically, they are designed to do for the surf fisherman what a rodholder does for the bass angler in a boat—hold his rod. The rod can be set in a sand spike when you stop fishing, or it can be used while fishing, in conjunction with a pyramid sinker and fish-finder rig. This is the still-fishing aspect of the surfcasting.

The sand spike is nothing more than a tube in which to set the butt of the rod and a spike on the tube to pierce the sand. The spike should be long enough to give the tube firm support and at the same time hold the butt above the sand and incoming water. In some models, the tube is pointed on one end and becomes the spike. In others, a piece of angle iron is bolted to a tube of aluminum or plastic pipe. Needless to say, materials that won't rust should be used for the tube. The spike material is not quite as important.

Pliers

One of the most important pieces of equipment that a fisherman in salt water can have is a good set of marine pliers. There are several models from which to choose, and there are two sizes. The best pliers are geared or levered so that the two faces move and meet in a parallel plane, rather than scissoring like simple hinged pliers. This makes them more useful when something must be evenly crimped or squeezed together. Most pliers of this type have indentations on their faces so that they can hold split shot without slipping. Also, on the back of the face, they should have a cutting device for cutting wire, hooks, and other materials. They should also have a good gripping surface on their handles, because your hands are likely to be wet whenever you use them. Lastly, they should be impervious to salt water and its corrosive effects. If not, they aren't worth a dime because they will rust shut the first time you set them aside. Even the best pliers should be given some care, and regular doses of silicone spray or oil are a must.

Knives

Most fishermen carry a small filleting knife on their belts. The knife can clean fish as well as do a host of other tasks. It should be made of metal that holds its edge, because a dull knife is worse than no knife at all. It goes almost without saying that it should be impervious to salt water. Large knives are not needed in the boat or in the surf; a blade of 4 to 6 inches is more than enough.

Billy club

Both the well-equipped boat and the well-equipped surfcaster or bank
fisherman should have a short club, with leather strap for ease of handling,
to put away big and ferocious fish. If the club is made of hickory, oak,
or other heavy woods, it may be heavy enough to pacify even the largest
bass. If it is made of a lighter wood, it should have a core of lead to give
it oomph. A hard blow isn't always needed to kill the biggest bass. A
well-placed blow is more desirous. A fish's brain is located just behind
a line drawn between the two eyes. A light tap in this spot is enough to
do in most bass. You can tell when you have hit correctly—a bass will
stiffen and the tail and fins will vibrate quickly for just a short time. It
is the most merciful way to finish the job.

Creepers and felt soles

Rocks, jetties, and extremely gravelly beaches are most safely and easily
fished when you are wearing creepers or felt soles. Many manufacturers
make felt sandles that slip over your wader foot and can be taken off
when you are in the sand. Creepers are spike-laden frames that also
strap onto your foot and were originally designed for walking on ice or
mountain climbing. At one time, you could purchase waders with built-in
metal spikes. Today, you can achieve much the same effect by buying
a pair of golfer's rubbers. They come equipped with spikes and can be
fitted snuggly over your wader boots and won't get lost in the wash. They
can be removed to save the points when you aren't teetering on a slippery
rock.

    Still other fishermen have devised their own felt soles, added spikes,
and then glued this affair to the soles of their boots. These provide the
ultimate in traction and can be replaced when the spikes wear or the
felt becomes solid with debris.

Flashlights

If you walk the surf at night your hands are usually filled with other
equipment, and when you begin fishing there isn't a hand left to hold
a light. Surfcasters have taken an idea from spelunkers and adopted a
headlight with headband for fishing the surf. It frees their hands to tie
on lures or to gaff a bass when it is ready to come ashore. Lights below
one's head in elevation are too often turned green by the effects of salt
water splashing or flooding them.

More surfcasting equipment. Filleting knife and belt case, long-nosed pliers, parallel pliers and cutters, long-handled gaff, two smaller boat gaffs, surf fisherman's gaff, and lead-core billyclub.

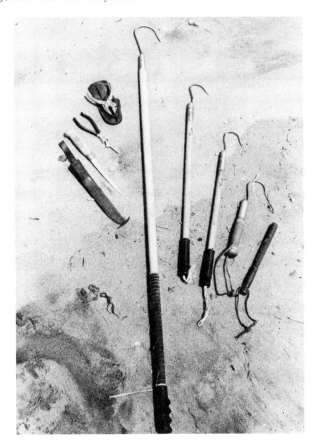

Lure carriers

Most fishermen who wade out into the surf find it difficult and dangerous to carry lures in their pockets. It's too long a walk back to the beach to get a new lure if one is lost, and early in the game many small side packs were improvised that would carry lures, snaps and swivels, and any other gear. But such packs were regularly washed by the surf. With the introduction of plastics, the entire kit was molded to hold lures, and equipped with a shoulder strap. Today, there are several sizes of bags and lure carriers available, some made of plastic, others of aluminum with canvas covers. All do the job and you can't go too far wrong with either variety.

20

The Bass Boat

Any boat will do for striped bass fishing, but some boats do a lot better than others. For a long time in the search for striped bass, it was the rowboat that accounted for the angler's getting to sea. During most of these early years, striped bass fishing from boats was restricted to bays and harbors that contained a minimum of current and to anglers with a strong back and light oars.

Striped bass fishing as a sport in small boats was well practiced during the later years of Cuttyhunk, along the Massachusetts coast, and as far west as New Jersey. The boats were large seaworthy dories that took a lot of row power to move. More often than not, they were manned by guides and fished by sports. Not until the turn of the century and the installation of small gasoline engines in the dories did boats specifically for striped bass begin to evolve.

MONTAUK BASS BOAT

There were only two boats built during the early years on the eastern end of Long Island that can be termed Montauk bass boats. They both carried the same name, *Pun'kinseed*. They were the end product of an earlier type of skiff first in use around Sandy Hook, N.J. The daddy of all of today's striped bass boats was a man named Otto Scheer. Originally from New Jersey, Scheer grew up with fishing deeply entrenched in his background. His father, William Scheer, has been credited with being one of the first anglers in the New York Bight to practice inshore fishing, and he pioneered fishing the Mud Hole for giant tuna before everyone else found out the big fish were there.

Otto Scheer, while still a youth, regularly rowed the waters on both sides of Long Island Sound. One summer, he and a companion devoted three weeks to rowing a double-oared boat from New Rochelle to New London, trolling for stripers all the way. As he grew older and wiser, Scheer became a leading international jeweler. His first love, however, remained striped bass fishing. Eventually, he headed east, spending more and more of his life at Montauk while it was still a primitive part of Long Island.

Otto was as rabid a striped bass angler as God ever made. In the beginning, he joined the early surfmen who had been hurling out their insides for years at the striped bass of Montauk. Sometimes he fished from the water or at other times from the bass stands that dotted the point. Scheer knew there had to be a better way, so he planned and executed a careful scientific campaign for the demise of the stripers.

His greatest discovery was that bass were lying inside the surf, and that when disturbed, they ran inshore, not off. The only way to get them was by boat, but no one in those days, during the early 1920s, fished Montauk by boat. There weren't any. After years of studying the Jersey boats like the Jersey skiff and Seabright dory, and after gaining a lot of experience in small boats, he built or had a hand in building a boat he designed. It had a special purpose in mind: fishing between the breakers and among the large boulders that surrounded Montauk. The boat was finished in the early 1920s. It was 18 feet long and had an 8-foot beam. It was only natural that she be named the *Pun'kinseed* because of her overall appearance.

This first boat did a lot of inshore as well as offshore fishing during the late 1920s. On one trip, John Sweeting captained the *Pun'kinseed* for Scheer and guided Otto to the first white marlin ever taken on rod and reel off Montauk. He also is credited with the first broadbill swordfish, taken in the little *Pun'kinseed*.

In 1929, Sheer built another version of the first boat which was destined to become the most famous small open fishing boat on the Atlantic Coast. The boat was completely open, with a coaming around the cockpit that came up to the hip of the average man. Like the first boat, it was 18 feet long but 8 feet 4 inches wide. It was powered by a 91-horsepower six-cylinder Gray engine—a lot of power in those days even for a large boat. In addition, it was extra heavily planked so that the hull could withstand a pounding on the rocks if the boat was steered in too tightly. Steering was accomplished from two positions, with long-handled tillers both fore and aft on her port sides. A locker was also fitted at the bow position to increase the height of the helmsman. The bow tiller gave the skipper immediate view of the rocks ahead and he could man the craft from that position while fishing.

For years after, the *Pun'kinseed,* with Otto Scheer on the rod and Capt. Bill Bassett at the helm, accounted for thousands of striped bass

The Pun'kinseed *at work. This is Otto Scheer's boat working the inshore waters under the Light at Montauk. The painting was done by Lynn Bogue Hunt, the angler on the port side of the boat. It was the cover for the March 1936* Field & Stream, *which carried a story by Hunt on striped bass fishing in the combers off this famous landmark.*

under Montauk's light. Gradually, the boat was copied and others joined the growing cadre of boats fishing striped bass in the surf.

During the big blow in the fall of 1935, while tied to her mooring in Great Pond, the *Pun'kinseed* sank. Scheer immediately raised her, and after installing a new engine, she was again fit for duty on the point. But three years later, September 21, the 1938 hurricane hit the village of Montauk with full force. Bill Bassett tried to pull her ashore, next to Jack Well's gasoline docks. There was no one else to help him, and he was in water up to his neck. The *Pun'kinseed* finally broke away from Bassett and the huge seas swept her away. They towered 6 feet over Well's dock, and the *Pun'kinseed* was last seen heading out to sea, battling the waves.

CUTTYHUNK BOATS

But before the *Pun'kinseed* was lost to the world a wise old Cuttyhunk skipper had been east to pay a visit to Montauk. He was especially impressed by the way the few boats there pursued the bass fishing, in on the shore and among the rocks. Coot Hall brought the idea back to Cuttyhunk, and soon the design was modified. Eventually, it emerged as the Cuttyhunk bass boat. Hall had three or four men working for him, all out of this style of boat, and for a while they dominated bass fishing on the Sow and Pigs Reef.

There's little difference today in the basic design of Cuttyhunk boats from those twenty-five years ago, or even from Scheer's boat. They are between 18 and 22 feet long with a beam somewhat less than the 8 feet 4 inches of the *Pun'kinseed*. The sides are rather vertical, with a fairly hard chine. The bow still carries semblances of the straight, almost knife-like bow of the *Pun'kinseed*.

The coaming is still an integral part of these open boats, and a fore-and-aft tiller is standard. The engine housing, an inboard, is amidships and a pair of chairs, sometimes light fighting chairs, are placed along each side of the housing or near the clear transom. There are no obstructions across the back, and rods are stored upright near a little cuddy cabin that is hidden under a bow deck. The boats are quite fast; 25 mph is a beginning speed.

At one time, most of the Cuttyhunk boats were of stripped-plank construction, but lapstrake quickly took over. Today, the boats are about evenly divided between lapstrake and plywood hulls, with a few fiberglass hulls now breaking through as "accepted" boats. There is a lot less care involved. Most of the older boats are Dodges, Prigs, and Lymans, with several custom jobs made by the South Dartmouth Yards in Massachusetts.

THE MODERN BASS BOAT

Distribution of boats like the Cuttyhunk bass boat was rather limited. They appeared in northern New Jersey, along eastern Long Island, and in parts of Connecticut and Rhode Island as well as the Elizabeth Islands. The boat was fine for a specific kind of water, but lacked the versatility to fish other areas and wasn't especially trailerable.

In 1963, Richard Fischer of Rockland, Mass., designed and introduced a boat that would become the mobile bass fisherman's dream, the Boston Whaler. It was a small boat, as far as boats designed for fishing tricky waters was concerned. It was only 16 feet long, but had a 4-foot width, a ratio rather close to that of the old *Pun'kinseed*. And like the

A pair of modern Cuttyhunk boats fishing the famous Sow and Pigs Reef on the west end of Cuttyhunk Island.

Pun'kinseed it had a tremendous amount of lift. It would not sink deeply into heavy seas or incoming waves. The hull design was basically that of a sled, or scow, and is quite close to the Chincoteague scows of Virginia's coastal waters. Unlike other scows, it had a trihedral hull, with sponsons on the chine that gave the boat exceptional lateral stability. There are better boats for specific seas than the Boston Whaler but there aren't any that can do as many jobs as well. It was designed as a general all-around boat, but striped bass fishermen took it to their hearts and it became the classic boat for years.

The Whaler was seaworthy beyond its dimensions. It was so buoyant that it rode above most rough seas. It was notorious for catching water with its sponsons, but in a following sea it would handle better than any boat afloat and it was great for working in close to the beach. The gunwales were shallow, but with the lift the boat afforded, deep gunwales would only catch wind.

The most unique feature, however, was a standup console used for steering the boat located just aft of center. It was a compromise to the Cuttyhunk boats with their dual steering. Because the boat was relatively small, it could easily be guided by a man in the middle.

This basic configuration or style then spawned a series of new boats that extended the fishing prowess of the boat-equipped striped bass

The Mako, a modern striped bass boat that is maneuverable in the water, fast, and trailerable.

angler. The most pressing need for advancement in the 16-foot Whaler was a longer hull so that it could work in larger seas.

Mako and Aquasport produced the next innovations in the bass boat. They retained the center-console concept of the Whaler but built their boats more on the deep-vee principle with hulls 17, 19, 22, and up to 23 feet long. This modern bass boat can handle a lot of water. Boston Whaler eventually produced the extended Whaler, a 22-foot model called the Outrage. The hull was changed in front to form a somewhat modified vee. The sponsons on the side were reduced and the bow raised to give it a greater sheer and produce a dry-running craft.

Another feature that is unique to this class of boats is that they are all self-bailing. This is achieved by building a double bottom in the boat with the top of the inner deck above the waterline. They work beautifully when underway but when loaded with gasoline and all the paraphernalia needed to do battle with striped bass, many will slosh water on their decks. However, it is a nice feature.

HOW TO RIG A BASS BOAT

Generally, this breed of inshore fishing boat is between 17 and 22 feet long, of an open construction, with steering and control console designed for stand-up operation near the middle of the craft. The boat is powered by one or two outboards and toted about from place to place on a tandem-wheeled trailer. The last item has not only freed the roving bass fisherman from working out of a single port but has also reduced the cost and gas consumption by allowing him to drive closer to his fishing, with a minimum of on-water running.

Nowadays, there is a wide range of selection of hulls from which an angler can choose and turn it into a bass fishing machine. The choice, however, can be a mind-muddling experience unless he first decides with himself just what kind of boat he wants. Before you ever go looking for the correct hull, first decide, truthfully, just what you want the boat to be able to do for you and then the maximum limit of your pocketbook. Prices of fiberglass hulls can vary from as little as $3,000 for a minimally equipped boat to $10,000 for a rig with all the extras you'll ever need loaded onto it. This great disparity is one of the nice features of this class of boat; you can manipulate the variables and really tailor-make a super bass boat.

There's no such thing as the perfect bass boat. We all are individuals, and our boats and their characteristics are likely to reflect this individualism. What equipment you feel you might need or its arrangement in a specific hull might be just great for you but to another angler it might feel all wrong. This is even evident in selecting the basic hull. That's why there is such a choice available. Your boat should match the fishing conditions of water over which you spend the greatest amount of time. After you pick the hull, then there is more room for us to agree upon and we can go on and build the perfect bass boat.

After the initial decision about which hull and which length to buy, the next most pressing question to be solved is the power plant or propulsion. You have three possible selections: inboards, inboard/outboards, or outboards. All possess advantages, but a quick comparison will show that outboards are preferred by most operators of such rigs. The reasons they give are: low initial cost, fuel economy, power selection, size, weight, and location in a craft, ease of replacement, and dependability.

A second consideration at this time is the use of dual power. A single unit is easier to handle, less complicated as far as installation is concerned, and more economical to run. With two units, you can figure that your troubles have doubled. However, when you are working in close to the surf or when you are making those long reaches between islands you have the assurance that if one engine should go down there is always a second. The single engine should be capable of putting the boat on plane and you'll be able to limp back at least at half speed. There are many bass boats with double engines, so there must be a need for them.

What size power? Most craft in this class are capable of handling a maximum of 200 to 250 horsepower. This doesn't mean that you must put the maximum on your transom. The actual engine ratings will be a

*Here is the author's striped bass boat, the 21-foot Outrage by Boston Whaler.
I consider this one of the most versatile crafts made for fishing inshore waters.
It is used as a model for outfitting the complete boat for striped bass fishing.*

factor of the size and weight of your craft. For a single installation, the choice can range from 85 to 135 horsepower. For dual installation, they can range from a pair of 50-horsepower outboards to a set of dual 100s. The final choice will depend on your budget, the speed you feel is necessary, the gas consumption, and possibly the weight of the engines.

ACCESSORIES

One man's necessities can be another man's frivolity, and when it comes to accessories, this can also be true. However, I've included what I feel is important to me when I go hunting for striped bass. I choose a 22-foot Boston Whaler Outrage because its general features suit what I like in a boat.

The first place I begin in rigging the craft is at the console, the heart of any such stand-up boat. Mine looks like it might be from the inside of a jet airplane's cockpit, but at one time or another, everything on it has a function. I like to go fishing all the time, whenever I can and often whenever I shouldn't. The instrumentation on the boat helps me get there and back.

The most important item, especially when you get out of sight of land or run long distances in the dark, is a compass. A long and established name in things that point north is Ritchie. I picked the Ritchie Navigator model, though even Ritchie has less expensive models. This one works well at almost all angles of heave, the card has a rather quick return, it is adjustable so that the compass can be swung, and most important of all, it is lighted by two (red) bulbs so that it can be seen while running at night. Even if you don't think you'll ever run at night, it is a good idea to have internal compass illumination for those unexpected times.

A boat's trim, both hull and engine, are controlled by the location of the center of the load within a craft and by engine tilt. The first can be adjusted, to a degree, simply by shifting about the heavy movable gear. Greater and more finite adjustments can be made by adjusting the angle of the engine with relation to the boat and water. Trim tabs located on the transom of a boat at the level of the bottom work well for big boats, but power tilt on the engine, actually adjusting the angle of the entire outboard, is an easier way to achieve the most accurate trim. Not only does power trim or tilt adjust the engine while under way, but when you are alone launching and retrieving a boat, the power trim lifts the engines out of the water while you still have one hand on the wheel.

Checking trim while the boat is underway can be done by eye, watching how the spray is thrown, and by feel. However, a much more accurate method is with the use of a tachometer. If a boat isn't trimmed properly,

Accessories. The close-up of the console of the Whaler shows the location of fathometer, tachometer, speedometer, bilge pump switch, gasoline tank gauge, light switches, power trim controls, gas and shift levers, and compass.

it will be pushing ahead of water before the hull and the engine is being overtaxed for the given amount of speed. By playing with the power trim and keeping one eye on the tachometer you can see the engine speed pick up without touching the throttle, when the engine and boat achieve their most efficient trim.

A tachometer's first job, however, is not so much to be a check on the boat's trim but to indicate the speed at which your engines are turning over. Dual engines work best when their speeds are exactly the same. You can tune them fairly well just by your ears alone, but you can be exact with a pair of tachometers. Tuned engines are a must because they help you stretch fuel, make steering easier, and keep one engine from working harder than the other.

A tachometer is also a fuel-saver when used in conjunction with a speedometer. After getting a boat onto plane by using the full or almost full force of the engines, you can often cut back several notches on the throttle and still maintain your same forward speed if you have a planing hull. Once a boat is stepped onto plane it takes less power to keep it there than it took to get it there. As you pull back on the throttle or throttles, the tachometer will slowly fall, telling you that the engines are turning over at a slower speed and that you are using less gas. How-

VHF radio used to communicate between other boats, the Coast Guard and the marine radio operator. Also carries marine weather forecasts.

ever, the speedometer will hold constant. If you continue to pull back, the speedometer will eventually begin a slow fall. At one point it will drop off abruptly. Put it back to the point just before it started the nose-dive and you'll be squeezing the maximum range and gas economy out of your boat.

It's foolhardy to run out of sight of land or far away from your home port without some sort of radio equipment. A goodly number of today's traveling bass boats are equipped with either Citizen Band radios (CB) or Very High Frequency (VHF) marine radios. The safety reasons are obvious, and that is why many skippers have both types. VHF equipment has a greater range. Its wattage is now limited to 25 and this restricts its broadcasting scope. In the past, marine radios could reach anywhere from 100 miles to halfway around the world, depending upon how much you paid for your increase in wattage. But the few number of frequencies available were so jammed because of this range that it was nearly impossible to get a call through or talk with someone even a few miles away. The Federal Communications Commission, the overseeing governmental agency, is phasing out all marine radios of this type and all new installations must be VHF radios.

VHF radios, under good transmitting conditions, can span 25 to 50 miles over water. On a radio with a good ground, it might even be doubled. There are nearly sixty possible channels of frequencies from which to choose, and each VHF radio has room for six to a dozen channels. While all channels are not working frequencies available to the public, there are still many more for the bass skipper to use than in the past. Quite a few are assigned to specific users; like the Coast Guard, commercial vessels, bridge masters, and gate tenders at the locks.

Most VHF sets today are nontunable. That is, each frequency is controlled by a crystal and picked up on a selector. You should equip your set with the channels that are most frequently used in your area. You can determine this by checking with skippers at your local dock or the electronics repair shop in your area or by visiting some of the marinas and yacht clubs. FCC regulations also require manufacturers to place certain channels on every set for distress calls. Channel 16 is used specifically for such messages.

The U.S. Coast Guard monitors Channel 16 but can also be reached on Channels 12, 21, 22, 23, and 83. Your local marine radio-telephone operator is also there if you need her help to call home, or anywhere else for that matter. There is a $1 service charge for marine hook-up calls and then the regular cost of telephone service. There is no place at sea to put your nickels, so out of necessity your call must be made collect or charged to a credit card number. Marine operators usually

Citizen Band radio.

monitor Channels 25, 26, 27, and 28. Most of your ship-to-ship communications should be done over Channel 6.

At the end of the choices of channel selection are WE-1 (162.55 MHz) and WE-2 (162.4 MHz). With these channels, your set will just have receiving crystals because all you can do on these is listen. They continually broadcast weather forecasts produced by the U.S. Dept. of Commerce's National Weather Service Office. These stations are strategically strung along our coasts so that you can always reach one. The slightly different frequencies are necessary because one station may have a range that overlaps the next. The stations' frequencies then alternate up and down the coast. You should have either one or the other, preferably both, so that you can always keep tabs on the weather conditions to come and marine surveys of existing conditions.

Your craft or "ship" will need to be licensed, and the agency that handles this is the Federal Communications Office. For an application you should request FCC Form 502 directly from the Secretary, FCC, Washington, D.C. 20554. The ship's license is valid only for that craft, and if you move your radio to another boat, you will need a new license. The license involves little more than filling out the form and sending in your money.

As an operator of a VHF radio, you too must be licensed. Like the station license, there is little effort except a short waiting period and paying your fees. The forms needed here are FCC Form 753A and can be obtained from a local FCC office.

Citizen Band radios are also extremely helpful and are found in greater use along our coasts than VHF, especially by small boat fishermen and anglers concentrating on inshore waters. Most fishermen prefer to use CB because it has a shorter broadcasting range and therefore affords channels that are less crowded. The average range can vary, depending upon the quality of your set, the antenna, how well it and the radio are grounded, and atmospheric conditions at the time. A good set should generally be able to reach between 10 and 25 miles. On exceptionally good days, they can broadcast up to 50 and 60 miles without skip, but these are exceptions.

The broadcasting range of CB is, like VHF, limited by its input wattage. CB sets had been regulated to a maximum of 5 watts by the FCC. Bass fishermen seem to prefer CB to VHF because the sets are more compact, cost about half as much, and offer a maximum of twenty-three stations or channels, all usable by the operator. Less expensive CB sets often have fewer crystals, from five to a dozen, instead of the full twenty-three complement.

Unfortunately, the Coast Guard does not monitor CB frequencies. However, most CB operators reserve Channel 13, or in other areas

Channel 8, as their distress channels. Here, the word is likely to be passed along quickly. It is seldom that you cannot raise another boat, possibly one with VHF, or a beach vehicle or even a shore station with a telephone nearby to call for help and the Coast Guard. You might even get a return call from the Coast Guard station on their more powerful CB radio if you are within their range.

Recently, the FCC has ruled that Channel 9 be reserved for emergency communications involving the immediate hazards to life or to property. This channel is also reserved for rendering assistance to motorists. This FCC ruling applies to both AM and SSB Citizen Band radios. However, it hasn't yet found wide acceptance because no one will monitor it. That is, no one talks on it unless it is an emergency and a service, like the Coast Guard, must monitor Channel 9 before calling on it can have any practical effect.

Unlike VHF, the CB station is not licensed. However, the operator is, and he must apply on FCC Form 505 for a Class D license to operate a CB set. These can be obtained from local FCC offices or from Washington.

Most charterboat skippers fishing on a daily basis out of New Jersey, New York, and New England ports make greater use of CB than VHF. If you keep tuned to them for a while, you can actually develop some idea where and when the fishing is great. Some skippers, like beach-buggy clubs, have developed their own code for fishing action and locations, and maybe you too can get in on it.

Next to the compass, the second most important navigational as well as fishing piece of equipment on your boat should be a fathometer, or depth meter. This device tells you how much water you have between the boat and the bottom. The simplest fathometer operates by sending a signal via a transducer through the water. The signal bounces off the bottom and is again picked up by the transducer and recorded as a flash on the dial of your machine. The signal is constantly emitted and thus you know, by looking on the screen, exactly the depth of the bottom on the scale. This is the basic form. Other forms will translate the transducer signal into a number and read out on a digital screen. Many flasher-type fathometers are also capable of reading any obstructions that might swim between you and the bottom. They are so sensitive that they can read individual fish or schools of smaller fish. Thus, many are fish-finders as well as bottom locators. The depth range of fathometers varies considerably but most can work between 50 and 300 feet.

More advanced and more expensive models of fathometers include a flasher but in addition print out the flash on a continuously moving chart. In scale, the chart eventually prints a facsimile of the bottom profile. This frees the angler from continuously monitoring the screen and

Recording fathometer. This device frees you from constantly monitoring the screen of your depth gauge and allows you to draw a profile of the bottom's contour by recording the soundings on a flowing piece of graph paper.

gives him a chance to watch what is going on about him. The chart records any fish that appeared on the screen and at the correct depth. It might be just that moment that you turn your head away from the screen that a fish appears. It also gives the angler some idea of the shape and distribution of a school over the bottom.

Recording fathometers cost more because of the added service. A flasher-type fathometer will cost between $100 and $250 while the recording type begins at about $300 and has almost no limit. Most commercial models start at around $1,000.

Striped bass are especially sensitive to water temperature. We know that bass are almost dormant when the water gets below 40 degrees. Between 50 and 65 degrees they are on the move. In water over 70 degrees, they start to panic, and you won't find bass in water over 80 degrees unless they are traveling real fast or dead.

There are two types of thermometers available for bass fishermen. The first is a surface meter that has its sensory unit mounted to the hull of the boat and measures the temperature of the top of the water. At times, this may be all you need to fish successfully. But at other times, when the water temperature is not uniform at all depths or you are fishing over great depths, then a meter that can go down is in order. There

are two types that do that easily. One is a mercury or alcohol thermometer that can be lowered on a string and measures the temperature at a
prescribed depth, and the other is an electric thermometer that can be
unwound off its holder. On the latter, the temperature change is noted
on a dial as the sensor descends and the depth measured on the calibrated
cord.

A variation of this last unit is an electric thermometer mounted on a
downrigger. The downrigger is a heavy weight lowered on a cable from
a large wheel to a depth that is read off on a meter attached to the reel.
The line used to lower the weight has an electric wire in it, and at the end,
to which the weight is attached, it is connected to a temperature sensing
device. The downrigger is usually trolled at a specific depth and a constant reading of the temperature can be made to find the layer at which
striped bass are apt to be located.

There is such a variety of extras and optional equipment that can
be added to a boat that the list becomes quite extended. The best approach might be to make a checklist. The following is what I normally
have on my 22-foot boat. You might want to add or subtract to suit your
particular needs. However, the following serves as a place to begin:

Checklist for the complete bass boat

_____ anchor
_____ anchor line and chain
_____ anchor line, extra
_____ bilge pump, automatic
_____ bilge pump, manual
_____ billy club
_____ Bimini belt
_____ binoculars
_____ bulbs, spare
_____ bumpers or fenders
_____ can opener (for oil)
_____ canvas, mooring cover
_____ canvas, navy top
_____ cleaning gear
_____ compass
_____ cooler (for food)
_____ cutting board
_____ deck shoes (or boots)
_____ distress-signal kit
_____ docking lines
_____ elastic hold-downs

_____ fathometer
_____ fighting chair
_____ fire extinguisher
_____ first-aid kit
_____ fish box
_____ fog horn or whistle
_____ foul-weather gear
_____ fuel-line hose, extra
_____ funnel, gas (with filter)
_____ fuses, assorted sizes
_____ gaffs, small and large
_____ gas cans, auxiliary
_____ gas mats, for cans
_____ gloves, for handling fish
_____ knife
_____ life jackets
_____ lights, deck
_____ lights, hand
_____ lights, spot
_____ live-bait box
_____ maps, navigational
_____ marker floats
_____ notebook (pencil, ruler, dividers)
_____ oar or paddle
_____ outriggers
_____ radio (CB or VHF)
_____ radio, weather
_____ rod holders
_____ rod storage racks
_____ scoop, plastic bleach bottle
_____ seat cushions
_____ storage lockers
_____ tackle boxes
_____ tool box
_____ water jug
_____ weighing scale (hand)

It might be appropriate to say a word or two about some of the items on the list:

Anchor

The type and weight will depend a lot on the type of bottom in your area. A Danforth is one of the best all-round anchors and is great in the sand,

and about the only one that will hold on this type of bottom. A navy anchor is a compromise, with its weight doing a lot of the holding and the flukes making a slight contribution. It will not foul as much among rocks as a Danforth. The grapple-type anchor has little or no holding power in mud or sand but is excellent in rocks and can be retrieved when a Danforth or navy anchor might stay lodged.

Anchor line and chain

For a boat between 16 and 24 feet in length you will need a fairly sturdy line of substantial length. The amount of line you carry will be determined by the depth of the water over which you normally fish. The scope is the amount of rode or anchor line you will have to pay into the water to get your anchor to take a bite, or hold, at that depth without letting the boat drift. There is a minimum ratio of depth of water to length of line needed that will let the anchor hold in fairly calm seas. It is 1:3. That is, for every 10 feet of water over which you anchor, you will have to let out 30 feet of line. If you hope to anchor in 100 feet of water you will have to carry 100 yards of line on your craft. The more you increase the ratio, the greater will be the holding power of the anchor.

The best lines are made of nylon or other synthetic materials, but hemp and other natural fibers are cheaper. The diameter will vary between 3/8 and 1/2 inch for easy handling and sufficient holding strength. Chain on the anchor, two to three feet long, will help lay the anchor on the bottom in a position in which the flukes can take a bite.

Anchor line, extra

If you find that you will be traveling or fishing in water deeper than you normally fish, you may have to increase the rode of your anchor line by stowing away an extra hank. It is discouraging to try to anchor a boat in deep water while your engines are down and have the anchor dangling under the boat as you drift. The extra line is a safety factor and it will more than likely come in for a hundred and one other uses.

Bilge pump, automatic

An automatic bilge pump is motor-driven and works off your batteries. It can often be operated automatically with a toggle switch that is controlled by a mercury float. When the level in the bilge rises to a certain point, the mercury in the float flows to a pair of exposed terminals and closes the circuit. The pump is turned on until the water is gone and the float returns to the low level. This is ideal if your boat is left at a mooring or tied to the docks. Any rainwater will automatically be removed. The automatic device is also handy when you are running steadily in rough seas and take spray over the boat. The spray builds up in the bilge if you don't remember to pump the water and throws off the trim of the craft with its added weight.

Bilge pump, manual

This is also a handy device to have aboard in case your electric pump fails or your batteries run low. It is a simple tube-and-piston affair that moves a surprising amount of water in a short stroke.

Billy club

This might also be called a pacifier. If the core is made of lead it carries a bit more weight. Big and even small fish should be tapped on the head to kill them after they are in the boat. This is especially true if you are trying to remove a plug with a gang of extra hooks on it. A sudden lunge by the fish could bury the hooks in your hand. The pacifier is also great on bluefish that get in the way while you are trying to concentrate on striped bass fishing.

Bimini belt

A Bimini belt is a must if you are working a trolling rod with a lot of line or wire, even without a fish. The butt of the rod sits in a portable rod holder that is mounted on a small platform that fits in your groin. The platform attaches around the waist with a belt. It is an inexpensive item and saves a lot of wear and tear on the bellybutton.

Bulbs, spare

Before you take your boat on the water you should go over the entire craft, making a list of every bulb in use. Check the running lights, as well as those for your instrumentation and your auxiliary or accessory equipment. Then buy duplicates and store them aboard your craft or in a tool kit.

Bumper or fenders

If you plan to pull alongside a dock for gas or leave the boat anywhere for an extended time, bumpers or fenders are a must. This is especially true if the wind is blowing. They are also indispensable for use between other boats and bulkheads

Weather canvas. The complete striped bass boat allows the angler to fish in almost any weather, and when weather is favorable, allows him the maximum in fishing room. The Boston Whaler Outrage comes equipped with a forward shelter, a navy top, and a large window. Not shown are side curtains as well as an after curtain to completely seal the cockpit. When not in use, all the canvas is folded and stored aboard the craft and out of the way.

Canvas, navy top

The navy top canvas illustrated in this book comes into its own in either hot or cold weather. During early-season fishing, the navy top can be zippered to a windshield to keep you out of the wind. It works equally well in rain. But it really pays off during the hot days of July and August, when even out on the water the noonday sun is just too much. Sun exposure can really wear you down and shorten a day.

Can opener

Not all oil cans have a pull-top, so an old-fashioned "church key" is still an integral part of every boat's operation. Who knows, it might even find its way to a can of beer.

Canvas, mooring cover

Whether your boat is tied to a mooring or rides on a trailer, a mooring cover over the entire works is a must if you like to keep a clean boat or protect the instruments. Most instruments are waterproof and weatherproof but if you've ever been caught in a rainstorm while trailering your boat down a highway, you know how dirty it can get. You'll swear you'll never do it again without a boat cover.

Cleaning gear

A clean boat is a much more efficient boat, and every craft should have aboard it an assortment of rags for wiping your hands or wiping salt water off the rods, reels, and other equipment as well as the boat. An old-fashioned scrub brush is a must on the deck, and if it comes on a long handle so much the better. Cleansers are needed on fish blood and other grime that builds up. Sponges and paper towels are useful.

Cooler, food

Food coolers, with enough room for ice, are a real must during an entire day of fishing. They can also double as a watertight box for your binoculars, cameras, and clothing that must stay dry.

Cutting board

This device can be no more than a simple 12-inch-square piece of wood that you can lay on the gunwale of your boat when you want to cut fish, bait, or line.

Deck shoes

Traction on a fiberglass deck is increased if you wear rubber-soled deck shoes. When the going gets wet, they grip all the better. And more, they don't leave black marks on your deck. One step better is short boots with a deck-shoe sole. These are indispensable in wet weather or rough seas and keep your feet dry beneath your foul-weather trousers.

Distress-signal kit

Like a first-aid kit, a distress-signal kit should be aboard every boat, no matter how large or how small. Most come sealed in a plastic bag ready for use and contain a few road-type flares and a smoke flare or two, and some even have flares that are fired into the air for help.

Fighting chair

My Boston Whaler Outrage has a chair behind the console with a back that can flip forward or aft. In the forward position, it is an excellent fighting chair for fishing off the stern. As an added chair, one fits in the forward section of the boat and comes equipped with rod gimbal and swings about easily. The coaming is used as a foot rest when fishing off the bow.

Fish boxes

These can be portable or fixed, but should be large enough to hold several big bass. They should also be self-draining, out the transom and not onto the deck. Many are constructed of only one skin of fiberglass. Those with double skins and foam insulation between are better and can have ice added to them to preserve fish during especially warm weather. They can also act as a second cooler for food.

Fog horn or whistle

Most states as well as the federal government require that every boat have aboard a sounding device that can be used to signal at night or in the fog. You might not think you'll ever need one aboard until the first time you find yourself broken down and in the fog, unable to move. Then you hear another boat bearing down upon you and there is no way to yell above the sound. Fog horns and whistles can be manually operated, run off the battery in your boat, or can have refillable compressed-air cans that blow a toot as big as a tugboat's.

Funnel, gas

Every craft should have a gas funnel aboard, one equipped with a screen that will filter out water. The bucket-type funnel is the best and aids in getting gas into your gas tank when it is poured from another can or tank. Nozzles are hard to find at sea when you are out of gas.

Fuses

Like light bulbs, you should make a list of all the fuses you have on your craft and then duplicate them with spares, set aside in your tool box or elsewhere aboard the boat.

Gaffs, small and large

The only safe way to bring a striped bass aboard your boat, especially when it has hit a lure loaded with hooks, is to gaff it. Every boat should be equipped with a small gaff that will work on most bass. But what about the time when you nail a 50-pounder and all you have is that little hook with you? I've seen few striped bass fishermen who can leave the dock in the morning and predict what size fish they'll be getting. Bring along both gaffs.

Gas cans, auxiliary

If your tank won't hold enough gas for a full day's running then you might have to take along spare cans. They should be stored out of your fighting area and used first. After they are empty, you can place them out of the way and somewhere where their weight will no longer affect your boat trim. Some anglers have been using the collapsible plastic gas containers that after they have been emptied can be folded up and stored completely out of the way. If you use metal cans, the bottoms should have rubber liners or they should be placed on rubber mats so that they stay put while you are underway and do not harm your deck.

Life jackets

Now that they are manditory and new regulations limit them to only the approved type, everyone carries life jackets aboard a craft. But too often, they are not readily accessible. Stow them where you can get to them in a hurry. The area should be one that is light, dry, airy, and easy to reach.

Lights

Every boat nowadays comes equipped with running lights, but there are several auxiliary lights that come in quite handy, especially if you spend many evenings fishing for bass . . . and you should. The most valuable are a set of deck lights. I have installed a pair under the gunwale on each side of the afterdeck of my boat. They flood only onto the deck and the lights don't shine in my eyes or in the water.

A spotlight is dandy if you are running into a strange port or in the fog. The intense beam can be more effective than a fog horn that cannot be heard by another skipper because of his own engine's noise. A hand flashlight is also a must in the dark, not only for finding your way around or locating equipment, but also for signaling.

Live-bait boxes

These items have become integral parts of this new class of boat. But I have found few that are really functional or can handle enough live baitfish for a trip. I designed the one illustrated here. It has its own pump for pulling in fresh seawater and circulating it. I let gravity, through a high standpipe, take care of getting the water out. Fresh seawater is much better than an aerator. The purpose of the aerator is to saturate the water with oxygen. Fresh seawater already has it at the saturation point, so why not use the real thing?

This live-bait box was designed by the author and built of fiberglass especially to hold bunker. The pump and the intake hose are shown in the foreground. The standpipe drain is inside. Overflow water runs out the bottom, through a hose, and over the transom.

A portable live-bait box or well like the one illustrated is also a smart item to have because when you aren't fishing with live bait, the box can be left at the dock or at home and the cockpit space used for other gear or fighting room.

Marker floats

These are handy little devices that can be purchased at a marine store or made yourself from a flat chunk of styrofoam and 100 feet (or more if needed) of 30-pound-test Dacron or nylon line. Add to the end of the line a 4- or 5-ounce lead sinker. The heavy lead will flip the styrofoam, un-winding the line, until it reaches the bottom. All you need do is toss it over the side when you strike a fish and return on another pass to pick up another bass.

Maps, navigational

Even if you are fishing in your back yard, a good coastal navigational map with all the contours and points of land as well as man-made landmarks can come in handy. One of the times they did for me was almost in my backyard when a fog suddenly formed and I needed a course for home. Nautical charts can be purchased at most marinas, tackle shops, or book shops or ordered directly from the federal government in Washington.

Outriggers

You shouldn't find much use for outriggers when striped bass fishing unless you like to fish live bait. I believe that live bunker, hooked and stemmed against the tide over a rocky shoal, are one of the most devas-tating baits for taking large striped bass. But live bunker or mackerel have a mind of their own and if you want to fish more than one line at a time you will have to spread the baits. The only way I know how is with outriggers designed for this class of boat.

Radio, weather

If you don't have a VHF radio on your boat with the weather channels you can still take advantage of the continuous weather broadcasts by the

RDF-weather radio. Several radio manufacturers produce portable radios with a unidirectional AM antenna that can be used as a directional finder. It can locate radio stations along the beach and give you their reading. Most such radios also come equipped with VHF bands so that you can listen to conversation on that frequency as well as tune into weather stations.

National Weather Office. Small portable FM radios, with only the weather band on them, are produced by several companies and for under $25 you can have all the weather you want.

Rod holders

Every well-equipped bass boat should have aboard a minimum of four rod holders. They should be placed as sets, two on each side of the gunwale—one pair near the transom and the second about amidships. Many anglers add additional pairs to their boats, on the backs of fighting chairs and even a series ahead of the console. Those on the console serve more as upright storage racks than as rod holders while fishing or trolling.

The angle at which the holders are set is quite important for the security of the rods, and for them to function while trolling. Those on the gunwale are usually slanted aft. Those on your console or seat should be tilted outboard of the gunwales. This will give you the ability to troll four lines separated as far apart as possible.

If you use outriggers, then the two sets amidship on the gunwale, though in line with those astern, can have their lines running off, to the side of the stern rods.

Rod storage racks

No boat should be without a permanent place to store rods. This is even more necessary when you are underway or when trailering the craft. Most are stored on each bulkhead against the gunwale of the boat. These vertical racks can accommodate from three to five rods on each side. They are hole-and-hook devices that keep the rods from bouncing out because of the boat's action. The butt fits into the hole portion and the tip is put over the hook. They alternate hooks and holes on the same side.

Storage lockers

Some boats come equipped with storage lockers. Most storage space on the center-console-type boat is either under the bow or in the console itself. On a few boat models the bow is enclosed with doors and wood-work so that the elements don't ruin the gear, and the doors can even be locked. Storage space is always at a premium aboard a boat. It can be extended if you add shelves or mount some of your equipment, like radios, to the top of the storage area and leave the bottom free for loose gear.

Tackle boxes

These are portable items that will usually be carried on and off the craft. I set mine on a pair of heavy rubber gasoline mats and they seem to last longer, resisting the pounding that comes while running in heavy seas. To keep them from bouncing about, I also secure them to the bulkhead with the elastic cords and hooks. My tackle boxes are always too heavy and can affect the trim of a boat, so I make sure that I place one on each side to balance it out.

Tool boxes

I have established a separate tool box for the boat and it always stays aboard. There are a host of items that can be added to it but there is a minimum amount for unexpected repairs. A pair of screwdrivers, both

Phillips and the slot type, are standard. Then you need a pair of pliers, a plug wrench, an adjustable wrench, a roll of electrical wire, wire trimmers and terminal posts, a set of box wrenches, and almost everything that is emptied, from time to time, from my pockets.

Water jug

If you don't have a fresh-water supply on board then you should carry a plastic gallon jug of water. I store it away in the forward compartment and may never use it during a season. But I know it is there if my batteries suddenly run down and I find they need water, or I become thirsty and coffee and Coke just won't do, or when my glasses need washing, or, most important of all, when I find myself drifting to sea with nothing to drink. This hasn't happened, but it might.

THE TIN BASS BOAT

They just don't make many tin boats today but surf fishermen still refer to the aluminum craft they use as a "tin boat." The tin boat is used primarily by surfcasters who can't stand to see the birds and fish breaking just beyond their casting range. But the surf is no place to try to launch a regular bass boat, so the best means of transportation from the beach

Not really tin today, but lightweight marine aluminum, tin boats can be carried on top of a 4-wheel-drive vehicle or towed on a trailer and launched in the surf to follow the fish.

to the fish has been the lightweight aluminum car-top boat. Not all are carried on cars nowadays—some fishermen use small trailers that a 4-wheel-drive vehicle can pull through the sand.

The primary element of this type boat is lightness, and the small, round-bottom craft vary in length between 12 and 14 feet. They are easily pushed by a light 6-to-10-horsepower outboard. There is little else in such a craft other than the gas supply—maybe an anchor and the rods for a pair of fishermen, strapped down in case the launch fails and all is swept back on the beach.

The scene at a tin-boat launching is reminiscent of the old days when lifesaving stations existed every few miles up and down our coasts. The service went out to rescue ships and persons foundering in the water. The tin boat is launched by two anglers, one on each side, with the motor running and sputtering in shallow water. As a wave dissipates on the beach they rush into the next one, hoping to get the engine in gear and under way before the next wave can turn them sideways and swamp the boat.

If the weather and water are warm, the whole effort can be a lot of fun, but striped bass have a peculiar way of appearing at times of the year when swimming isn't too healthy and a swamping can be dangerous.

Getting the boat back isn't too difficult if the motor is fast enough to outrun a tumbling wave. The skipper just runs it full throttle up the beach. Of course, the engine needs a rinsing and flushing in fresh water to get the sand out of the impeller or the water pump will eventually be ruined.

21

The Beach Vehicle

The beach vehicle is a primary tool of the surf fisherman. It provides him with a speedy way to cross miles of sand without effort and usually in comfort. It allows him to take along all of the paraphernalia necessary for him to practice his sport in the manner he likes. The beach vehicle has opened hundreds of miles of striped bass waters that would normally be out of the reach of fishermen today if the buggy hadn't evolved into the vehicle we now know.

Before the advent of the beach vehicle there was very little surf fishing except at access points where you could drive with a horse and buggy or where the pavement was close to the surf. To take a car onto the sand was unheard of. First of all, automobiles cost too much and were put to better use. Secondly, the early automobiles wouldn't hold up very long to the corrosive effect of salt water.

The angler had to wait until the automobile became old, or used. It was the used car, one with very little resale value, that could be considered for beach use. The first automobiles to become old were the first ones mass-produced in the United States, Henry Ford's Model T and Model A. Not only was the Ford a good used car, with many miles of use left to it, but it was well suited for going over the sand. The front end was relatively light with a small but powerful engine, and the entire car didn't sink very deeply into the sand. With oversized tires, it could literally float over the softest sand. Not only that, if anything went wrong on an isolated beach, it was usually easy to fix because there wasn't much that could go wrong with Ford's automobile.

The first appearance of the Model A as a beach vehicle was just before World War II, during the late thirties and into the forties. It coincided with the rediscovery by the average American of saltwater fishing that had begun during the Depression.

World War II had a great effect on the development of the beach vehicle. Most of it began with the attitude of the fishermen, ex-servicemen who knew what they wanted and figured out every means to serve their ends. The war also spawned a number of all-terrain vehicles, but the only one that amounted to much, as far as the coastal fisherman was concerned, was the universal jeep. Many ex-servicemen had come to know it intimately, and it was only natural that they should turn to the jeep when the going (in the sand) got tough.

Another factor encouraging the use of the jeep and other vehicles for beach use was the great supply of war-surplus materials. The jeep was sought everywhere as a vehicle to get the sportsman where he wanted to go. If a jeep couldn't be had, then the surfmen would use other vehicles. The beach buggy was born. In most instances, the beach buggy was often a Model A or early-vintage Chevrolet or Plymouth, cars lighter than the average and equipped with large tires run at low pressure. It took a bit of learning to drive in the sand, and the fact that these vehicles moved over sand amazes modern beach vehicle owners, who rely almost entirely on four-wheel drive.

Because most of these vehicles had seen a lot of use, it didn't matter much what you did in the way of alterations or innovations. A buggy's real value lay in how well it moved along the sand and not what it might bring when resold. The beach vehicle was terminal, used until so much was wrong with it that it was beyond repair and eventually finished up behind some gas station near the beach.

Today, the main purpose of most beach vehicles is to get an angler to the fishing and back again, all within a day. But the earlier anglers took more time with their sport, and a fishing trip usually lasted for two or more days. This meant that his vehicle had to provide the basics for food, shelter, and comfort. The innovators went to work and the early beach buggies acquired bunks, sinks, and stoves. At first, the gear was just carried inside and the stoves were set up on the beach and the bunks set alongside the dark side of the vehicle. The heat was no more than a score of blankets.

As the demand for more and more facilities in a buggy grew, the thinking surf fishermen discovered the old bread vans and delivery wagons were just what they needed. By the 1950s, there were enough "old" or "used" vans of this nature to make them perfect targets for the surfmen, and their conversions began to sprout along the beaches. The sport of building or rebuilding beach buggies had spread up and down

The modern beach vehicle cannot really be called a buggy. But during the beginning and developmental years of vehicles in the surf, old buggies were converted for service on the sand by the use of oversized and deflated tires. This early Model A Ford was converted by Dick Woolner.

our Atlantic Coast. Where there once had been but a handful of vehicles parked on a point, there were now thousands leaving their track from Florida to Maine.

Along with this explosion of beach vehicles came a new problem. These vehicles could pose a serious threat to the stability of fragile marine flora along the beaches, and unthinking fishermen often left heaps of refuse and litter at their favorite meeting spots. Local municipalities began to pass restrictive ordinances and caught many of the buggy operators by surprise.

However, the Massachusetts group that rode the sand of Cape Cod and adjacent beaches saw the future with dark glasses. They organized into an association to police their own members and adopted a code of ethics. The code was written by an ex-GI named Francis W. Sargent. Sargent later went off to become governor of the State of Massachusetts, and still sports MBBA No. 1 on his vehicle. The secretary and treasurer picked Number 13 for good luck. He is Frank Woolner, now the editor of *Salt Water Sportsman* magazine.

Similar beach-buggy associations sprang up in New Jersey, in Virginia, and on Lond Island, and today they exist along most of our Atlantic Coast states. They have, in part, adopted the code of ethics of the Massachusetts Beach Buggy Association and together pay more heed to the condition of the beaches than many local parks and recreation departments.

Walk-in vans heralded a new aspect in the life of a surf fisherman. He no longer had to rough it in tents or sleep stretched across the seats of his vehicle. Inside bunks, a sink with running water, a propane heater, and a table gave him most of the comforts of home. But a van with all this extra weight meant that the tires had to grow larger and softer and four-wheel drive was needed. Very few vans had four-wheel drive, and those which did were so expensive as to be beyond the reach of most surfmen.

The panel truck began to appear on the beaches as these commercial vehicles also became old or too worn for efficient use in business. Many, like the Dodge trucks, came with four-wheel drive and when modified inside, could sleep a pair of fishermen and carry all their gear for a few days on the sand.

The affluence of the American surfcaster grew during the 1950s and his leisure time increased correspondingly into the 1960s. Fishermen were now capable of affording a new unit to take onto the beach. Besides, most of the Model As and early Chevies and Plymouths were now too far gone for the beach or had become collector's items. They were far too valuable to run in salt water. The need was still there, and Kaiser-Jeep developed its Jeepster and then the Wagoneer, a Jeep station wagon, all with four-wheel drive. Though there is today a rash of similar vehicles on the beach, I don't think I would be too far wrong if I said that the Wagoneer is still the most popular vehicle. In its early days, it was a compromise vehicle for the fisherman. It was both a buggy for the beach and a station wagon which the wife could drive. It worked just as effectively on the sand as in the suburbs and in shopping centers. Its early success in the 1960s encouraged other manufacturers to produce more such multiple-use vehicles, and Jeep today shares the beach with Chevrolet, Dodge, Ford, GMC, International, and several foreign manufacturers.

TYPES OF VEHICLES

Beach vehicles today can roughly be divided into five classes based on size and expected performance. The old beach buggies are, for the most part, a thing of the past. Very few two-wheel-drive vehicles now appear on the beaches.

Day vehicles

For want of a better name, the smallest beach vehicles are grouped as day vehicles, intended mainly for transportation and carrying only the equipment needed to fish and make the angler comfortable while he is on the beach. The classic example is the Jeep Universal, a somewhat enlarged version of the old Army jeep. It has been increased in size so that the rear compartment can handle most of the angler's gear, or even tote two additional fishermen. Other similar units are the Bronco by Ford and the Scout by International. Toyota and Land-Rover also produce smaller units comparable in size and performance.

Mid-range vehicles

Only one unit can be classified in this group: the Jeepster by American Motors. More recently, the Jeepster has been supplanted by the Commando by American Motors. This is still a day vehicle in the real sense because it isn't large enough for sleeping or eating quarters and its carrying space is still somewhat limited. Also, it is less adaptable to general use and thus isn't practical for the family which can afford but one car.

Station wagons

This group, the largest, has burgeoned during the last decade. At one time it was the almost exclusive realm of the Jeep Wagoneer. The beach station wagon is a multiple-use vehicle that can double as the family car when not on the beach. In addition to the Wagoneer, there are the GMC and Chevrolet Blazers, somewhat similar in construction to the modified panel trucks and not quite as adaptable as a family car as the Wagoneer, and International's Travelall wagon. New to this class and similar to the Blazer are the Dodge and Plymouth Ramchargers with either soft or hard tops. Toyota has a crusier in this class and Land-Rover has a larger version of its smallest all-terrain vehicle, but it is not as adaptable to the one-car family as the Travelall and Wagoneer.

The Jeep Wagoneer was so popular that it inspired other auto manufacturers to produce multiple-use beach vehicles. It is at home at the shopping center as well as alongside the surf. Here, two Wagoneers line up for the ferry from Hatteras to Ocracoke Island, N.C.

Pickup trucks

A large number of surf fishermen who require a pickup truck in their work purchase them equipped with four-wheel drive so that they can be used in the sand or off a hard road. An empty pickup truck has extremely poor rear-end traction and will spin out on a wet or muddy surface. But if the box is loaded and weight is placed on the rear wheels, it will go much better. However, a loaded pickup without four-wheel drive will not make much headway on the beach. A four-wheel-drive pickup, even when empty, has the bulk of its weight on the front drive system and has no problem on the beach.

Camper-pickups

The ultimate beach vehicle should provide a surf fisherman with transportation over the sand, a place for him to sleep comfortably, a kitchen in which he can prepare his meals when a long stay is in mind, all the space needed to carry his unmanageable equipment and maybe even a boat, and communications equipment. In reality, the complete beach vehicle is much like the complete boat and does for the surf fisherman what a boat does for the floating angler.

The only beach unit capable of approaching this ideal and meeting the demands of such an angler is the pickup truck equipped with a camper unit on its bed. The normal quarter-ton pickup is often too small except for the lightest of box units. Instead, most fishermen who intend to take it all with them select a half-ton or even three-quarter-ton pickup, and always with four-wheel drive. To help spread the load over a wider surface of sand, extra-large, often balloon tires are used on such units. These tires are not well suited for hard roads, and camper-truck owners often have a set of regular tires to use when prolonged hard-surface travel is in order.

The majority of camper units slide onto the box so that the pickup truck can be used for other jobs. The unit can be taken off and stored in the driveway when not in use. However, a considerable number of units are chassis-mounts. This gives the camper-surf fisherman a lot more room in the camper, but at the same time means that its only use will be on the beach or in other camping situations. This requires a considerable outlay of money but apparently enough anglers are willing and able to spend it because there are quite a few on the beaches.

HOW TO RIG A BEACH VEHICLE

Outfitting a beach vehicle used to be a very personal affair because the unit itself had little value other than its ability to travel over sand. Today, however, with new vehicles going into the saline world, a lot of care is taken of such units, with a thought to second sales, and therefore modifications that won't please a potential buyer are not made. Also, many modifications can be factory-made or purchased; not all improvements are left to the art or skill of the surf fisherman.

Proliferating on the beaches as well as in inland camping areas are the campers on pickup-truck bodies. Either the slide-on or box mount, illustrated here, or the chassis mount can provide the surf fisherman with all the comforts of a boat or home away from home.

Factory options

Before you ever take delivery of your vehicle, you can have it half-designed for the beach. The first consideration is the four-wheel-drive aspects. Of course you are getting four-wheel drive. How it goes into four-wheel is another matter. Wagoneers are built with full-time four-wheel traction. As the load on the engine and traction on the rear end demand it, the vehicle is automatically shifted in and out of four-wheel drive. In other models, you have the option of automatic four-wheel drive that is engaged from inside the unit, or manually, getting outside and locking the front hubs for four-wheel operation.

Locking hubs engage the axle to the wheel and they spin together. Unlocked, the axle doesn't move and there is less wear on it. With the hubs locked the axle spins with the turning of the wheel. However, not until you shift it into four-wheel drive do you have power turning the front axle. Thus, you have an option of three methods for achieving four-wheel drive. The manual-locking hubs are the most popular in use today.

In addition to front-axle drive, you can get a positive form of traction for the rear wheels. If one wheel is spinning, the other won't stop but will turn to help pull out the spinning wheel. This is done automatically without your having to think or act and is a handy option in most vehicles.

Cooling systems found in most beach vehicles are adequate for fall, winter, and spring driving. However, if you are on the beach during the summer, driving in soft sand and forced to stay in low gear, the engine is working hard and overheating. The fan and water pump are not capable of keeping your coolant cool at slow speeds. An oversized radiator is a must, even if you don't intend to get into hot situations. And if you can get along without an air conditioner, do it. The air-conditioner radiator or cooler sits in front of your engine's radiator and not only stops the cool air from hitting it but adds its own heat load to the car's radiator.

An oil cooler is also handy when you do a lot of beach traveling during the summer. If you are driving a pickup-camper unit, it is a must. It prolongs the life of your oil as well as that of your engine. It is easy to install and not expensive.

The electrical system is also being taxed on the beach. Start out by selecting a heavy-duty battery, one of 50 or more amps, and get a heavy-duty alternator to help keep it up to snuff. At slow beach speeds, a generator or normal alternator may not be able to keep it fully charged. When you add a CB radio, extra lights, and electricity for a camper if you are carrying one, the heavy-duty electrical system is not an accessory but a necessity.

If you can get a larger gas tank on your unit, do it. It will save you a lot of future headaches. There are few gas stations near the beach and on some really isolated strands, you might even have to tote along jerry cans. The bottom of the unit should be protected in two ways. On many, you can get skid pans that protect your oil pan and gas tank. You are liable to be trafficking over a lot of debris washed onto the beach and you need the bottom protection. Undercoating is another must if you run in the surf or anywhere near it. If you can get it done locally rather than at the factory, you can talk the man into an extra-heavy coat.

Most beach traffic is over bouncy rut situations and your vehicle is sure to need heavier shocks and springs. Adjustable shocks are a great idea and a little more expensive. If you have a camper unit, you will automatically be encouraged to get the heavy-duty equipment by the auto salesman. Don't argue with him on these items. They really are needed.

At one time, beach-buggy addicts shunned automatic transmissions. However, experience has shown that they produce a smooth, even start, get the operator stuck less often, and hold up better than a standard transmission. Power brakes are good, but most braking on the sand is done by engine compression or just taking your foot off the gas pedal. Power steering, however, is another story. When you try to follow a wheel set wider than yours, you need full-time power steering. When running on soft sand, power steering takes some of the constant strain off your arms. If the wife will be doing some of the driving, get her power steering. It pays for itself in your own well-being.

The powerplant, your engine, should be able to carry you over the sands without overexerting itself. It is therefore far wiser to have more engine than you think you need and allow it to work at a more leisurely pace rather than to get a smaller engine and make it work at its maximum all the time. Going through sand is tough work, even for something as impersonal as a car engine. But give it a break and you'll have less to worry about in new parts and repairs. A V-8 is almost standard on most vehicles, but smaller units can get by with a straight 4 or a V-6. Make sure that they run smoothly on regular gas for economic reasons.

Tires

The rubber on your vehicle is the main link between you and the outer world, or the sand on the beach. Tires can make you go or stop you dead in your tracks. Tires, their treads, shape, pressure and construction, are crucial to your mobility. The more tire surface you have spread over the sand, the less you will sink and the less will be your friction per square inch . . . all letting you move more easily over the beach and your engine work at a reasonable stride.

Snow or mud treads with their knobs have no place on the sand. They have a tendency to dig and bury the wheels. Regular suburban tires on all four wheels are all that you need in the sand. In fact, less tread on them, as they wear, will provide you with better go-power.

To have four wheels turning is not always enough to get you through the sand. You may not have sufficient flotation. You achieve flotation in two ways: by purchasing and equipping your vehicle with as wide a tire as possible and by deflating the tire so that its profile changes and more of it appears flattened at the bottom, increasing your contact area. The most disheartening sight to see is the owner of a new 4x4 taking his vehicle onto the sand for the first time, slipping it into four-wheel drive, and getting stuck 10 feet off the hardtop.

Most tires are rated to a maximum air pressure of 32 pounds per square inch (psi). At this pressure, the tires are hard as wood and last a long time. But on the beach, they should be deflated down to 18 or 20 pounds for normal going. If the engine's temperature gauge begins climbing, you know the engine is working too hard and the needed flotation just isn't there. You can deflate your tires down to 10 or 12 pounds and the vehicle will travel with a lot less strain. You can even deflate them to 8 pounds in special situations but you must be careful.

There is a minimum deflation pressure and it is close to 8 psi for most tires. The reason involves the sidewall of a tire. This portion isn't designed to take the flexing that the bottom can withstand. At low pressures, the sides of the tire bulge and work constantly. As they do, the rubber begins to heat. Eventually this leads to cracking and a shortening of the tire's life. That is why, as soon as you are off the sand and onto a hard surface, you should inflate your tires before traveling at high speeds.

Sidewall bulge is desired on the beach and necessary. This is more difficult to obtain with tires with six or more plies, and as a result, most vehicles should be equipped with the four-ply versions suitable for the majority of automobiles. The six-ply is just too stiff and you don't get the deflation advantage with it that you do in a four-ply tire.

Wheel size should be as large as possible, and 15-inch is what most vehicles can handle. This gives you a higher lift above the sand with your chassis. In addition, it also means more tire surface on the tread in contact with the sand and hence more flotation. Width of tread is still another tire variable, and the widest most rims can handle is the current L-70. Tire-width terminology has changed a couple times during the last decade and if you aren't sure of what you want and are getting, don't feel lonely. Here you'll have to trust to the experience of your tire dealer.

For large beach vehicles and truck-camper units, special tires, some verging on balloons, are necessary. These call for extra-wide rims that must be specially ordered, and they increase the cost of a beach vehicle. But if you want to take your home with you, that is the price you must pay.

Fishing accessories

The first accessory equipment you must add to your new beach vehicle are holders for your rods. There are two types and you'll need both in most cases. The first are permanent or traveling rod holders to hold the wands when they are not in use. A series of holders over the top of the unit, similar to a ski rack, will do and are the type often used. The rods are held parallel to the length of your vehicle and across its top. If you plan to tote a box on the top, then you can install rod holders along each rain gutter.

Some units come equiped with inside holders, mounted to the inside roof of the vehicle, while still others have holders along one side of the window. However, because most surf rods are so long and often are produced in one piece, the inside holders don't work with the back window closed.

The second type of required holder is the temporary holder for while you are fishing. A few fishermen take actual boat holders and secure them to the sides of their vehicle, but most go for a bumper-type holder. This holder is basically a piece of 2x12 wood, bolted across the front of the bumper, to which any number of holders are secured. The rods are carried upright across the front of the vehicle. Short lengths of 2- or 3-inch PVC tubing will do as well as the regular holders and cost a lot less. Or you can take the easy but expensive way out and buy a bumper rod holder—but I doubt if you can get a good one for less than $100.

One of the most efficient methods of carrying rods is to attach a series of rod holders on a large plank mounted on the bumper of your vehicle.

The next item you need is a place to carry your fish. After a while, you'll become tired of fish flopping around on the floor of the unit or in the back and you'll get a fish box. Some boxes are no more than a wooden box bolted to the front or the back of the vehicle on a special frame. Others are large, insulated coolers that can hold ice and keep your fish from spoiling during warm weather. You can carry the big cooler inside the vehicle, but this eats up a lot of space that could be used to better advantage.

Most dedicated beach fishermen eventually build a platform on the roof of their vehicle and box it in so that they can carry a lot of the bulky gear—waders, hipboots, lanterns, rain gear, sand spikes, and the like—on top. There may even be enough room to add your fish cooler to this box.

A number of such vehicles have top boxes constructed with collapsing sides. When the sides are down, they expose a pair of crossbars on which a light car-top boat can be carried. If you regularly carry a cartopper you will need an engine bracket welded to the side or back of your vehicle so that the outboard can be carried upright, outside, and always ready for use.

If everything that can possibly be carried on the side is out there, you then have room for a few collapsing bunks. These can fold against the side when not in use. A small propane heater is a must if you aren't carrying a camper. Propane bottles can be mounted on top or in the back. If you use a lot of fuel or have a camper, select a unit that has two bottles rather than one. Not that their capacity might be greater; it's just that you can use one until it runs out and then switch to another. In a one-bottle rig it's impossible to tell when you are about to run out of fuel unless you take the bottle off and weigh it.

Miscellaneous accessories

Most beach vehicles keep in touch with other units and keep tabs on what the boats are doing offshore by installing a Citizen Band radio. Not only are they great as information gatherers but if you bury your rig below the high-tide mark and the water is coming in, you'll be able to call for help with a CB set in your cab.

A few fishermen still rig their beach vehicles with spot lights, and though lights on the water are taboo at night, they can be helpful when traveling on the beach or helping someone get out of a jam. Even better are fog lights or a pair of extra lights mounted under the front bumper of the car. Fog can be as blinding at night on the beach as it is on the water, and when you don't have someone else's rut to follow, the low-slung lights are extremely helpful.

If you do a lot of beach riding during the off season, when few other vehicles are out, or work in areas where very few other fishermen frequent, then a power winch on the front of your unit can be the only insurance against getting stuck. Most beaches where there is enough sand to require a beach vehicle have few boulders to tie onto to let your winch pull you out. But, a large Danforth sand anchor and a stout cable or line will get you out of a hole.

If you plan to fish the surf from a small boat carried on a trailer, then a ball and hitch is a necessity. A factory hitch is usually best because it is either welded or bolted to the chassis while the unit is being built. Even if you don't plan to use a boat, the hitch is a great place to attach a cable for towing another vehicle and it increases the resale value when you are ready for a new vehicle.

Emergency kit

You may be beach-wise enough so that you never need your own emergency kit but too often you are likely to come across someone who isn't, and if you want to give him a hand, you'll need some added items.

Foremost among these is a towing chain or heavy line. You will need to know how to tie a bowline in the line or you'll never get loose without cutting it after you are free. Next, add a shovel. A collapsing army shovel is great, though it won't carry a lot of sand. Though this smaller shovel may take longer to dig you out, it doesn't require a lot of storage space.

If you are traveling into isolated country, a pair of planks or some carpeting can help you out of tight situations. An extra bumper jack is also a great help. If you really bog down in rotten sand, one of the best techniques is to jack both rear tires off the ground and then push the vehicle forward, off the jacks. Stand clear when it's falling. If you can fill the hole with sand before you let go or add a few planks, you'll get out sooner and easier.

During really hot weather, it's a good idea to carry a few plastic gallon jugs of water for the radiator. If you do boil over, you can use salt water in an emergency, but you'll have to flush the cooling system thoroughly. A spare water jug is a better way to meet the problem.

Inflating your tires can be a problem in some areas, and if you don't need gas, the service-station operator may give you a hard time. A spark-plug pump is available if you want to pump your own. One plug is removed and a device placed in the head of your engine. The other, via a long tube, goes to your tire's valve stem. You must have a good tire-pressure gauge in the glove compartment of your car.

An extra fan belt, maybe a spare water hose, and assorted bits of wire and tools should also find their way into your emergency kit. In addition, you should always have a first-aid kit and a fire-extinguisher stored under the seat of your car.

DRIVING THE TRACK

There's only one way to develop the knack of handling a vehicle in sand, and that is by driving it in sand. There are a few tricks you can pick up immediately by imitating other drivers. The first is to overcome the feeling that your adventurous spirit is being stifled if you follow a rut rather than make your own marks in the sand. A vehicle that has gone on before you has already knocked down the sand and partially compressed it for you. It will be easier driving and you can go somewhat faster if you stay in the track. Make new tracks only if there aren't any where you want to go. If there are any hazards on the beach or in the sand, then the guy before you has experienced them. Learn by his tracks.

Next, get to read the sand. Sometimes the color can be a key to its consistency. Some sand will pack easily under weight and this makes for easier going in your vehicle. Other sand won't pack at all, particularly if it is fine and without moisture. This type is called rotten sand and all you can do is slowly plow through it. Maintain a constant speed and forward motion and you'll stay on top. If you drive too slowly, you are making your engine overwork and you are giving the vehicle time to sink into the sand.

When you turn out of someone's tracks, do it quickly and then return the wheels to a parallel course. It will make breaking out of the rut easier. Otherwise, you can have your wheel partially turned and still be stuck in the rut. Don't use your brakes to stop unless you are too close to what you want to avoid. Heavy braking will cause your tires to dig into the sand and you may not be able to get going again easily. The best way out of this situation is to back down in your tracks and make a running start over the holes you just created.

Running the beach below the high tide can be tricky and it takes some experience. The sand left behind by a falling tide is usually better packed than that above high tide and your car can run easier on it. But never stop or lose your forward momentum while traveling below the high-tide mark unless you are certain you can get out again. There's nothing that will make a man cry harder than watching the tide come into his cab.

Don't cross barrier beaches or sand dunes where vegetation is growing. In many states and federal parks it's illegal as well as thoughtless. These wild grasses hold the dunes together and keep the beach in place. If ramps are not available over such areas, then cross only where tracks have previously been made. This means that you won't always be able to get on or off the beach where you want, without some extra running, but it won't make you unpopular with local officials or other beach buggy operators. It means that you and he will be able to continue to use the beach in a vehicle. It's better than walking.

Many municipalities and parks have placed restrictions on the use of the beach by vehicles, especially during the months when bathers swarm into the surf. Become familiar with these regulations, abide by them, and obtain the beach permit when necessary. You might get all the information you need by contacting the beach-buggy association in your area. If you can't find one, then write United Mobile Sportfishermen, Inc. P.O. Box 74, Forestville, Conn. 06010 and ask for help.

22

Striped Bass Cookery

The proof of the pudding is in the tasting, and the taste of striped bass, properly served up, makes all those early reveilles and rain-soaked days worth the effort. Cooking and eating your own striped bass seems to make the catching so much more pleasurable. If you haven't tried it, you've missed one of the better parts of striped-bass fishing. Nor is there any fish comparable to a freshly caught bass, rushed to the frying pan and then served while a little wiggle is still left. You'll never visit a fish market again.

STORAGE

Striped bass are firm-fleshed fish with flaky meat that will take some abuse before it begins to deteriorate. But it's still best to take care of the bass immediately after it has been unhooked. During the early and later part of the striped bass season, outside temperatures are usually cool enough so that you don't have to worry about bacteria immediately attacking your fish. But in the warmer months of the year, you'd better pay attention or most of the flavor will be lost in the first hour.

Striped bass should be immediately placed in a cooler or ice chest if it is warm outside. The fish shouldn't be allowed to soak in their own blood and salt water, even in a cooler. Water, warm or cold, will immediately begin to soften the firm meat. Drain your cooler regularly.

If you don't have refrigeration in your boat, store the fish out of the direct rays of the sun and in an area where they are exposed to the air. You can cool them slightly by covering your bass with a burlap bag and regularly splashing it with water. Air passing over the burlap will evaporate the water and slightly lower the temperature of the fish. If you are on the beach, you can bury your bass in the sand. Make sure that you dig deep enough to reach cool, wet sand and that it isn't too far below the high tide mark or you may have a difficult time finding it. Mark it with a stick, just to be sure.

CLEANING

If you plan to scale your fish, it is easiest done as soon as the fish is caught. The longer you wait, the more difficulty you will encounter, especially if the scales are given the chance to dry. However, even the driest striped bass scales aren't especially difficult to scrape off. You can do it with a scaling device or simply use a sharp knife with a rather stiff blade. Hold the tail firmly and work your way toward the head, against the grain of the scales.

If you are going to fillet the fish and don't need the skin, you can forget about scaling it. It will all come off with the skin. To fillet a fish, you need a sharp pointed knife, often known as a filleting knife. The spine on the knife is rather thin and the blade somewhat flexible to help you cut around the curves and get all the meat possible. The first step is to cut a parallel line down each side of the dorsal spine or fin, from head to tail. The incisions should not be deep, at first. After the skin is pulled off they can be deepened. The next incision, also just skin deep, is just behind the head, from the back, over the sides of the bass, behind the pectoral fin and then across the belly toward the vent. The line is then extended to the base of the tail. The cut across the sides of the belly shouldn't be deep enough to cut into that cavity. If you do it correctly, you'll miss spilling the insides.

With your filleting knife, pry the skin from the muscle near the head, against the back. When you have freed enough to grasp the skin with a pair of pliers, hold the head of the fish firmly against the table and quickly strip back the skin. Once you get the hang of it, all the skin will come with one stroke. Pull the skin off the fillet all the way to the tail and cut if free. Now separate the fillet on one side by deepening the first incision along the dorsal fins and spines, all the way from the head to the tail as deep as the back bones.

Much of it can be freed by slipping your finger down along the spine. Next, cut the fillet away from the head and follow closely the contour of the ribs that bulge out to protect the stomach. Don't try to save the belly meat — it is thin and tough. Work the tip of your knife over the side of the spinal column and then down the side to the ventral line. The fillet is almost free except for the tail, and that is cut at right angles. Follow the same procedure for the other side. You have almost 95 percent of the bass's flesh, and without any bones.

Filleting works best for small bass, 3 to 10 pounds. You can also fillet larger bass, but the pieces of meat are so thick that to cook evenly

Filleting a striped bass. The first incision is made, just skin deep, along the back, from base of head to base of tail. The cut is made on each side of the dorsal spine.

Then another incision is made over the side of the bass, just behind the head, from the cut on the line to a spot just past the ventral fin.

The incision is then followed along the bottom or belly of the fish, still just breaking the skin, all the way back to the base of the tail.

With a filleting knife, cut away the skin from the flesh in the area shown in the photograph.

When you have freed enough skin from the flesh to grasp it with your pliers, hold the head and flesh down with one hand and quickly pull the skin off the flesh with the other. Pull it all the way to the base of the tail.

With the filleting knife, deepen the incision on the back, following the long spines in to the backbone. Free the fillet from head to tail along the backbone.

Cut over the rib bones protecting the intestine and then free the fillet below the backbone all the way to the tail. Cut it free at the base of the tail. Now you have a fillet entirely free of bones and no scaling was required. Flip over and fillet the other side.

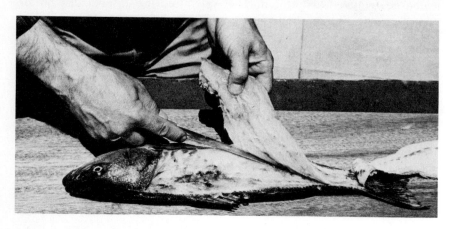

they must be sliced into thinner fillets or cut across to make strips or fingers of fish. Fish for baking are also best selected from bass about 3 to 10 pounds in weight. They are first prepared by scaling. Then remove the dorsal fins by incisions on each side and one cut on an angle to sever the spiny bones from the vertebral column. The anal and caudal fins are cut at their bases and the pectoral fins are usually removed with the head and stomach.

The head is cut on an angle from the top, behind the pectoral fin, in much the same manner as in preparing for skinning. The knife is forced through the backbone of the spine or broken by hand. The fish is cut along the bottom to the vent and the entire head and entrails can be pulled free in one piece.

Almost every bit of the bass fillet is good to eat. The only exception is a small strip along the sides in the area of the lateral line. This can be distinguished by its dark, liverlike color. It is rich in oils and gives the bass an excessively fishy flavor if cooked while still on. It is easily removed, rather shallow in depth, and doesn't leave much of a hole.

If you plan to use the fish immediately, don't wash it in water, but clean it with a paper towel and dry out the inside. If it is to sit awhile, sprinkle the inside with salt and let it stand. If your striped bass is to be frozen, separate the fillets into whatever size portions you want and freeze them together. If you thaw too much, you cannot refreeze it. A great way to ensure almost perfect freshness is to place your fillets in a plastic bag and then fill the bag with water. The bag should be placed in a milk carton or something similar to give it shape, and then when frozen it can be removed and stored. The water freezing ensures that no air will ever get to the meat and give you freezer burn. Also, the ice seems to lock in the bass's flavor.

Really large bass can be treated as fillets, as we mentioned earlier, or they can be steaked. If they are to be steaked, they should be cleaned like a bass to be baked, with the skin in place. The steaks are cut across the body, going from head to tail in parallel slices. The thickness will depend a lot upon your personal preferences, but a bass steak 1 or 1½ inches thick is easily cooked and handles well in the broiler or frying pan. Smaller sections are apt to fall apart because the flesh is rather flaky. Thicker slices might not be sufficiently cooked in their centers.

The baked striped bass, garnished with lemon, cherries, sweet and white potatoes, and parsley and ready to serve.

COOKING

The striped bass is a gourmet's delight. The flesh of a striper can be prepared in a great variety of ways. Bass can be fried, broiled, boiled, poached, and baked, as well as made into a pudding or a salad or chopped into bass fingers. Because of the fine texture of their flesh and the firmness when properly handled and prepared, striped bass can be used as *the* fish in almost any of your favorite seafood recipes. They mix well with your imagination and it is difficult to do a bass in by cooking.

Broiled striped bass

This recipe is adapted from an old Alabama recipe for red snapper. But because the striped bass is also an Alabama fish the same preparation has often been used and has proved to be a delightful method for the preparation of stripers.

ALABAMA STRIPER DELIGHT

The striped bass is filleted and then the pieces basted with fresh orange juice; sprinkled with soy sauce; then broiled to a tender, juicy perfection. Try this one if you want some elegant but easy dining enjoyment.

2 pounds bass fillets, fresh if possible	1 tablespoon soy sauce
1/3 cup orange juice	1 teaspoon salt
1/4 cup butter or margarine, melted	Dash pepper

Cut the fillets into serving-size portions. Combine the ingredients and mix thoroughly. Put the fish, skin side up if it has been scaled, into a well-greased broiler pan and brush fillets with the sauce. Broil about 3 inches from source of heat for 4 to 5 minutes. Turn carefully and brush with sauce. Broil 4 to 5 minutes longer, basting occasionally, until fish flakes easily when tested with a fork. This should serve about six.

Baked striped bass

Prepare the bass for baking by scaling, removing fins and viscera. The head and tail are often left on when a bass is to be baked. The cavity of a bass can be filled with whatever stuffing you prefer. Because the striped bass is usually a somewhat dry fish—that is, without a lot of naturally occurring fats or oils—fats or oils must be added. Cut three or four gashes in the side of the fish, depending upon its size, and insert pieces of salt pork. Or, you can substitute strips of bacon that are secured by tying them on with pieces of string. This also helps keep the stuffing inside the cavity.

Brush oil over the skin of the fish and place the bass on its belly, on an oiled baking sheet or pan. Bake in an oven at 450 degrees for the first 15 minutes, then reduce to 350 degrees and allow 45 to 60 minutes baking time for a 5-pound fish. Baste from time to time with some extra pork or bacon fat. Serve with Hollandaise or Sauce Allemande.

BAKED FILLETS ORIENT

Take a bass fillet and cut into individual servings, each about ⅓ pound in size. Then dip each piece in salted milk and roll in finely sifted bread-crumbs. Place the fillets in an oiled pan and bake in a hot oven (between 450–500 degrees) for ten minutes. Serve with Tartare Sauce.

BAKED FILLETS IN CLAM NECTAR

2 pounds fillets	2 tablespoons oil
½ cup clam juice	3 tablespoons flour
1 cup cream	4 tablespoons butter
1 cup milk	1 onion, finely minced
1 teaspoon Worcestershire	1 small garlic clove, bruised
sauce	1 tablespoon minced parsley
Salt and paprika	Lemon juice to taste

To the heated oil add the minced onions and garlic, stirring constantly. Allow them to fry but not brown, then place on lid and cook for 10 minutes. Oil a baking pan and put the bass fillet in it, sprinkling them with salt, pepper, and lemon juice. Then spread the cooked onions and garlic over the fillets. Heat the clam broth, add ½ cup of boiling water with 2 tablespoons of butter, and bake the fish at 375 degrees for 20 minutes or until done. Heat the milk, melt the other 2 tablespoons of butter, sift in the flour, and cook together, adding the hot milk, and beat. Then add the seasoning and cream. Lift the fish onto a hot platter, add the liquid under the fish to the sauce, stir in the chopped parsley, and pour over the fillets and serve at once.

Poached striped bass

Poached striped bass recipes are extremely numerous, and perhaps this is about the best manner of preparation. Poaching often requires added sauces, and some of these are found at the end of this chapter.

LE BASSE BAR DE GASPE

This recipe is the work of Joseph Hyde, a renowned New York chef. It is an elegant method of preparing and serving striped bass, whether it comes from the Gaspé or Cuttyhunk.

The fish must be fresh for this method. Poaching a large striped bass with its head and tail requires a long poacher with rack, and, of course, a large platter upon which to serve the finished striper. With head and tail intact is the ideal way to cook a striped bass because the water surrounds the unbroken skin and the skin in turn holds in all the juices of the bass. Seawater is the preferred salt water for this poaching technique, or you can make a court bouillon, which will also give a fine flavor to the fish.

The vegetables for the court bouillon are sliced finely and cooked for ½ hour in the fish poacher with the other ingredients except for the vinegar or lemon juice, which is added with the fish. As the bass cooks, the water should be just barely simmered. The poaching time varies in relation to the thickness of the fish, about 15 minutes for every inch of thickness. If the fish is to be served cold, it need cook only 10 minutes to every inch.

The bass must be cooled and refrigerated in the court bouillon. This takes a large refrigerator. It can be cooled with ice cubes in a portable cooler, but water must never touch the bass. Cooling the fish in this manner is important because it keeps in the juices. When the fish is very cold, the juices congeal and the meat of the bass will not be dry; instead it will be moist and flavorful. This is a complicated method for the preparation of a striped bass but it makes for delicious eating and an impressive presentation.

POACHED BASS ABERCROMBIE

6 1-pound bass steaks	1 lemon
1 quart water	2 teaspoons salt
1 cup dry white wine	

Bass for this recipe should be steaked—that is, cut at right angles through the backbone. The steaks should be snuggly fitted into a deep pan that just contains them rested on their sides. For every quart of water that it takes just to cover the bass, add the juice of one lemon, 1 cup of dry white wine, and two teaspoons of salt. Simmer the affair for 10 minutes for pieces 2 inches thick. Increase the simmering time 15 minutes for each additional inch of bass.

POACHED FILLETS IN CURRY

2 pounds fillets	Salt and pepper
1 teaspoon curry powder	1 cup fish stock
3 tablespoons oil	1 cup milk
2 tablespoons butter	½ cup cream

Place the fillets in a shallow pan, and cover with boiling court bouillon. Bring all to a boil, then allow to simmer for only 15 minutes. Then heat the milk and fish stock. Heat the oil and sift in flour and curry powder, cook together, then add the milk and fish stock, beating the mixture until smooth. Add butter, a spoonful at a time. Beat in well and then add the cream and season to taste. Lift out the poached fillets to a platter and pour the curry over them.

POACHED FILLET OF BASS À LA CREOLE

2 pounds fillets	2 onions, finely minced
2 cups strained tomatoes	1 large or 2 small green
¼ cup oil	peppers
3 tablespoons flour	1 garlic clove, thinly sliced
2 tablespoons butter	1 tablespoon minced parsley
1 teaspoon chili powder	Salt, paprika, sugar

Poach the fillets in a shallow pan in salted water. Heat the oil and put in the onions, green peppers (minced), and garlic. Allow to cook for a few minutes, without browning or burning, then add the tomato and season with salt, paprika, and sugar to taste. Let these simmer together under a lid while the fish is cooking. Melt the butter, add the sifted flour and chili powder, cook together, then add to the tomato mixture, stirring until smooth. Then add the parsley. Place the fillets on a platter and pour sauce over them.

Boiled striped bass

Scale, clean, and cut off the fins of a striped bass and then place on oiled rack of a large kettle, or coil the bass in a large frying basket. Cover the entire fish with well-flavored court bouillon and bring to a boil. Then remove it from the heat to another burner and simmer until the flesh is ready to separate from the bone, about 6 to 10 minutes to the pound, according to the thickness of the fish. Slip off the skin and place the bass on a hot platter with your choice of garnishings. Dutch and Sauce Supreme are rich sauces for a striped bass.

STRIPED BASS PUDDING

1½ cups boiled striped bass, free from skin and bones	Salt and paprika
3 eggs, yolk and whites separated	1 teaspoon onion juice
	1 teaspoon Worcestershire sauce

    1 cup cream   1 pinch nutmeg
    ½ cup cracker crumbs   1 teaspoon lemon juice

Work the baked bass and butter to a cream. Add the yolks of eggs, cream, and cracker crumbs. Add the seasoning and taste carefully, as the success of this dish is in getting it well flavored. Beat the whites of the eggs very stiff and *fold* them into the mixture. Pour into a buttered mold and allow a little room for rising or expansion as it cools and sets. Steam for two hours. Place in a warm oven to dry out so that the mold can easily be removed, put on a platter, and garnish.

This pudding may be served hot with a rich sauce, or cold with Tartare Sauce or Norwegian Sauce. It may also be baked in the oven, placing the baking dish in another containing hot water. Bake about 40 minutes and serve with a sauce similar to that used for steamed pudding.

STRIPED BASS SALAD

    1 cup boiled flaked bass,   1 cup finely minced celery
      free from skin and bones   1 head lettuce
    3 tablespoons minced olives   Salt and paprika
    Mayonnaise to mix   Lemon juice

Mix the fish, celery, olives, and mayonnaise together, and season with salt and lemon juice. Line a salad bowl with leaves of lettuce. Place the salad in the center and dust with paprika.

Striped bass fingers

Still another delicious way to prepare striped-bass fillets, which happens to be a favorite of my wife's and mine, is as strips or chunks of striped bass fried in butter. Cut the striped-bass fillets into fingers that are as wide as they are thick and place into a buttered frying pan with just enough butter or margarine so that the fish won't stick. Fry until one side is nicely browned and then turn to complete the other side. Serve hot and eat immediately, with dashes of fresh lemon.

Sauces and dressings

Striped bass alone make great eating, but the gourmet is well aware that the correct seasonings and sauces can enhance the flavor of a bass and turn it into a delight.

COURT BOUILLON

Court bouillon (French for "quick" or "short sauce") is a broth that can be made quickly and often adds the real flavor to what might be a rather bland adventure when a bass is boiled or poached. Court bouillon has many variations. The simplest form comes from Brittany. It consists of equal parts of milk and water, with some salt. The court bouillon is made in advance of the fish to be cooked and must be boiled for at least ½ hour before being added to boiled or poached striped bass. The bass is covered completely and simmered gently until cooked (with a lid on).

The following is a more elaborate recipe for the poaching of a large striped bass (8 to 10 pounds) and can be reduced proportionately for smaller fish.

2 gallons water	1 stalk celery
2 carrots	2 tablespoons peppercorns
4 medium onions	½ cup red wine vinegar or
3 tablespoons salt	⅓ cup lemon juice
3 bay leaves	

SAUCE VERTE

This sauce is composed of homemade mayonnaise and a collection of blended herbs. Beat the egg yolks with a whisk or beater (the advantage of a whisk is that you have a hand free to add oil). Add the mustard, vinegar, and a little salt to taste. Beat this together, then add oil in a thin stream, whisking constantly. If the mayonnaise is too thick, a little more vinegar may be added.

MAYONNAISE

3 egg yolks	1 cup peanut oil
1 tablespoon mustard	Dash of cayenne
3 tablespoons red wine vinegar	Salt to taste.

HERBS

The herbs can be made of ½ cup parsley branches and either ½ cup tarragon leaves or ¼ cup tarragon leaves and ¼ cup chervil leaves. Put these in a blender with ½ cup of oil and use a wooden spoon to help push the herbs into the blades. This mixture is then added to the mayonnaise.

Index

Note: Page numbers in italics indicate illustrations.

abundance, 85–88; *87*
  records, 86–88
accessories, boat, 310–329; *311*
  anchor, 318–319
  bilge pump, 319–320
  canvas, top, 321
  check list, 317–318
  compass, 310
  fathometer, 315–316; *316*
  fighting chair, 323
  live-bait tank; 266, 325; *325*
  radio, CB, 138, 314; *313*
  radio, VHF, 312–314; *312*
  radio, weather, 326–327; *327*
  tachometers, 311–312; *311*
  thermometers, 316, 317
accessories, fishing, 298–301; *296, 301*
  billy club, 300
  Bimini belt, 298, 322
  creepers, 300
  flashlights, 300
  gaffs, 298, 324
  knives, 299
  lure carriers, 301
  pliers, 299
  sand spikes, 299
Alabama, 34, 73, 104
American Angler's Guide, The, 114

American Fishing Tackle Manufacturer's Association, 172
anadromous fish, 24
Anadromous Fish Conservation Act, 109
anatomy, 14–18
  coloration, 17
  eyes, 15, 18, 191
  external, *15*
  fins, 15, 16
  internal, *16*
  kidneys, 25
  scales, 16, 17; counts, 43; annulus, 58, 60
  skull, *17*
  stomach, 63
  stripes, 16, 17
  teeth, 17
anchors, 318
  chain, 319
  line, 319
Aquasport boats, 307
Arizona, 77–78, 104
Arkansas, 79, 104
Atlantic States Marine Fisheries Commission, 108–109

baits, live and natural, 235–275
  blue crabs, 253–255; *254*

blue mussels, 246–247
bloodworms, 240–241; *237*
bullheads (sculpin), 273–274; *273*
butterfish, 268
calico crabs, 255–256; *254*
eels, 20, 197, 198, 269–271; *264–265, 269, 271*
fiddler crabs, 256; *254*
green crabs, 256; *254*
hermit crabs, 256–257; *257*
killifish, 258–259; *258*
mackerel, 272
menhaden, 260–268; *261, 262*
razor clams, 246
ribbed mussels, 247
ribbonworms, 241–242
sand bugs, 256–257; *257*
sand eels, 259–260
sandworms, 236–239; *237, 239*
sardines, 274–275; *274*
shrimp, edible, 252–253
shrimp, grass and sand, 251–252; *251*
skimmer clams, 244–245
soft clams, 245–246
spearing, 259
squid, 247–250; *248*
bait fish
as chum, 186
for freshwater stripers, 200
banks, fishing from, 144–146; *145*
casting from, 146
chumming, 146
rods, 146
waders, 146
Bassett, Capt. Bill, 303–304
beaches, 131–136
bars, 132–133
current along, 134
scouring, 131–132; *131*
slope, 131
tide effect on, 134–136

beach vehicles, 331–345
driving, 344–345
fishing accessories, 341–343
how to rig, 337–341
types, 335–337
Bimini belt, 298, 320
Binghamton, N.Y., 36
bird watching, 137, 138, 200–201; *137*
boats, 155–166; *see also* boats, bass
boating a bass, 164–166; *165*
bottom fishing from, 163–164
casting from, 159
fly fishing from, 178–179
handling, 155–158
jigging from, 162–163
trolling from, 159–162
boats, bass, 302–330
check list, 317–318
Cuttyhunk, 305; *306*
how to rig, 307–329; *309*
modern, 305; *307, 309*
Montauk, 302–304
tin bass boat, 329–330; *329*
Boston Whaler, 305–306
bottom fishing, 163–164; *see also* still fishing
chumming, 164
bridges, fishing from, 152–154; *152*
locations, 153
tackle, 153–154
British Angler's Natural History, 13
Brooks, Win, xiii
bullheads (sculpin), 273–274; *273*
bunker: *see* menhaden
butterfish, 268

California, 47, 61, 68
commercial fishing, 96
freshwater, 77–78
migrations, 69
regulations, 104
spawning, 69–70

California Current, 134
Canada
  distribution of bass, 28
  regulations, 107–108
Cape Cod Spinner, *239*
Cape Hatteras, 36
Carboloy guides, 214
casting, where to, 139, 159
casting platforms, 121; *122, 123*
catadromous fish, 24
Chesapeake Bay, 32, 37, 39–43, 45, 46, 63, 100, 181, 186
Chincoteague scow, 306
chumming, 180–190
  Chesapeake Bay, 181
  current, 182–183
  fishing tackle, 187–190
  fishing technique, 187
  from sod bank, 146
  in the past, 180–181
  Long Island, 181
  purpose, 181–182
  rate of, 184
  types, 185–187
  water depth, 183
  with clams, 182
  with shrimp, 181
  where to, 183–184
Church, Charles B., 23, 125, 126–127
Cinto, Charles B., 126; *127*
clams, 244–246
  as chum, 181, 186
  razor, 246
  skimmer, 244–246
  soft, 245–246
clamworms, 237
classification of striped bass, 11–14
cleaning striped bass, 347–351; *348–351*
clothing, 293–297
clubs, fishing, 117, 121–125, 180; *124, 125*

Colvin, Cap, 176
commercial fishing, 96–98, 103
compass, 310
concentration, 139
Connecticut, 30, 104
cookery, 346–357
  cleaning, 347–351; *348–351*
cooking striped bass, 351–357
  baked, 352–353
  boiled, 355–356
  broiled, 352
  fingers, 356
  poached, 353–355
  sauces and dressings, 356–357
Coos Bay, 1, 67
Coriolis Effect, 266
crabs, 186, 253–257
  as chum, 186
  blue, 253–255; *254*
  calico, 255–256; *254*
  fiddler, 256; *254*
  green, 256; *254*
  hermit, 256–257; *257*
crustaceans, 250–257
current, 134, 139, 182–183, 266
  affecting eggs, 92
Cuttyhunk bass boat, 305; *306*
Cuttyhunk Club, 121, 123–125; *123, 124*

dams, 26, 73–74, 78, 204; *205*
Delaware, 31–32, 105
Delaware River, 37, 40
digestion, 63
Dingell-Johnson Program, 109
distribution of striped bass, 27–35; *25, 26*
  Alabama, 34
  California, 35, 68–69
  Canada, 27, 28
  Chesapeake Bay, 32
  coastal, 26–27
  Delaware, 31–32

Florida, 33–34
Louisiana, 34–35
Mississippi, 34
New England, 28–30
New Jersey, 31
New York, 27, 30–31
North Carolina, 32–33
Oregon, 35, 71–72
Pacific Coast, 35
South Carolina, 33
summer, *41*
winter, *42*
Washington, 72
dominant year class, 93–94
Doroshev, Dr. S. I., VIRNO, USSR,
    55
drift (eggs), 92

eels, 20, 197, 198
rigging, 269–271; *264–265, 269,
    271*
eggs (ova)
current, 92
drift, 92
maturation, 51–55; *52, 53*
salinity, 92–93
size, 49
Elizabeth Islands, 117, 180, 186
environment, 90
evolution, 26, 56

fecundity, 49–50
Federal Communications Commis-
    sion, 312, 314
feeding, 63–65, 191, 193
frequency, 63–64
habits, 63
habits of food fish, 193
specificity, 64
time, 64, 191
temperature, 64–65
Field & Stream, 304
finding striped bass, 136–137

gulls, 137
immediate signs, 136–137
Fischer, Richard, 305
fishermen, 113–114, 121–128
colonial, 113–114
Indian, 114
recent, 121–128
*Fishes in the Vicinity of New York
    City,* 17
Fishing in American Waters, 116
fishing pressure, 95–98; *96*
colonial, 97
commercial, 97–98
during the day, 191
Santee-Cooper, 96
sportfishing, 98; *99*
flashlights, 300
flies, saltwater, 174–178
bucktails, 176–177; *176*
popper flies, 175–176; *175*
streamers, 177; *178*
floats, 238
Florida, 33–34, 47, 79, 105
fly-rodding for striped bass, 167–
    179
from boats, 178–179
locations, 168–170
technique, 170
Forester, Frank, 116
freshwater striped bass, 73–84,
    199–205
Arizona (Calif.–Nev.), 77–78
Arkansas, 79
bait, 200
Florida, 79
foods, 200–201
Georgia, 79–80
in rivers, 204–205
jigging, 201
Kentucky, 80–81; *78*
life cycle, 199
locating, 202–204
Oklahoma, 81–82

seasons, 200–201
South Carolina, 73–76
tackle, 201–202
Tennessee, 81
Texas, 82
versus saltwater striped bass, 84
Virginia, 82–83
food, 61–64
  cannibalism, 62
  fish, 62–63
  larval, 62
  sandworms, 63
  shellfish, 62
foul-weather clothing, 294; 295
future of striped bass, 85–110

gaffing a fish, 166
Georgia, 33, 79–80, 105
glasses, polaroid, 142
growth, 57–61; 59
  age-length relationship, 61
  freshwater, 58
  males, 57–58
Gulf Stream, 134

hatcheries, 83–84
  Havre de Grace, 83
  Moncks Corners, 76
  North Carolina, 75
  Russian, 83–84
  Santee-Cooper, 73–76
hatching time, 48
haul seining, 96, 103
hermaphrodism, 49
hats, 297
Hawaii, bass stocking, 68
Hell Gate, 118–121; 120
Herbert, William Henry, 116
Hollis, Dr. Edgar, 100
hooks, 232–234; 232–233
Hudson River, 37, 40, 45, 47, 104; 44
Hunt, Lynn Bogue, 304

Hydron (Woodstream Corp.), 277

International Game and Fish Commission, 126–127, 213, 223, 226

Jeep, 334, 335
jetties, fishing from, 149–152; 150
  rods, 151
  safety, 151–152
jigging, 162–163
  drift, 163
  jigs, bucktailed, 284–285; 285
  jigs, diamond, 285–286; 286
  rods, 214

Kentucky, 80–81, 105; 78
Keystone Reservoir, 204
killifish, 258–259; 258
Kirker, Edward J., 124–126
knives, 299
knots, 227, 229; 228
  Bimini hitch, 227
  blood, 227
  clinch, 227
  finishing, 227
  haywire, 227
  in wire, 225
Kronuch, John, 214

larvae, 53, 55
leaders, 226
  fly-fishing, 172–173
legislation, 101–110
  early acts, 101
  effects of, 101–104
  federal, 108–109
  interstate, 108–109
  motivation, 103–104
legislation by states and provinces, 104–107
  Alabama, 104
  Arizona, 104

Arkansas, 104
California, 104
Connecticut, 104
Delaware, 105
Florida, 105
Georgia, 105
Kentucky, 105
Louisiana, 105
Maine, 105
Maryland, 105
Massachusetts, 105
Mississippi, 105
New Brunswick, 107
New Hampshire, 105
New Jersey, 105–106
New York, 106
North Carolina, 106
Nova Scotia, 107
Oklahoma, 106
Oregon, 106–107
Pennsylvania, 107
Prince Edward Island, 108
Quebec, 108
Rhode Island, 107
South Carolina, 107
Tennessee, 107
Texas, 107
Virginia, 107
lines, 222–226
cotton, 114, 115
Dacron, 223
flylines, 171–172
lead-core, 224
Monel, 214
monofilament, 222–223
nylon, 223–224
squidding, 115, 116, 224
stripping, 170
wire, 224–226; *225*
live-bait tank, 266, 325; *325*
locomotion, 18
Long Island, fishing, 100, 103, 114–115, 263, 266–268
Louisiana, 34–35, 105

lures, artificial, 276–292
carriers, 301
copy-cat, 290–291; *290*
jigs, 284–286; *285, 286*
plugs, 278–282; *279, 280, 281*
selecting, 291–292
spoons, 282–284; *283*
tube, 286–287; *287*

mackerel, 272
Maine, 105
distribution of bass, 29
Mako boats, 307
Mansueti, Romeo, 92
maps, 202, 203, 326
Martin, Roland, 201, 204
Maryland, 102, 105
Massachusetts, 29, 101, 105
Massachusetts Bay Colony, 101
Massachusetts Beach Buggy Association, 334
menhaden (bunker), 121, 260–268; *261, 262*
meristic features, 43
Merriman, Dr. Daniel, 102
metabolism, 22, 203
migration, 24–43
Chesapeake Bay, 39–43
coastal, 37
Delaware River, 37, 40
Hudson River, 37, 40; *44*
Oregon, 71–72
post-spawning, 39
Roanoke River, 36
routes, *38, 39*
Sacramento River, 36, 69
seasonal, 36, 43
spawning, 35–37
speeds, 18
Susquehanna River, 36
Miner, Col. Francis W., 23
Mississippi, 34, 73, 105
missuckeke, 12
mollusks, 242–250

Montauk, 115, 135–136, 191, 288; *136, 142*

Montauk bass boat, 302–304; *304*

Morone labrax, 13, 14; *13*

Morone saxatilis, 11–14

Morton, Thomas (1632), 85

Moutrie, Lake (and Marion, S.C.), 73–74

mussels, 246–247
    blue, 246–247
    ribbed, 247

Naimoli, John, 284

names for striped bass, 12–13

Nereis virens, 236–239; *237, 239*

Nevada, 77–78

New Brunswick, 107, 114

New Hampshire, 29, 105

New Jersey, 31, 105–106, 262

New York, 30–31, 101, 102, 106

Nichols, John Treadwell, 17

night fishing, 64, 191–198
    at anchor, 197–198
    baits, 198
    in the surf, 194
    lures, 194
    navigation, 195
    trolling, 195–197
    why, 191, 193

night vision, in bass, 18

Nissequogue River, 168, 192–193

Noctiluca milaris, 196

North Carolina, 32–33, 106

Nova Scotia, 107

oil slicks, 138

Oklahoma, 81–82, 106

Ontario, Lake, 117

ontogeny, 56

Oregon, 37, 67, 71–72
    migration, 71, 72
    regulation, 106
    spawning, 71, 72

Oregon Inlet, N.C., *332*

Orient Point, L.I., 136

Outrage, Boston Whaler, 307; *309, 321*

outriggers, 326

Pacific Coast, 35, 49

Palma, Lou, 290

patterns, fly, 177

Pennsylvania, 106

piers, fishing from, 147–149; *147*
    landing a fish, 148
    tackle, 149

phosphorescence, 196

phylogeny, 56

pliers, 299

plugs, 276, 277
    deep-diving, 281–282; *281*
    medium-depth, 280–281; *280*
    top-water darters, 279
    top-water popping, 278–279; *279*

Plum Gut, 4, 163, 214

Plymouth Colony, 85

pollution, 94–95

populations, 77–83, 90–100
    equilibrium, 93–94
    factors affecting, 90–98
    freshwater, 77–83, 84; *77*
    fluctuations, 100
    forecasting, 99–100
    physical limiting factors, 94–95
    recruitment, 100

pork rind, 284

Potomac River, 39–40

Prince Edward Island, 108

Pun'kinseed, 302–304, 305, 306; *304*

predation, 91–92

quahogs, 245

Quebec, 108

races, 43–45

Raphael, Dr. Ernest, 129; *v*

recipes, striped bass, 352–357

records, 23, 57–58, 86, 125, 126, 127; *125, 127*
recruitment of striped bass, 100
reels, 116–119, 173–174, 215–221
  bait-casting, 219–220
  conventional, 218–219; *219*
  backing, 173
  development, 116, 117, 118, 119
  fly, 173–174; *174*
  spinning, 215–218; *215*
  trolling, 220–221; *221*
regulations, 50–51
reservoirs, 77
retrieve speeds, 140, 216, 291
Rhode Island, 30, 106
Rinefelder, Al, 290
rips, 136, 157
rivers, striped bass in, 204–205
Roanoke Rapids, 36, 205
Roanoke River, 23, 36, 46, 47
rockfights, 48
rocks, fishing from, 141–142; *142*
rods, 117–119, 170, 211–214
  bank, pier and jetty, 211–212
  boat, jigging, 214
  boat, spinning, 212–213
  boat, trolling, 213–214
  boat, wire-line, 214
  butt lengths, 211
  conventional, 210–211
  development, 117, 118, 119
  fly, 170
  guides, 210
  length, 209
  spinning, 210
  surf, 209–211
Russia, 83–84

Sabatowski, Capt. Frank, 126
Sacramento River, 36, 69
safety in the surf, 142–143
St. Lawrence River, 45, 47
Salt Water Sportsman, 334
sand bars, 132–133

sand bugs, 256–257; *257*
sand spikes, 299
Sandy Hook, 191
San Francisco, 37, 66; *39*
Santee-Cooper, 45, 73–76, 96; *76*
sardines, 274–275; *274*
Sargasso Sea, 20
Sargent, Francis W., 334
Schaefer, Richard, 100
Scheer, Otto, 302–304; *304*
Schrier, Fred, 177
Scott, Genio C., 27, 117–121, 209
sea basses, 11
seaworms, 186, 236–242
  as chum, 186
  bloodworms, 240–241; *237*
  ribbonworms, 241–242
  sandworms, 236–239; *237, 239*
senility in bass, 50–51
senses, 18–21
  hearing, 20–21
  taste, 21
  sight, 18–19
  smell, 19–20
Shining Tide, xviii
shoes, 143, 297
shrimp, 185, 251–253
  as chum, 185; *181*
  edible, 252–253
  grass and sand, 251–252; *251*
sinkers, 230–232
  shapes, 231; *231*
size of striped bass, 23, 58–59; *22*
  records, 23
Smith, Capt. John, 85
snaps, 229; *230*
Snyder, George, 116
South Carolina, 33, 107
Sow and Pigs Reef, 136, 191, 238
spawning, 46–51
  act of, 48–49
  California, 69–70
  duration, 50–51
  fecundity, 49–50, 51

migrations, 35–37
populations, 36
salinity, 47
seasons, 46–47
sites, 47–48
survival, 40
temperatures, 47
spearing, 259
spinning, 158, 159; *see also* casting
Spohn, Dave, 289
spoons, 282–284
    heavy, 283–284; *283*
    light, 282; *283*
sportfishing, 98, 99; *99*
squid, 247–250; *248*
    tin, 115, 276, 283–284
squidding, 114–115; *115*
stemming, 157
still-fishing, at night, 197–198; *see also* bottom fishing
stocking, Pacific Coast, 66
Stone, Livingston, 66
storage of striped bass, 346–347
stripping line, 170
surf, nature of, 129
    creation, 130
    currents, 134
    swells, 133–134
    wave patterns, 130; *130*
    wind effect on, 133
surfcasting, 131, 128–144
    at night, 194–195
Susquehanna River, 36, 63
swells, 133–134
swivels, 229; *230*

tapeworms, 236, 241–242
taxonomy: *see* classification
temperature
    feeding, 64–65
    freezing, 22, 203
    hatching, effect on, 48
    optimal, 23, 47
    population affecting, 90–91

sensitivity to, 21–23
    spawning, 47
Tennessee, 81, 107
Texas, 82, 107
Thames River (Conn.), 65
Throckmorton, Stephen Rush, 66
tides, 134–136
tires (beach vehicles), 340
Toledo Bend, 82
transplantings, Pacific Coast, 66–68
trawlers, 103
trim tabs, 310
trolling, 159–162
    at night, 195–197
    speed, 161–162
trout, eastern brook, 24
tube lures, 286–287; *287*
    umbrella rig, 287–289; *288, 289*
turbidity, 93

umbrella rig lure, 287–289; *288, 289*
United Mobile Sportfishermen, Inc., 345
U.S. Coast Guard, 313, 315
U.S. Dept. of Commerce, National Weather Service Office, 314, 327
U.S. Fish & Wildlife Service, 109

Virginia, 82–83

waders, 143, 294, 296
Wadsworth, Capt. Tom, *214*
Washington, 72
Watch Hill, 191
waves, wind effect on, 133
West Island, 121
when to fish, 140
Williams, Roger, 12
wind, 133, 170
Wood, William, 113–114
Woolner, Dick, *333*
Woolner, Frank, 334

Photo Credits